A HISTORY OF MOSAICS

A HISTORY OF
MOSAICS

by

EDGAR WATERMAN ANTHONY

REPRINTED BY
HACKER ART BOOKS
NEW YORK
1968

FIRST PUBLISHED
1935

Printed in the United States of America

To
A. Kingsley Porter
and
Lucy Kingsley Porter

PREFACE

No general history of mosaics has been written since Gerspach's little book, *La Mosaïque,* appeared over half a century ago, and that was never translated into English. Mosaics, for the most part, have been treated in general histories of art or painting. They deserve to be studied for themselves, and there ought surely to be a wider knowledge of one of the greatest artistic expressions of the early Christian period and the Middle Ages. It seems, moreover, worth while to continue their history to the present day, rather than to terminate it abruptly at the point when they ceased to be æsthetically good, especially when we consider the revival of interest in the art, as an art and not a craft, that has occurred in recent years.

A word as to the illustrations. The photographs have been chosen to show the best and the most characteristic of all the earlier mosaics of the great periods, and to show selected examples of later work in order to give an idea of the continuity of development. Mosaics, even more than painting or sculpture, lose in reproduction. They ought, of course, to be seen in place, in their architectural setting where the subdued light brings out the glowing, vibrating color. They cannot be well studied in museums, and, fortunately, very few of them have found there way there. But although photographs may be inadequate, they are usually better than the falsely colored reproductions which are sometimes published. It is to be regretted that more illustrations could not be included.

A glance at the notes and bibliography will show how great is the debt I owe to the researches and critical judgments of the many scholars, both of the past and the present, who have written about mosaics. I crave indulgence in advance for those instances where I may have inadvertently failed to give due credit for sources of information. I have tried to assemble as complete a bibliography as possible, for, as far as

I know, this has never been done before for mosaics. As a good many items have now been largely superseded, I have attempted to indicate the most important and essential material in the notes. Without the excellent photographs of Alinari, Anderson, Brogi, Sebah and Joaillier, Marguerite van Berchem, Thomas Whittemore, and others too numerous to mention, it would have been impossible to illustrate this book.

I wish to thank especially Mr. and Mrs. Bernhard Berenson, as well as Miss Niki Mariano and the Baroness Anrep for their unfailing interest and help and for the delightful hours I have spent in the library of "I Tatti" gathering material. Miss Marguerite van Berchem graciously read a part of my manuscript and gave valuable suggestions. To many friends in Rome I am under deep obligation; above all, to Mrs. S. Arthur Strong, to Commendatore Biagio Biagetti, Director of the Vatican Studio of Mosaic, to Dr. Randall MacIver, to the Countess Caroline Lanckoronska of the Polish Academy, and to the late Professor Ernst Steinmann, Director of the Biblioteca Herziana. To Professor Lawrence Moore of Robert College I am indebted for the great kindness he showed me during my recent visit to Constantinople. I am most grateful to Mrs. William H. Moore and Miss Margaret Enders for procuring the photograph of the mosaic at Marienburg.

I cannot thank Professor Paul J. Sachs, Miss Elizabeth Clarke, Miss E. Louise Lucas and other members of the staff of the Fogg Museum, enough, for their constant help and kindness in connection with my work. I first became interested in the study of mosaics while a pupil of the late A. Kingsley Porter and it is due to him more than to anyone else that this book has been written.

EDGAR WATERMAN ANTHONY

Manchester-by-the-Sea
Massachusetts
June, 1935

TABLE OF CONTENTS

                                                                                   PAGE

I. THE ORIGIN AND SPREAD OF MOSAIC 25

      Mosaics defined; one of the most widespread and earliest of techniques—Roman and Christian Mosaics only one category in this development—Earliest mosaics: Sumerian mosaics of five thousand years ago:—Warka—the 'al Ubaid Temple—The "Standard" of Ur—Egyptian Mosaics—Crete—Mohammedan Mosaics—Persian and Moorish Mosaic Tiles—*Opus Sectile*; its relation to mosaic—Florentine and Mogul intarsia—Early Mexican mosaics.

II. THE CHARACTERISTICS AND TECHNIQUE OF CLASSICAL AND CHRISTIAN MOSAICS 33

      Distinguishing qualities—Primarily an architectural decoration—Comparison with painting and with stained glass—Possibilities and limitations—Technique: materials, methods and processes.

III. HELLENISTIC AND ROMAN MOSAICS 45

      Mosaics of classical Greece; the pebble mosaics of Olynthus—Late Hellenistic and Roman pavements from Syria to Britain—Varieties of mosaic as understood by the Romans—Résumé of Roman pavements and their influence upon Early Christian mosaics—Palestine, Syria, Northern Africa—The earliest Wall mosaics—the "Silvanus" from Ostia—Catacomb mosaics—Changes brought about by the recognition of Christianity.

IV. ROMAN MOSAICS FROM THE FOURTH TO THE SEVENTH CENTURIES 57

      Official recognition of the Church a great impetus to art.—Origin and development of Early Christian iconography: Eastern and Western influences: theories and facts.—The new iconography defined.—Lost mosaics of the Holy Land.—Santa Costanza.—Santa Pudenziana.—Santa Maria Maggiore.—Santa Sabina.—San Paolo-fuori-le-mura.—The Lateran Baptistery.—SS. Cosma e Damiano.—San Lorenzo-fuori-le-mura.—Lost mosaics: Old St. Peter's and the Lateran, Sant'Agata dei Goti, Sant'Andrea Catabarbara.—Summary of the styles.

V. THE MOSAICS OF RAVENNA 85

In the 5th and 6th centuries Ravenna the most important city in Italy and in the development of mosaics.—Three great personalities, Galla Placidia, Theodoric and Justinian.—The Mausoleum of Galla Placidia.—The Baptistery of the Orthodox.—Sant'Apollinare Nuovo.—San Vitale.—The Archiepiscopal Palace.—Sant'Apollinare in Classe.—The Arian Baptistery.—San Michele in Affrisco.—Lost mosaics.—The salient points of the style and their probable origin.—The influence of the style elsewhere.

VI. OTHER EARLY MOSAICS TO THE SEVENTH CENTURY . 105

Salonika the second city of the Byzantine Empire and its mosaics: St. George, St. Demetrius, the Eski-Djouma, and the recently discovered mosaic in St. David.—Constantinople: the problem of St. Sophia, the mosaics of the Narthex.—The Church of the Holy Apostles.—Mount Sinai: the Monastery of St. Catherine.—Parenzo.—Pola: Santa Maria del Canneto.—Milan: San Lorenzo and the Chapel of St. Victor in Sant'Ambrogio.—Albenga: the Baptistery.—Casaranello.—Naples: San Giovanni in Fonte.—The lost mosaics of Nola.—Capua: San Prisco.—North Africa and Spain.—Summary of the Early Christian style in general.—Antioch as a radiating center?

TABLE OF CONTENTS 11

VII. THE SEVENTH AND EIGHTH CENTURIES 125

 Jerusalem: the "Dome of the Rock".—Damascus: the Great Mosque.—Spain: the Sanctuary of the Mosque at Cordova.—The Roman group: reasons for the strong Eastern influence.—Sant'Agnese.—Oratory of St. Venantius.—Santo Stefano Rotondo.—San Pietro in Vincoli.—Oratory of John VII.—San Teodoro.—St. Sophia, Salonika.

VIII. THE ROMAN SCHOOL OF THE NINTH CENTURY . . 141

 Peculiarities of the style: Eastern and Western influences.—SS. Nereo ed Achille.—The Triclinium of the Lateran.—The Christ from the Vatican crypt.—Santa Maria in Domnica.—Santa Cecilia.—Santa Prassede.—San Marco.—Influence of the Roman School elsewhere; Germigny-des-Prés, Aix-la-Chapelle.

IX. THE ELEVENTH CENTURY IN THE NEAR EAST . . 155

 The great revival in Byzantine art and the impetus given to mosaics.—The new style and its iconography defined.—Constantinople: the New Church of Basil I. and the Church of the Holy Apostles.—Cyprus: the Panagia Angelokistos, the Panagia Kanakaria.—The Lunette of Leo VI in St Sophia.—Hosios Lucas in Phocis.—Kiev: St Sophia and St. Michael.—Nicæa: the Church of the Dormition.—Salonika: St. Sophia.—Chios: Nea Moni.—Macedonia: Seres.—Vatopedi: the Catholicon.—Grottaferrata.—Daphni.—Bethlehem: the Church of the Nativity.—Jerusalem: the "Dome of the Rock" and the Mosque of El-Aksa.—Byzantine miniature, or portative mosaics.

X. SICILIAN MOSAICS 177

 Saracenic and Byzantine influences under the Normans which produced the mosaics.—Cefalù.—The Martorana.—The Cappella Palatina.—Secular decoration: La Zisa and the *Camera di Ruggero*.—Monreale, etc.—Messina: the Cathedral; San Gregorio.—Sicilian influence on the mainland: Salerno; Capua; Santa Restituta at Naples.

XI. Venetian and Florentine Mosaics 189

The Venetian School.—The early work in St. Mark's.—The Genesis cycle of the narthex.—The influence of Venice elsewhere.—Torcello.—Murano.—SS. Maria e Donato.—Ravenna: the Madonna now in the Archiepiscopal Palace.—Trieste. Venetian influence in Milan: the apse of Sant'Ambrogio.—Venetian influence in Tuscany: the Florentine Baptistery; the Duomo; San Miniato; San Frediano at Lucca; the apse of the Cathedral of Pisa.—Genoa: San Matteo.

XII. Roman Mosaics of the Twelfth and the Thirteenth Centuries 207

The revival in Rome.—The combination of early traditions with the Byzantine style.—San Clemente.—Santa Francesca Romana.—Santa Maria in Trastevere.—Christ between St. Peter and St. Paul from the Vatican crypt.—San Bartolomeo all'Isola.—Restoration of the apse of Old St. Peter's.—San Paolo-fuori-le-mura.—San Tommaso in Formis.—Civita Castellana.—Spoleto: the *Deesis* on the façade of the Cathedral.—The vault of the Sancta Sanctorum; the Cosmati and their influence.—Santa Maria sopra Minerva; the tomb of Durande di Mende.—Santa Maria Maggiore; the tomb of Gonsalvo Rodriquez.—Palazzo Colonna: Madonna and Saints.—Santa Maria in Aracœli; the Cappella di Santa Rosa; the Madonna in the lunette.—The Brooklyn Museum Madonna.—Santa Sabina; the tombstone of Munio da Zamora.—San Crisògono; Madonna and Saints.—Jacopo Torriti; the Lateran apse; the apse of Santa Maria Maggiore.—Rusuti and the façade of Santa Maria Maggiore.—Assisi.—Cavallini; his work in Santa Maria in Trastevere.—Giotto; the "Navicella."—Reasons for the abrupt ending of the Roman school in the early fourteenth century.

XIII. THE FOURTEENTH CENTURY 225

The Byzantine Renaissance; character of the new style.—Constantinople: the Kahrie Djami.—Arta: Church of the Parigoritissa.—The Fetiye Djami.—The changing character of mosaics and the influence of painting, etc.—St. Mark's: the Baptistery and the Chapel of St. Isidore.—The façades of the cathedrals of Orvieto and Siena.—Mosaics in Northern Europe: Prague; Marienwerder; Marienburg.

XIV. FROM THE RENAISSANCE TO THE NINETEENTH CENTURY 235

The increasing influence of painting and the relationship of the painters of Venice and Rome to the mosaicists.—St. Marks': the Chapel of the Mascoli; Giambono.—Florence: Baldovinetti and Ghirlandaio.—Rome: Santa Croce in Gerusalemme, the Cappella di Sant'Elena.—Santa Maria del Popolo: the Chigi Chapel; Raphael and Luigi de Pace. Venice; the influence of Titian, Tintoretto and others.—The trial of 1563; the Bianchini and the Zuccati.—The lowest ebb of the art.—Revival under Leopoldo dal Pozzo.—The Vatican Studio: Muziano da Brescia. —Decoration of St. Peter's; the altars.

XV. NINETEENTH CENTURY AND MODERN MOSAICS . . 249

The Romantic Movement and the new interest in the Middle Ages; the influence upon mosaics.—Mosaics and archæology; restorations.—Venice: the Salviati.—The Vatican Workshop;

the Restoration of St. Paul's, etc.—Other nineteenth century restorations in Italy.—The revival of interest in mosaics in Northern Europe.—Russia.—France; Belloni and the "Pompeian School"; Charles Garnier and the Paris Opèra.—Later mosaics.—Germany. — England. — America. — The revival of mosaic as an independent art; influences from the past; its relation to modern painting.—Recent work in Germany, Denmark, Norway and Sweden.—England.—Recent work in America.—The future of mosaic as architectural decoration.

Notes 263

Bibliography 299

Glossary 315

Index 315

Illustrations 333

ILLUSTRATIONS

1. Naples Museum. Academy of Plato from Torre Annuziata. (Anderson 25783)
2. Rome. Museo delle Terme. Head of Medusa. (Alinari 30169)
3. Pompeii. Reclining Dog. New excavations.
4. Rome. Lateran Museum. Pavement from the Baths of Caracalla. Detail. (Moscioni 8281)
5. Rome. Capitoline Museum. "Pliny's Doves." (Brogi 7109)
6. Timgad. Pavement in "Carpet Style". *Mosaïque de la Piscine.*
7. Zliten (Tripoli). Detail of Pavement. (Aurigemma)
8. Pompeii. Fountain Niche. (Brogi 5265)
9. Naples Museum. Fountain Niche from Pompeii. (Anderson 25779)
10. Naples Museum. Mosaic Column from Pompeii. (Anderson 25764)
11. Rome. Lateran Museum. "Silvanus" from Ostia. (Moscioni 2983)
12. Rome. Santa Costanza. Ciampini's Engraving of the Dome.
13. Rome. Santa Costanza. View of the Vault. (Alinari 6086)
14. Rome. Santa Costanza. Detail of the Vault. (Brogi 15856)
15. Rome. Santa Costanza. Detail of the Vault. (Brogi 15858)
16. Rome. Santa Costanza. Left Apse. (Alinari 28515)
17. Rome. Santa Costanza. Right Apse. (Alinari 28516)
18. Rome. Santa Pudenziana. Apse. (Brogi 17131)
19. Rome. Lateran Baptistery. Apse. (Brogi 15698)
20. Rome. Santa Maria Maggiore. General View of the Nave (Alinari 5875)
21. Rome. Santa Maria Maggiore. Abraham and the Three Angels. (Alinari 30125)
22. Rome. Santa Maria Maggiore. Separation of Abraham and Lot. (Alinari 30126)
23. Rome. Santa Maria Maggiore. Marriage of Moses and Sephora. (Alinari 30142)
24. Rome. Santa Maria Maggiore. Triumphal Arch. (Anderson 17653)
25. Rome. Santa Maria Maggiore. Detail of the Arch. (Alinari 30122)
26. Rome. Santa Maria Maggiore. Detail of the Arch. (Alinari 30121)
27. Rome. Santa Maria Maggiore. Detail of the Arch. (Anderson 31228)
28. Rome. Santa Sabina. Mosaic. (Brogi 17982)
29. Rome. Santa Sabina. *Ecclesia ex Circumcisione.* (Alinari 27956)
30. Rome. Santa Sabina. Ciampini: Destroyed Mosaic of the Arch.
31. Rome. San Paola fuori-le-mura. Apse and Triumphal Arch. (Alinari 7153)
32. Rome. Lateran Baptistery. Detail of the Vault. (Moscioni 6680)

33. Rome. SS. Cosma e Damiano. Apse and Triumphal Arch. (Brogi 17082)
34. Rome. SS. Cosma e Damiano. Christ, Detail.
35. Rome. SS. Cosma e Damiano. Right Half of the Apse. (Alinari P.2.N. 7179)
36. Rome. SS. Cosma e Damiano. Left Half of the Apse. (Alinari P.2.N. 7180)
37. Rome. San Lorenzo fuori-le-mura. Triumphal Arch. (Alinari 7150)
38. Ravenna. Mausoleum of Galla Placidia. Exterior. (Alinari P.1.N. 18106)
39. Ravenna. Mausoleum of Galla Placidia. Interior. (Alinari 18108)
40. Ravenna. Mausoleum of Galla Placidia. Stags Drinking. (Alinari 18265)
41. Ravenna. Mausoleum of Galla Placidia. St. Lawrence. (Alinari 18263)
42. Ravenna. Mausoleum of Galla Placidia. The Good Shepherd. (Anderson 27656)
43. Ravenna. Baptistery of the Orthodox. Dome. (Alinari P.2.N. 18228)
44. Ravenna. Baptistery of the Orthodox. Baptism of Christ (Alinari P.2.N. 18229)
45. Ravenna. Baptistery of the Orthodox. Interior. (Alinari P.2.N. 18043)
46. Ravenna. Sant'Appollinare Nuovo. Left Wall of Nave. (Alinari P.N.1. 18059)
47. Ravenna. Sant'Apollinare Nuovo. Right Wall of Nave. (Alinari P.N.1. 18058)
48. Ravenna. Sant'Apollinare Nuovo. Detail of Left Wall. (Alinari 18233)
49. Ravenna. Sant'Apollinare Nuovo. Detail of Right Wall. (Alinari 42098)
50. Ravenna. Sant'Appollinare Nuovo. The Multiplication of Bread. (Anderson 27473)
51. Ravenna. Sant'Apollinare Nuovo. The Separation of the Sheep from the Goats. (Anderson 27465)
52. Ravenna. Sant'Apollinare Nuovo. The Last Supper. (Anderson 27475)
53. Ravenna. Sant'Apollinare Nuovo. The Kiss of Judas. (Anderson 27477)
54. Ravenna. Sant'Apollinare Nuovo. Virgin Enthroned. (Alinari P.2.N. 18237)
55. Ravenna. Sant'Apollinare Nuovo. Christ Enthroned. (Alinari P.2.N. 18243)
56. Ravenna. Sant'Apollinare Nuovo. Portrait of Justinian. (Anderson 27488)
57. Ravenna. San Vitale. Christ Enthroned. (Alinari P.2.N. 18223)
58. Ravenna. San Vitale. Vault. (Alinari P.2.N. 18222)
59. Ravenna. San Vitale. St. Matthew and St. Mark. (Alinari 18033)
60. Ravenna. San Vitale. Abel and Melchisedek, Moses and Isaiah. (Alinari 18216)

61. Ravenna. San Vitale. Abraham and the Three Angels, The Sacrifice of Isaac with Jeremiah and Moses above. (Alinari 18219)
62. Ravenna. San Vitale. Soffit of the Arch. (Alinari P.2.N. 18211)
63. Ravenna. San Vitale. Justinian and His Court. (Brogi 3919)
64. Ravenna. San Vitale. Theodora and Her Court. (Brogi 3918)
65. Ravenna. San Vitale. The Empress Theodora and Attendants. (Alinari 18227)
66. Ravenna. Archiepiscopal Palace. Vault. (Alinari 18267)
67. Ravenna. Archiepiscopal Palace. Interior. (Alinari 18137)
68. Ravenna. Archiepiscopal Palace. Vault and Apse. (Alinari 42124)
69. Ravenna. Archiepiscopal Palace. Busts of Female Saints. (Anderson 27366)
70. Ravenna. Archiepiscopal Palace. Christ. (Alinari 42126)
71. Ravenna. Sant'Apollinare in Classe. Apse. (Alinari 42103)
72. Ravenna. Sant'Apollinare in Classe. Detail, St. Ursus. (Alinari 18205)
73. Ravenna. Sant'Apollinare in Classe. Constantine IV and Reparatus. (Alinari 18202)
74. Ravenna. Sant'Apollinare in Classe. Sacrifice of Melchisedek. (Alinari 18203)
75. Ravenna. The Arian Baptistery. Cupola. (Alinari 18245)
76. Ravenna. San Michele in Affricisco. Apse. (Kaiser Friedrich Museum, Berlin)
77. Salonika. St. George. Decoration of the Dome. (Tsimas)
78. Salonika. St. George. Detail, Leo and the Flute-Player Philimon. (Tsimas)
79. Salonika. St. Demetrius. St. Demetrius and Two Children. (Tsimas)
80. Salonika. St. Demetrius. St. Demetrius and the Founders. (Tsimas)
81. Salonika. St. David. Vision of Ezechiel. (Tsimas)
82. Constantinople. St. Sophia. Narthex. Vault. (Whittemore)
83. Constantinople. St. Sophia. Narthex. Cross. (Whittemore)
84. Sinai. Monastery of St. Catherine. Detail of the Apse. (Savignac)
85. Parenzo. Façade. (Alinari 21227)
86. Parenzo. Apse. (Alinari 21236)
87. Parenzo. Detail of the Apse. (Alinari 21252)
88. Parenzo. Annunciation. (Alinari 21253)
89. Parenzo. Visitation. (Alinari 21254)
90. Milan. San Lorenzo. Christ and the Apostles. (Anderson 12825)
91. Milan. San Lorenzo. Apse. (Anderson 12827)
92. Milan. Sant'Ambrogio. Chapel of St. Victor. Cupola. (Wilpert)
93. Milan. Sant'Ambrogio. Chapel of St. Victor. St. Ambrose. (Wilpert)
94. Albenga. Baptistery. Detail. (Wilpert)

95. Casaranello. Cupola. (Wilpert)
96. Naples. San Giovanni in Fonte. Christ and Angel. (Alinari 33748)
97. Naples. San Giovanni in Fonte. The Lion. (Anderson 25219)
98. Capua. San Prisco. Cappella di Santa Matrona. Christ in lunette. (Wilpert)
99. Capua. San Prisco. Cappella di Santa Matrona. The Vault. (Wilpert)
100. Tarragona. Tombal mosaic.
101. Jerusalem. The "Dome of the Rock." Octagonal Arcade. Detail. (Van Berchem)
102. Jerusalem. The "Dome of the Rock." Circular Arcade. Detail. (Van Berchem)
103. Jerusalem. The "Dome of the Rock." The Drum. Detail. (Van Berchem)
104. Damascus. The Great Mosque. The Great Panel. (de Lorey)
105. Damascus. The Great Mosque. The Four Trees. (de Lorey)
106. Cordova. Mosque. Façade of the Mihrab. (Senan y Gonzalez)
107. Rome. Sant'Agnese. Apse. (Brogi 15852)
108. Rome. San Teodoro. Apse. (Moscioni 6682)
109. Rome. Oratory of St. Venantius. Apse and Triumphal Arch. (Alinari 7173)
110. Rome. Oratory of St. Venantius. Group of Saints on the Left. (Brogi 15696)
111. Rome. Oratory of St. Venantius. Group of Saints on the Right. (Brogi 15697)
112. Rome. Santo Stefano Rotondo. Apse. (Moscioni 6705)
113. Rome. San Pietro in Vincoli. St. Sebastian. (Moscioni 10988)
114. Rome. Oratory of John VII. Façade of the Oratory from Ciampini.
115. Florence. San Marco. Virgin as Orant. (Alinari 4571)
116. Rome. Museo Petriano. Portrait of John VII. (Alinari 26381)
117. Rome. Museo Petriano. St. Peter Preaching. (Anderson 20315)
118. Rome. Lateran Museum. The Washing of the Infant Christ. (Alinari 29870)
119. Rome. Santa Maria in Cosmedin. Adoration of the Magi. (Alinari 26569)
120. Salonika. St. Sophia. Virgin in the Apse. (Tsimas)
121. Rome. Triclinium of the Lateran. Apse. (Alinari 17497)
122. Rome. Vatican Crypt. Christ Blessing. (Alinari 26420)
123. Rome. SS. Nereo ed Achille. Triumphal Arch. (Alinari 7251)
124. Rome. Santa Prassede. The Apse and the Triumphal Arch. (Brogi 17122)
125. Rome. Santa Prassede. The Heavenly Jerusalem. (Alinari 26707)
126. Rome. Santa Prassede. The Twenty-four Elders. (Alinari 26709)

LIST OF ILLUSTRATIONS

127. Rome. Santa Prassede. Façade of the Cappella San Zeno. (Alinari 26712)
128. Rome. Santa Prassede. Vault. (Brogi 17129)
129. Rome. Santa Prassede. Female Saints. (Brogi 17125)
130. Rome. Santa Maria in Domnica. Apse. (Anderson 2386)
131. Rome. Santa Cecilia. Apse. (Brogi 17062)
132. Rome. San Marco. Apse. (Alinari 26529)
133. Germigny-des-Prés. Apse. (Photo.Arch.photo.d'art et d'hist. 72457)
134. Aix-la-Chapelle. Cathedral. Decoration of the Dome. (from Ciampini)
135. Constantinople. St. Sophia. Narthex. Lunette over the Royal Door. (Whittemore)
136. Constantinople. St. Sophia. Narthex. Lunette over the South Portal. (Whittemore.)
137. Phocis. Hosios Lucas. The Pantocrator. (Diez)
138. Phocis. Hosios Lucas. The Madonna and Child in the Apse. (Diez)
139. Phocis. Hosios Lucas. Descent of the Holy Ghost.
140. Kiev. St. Sophia. The Pantocrator. (Diez)
141. Kiev. St. Sophia. Communion of the Apostles. (Diez)
142. Nicæa. Church of the Dormition. Virgin of the Apse. (Schmit)
143. Nicæa. Church of the Dormition. Archangels. (Schmit)
144. Nicæa. Church of the Dormition. Virgin as Orant. (Schmit)
145. Salonika. St. Sophia. Cupola. (Tsimas)
146. Chios. Nea Moni. Baptism. (Diez)
147. Chios. Nea Moni. *Anastasis*. (Diez)
148. Seres. Communion of the Apostles. (Diez)
149. Grottaferrata. Pentecost. (Moscioni 10401)
150. Grottaferrata. *Deesis*. (Brogi 17215)
151. Daphni. Pantocrator.
152. Daphni. Transfiguration. (Alinari 24698)
153. Daphni. Entry into Jerusalem. (Alinari 24687)
154. Daphni. Crucifixion. (Alinari 24686)
155. Daphni. *Anastasis*. (Alinari 24689)
156. Daphni. Prayer of St. Anna. (Alinari 24691)
157. Florence. Opera del Duomo. Panels of the Twelve Feasts. (Brogi 7675)
158. Florence. Bargello. Christ. (Brogi 22169)
159. Paris. Louvre. Transfiguration. (Giraudon 17761)
160. Cefalù. Cathedral. Apse. (Anderson 29586)
161. Cefalù. Cathedral. Vault. (Anderson 29591)
162. Palermo. The Martorana. Interior. (Anderson 29106)
163. Palermo. The Martorana. Cupola. (Brogi 11369)
164. Palermo. The Martorana. Nativity. (Brogi 11373)
165. Palermo. The Martorana. Dormition. (Brogi 11372)

166. Palermo. The Martorana. King Roger Crowned by Christ. (Brogi 11374)
167. Palermo. The Martorana. SS. James and Paul. (Anderson 29095)
168. Palermo. Cappella Palatina. Interior. (Alinari 33102)
169. Palermo. Cappella Palatina. Cupola, Christ and Archangels. (Brogi 11391)
170. Palermo. Cappella Palatina. Apse, the Pantocrator. (Alinari 33112)
171. Palermo. Cappella Palatina. Nave, Creation of Adam and Eve. (Alinari 33137)
172. Palermo. Cappella Palatina. Nave, Entry into Jerusalem. (Brogi 15445)
173. Palermo. Cappella Palatina. Nave, Scene from the life of St. Paul. (Alinari 33128)
174. Palermo. Cappella Palatina. Nave, Head of St. Gregory. (Anderson 29018)
175. Monreale. Cathedral. Apse. (Alinari 33295)
176. Monreale. Cathedral. Nave, Old Testament scenes. (Alinari 33274)
177. Monreale. Cathedral. Nave, detail of the Creation. (Alinari 33242)
178. Monreale. Cathedral. William II offers the church to the Virgin. (Brogi 15419)
179. Monreale. Cathedral. Christ crowning William II. (Brogi 15420)
180. Palermo. La Zisa. (Anderson 29722)
181. Palermo. La Zisa. Detail of frieze. (Anderson 29718)
182. Palermo. Palace. Camera di Ruggero. (Alinari 33087)
183. Palermo. Palace. Camera di Ruggero, detail. (Anderson 29530)
184. Messina. Cathedral. Main Apse. (Photo. Min. della istruz. pubbl.)
185. Messina. Museum. Virgin and Child from San Gregorio. (Anderson 29962)
186. Salerno. Cathedral. Façade. St. Matthew. (Anderson 26628)
187. Naples. S. Restituta. Virgin and Child. (Anderson 25216)
188. Venice. St. Mark's. Interior. (Alinari 12377)
189. Venice. St. Mark's. The Ascension Cupola. (Alinari 13745)
190. Venice. St. Mark's. The Ascension Cupola. The Virgin. (Alinari 38677)
191. Venice. St. Mark's. The Pentecost Cupola. (Alinari 13742)
192. Venice. St. Mark's. The Christ Emmanuel Cupola. (Alinari 13746)
193. Venice. St. Mark's. The Christ Emmanuel Cupola, Detail of Prophets. (Alinari 38676)
194. Venice. St. Mark's. *Deesis*. (Alinari 13739)
195. Venice. St. Mark's. Entry into Jerusalem. (Alinari 13896)
196. Venice. St. Mark's. *Anastasis* and Incredulity of Thomas. (Alinari 13743)
197. Venice St. Mark's. The Body of St. Mark carried to the Ship. (Alinari 32398)

LIST OF ILLUSTRATIONS

198. Venice. St. Mark's. Angels above the Treasury Door. (Alinari 20733)
199. Venice. St. Mark's, Narthex. The Creation Cupola. (Alinari 13721)
200. Venice. St. Mark's, Narthex. The animals going into the Ark. (Alinari 38684)
201. Venice. St. Mark's, Narthex. Cupola. Life of Abraham. (Alinari 13728)
202. Venice. St. Mark's, Narthex. Cupola. Life of Moses. (Alinari 13738)
203. Venice. St. Mark's, Cappella San Zeno. Scene from the life of St. Mark. (Alinari 32406)
204. Venice. St. Mark's, Façade. Translation of the Body of St. Mark. (Alinari 13720)
205. Torcello. Cathedral. Vault. (Alinari 13834)
206. Torcello. Cathedral. Central apse. (Alinari 13836)
207. Torcello. Cathedral. Lateral apse, Christ, Saints, and Archangels. (Alinari 13835)
208. Torcello. Last Judgment. (Alinari 18281)
209. Murano. SS. Maria e Donato. Apse. (Alinari 13833)
210. Trieste. Cathedral. Cappella del Sacramento. Apse. (Alinari 21135)
211. Trieste. Cathedral. Cappella del Sacramento. Detail. (Alinari 21138)
212. Trieste. Cathedral. Cappella di San Giusto. Apse. (Alinari 21129)
213. Ravenna. Archiepiscopal Palace. Virgin as Orant. (Alinari 18268)
214. Ravenna. Archiepiscopal Palace. Head of St. John. (Alinari 42127)
215. Milan. Sant'Ambrogio. Apse. (Alinari 14500)
216. Florence. Baptistery. Vault of the "Scarsella." (Alinari 20451)
217. Florence. Baptistery. Madonna and Child, detail. (Alinari 20452)
218. Florence. Baptistery. St. John the Baptist. (Alinari 20453)
219. Florence. Baptistery. General view of the dome. (Alinari 3738)
220. Florence. Baptistery. Decoration below the lantern. (Alinari 17249)
221. Florence. Baptistery. Christ enthroned. (Alinari 3746)
222. Florence. Baptistery. Detail of the "Hell." (Alinari 17246)
223. Florence. Baptistery. Birth of St. John. (Alinari 17242)
224. Florence. Baptistery. Detail of a head by Cimabue(?). (Alinari 17243)
225. Florence. Baptistery. The Prophet Joel. (Brogi)
226. Florence. Cathedral, lunette. Coronation of the Virgin. (Brogi 420)
227. Florence. San Miniato. Apse. (Brogi 2265)
228. Florence. San Miniato. Façade. (Brogi 2266)
229. Lucca. San Frediano. Façade, Ascension. (Alinari 8424)
230. Pisa. Cathedral. Apse. (Brogi 19450)
231. Rome. San Clemente. Apse and Triumphal Arch. (Brogi 17081)
232. Rome. San Clemente. Apse, detail. (Alinari 7177)
233. Rome. Santa Francesca Romana. Apse. (Alinari 27823)

234. Rome. Santa Maria in Trastevere. Apse. (Brogi 15667)
235. Rome. Santa Maria in Trastevere. Apse, Jeremiah and Isaiah. (Alinari 28421)
236. Rome. Santa Maria in Trastevere. Detail of the façade. (Alinari 28401)
237. Rome. St. Peter's. Fresco of the Old Apse. (Anderson 20309)
238. Poli. Cappella Conti. Head of Innocent III. (Moscioni 9077)
239. Rome. San Paolo fuore-le-mura. Apse. (Brogi 17888)
240. Rome. San Paolo fuore-le-mura. Head of Apostle in the Sacristy. (Anderson 20999)
241. Rome. San Tommaso in Formis. Medallion of Christ and two Slaves. (Venturi)
242. Civita Castellana. Lunette in the Atrium of the Cathedral. (Alinari 35881)
243. Rome. Sancta Sanctorum. Vault. (Alinari 26676)
244. Rome. Santa Prassede, Cappella di San Zenone. Virgin and Child. (Brogi 17123)
245. Rome. Sta. Maria sopra Minerva. Tomb of Durande. (Alinari 27887)
246. Rome. Sta. Maria Maggiore. Tomb of Rodriguez. (Alinari 7151)
247. Brooklyn Museum. Madonna.
248. Rome. Sta. Sabina. Tombstone of Zamora. (Brogi 17983)
249. Rome. San Crisògono. Madonna and Child. (Alinari 27994)
250. Rome. Sta. Maria in Aracœli. Madonna and Child in the lunette. (Alinari 26691)
251. Rome. The Lateran. Apse. (Brogi 15694)
252. Rome. Sta. Maria Maggiore. Apse. (Alinari 7152)
253. Rome. Sta. Maria Maggiore. Apse. Detail. (Alinari 28272)
254. Rome. Sta. Maria Maggiore. Dormition. (Alinari 28273)
255. Rome. Sta. Maria Maggiore. Façade, Christ, enthroned. (Alinari 28278)
256. Rome. Sta. Maria Maggiore. Façade. Dream of Pope Liberius. (Alinari 28282)
257. Rome. Sta. Maria in Trastevere. Cavallini. Birth of the Virgin. (Alinari 28415)
258. Rome. Sta. Maria in Trastevere. Cavallini. Nativity. (Alinari 28417)
259. Rome. Sta. Maria in Trastevere. Cavallini. Dormition. (Alinari 28420) 28420)
260. Rome. St. Peter's. The "Navicella.". (Alinari 7155)
261. Rome. Boville Ernica. S. Pietro Ispano. Angel. (Muñoz)
262. Constantinople. Kahrie Djami. Cupola. Christ and Prophets. (Sebah and Joaillier)

LIST OF ILLUSTRATIONS

263. Constantinople. Kahrie Djami. Theodore Metochites at the feet of Christ. (Sebah and Joaillier)
264. Constantinople. Kahrie Djami. Dormition. (Sebah and Joaillier)
265. Constantinople. Kahrie Djami. The Magi before Herod. (Sebah and Joaillier)
266. Constantinople. Kahrie Djami. Annunciation. (Sebah and Joaillier)
267. Constantinople. Kahrie Djami. The High-Priest Gives the Wool to the Virgin. (Sebah and Joaillier)
268. Constantinople. Cupola of the Fetiye Djami. (Sebah and Joaillier)
269. Constantinople. Cupola of the Fetiye Djami, Detail of Christ. (Sebah and Joaillier)
270. Venice. St. Mark's, Baptistery. Christ surrounded by angels and Seraphim. (Alinari 13761)
271. Venice. St. Mark's, Baptistery. Herod's Feast. (Alinari 13763)
272. Marienburg. Marien-Kirche. Virgin and Child.
273. Venice. St. Mark's, Chapel of the Mascoli. Birth of the Virgin and Presentation. (Alinari 13898)
274. Venice. St. Mark's, Chapel of the Mascoli. Dormition. (Alinari 13900)
275. Florence. Cathedral. Annunciation. (Brogi 11408)
276. Florence. Museo del Opera. St. Zenobius. (Brogi 7674)
277. Rome. Sta. Croce in Gerusalemme, Cappella di Sta. Elena. Vault. (Alinari 20134)
278. Rome. Sta. Maria del Popolo, Cappella Chigi. Cupola. (Alinari 7248)
279. Venice. St. Mark's. Detail of the Paradise. (Alinari 13748)
280. Venice. St. Mark's. Mosaic on Façade by Leopoldo dal Pozzo. (Alinari 32422)
281. Rome. St. Peter's. Detail of the Dome. (Alinari 26463)
282. Rome. Façade of San Paolo fuori-le-mura. (Brogi 18604)
283. Rome. Apse of the American Church by Burne-Jones. (Alinari 26497)
284. Detroit. Church of the Holy Redeemer. Detail by R. Scheffler. (Ravenna Mosaics, Inc.)
285. St. Louis. Cathedral. Detail. (Ravenna Mosaics, Inc.)
286. New York. St. Bartholomew's. Detail. (Ravenna Mosaics, Inc.)
287. Paris. Sanctuaire de Ste. Thérése de l'Enfant Jésus. Detail of Mosaic by the Brothers Maumejean.
288. The Hague. Mosaic by Thorn-Prikker. (Ravenna Mosaics, Inc.)
289. Germany. The Three Wise Men, by Ewald Duellberg. (Ravenna Mosaics, Inc.)
290. Frankfurt-am-Main. Tower of the Frauen-Friedenskirche. (Ravenna Mosaics, Inc.)

291. SS. "Bremen", Mosaic in Ball-Room by Maria May. (Ravenna Mosaics, Inc.)
292. Stockholm, Town Hall. The "Golden Hall" by Einar Forseth. (Ravenna Mosaics, Inc.)
293. London. 35 Upper Brook Street. Pavement by Boris Anrep.
294. London. Pavement by Boris Anrep. National Gallery.
295. Rochester, New York. Rochester Savings Bank. (Ravenna Mosaics, Inc.)
296. New York. International Telephone and Telegraph Building. Mosaics by Victor White. (Ravenna Mosaics, Inc.)
297. Ottawa. Metropolitan Life Insurance Building. Detail by Barry Faulkner. (Ravenna Mosaics, Inc.)
298. Cincinnati. Union Terminal Station. Mural. (Ravenna Mosaics, Inc.)
299. New York. Irving Trust Building. Reception Room. (Ravenna Mosaics, Inc.)
300. New York. Rockefeller Center. Mural. (Ravenna Mosaics, Inc.)

THE ORIGIN AND SPREAD OF MOSAIC

THE ORIGIN AND SPREAD OF MOSAICS

Mosaics defined; one of the most widespread and earliest of techniques—Roman and Christian Mosaics only one category in this development—Earliest mosaics: Sumerian mosaics of five thousand years ago: Warka—the al 'Ubaid Temple—The "Standard" of Ur—Egyptian Mosaics—Crete—Mohammedan Mosaics—Persian and Moorish Mosaic Tiles—*Opus Sectile;* its relation to mosaic—Florentine and Mogul intarsia—Early Mexican mosaics.

I.

THE ORIGIN AND SPREAD OF MOSAIC[1]

Mosaic in its broadest interpretation may be termed a method of placing small pieces of differently colored materials closely together so as to form a surface, usually with a pattern or a pictorial representation. These spots of pure color when viewed at a certain distance tend to fuse together upon the retina of the eye and produce a result which may be called "impressionism". The materials composing a mosaic must be fastened upon or set into a base or foundation which will hold them in place and thus, the result may be defined as a kind of inlay. Although it is difficult to draw a sharp line between inlays which are or are not mosaics, the method at least was in use in Mesopotamia as early as the fourth millennium B. C., and decoration which may with certainty be called mosaic existed at that time. Dalton, who follows Strzygowski, is of the opinion that all mosaics originated as imitation, in a more durable form, of carpets and hangings, but this as yet cannot be proved.

It is probably from such early traditions that Hellenistic and Roman pavements and the Early Christian wall mosaics were ultimately evolved, and it is with these mosaics that we are chiefly concerned, but we should bear in mind that viewed in true perspective they are but one phase of a method of decoration which may be nearly as ancient as art itself.

Five thousand years ago or possibly even earlier, in Southern Mesopotamia, the Sumerians covered walls with mosaics. Among the débris of houses of the al 'Ubaid period are found cones of baked clay, shaped somewhat like pencils with the blunt end painted red or black, or sometimes left plain. These cones were used for wall mosaics. None are *in situ* but their use is proved by examples of the same technique of a later date.

At Warka (Uruk) the Germans have excavated a Ziggurat tower with a high stepped platform constructed of mud bricks. The upper part of the walls is decorated in panels with a mosaic of large clay cones, hollow like vases, and sunk in the mud plaster. A very striking effect is obtained by the white rims and the dark shadow of the interiors. As Woolley says, "In this case the size of the 'inlay' is determined by the height of the building—seen from so far away the small solid cones would have been ineffective—and the hollows take the place of color".

In another building at Warka there is an example of the small-cone technique. Here, there is a great courtyard enclosed by a wall with half columns and at one end steps lead to a terrace with a columned hall. The columns, the façade of the terrace and the whole of the courtyard wall were covered with a mosaic, red and black and white, made up of the same little pencil-like cones as are found in the débris of the al 'Ubaid houses. To quote Woolley again, "On every half-column the pattern is different; the panels of the platform front, framed by pilasters in relief, are filled with delicate designs; as in the case of the painted pottery, the elements are simple, zigzags, triangles and lozenges, but these are combined into an intricately varied scheme of decoration, and though the colors are faded now the general effect is wonderfully rich..." Woolley thinks that these mosaics were used instead of paint to preserve the mud plaster of the walls as they formed an almost waterproof covering as well as a permanent decoration.

The earliest mosaics were made with clay cones only. In time, animal motifs were combined with the early geometric patterns and later these were made in one piece—silhouetted figures of baked clay—and set against a background of cone mosaic. According to Woolley the final step was "to extend the technique of the figures to the background also, and instead of the long pencil-like cones imbedded in the plaster we find a mosaic of large or small pieces of flat stone secured by copper wire and bitumen to a wooden backing, or the figures might be inlaid in slabs of solid stone, as is the case with some of the Kish palace decoration".

At al 'Ubaid a remarkably ornate little shrine of the First Dynasty of Ur, 3100-3000 B. C., the so-called Temple of A-anni-padda, can be reconstructed from the many fragments which have been uncovered. The entrance was flanked by palm-columns covered with a mosaic of red and black stone and mother-of-pearl—lozenges and triangles—anticipating to some extent the mosaic columns of Pompeii. On the walls were mosaic freizes—a dairy scene, rows of cattle, and birds—the figures of shell or limestone against a background of black stone.

The Sumerians also decorated various objects, harps, gaming-boards, furniture with silhouetted figures cut from the solid portion of the conch-shell and set against a background of lapis-lazuli mosaic. This technique is in the old tradition of the wall mosaics reduced in scale. The most remarkable example is the extraordinary "Standard of Ur" with its rows of men and animals portraying a field of battle and the celebration of victory.

Woolley thinks that the early Sumerian reliefs were strongly influenced by the old tradition of mosaic as they are separated from the plane of the background by an almost vertical edge and the background must have been originally filled with a colored paste or mosaic.

Work which may be classed as a kind of mosaic existed at a comparatively early date in Egypt. Numerous objects belonging to the minor arts show a minute inlay of colored glass, lapis-lazuli, and other stones in small compartments of ivory, and similar work on a larger scale as a decoration for the capitals of columns has been found at Tel-el-Yehudia in Lower Egypt. Here, bits of colored glass and earthenware have been inserted into sinkages to form lotus and other patterns. In a temple of Rameses II, near Heliopolis, there are some wall reliefs with an inlay of glass paste.

The early Minoans were also familiar with the methods of mosaic. Sir Arthur Evans discovered a rough stone box in the Lesser Palace at Knossos containing small tesseræ of crystal, amethyst, beryl, lapis-lazuli, and solid gold which must have been used for very fine work resembling the later miniature mosaics of the Byzantines. For their pavements the

Ægeans also imbedded pebbles in a hard clay, sometimes using different colors to form simple patterns and such work may have led directly to the Greek pebble mosaics, such as those found recently at Olynthus and which we shall consider later.

In Mohammedan countries the native artists seldom imitated cube mosaics of the Roman or Byzantine type. The few surviving examples such as those in "The Dome of the Rock" at Jerusalem, the Great Mosque at Damascus, or the Mosque at Cordova were done by Early Christians or Byzantines. But the Mohammedans inherited the great ceramic traditions of Mesopotamia and Persia, the glazed and enamelled brick of the Chaldeans and Babylonians which had been continued by their successors, and from these traditions came wall tiles. Persia, in addition to the purely faience or lustre tiles, developed a mosaic tile, which from the fourteenth to the seventeenth centuries was used in some of the most beautiful polychrome decorations in existence. The technique consisted of cutting large tiles of solid colors into small shaped units which were then assembled into rich and complex patterns. The dominant color was a deep blue with turquoise as a foil, and other tones—light emerald, saffron, a rich black, and white—were used for outlines and accents. The patterns followed the intricacy and finesse of the Persian miniaturists. Remarkable examples are found in the mosque at Veramin of the early fourteenth century, the mosque of Chah-Sindeh at Samarkand, 1392, and at Isfahan, especially, the great portal of the Masjid-i-Shah.

Further west in Northern Africa and Spain the Mohammedan potters developed a slightly different type of mosaic faience which later became Spanish *azulejos* and which we find in the Alhambra, the House of Pilate at Seville and elsewhere. Persian mosaic faience found its way to India in the wake of the Moslem conquerors and there are still fine examples in old tombs and mosques, notably at Delhi. A similar technique was used on the great entrance arch and loggia of the Chinili Kiosk for the Seraglio at Constantinople, erected from 1466 to 1470.

However, in Persia and the rest of the East mosaic tiles were gradually abandoned in favor of those of painted faience.

We may also mention the small scale geometric inlay of wood, often combined with ivory and mother-of-pearl, used throughout the Mohammedan world for the decoration of furniture and panels, and which may be called a kind of mosaic.

A technique closely related to mosaic, called *opus sectile* by the Romans, consists of an inlay in which the materials are cut to fit the contours of the design. It was much employed by the Romans, as we shall see later, and revived in the well-known Florentine intarsia of the sixteenth and seventeenth centuries. It was most brilliantly developed under the Moguls in India in their buildings at Agra and Delhi where the most intricate patterns are formed in the cut marble and color is furnished not only by colored marbles but by precious and semi-precious stones.

But mosaics were not confined solely to the civilizations which grew up in Mesopotamia and about the Mediterranean. They also played an important rôle in the early cultures of Central America and Mexico. Included in the loot of the first Spanish conquistadores, the expeditions of Juan de Grijalva in 1518, and Cortes in 1519-1525, were shields, helmets, statucttes and other objects covered with extraordinary turquoise mosaics. Some of these found their way to Spain and Italy and may be seen in the Ethnographic Museum in Rome and elsewhere. More recent archæological expeditions have greatly increased the number and splendid examples may now be found in several museums.

These so-called turquoise mosaics so prized by the Aztecs were used to cover masks, shields, plaques, helmets, and many other objects. Sometimes, as in Mesopotamia, they were employed as a background for figures in flat relief. Although turquoise predominates, other materials were used—jadeite, malachite, quartz, beryl, garnet, obsidian, marcasite, gold, bits of colored shell, mother-of-pearl. These materials were fixed to a base of wood or stone, or even gold or shell or pottery, and held in place by a vegetal pitch or gum, or a kind of cement. Designs formed of the actual pieces were of less importance than the general effect of rich vibrating color, but some of the plaques have simple patterns of concentric circles and geometric motifs. The extraordinary feature is that the pieces employed, roughly square or rectangular in shape, are like those used in the Roman and Christian mosaics, and they may be called tesseræ or cubes in the actual sense of the word. In fact, the two techniques are so similar that it is difficult to believe that they are not related even though they developed so for apart.

These mosaics were still flourishing under the Aztecs at the time of the Spanish conquest but they go back in origin at least to the early Mayan civilization. There is a remarkable plaque of turquoise set in black cement or gum on sandstone, at Chichen Itzá in Yucatan, from the so-called "Altar Cache" of the Temple of the Warriors. Somewhat similar work, though cruder, has also been found with ancient remains of the Pueblos of Arizona and New Mexico and incrusted objects have been discovered in connection with early burials on the coast of Peru.

The Aztecs also adorned garments, and objects for warfare or religious ceremonies with mosaics made of tiny bits of feathers applied to wood, skin or paper with glue. These less durable feather mosaics have, of course, almost entirely disappeared. We may mention that the Chinese have also made feather mosaics.

Thus, we see that mosaics are not confined to one area or one period. Various peoples during the last few thousand years have used them as a means of artistic expression. But the great art of mosaic which developed and spread about the shores of the Mediterranean and has left us so much of the really permanent beauty of the past is our primary concern in the following chapters.

THE CHARACTERISTICS AND TECHNIQUE
OF CLASSICAL AND CHRISTIAN MOSAICS

THE CHARACTERISTICS AND TECHNIQUE OF CLASSICAL AND
CHRISTIAN MOSAICS

Distinguishing qualities—Primarily an architectural decoration—Comparison with painting and with stained glass—Possibilities and limitations—Technique: materials, methods and processes.

II
THE CHARACTERISTICS AND TECHNIQUE OF CLASSICAL AND CHRISTIAN MOSAICS

Mosaic as here considered is a surface decoration made by setting small pieces of differently colored stone or glass in a bed of cement. It is well to bear in mind how it technically differs from painting, for its special processes give it its individual character. It is primarily an architectural decoration whether used as a pavement or upon walls, in fact, it cannot well exist without its architectural setting; small portative mosaic panels or pictures are an off-shoot of the major art, and with these we shall not be much concerned here.

Nearly all the earliest mosaics which have survived are pavements, composed of tesseræ, or cubes, of variously colored marbles, and, in fact, in ancient times pavements of mosaic were probably used much more extensively than wall decorations, although the latter were not unknown. With the beginning of an officially recognized Christian art in the fourth century, wall mosaics take on a greater importance, and differ essentially from the pavements on account of their being almost entirely composed of tesseræ of colored glass. Pavements of mosaic continue, of course, but they tend to follow the older traditions both in design and technique, and, in general, become a separate branch of the art, having little or no influence upon wall decorations. The study of later pavements is, therefore, a special subject which will only concern us here in so far as it throws light upon the early development of the art as a whole.

On account of their possibilities for color, mosaics have never been surpassed as architectural adornment on a large scale, and in the early Christian period, and for the greater part of the Middle Ages, throughout the Byzantine Empire and in Italy, they were the chief murals; frescoes occupying a secondary position. The broad, simple treatment and the tendency towards abstraction and formalization, characteristic of all early mediæval art, and, especially that of the Near East, were eminently suited to the technique of mosaic and to subjects which were to be seen at a distance. During the great periods of the art until the fourteenth century, the mosaicists possessed a knowledge of their craft, an understanding of the possibilities as well as the limitations of the medium, equal to that of the great painters.

Mosaics are best suited to dimly lighted interiors and to constantly changing surfaces, such as the curves of an apse. As they reflect so much light themselves, the light which strikes them should never be too direct or too intense. The great mosaic interiors like St. Mark's at Venice, Torcello, the Florentine Baptistery, the Dome of the Rock at Jerusalem, and the Sicilian apses are all dimly lighted. The few examples we have of exterior mosaics are less successful.

The qualities of the best mosaics have, perhaps, never been better described than by John Addington Symonds, in the frequently-quoted passage from his "Sketches in Italy": "The superiority of mosaics over fresco as an architectural adjunct on this gigantic scale is apparent at a glance in Monreale. Permanency of splendor and glowing richness of tone are all on the side of the mosaics. Their true rival is painted glass. The jewelled churches of the South are constructed for the display of colored surfaces illuminated by sunlight falling on them from narrow windows, just as those of the North—Rheims, for example, or Le Mans—are built for the transmission of light through a variegated medium of transparent hues. The painted windows of the Northern cathedral find their proper counterpart in the mosaics of the South. The Gothic architect strove to obtain the greatest amount of translucent surface. The Byzantine builder directed his attention to securing just enough light for the illumination of his glistening walls."

Roger Fry[2] in an interesting article emphasizes what he calls "the unique power of mosaic in the realization of vision. The vibrancy of effect produced by decidedly broken color creates a definite æsthetic stimulant which in the right surroundings, quickens religious emotion." This vibration of color, a kind of super-impressionism, from the juxtaposition of a variety of spots of distinctly different tones, is what gives mosaic its most individual quality and differentiates it from fresco.

Mosaics show a kind of collective inspiration, common to nearly all early mediæval art. The personality of the artist does not emerge; no work is signed until the thirteenth century. The early examples were often done by groups of artists, as in the old Cathedral of Ravenna, the Basilica Ursiana, where four mosaicists worked: Eusebius and Paulus on the left half, and Statius and Stephanus on the right. [3]

The art of mosaic is vital and independent until the fourteenth century. From that time on, it becomes gradually submerged by the dominating influence of painting, and continues to exist, almost as a mere craft, only at Venice and at Rome. There is a certain revival of interest in the nineteenth century, but this is unaccompanied by any real appreciation of its inherent qualities as an art, as far as actual production is concerned. It is only in our own day that there are signs of a true revival.

We shall trace its growth through Early Christian times to the splendid culmination of the fifth and the sixth centuries at Ravenna and elsewhere, and continue through the further developments which bring about the second great period of the twelfth and the thirteenth centuries in Greece, Venice, Sicily and Rome; we shall then pass in review more briefly its losing struggle against the constantly increasing adverse conditions beginning with the Renaissance.

Some knowledge of the technique[4] is necessary to rightly understand such a highly specialized art, which depends so much upon proper execution for its effect. The surface to be decorated, wall, vault, or cupola, was rusticated and covered with a coat of cement, often several inches in thickness, to provide an even ground. Upon this foundation, a second coat of very strong cement was applied to receive the actual mosaic. Sometimes as many as three coats were used if the foundation had not properly prepared the surface. A problem arose which was somewhat similar to that in fresco painting. On account of the comparatively rapid drying of the cement, only that amount of the final coat could be laid in which the tesseræ could be imbedded at one time. The best mortar was usually considered to be a combination of powdered marble, lime and a kind of natural Portland cement. The Romans used the volcanic substance known as *pozzulana* which has many of the qualities of Portland cement. At the end of the sixteenth century, Muziano da Brescia, the director of the work in St. Peter's, invented a slow-drying cement, or mastic mixed with oil, which was used to some extent in St. Peter's and elsewhere, and since then there have been many experiments to try to improve the binding material.

It has been proved that in some of the best work which has successfully resisted for centuries the ravages of time the coats of cement are very thin, the first being little more than one inch in thickness, and the second hardly one quarter of an inch. With cement of the best quality mosaics are practically indestructible and merit the definition which Ghirlandaio is said to have applied to them, *"La pittura per l'eternità"*; a good deal of the destruction which has necessitated so much restoration, even in the early mosaics, has been caused by the cement becoming detached from the walls; oftentimes due to the fact that the foundation coat was not moistened when the second coat was applied.

Every age in the past has notoriously despised the work of its predecessors, and restorations were often an excuse for destruction; but, nevertheless, in the case of many mosaics almost constant renewal has been necessary on account of the poor quality of the foundation.

For example, in the recent restoration of the triumphal arch of Santa Maria Maggiore at Rome, a work of the fifth century, it was discovered that the foundation coat of cement, at least five centimeters thick, had been applied to a perfectly smooth brick wall to which it had not bound sufficiently. In addition, the surface coat of cement in which the tesseræ were imbedded had in places separated from the foundation coat. In order to preserve the work it was necessary to remove the surface very carefully in pieces so as not to disturb the position of the tesseræ in the slightest degree, and then to entirely renew the foundation. In the thirteenth century apse of this same church it has also been found that Torriti studded the foundation cement with iron nails in order to strengthen it. These nails have rusted away during the course of the centuries and have not only stained the surface of the mosaic but have caused the cement to disintegrate so that some time a very drastic restoration will be necessary in order to preserve the work.

In 1648[5] a decree was passed in Venice forbidding salutes of artillery and fireworks on the Piazza of St. Mark's, as it was found that the resulting vibration caused damage to the mosaics in the basilica. In 1697 it was found necessary to enforce this decree even more rigorously.

The surface having been prepared, the tesseræ were squeezed into it, not too closely together, with the result that some of the cement was usually pushed up between the joints, and colored if the white showed too strongly. The tesseræ varied in size and shape. As a rule they were roughly rectangular or square, and from an eighth of an inch to three quarters of an inch in size. The smallest were usually employed for faces and hands and other details, while the larger ones were used in the backgrounds and draperies. We speak of them either as "cubes" or "tesseræ", but "cube" should not suggest that they are square in the strict sense of the word. Every appearance of mechanical precision was avoided and the pieces always have the irregularity which comes from the chipping.

Mosaics depend, perhaps, more than anything else upon the proper reflection of light. If the cubes were merely pushed in flush with the surface there would be, in many cases, an over-reflection. To avoid this, they were often tilted at an angle, usually of about thirty degrees, depending upon their position and the amount of light. This has been noted by Boni at Parenzo, by Walter George at St. Irene in Constantinople, and by Marguerite van Berchem at Jerusalem and Damascus,[6] and recently by Thomas Whittemore in the narthex of St. Sophia. A clear understanding of tone values tended to leave the cubes of lighter color slightly raised above those which were darker; in most of the good work the blacks and other dark tones are always more deeply set than the rest.

In the Roman pavements the tesseræ were usually of Greek and Luna marbles, with other stone employed occasionally. Thus, the color-scale was very restricted; black and white, red, yellow, and an olive-brown were the chief tones. Cubes of glass enamel and even gold cubes were, however, sometimes employed in the wall decorations, as in fountain niches at Pompeii and elsewhere, and perhaps their use was even more extensive than we now realize, as nearly all traces of wall coverings of this character have, of course, been destroyed. In many of the Roman pavements the tesseræ have been closely fitted together, giving the polished effect of modern work, but the few fragments of wall mosaics which have come down to us are better in this respect. Seneca mentions walls hidden by glass, and the historian Flavius Vopiscus, writing at the beginning of the fourth century, speaks of a wealthy Roman who had his house decorated with squares of glass set in bitumen.[7] The basilica of Junius Bassus on the Esquiline had glass mosaics, and it is probably fragments of these which still exist in the Palazzo del Drago in Rome. The Museo delle Terme has a few fragments which are similar to those in the early Christian basilicas. Therefore we cannot say that the Christians were the first to use glass mosaics.

Although the art probably originated in the East, the early Christians must have found the technique ready to hand in the buildings of pagan Rome; but they were, apparently, the first to make use of it as mural decoration on such a large scale and to realize the full splendor of its color effects.

The glass used in the manufacture of the tesseræ was generally colored by the introduction of metallic oxides. Oxide of tin was used from very early times to make the color opaque; oxide of copper was used for the blues, chromium for the greens, and so on. The manufacture of gold and silver cubes is more complicated, and the process still in use at Murano probably represents a very old method; at least, it is similar to that used in the manufacture of the Early Christian figured, gold glasses. A thin piece of glass is taken, shaped somewhat like a watch-crystal. Gold foil is applied to the concave side and the glass is then subjected to a certain amount of heat. Then, some fused enamel, usually dark red or green, is poured into the concave side; the whole is flattened, fired again, and allowed gradually to cool. Thus, when it is cut up, there are three layers; the enamel base, the gold foil, and the thin transparent film which protects it. This protective film, in process of time, is apt to fall off, causing those dark spots which we so frequently see in the gold backgrounds. In the earliest times, the enamel base was usually of a colorless glass, but from about the eighth century it was the custom to use red glass as it gave a richer effect to the gold.

In the earliest mosaics the backgrounds are usually light, and marble tesseræ are used in connection with the glass. The mosaics of Santa Costanza and those of the nave of Santa Maria Maggiore have light backgrounds in the classical manner. Blue backgrounds were also used as early as the fourth century, and they never wholly died out. The most beautiful example is, perhaps, the vault of the Mausoleum of Galla Placidia, and almost equally fine is the sixth century apse of SS. Cosma e Damiano. In the fifth and the early sixth centuries the use of gold backgrounds became almost universal and has persisted ever since. The names San Martino a Cielo d'Oro, now Sant'Apollinare Nuovo at Ravenna, and San Victor a Cielo d'Oro at Milan bear witness to the success of this new method.

The range of colors employed even in the earlier wall mosaics was not large. In the nave of Santa Maria Maggiore there were forty-eight different tones comprising shades of red, blue, rose, green, yellow, gray, in addition to black and brown. The number was varied and extended as time went on, but in the best work only a comparatively few strong colors were used. It is the very essence of mosaic, which is meant to be seen at a distance, and relies so much upon the vibration of color, to employ only a few strongly contrasted tones to obtain brilliancy of effect. Audacious spotting of intense color in clearly defined areas gives the best of the early mosaics an extraordinary carrying power. It is only later when the art strove to imitate the methods and appearances of painting that the gradations were so enormously multiplied, so that today the Vatican studio boasts of over twenty-eight thousand different shades.

Thomas Whittemore in his careful study of the mosaics of the narthex of St. Sophia at Constantinople has taken accurate note of all the colors used there. In the marble tesseræ he found a white and a neutral tint, yellow ochre, yellow brown, cadmium orange, rose madder and Rubens madder. The colors of the glass tesseræ are: lemon yellow, red ochre, red brown, indigo, purple lake, Van Dyke brown, rose brown, raw umber, burnt umber, cobalt blue, ultramarine, veridian, cobalt green, chrome yellow, chrome green and haematite black. Thus, we find a rather restricted range of color even in a series of the most splendid Byzantine mosaics.

In the mosaics of "The Dome of the Rock" at Jerusalem, unsurpassed for the richness of their color effects, Marguerite Van Berchem has noted the following tones: the dominating notes are green, blue, and gold—the greens and the blues by their splendid tints recalling those of Persian ceramics. To these three fundamental colors are added, but in small quantities, several shades of red, silver, grey, violet or mauve, brown, black and white. All of the tesseræ are of glass except those of white, grey, and rose which are of stone.

Marble and stone tesseræ continued throughout the whole period to be used to a large extent for the faces and the hands. It is sometimes very difficult to distinguish between the grayish-white cubes of opaque glass which were often used, and those of marble. In the sixth century other materials—mother-of-pearl, even semi-precious stones—were sometimes employed for richness and variety of effect, as in San Vitale at Ravenna. A good many marble and stone tesseræ are used in the Venetian mosaics and Torriti uses marble tesseræ in the apse of Santa Maria Maggiore at Rome.

From the time of the Roman pavements to the Renaissance special local materials were also employed in conjunction with marble or glass. For example, in France, a black bituminous schist and a white and reddish limestone found near Autun were used in the pavements of that region. Mosaics from Boulogne-sur-Mer contain black and white cubes which come from nearby quarries, and bluish cubes in a mosaic from Anthée (Namur) are of a marble found in the vicinity of Dinant. At Salerno in Southern Italy, pebbles from the gulf were used for the whitish portions of the mosaics, and in the mosaics of St. Mark's at Venice we find pebbles from the river Piave. Later, at St. Peter's at Rome, a stone from Cotanello was employed for certain flesh tones. Tesseræ of terra-cotta are often found—and even egg-shells.

Early mosaics were always executed *in situ*. It is a question as to how much of the actual design was indicated on the surface as a guide for the placing of the cubes. In some cases plaster was laid on the foundation coat of cement, and on this the principal features of the design were drawn and colored. This was removed little by little as the work progressed, and the binding cement and tesseræ substituted for it. It seems, however, to have been more usual to scratch the design upon the cement, occasionally indicating the larger areas of color as a guide. We now have proof that on the triumphal arch of Santa Maria Maggiore the cartoon for the mosaic was rather carefully drawn and indicated in color on the plaster below and Torriti followed the same method eight centuries later in the apse. In any case, the designs, carefully thought out beforehand, must have been produced by a master mosaicist who controlled the work, and the tesseræ arranged upon some sort of cartoon, following much the same method that was employed in mediæval stained glass. Details and much of the actual placing of the cubes were left to assistants, highly trained in their craft, who manipulated the tesseræ in the same intelligent way that the painter used his brush. We may mention that the cement which showed between the tesseræ was sometimes stained to blend with the colors of the tesseræ themselves and was sometimes left a neutral gray. A fairly common practice seems to have been to stain the cement of the gold backgrounds red in order to enhance the effect, as in the narthex of St. Sophia at Constantinople and at Nicæa.

Later, when the designs were controlled by the painters, elaborate cartoons were provided, worked out in minute detail. They were usually pricked through or stencilled upon the surface to be decorated. All the mosaicist had to do was to mechanically copy a pattern. The final stage was to paste the cubes face downwards upon a paper model, transport them in sections, and put them in place. This lifeless method is still followed today, but the tendency now is to break away from it.

An understanding of the ways by which the best mosaics were produced ought to help one to appreciate them more fully. Technique in itself does not make a work of art, but in the case of mosaics, its degradation from the time of the Renaissance has almost prevented the accomplishing of anything of real excellence, so that it does not seem out of place to discuss this development in more or less detail.

HELLENISTIC AND ROMAN MOSAICS

Hellenistic and Roman Mosaics

Mosaics of classical Greece; the pebble mosaics of Olynthus—Late Hellenistic and Roman pavements from Syria to Britain—Varieties of mosaic as understood by the Romans—Résumé of Roman pavements and their influence upon Early Christian mosaics—Palestine, Syria, Northern Africa—The earliest Wall mosaics—the "Silvanus" from Ostia—Catacomb mosaics—Changes brought about by the recognition of Christianity.

III.

HELLENISTIC AND ROMAN MOSAICS

It was long thought that the Greeks of classical times did not employ mosaic, but recently a very interesting series of mosaic pavements have been uncovered at Olynthus in Macedonia, dating from the fifth and the fourth centuries B. C.[8] This discovery fills an important gap in the early history of the art, but it is too soon as yet to say just how much direct influence work of this kind had upon the later Hellenistic pavements of cube mosaic. These Olynthus mosaics are composed of pebbles of red, white, blue, green, and purple. Mythological scenes and other designs are represented. One of the earliest, in blue and white natural pebbles, shows Bellerophon on the winged Pegasus, hurling a spear at the Chimæra beneath him. Another represents two griffins tearing to pieces a stag; another a warrior with a yellow helmet attacking a centaur. Others show a lion devouring a stag, two winged griffins on either side of a deer, birds and animals, and floral designs. Although these pavements are very different technically from later mosaics, the transition from pebbles to cubes is not an abrupt one, but rather, the refining of a cruder method.

It is, however, in Egypt, in the time of the Ptolemies, that the fashion of decorating pavements and walls with tesseræ of marble and other materials seems to have developed into an independent art which spread into the rest of the Near East—Syria, Asia Minor, and Constantinople, and to the Roman provinces of the West. Two qualities especially inherent in mosaic—splendor of color and durability—must have strongly appealed to the Romans, for the quantity of pavements found in every province, stretching from Mesopotamia to Germany and England, is almost numberless.

Very few of these remains can be dated earlier than the first century before Christ, although there are a few late Hellenistic pavements at Delos and elsewhere; the great majority of them are of the time of the

Empire. Egyptian, especially Alexandrian influence, is strong in all the Imperial Roman mosaics, whether in Pompeii, Palestine, Northern Africa, or the other provinces. This is seen especially in the representations of the aquatic life of the Nile with the native fauna and flora, and, also, in the types of more conventional decoration.

The Romans classified mosaics into several categories [9], according to the kinds and the forms of the materials used. *Opus tessellatum* was composed of cubes of marble or stone, regularly placed in simple geometric patterns, and most of the Roman black and white pavements were carried out in this technique. *Opus vermiculatum* employed cubes of colored marbles or glass in a more irregular way to obtain a pictorial effect, and when this method was applied to walls and vaults it was more properly called *opus musivum*. It is from these last two methods that the mural mosaics of the Early Christians develop.

The work which the Romans designated as *opus sectile* does not come under the head of mosaic, although it has sometimes been thus classified. It is a marquetry in marble or other colored material, in which the pieces are cut in irregular patterns following more or less closely the outlines of the objects represented. The most famous early examples are the panels representing fighting beasts from the Basilica of Junius Bassus, now in the Capitoline Museum, and the more elaborate Hylas and the Nymphs and the Consular Chariot from the same basilica, now in the Palazzo del Drago. In the Tigress and the Bull from the Capitoline, the background is of green porphyry and the skin of the tigress is of *giallo antico* with stripes of the same green porphyry. The bull is in different shades of marble varying from cream to brown; various browns are used for the earth and the trees; white marble is used for the leaves, and the eyes of both beasts are of mother-of-pearl. This technique, employing comparatively large pieces of marble cut to fit the contours of the design, had no influence upon the Early Christian wall mosaics which, as we have seen, are executed in *opus vermiculatum* or *opus musivum*.

Roman pavements of the first two centuries are almost entirely Hellenistic in inspiration, and Alexandria was probably the center of this radiating influence (1, 2 and 3). We find all the scenes of classical mythology, landscapes illustrating the idylls of Theocritus, as well as the exceedingly popular scenes of life on the Nile, and other genre subjects. It will be sufficient to mention the famous mosaic from Palestrina with its great variety of Nilotic subjects, naturalistically treated; the Academy of Plato from Torre Annunziata and the Battle of Issus from Pompeii, both now in the Naples Museum. Later, in the period of the Antonines and the third and fourth centuries, the subjects often have a more native flavor and more realism; one will recall the boxers and gladiators from the Baths of Caracalla (4).

Sometimes, a separate mosaic picture,[10] or *emblema,* a miniature copying of some popular painting, was inserted in the center of a frame with a border of geometric or floral designs. One of the best known of the *emblemæ* is the famous "Doves" of the Capitoline Museum, found at Hadrian's Villa (5). In its minute technique and striving to imitate the naturalistic effects of painting, this is not unlike the later Roman mosaics of the seventeenth century. It may even be a copy of the mosaic so much admired by Pliny, executed by a Greek artist, Sosos, from Pergamon.

Many of these *emblemæ* discovered at Pompeii or Herculaneum, may be seen in the Museum at Naples, others in the museums of Rome and elsewhere. They were common throughout the empire. One of the most widely known, now in the Naples Museum, is signed by Dioskourides of Samos, and probably copies a Hellenistic painting of the fourth century B. C. More charming than this is a panel showing a group of actors and musicians in front of stage scenery. This is also in Naples. Most characteristic are the many genre scenes, animals, still-life, in fact, all the repertoire so dear to the Dutch painters of the seventeenth century. They appealed to a popular taste which was impressed by a certain facile technical skill in imitating the light and shade and the minute gradations of paint. They have, of course, little or no influence upon the later development of wall mosaics which sought to give an entirely different impression.

Pavements, as we have seen in our discussion of technique, were nearly always composed of tesseræ of marble, or stone, with a limited number of colors. Glass cubes were occasionally used, as in the early pavement from the House of the Faun at Pompeii, but this is almost an isolated example. However, in the wall mosaics which have disappeared glass tesseræ were used to a considerable extent, if we may believe the early writers, such as Seneca and Flavius Vopiscus. It seems probable that this custom of employing glass tesseræ also originated in Hellenistic Egypt [11] along with the manufacture of pavements. The Egyptians were also famous for their great fondness for decoration in color.

We have not the space to consider in detail the interesting pavements of Northern Africa [12], of Syria—especially Antioch—and the Holy Land [13], nor, indeed, of all the territories where Roman civilization held sway for any length of time, from the British Isles to the Black Sea. Often, they have great intrinsic merit and are well adapted for their purpose; simple effective designs of black and white; the motifs of the borders, frets, meanders, garlands, masks, in the best classical traditions. Others show an over-fondness for naturalistic representation, an indiscriminate strewing of the surface with unrelated objects which may even descend to the utmost depths of vulgarity and naïveté, as, for example, a large mosaic in the Lateran Museum which may be a copy of the famous pavement of Sosus of Pergamon, described by Pliny, upon which the débris of a feast—bones, egg-shells, mice carrying off scraps of food—were painstakingly displayed; a permanent record of bad taste and bad table manners.

On the whole, they continue as a separate tradition. From their very nature—they are to be trodden upon—only the more durable materials, such as marble or stone are employed, and this tends to confine them within certain limits and to divide them more and more from the wall mosaics. Here, they interest us principally as a link in the development of the art, and for their influence upon the first Christian wall mosaics of the fourth and the fifth centuries.

Among the hundreds of pavements scattered throughout Europe as far north as Roman civilization held sway we may mention a few outstanding examples. In France, a villa discovered at Jurançon contains one of the most extensive series of paved rooms in existence. A great mosaic at Lillebonne has a central *emblema* with Diana and Callisto, surrounded by a border of hunting scenes. There are other fine mosaics at Rheims, especially the "Mosaic of the Promenade", at Aix-en-Provence, Lyon, Cherchel, Sainte-Colombe, near Vienne and many other places. In Germany we have the remarkable mosaic at Nennig, near Trier, with combats of gladiators and *bestiarii* in hexagonal panels, and at Trier itself, the third-century mosaic signed by Monnos—a pavement nineteen feet square, about two thirds preserved, with representations of the Muses, famous writers of antiquity, and the Months. The Woodchester pavement in England—nearly fifty feet square—was discovered in 1797. In the center was a figure of Orpheus surrounded by compartments filled in with guilloches, scrolls and frets. Orpheus was a favorite subject in British mosaics and occurs at Cirencester in Gloucestershire and at Brading in the Isle of Wight. Quite recently other interesting Roman pavements have been discovered in England.

In Northern Africa, especially, the whole development of this art may be traced from the earlier pavements of a purely classical tradition to the tombal mosaics of the fourth and the fifth centuries, such as those at Tabarka, which are already in what might be called that general Mediterranean style prevalent in the Near East and Italy, and even in Spain, as we shall see later.

Many of these Northern African pavements, especially those found at Uthina (Oudna), Timgad, and Cyrene show a development of floral designs in all-over patterns which are carried out with an astonishing richness of color, and which almost anticipate the splendor of the Early Christian wall mosaics. Some of these date from as early as the second century, but they are quite different from the typical Roman pavement of two or three tones with the *emblema* in the center. A charming vintage scene from the Villa of the Laberii at Uthina [14] shows Dionysus in the center giving the vine to Ikarios, King of Attica. Over the background, interlacing vines grow in pairs from four vases in the corners, strikingly similar to a design on the ring-vault of Santa Costanza at Rome. The whole is enclosed in a heavy border of fruits and flowers with four masks.

At Timgad [15] we have even more elaborately developed all-over patterns in the "carpet style", so-called from the resemblance to richly woven textiles. The motifs consist of scrolls, conventionalized flowers and foliage, interspersed with birds, animals, and vases with sometimes a panel in the center representing a mythological scene. Fine examples are the pavement from the House of Sertius, now in the Museum of Timgad, the *"Mosaïque de la Piscine"*, (6) and in a more conventionalized manner, the pavement from the baths of a society known as the *Filadelfi*. The predominating colors in these mosaics are blue, green, and red, with less use of black, white, gray and yellow.

Some fine pavements dating from the first or the second century have been found in a Roman villa at Zliten,[16] in Tripoli near the border of Tunis. The most famous represents a series of gladiatorial combats, but more beautiful is one composed of magnificent acanthus scrolls, recalling the *Ara Pacis* at Rome, with birds and animals on the branches (7). This and the other African pavements we have mentioned show that richness of color was not unknown to the mosaicists of classical times. The designs of these carpet style mosaics recall the early textiles discovered at Antinoë and elsewhere in Egypt, and we may well suppose an Alexandrian influence here.

The series of over forty pavements uncovered since 1932 at Antioch show in striking fashion the progress of mosaic in that center during the first six centuries. The subjects remain pagan even in those which may be ascribed to a late date. There is a great fondness for mythological scenes and, especially, personifications. Here, as in Northern Africa, one may trace a gradual breaking away from a servile copying of contemporary painting with its gradations of tone to a bolder, more stylized technique, more expressive of the medium. One of the finest, a beautiful head of Thalassa from the fifth century may be compared with the early wall mosaics—Ravenna or Salonika—and the Arab mosaics of Jerusalem and Damascus are in a broad sense a later development of these Syrian traditions.

There are tantalizing references to mosaics in a number of the ancient writers and these would be an inestimable aid in forming a clearer idea of the development of the art, if even a few fragments of such work remained. A pavement on a vessel belonging to Hieron II, king of Syracuse, in the third century B. C., told the story of the Iliad in a series of panels. Ptolomey Philopator, 222-205 B. C., had a figured pavement on one of his pleasure boats for the Nile. Possibly the fragments found in the lake of Nemi and now in the Museo Nazionale at Rome, composed of very small tesseræ of glass, serpentine, and porphyry belonged to a similar pavement for one of the pleasure galleys of Caligula. According to Spartian, one of the authors of the *Historia Augusta*, there was a mosaic in the vault of a portico in the gardens of Commodus which portrayed Pescennius Niger, who became emperor in 193, in the midst of his friends and holding the sacred objects of the cult of Isis.

The fact that the early wall mosaics, as those of Santa Costanza and the nave of Santa Maria Maggiore, have light backgrounds may show that they started from the same tradition. Moreover, some of the motifs in the vaults of Santa Costanza are similar to those of the pavements. The recently discovered pavement at Aquileia,[17] one of the most extensive and beautiful examples which has come down to us, is a Christian work of the early fourth century. In its combination of genre subjects, fishing scenes, realistic portraiture, and the symbolism of the catacombs, it clearly anticipates the style of the mosaics of Santa Costanza, executed a little later. The popular Nilotic scenes were taken over by the early Christians in the dome of Santa Costanza, and in the apses of the Lateran and Santa Maria Maggiore; and Choricus of Gaza, writing in the fifth century, describes a similar scene in a church in his native town.[18] The naturalistic backgrounds in the Old Testament scenes of Santa Maria Maggiore are in the same general tradition as the Pompeian frescoes and the Theocritan idylls of the pavements. Even the strongly-modelled, colorful heads of the Apostles from the Baptistery of the Orthodox at Ravenna have a certain affinity with the pugilists from the Baths of Caracalla; and many other resemblances might be pointed out.

These points in common between classical pavements and the first Christian mosaics merely show that the early decorators of the churches took over a process that was already at hand, and with it, certain traditional modes of representation. But the aims of the two were widely divergent, and almost from the first, the older classical traditions exist almost as anachronisms, or survivals tending to disappear. The Christian artists had a sense of color which the Romans probably never possessed; the pale backgrounds became richer and soon changed to blue or gold.

The few remaining traces of wall mosaic before the fourth century and Santa Costanza are so scanty that it is difficult to form an idea of the actual appearance of such work. All that do survive are on a small scale, such as the niches for fountains discovered at Pompeii (8 and 9), with classical motifs in a few strongly contrasted tones. In Pompeii, even columns were covered with mosaic (10). The ground was usually blue; reds were obtained by cubes of pottery, lava, and ferruginous stone; even shell was used in some of the compositions. The use of gold cubes was extremely rare at this period.

Even more dependent upon pavement technique than these Pompeian mosaics is a vault decoration discovered at Hadrian's Villa. There is a floral-geometric design in black on a ground of white marble tesseræ. This vault belongs to a house which has been dated as early as republican times, later incorporated by Hadrian in the imperial residence, and, therefore, this may be the earliest extant example we have of the application of mosaic to walls or ceilings. Another example of the second century A. D., still showing a close relationship to the pavements, is the vault of a circular domed nymphæum near the Via Tiburtina in Rome, which is completely covered with a ground of white marble tesseræ. Corrado Ricci [19] suggests that the Romans were led to use mosaic instead of painting on walls as they had discovered its resistance to dampness and water in pavements and in the pools of the baths. It was, therefore, an easy step to employ it in fountain niches as at Pompeii. In these niches we have our first apse decorations on a small scale.

For more extensive wall mosaics we have to fall back upon literary references. St. Augustine in his *De Civitate Dei* describes mosaic pictures on the esplanade of the harbor of Carthage which were probably in the realistic, picturesque style of the Alexandrian landscapes, seen in the Pompeian frescoes and some of the pavements; the style which lingers on in the nave mosaics of Santa Maria Maggiore.

Trebellius Pollio tells us that the house of Tetricus, the Gallic emperor conquered by Aurelian in 273, still existed on the Coelian Hill at the time of Constantine. Here there was a mosaic of Aurelian receiving the sceptre and the civic crown. Procopius relates an extraordinary legend about a mosaic of Theodoric the Goth displayed in the Roman Forum. The head of this figure fell a short time before the death of Theodoric. Eight years later more of the figure disappeared at the time of the death of his successor Athalaric, and still more disappeared when the queen Amalasuntha perished. What little remained entirely vanished when the Goths were driven from Rome. There was still another mosaic of Theodoric on the façade of a church at Pavia. The king was represented as fully armed with lance and shield.

The so-called "Sylvanus" of the Lateran,[20] originally discovered at

Ostia, is one of the few existing wall mosaics of pagan origin. The figure (11), draped in white, stands out against the blue background, impressive in its simplicity. This is probably a work of the fourth century, contemporary with the mosaics of Santa Costanza.

Although it was only after the triumph of the Church that Christianity seized upon mosaic as one of its great mediums of expression, a few examples from the Catacombs have come down to us.[21] The crypt of St. Eusebius had a cantharus flanked by birds. In St. Calixtus, a lost mosaic, described in the eighteenth century, showed Christ seated on a globe between St. Peter and St. Paul, the Resurrection of Lazarus, and another scene. The two portraits of Maria Simplicia and Flavius Julius Julianus from the Catacomb of Ciriacus, now in the Biblioteca Chigi, are so much restored that they have little value. They are typical of the late-Roman manner of the early fifth century.

This brief discussion of the probable origins of the art and of the early pavements will serve as an introduction to the subject with which we are primarily concerned—the Christian wall mosaics.

We have now arrived at the point where the Church is to emerge from obscurity and revolutionize the art of the Roman world. We shall see, in regard to mosaic, how this essentially pavement technique of the Romans was transformed by a diversity of influences and an interplay of, seemingly, the most antagonistic traditions, into a vehicle for expressing with incomparable splendor the profoundest convictions of the Middle Ages.

ROMAN MOSAICS FROM THE FOURTH TO THE SEVENTH CENTURIES

Roman Mosaics from the Fourth to the Seventh Centuries
Official recognition of the Church a great impetus to art.—Origin and development of Early Christian iconography: Eastern and Western influences: theories and facts.—The new iconography defined.—Lost mosaics of the Holy Land.—Santa Costanza.—Santa Pudenziana.—Santa Maria Maggiore.—Santa Sabina.—San Paolo-fuori-le-mura.—The Lateran Baptistery.—SS. Cosma e Damiano.—San Lorenzo-fuori-le-mura.—Lost mosaics: Old St. Peter's and the Lateran, Sant-Agata dei Goti, San'Andrea Catabarbara.—Summary of the styles.

IV.

ROMAN MOSAICS FROM THE FOURTH TO THE SEVENTH CENTURIES[22]

When the Emperor Constantine officially recognized Christianity in 313, the art of the catacombs came up from hiding underground and began that remarkable transformation which it was to undergo during the next three hundred years. The earlier impressionism and symbolism, based upon the Pompeian-Alexandrian tradition prevalent under the Late Empire, was no longer adequate to express the ideals of a triumphant Church, the self-confidence of an already remarkably organized and wealthy religion which was constantly growing. A more splendid and luxurious art was required to crystalize ideas and to spread faith.

The new monumental style is in marked contrast to the symbolic art of the Early Christians. It is formal, abstract, and of solemn grandeur, with little or none of that naïve, appealing quality which we find in the frescoes of the catacombs. Figures predominate in the compositions and are not merely incidents in the decorative scheme. New types are evolved, Our Lord, the Apostles, historical scenes from the Old and the New Testaments, and many others which we shall see in mosaics of the first centuries.

What was the origin of this new style? [23] For the past thirty years, research has increasingly shown the tremendous rôle played by the Near East in the development of Christian art, both as to style and iconography. Its roots go back to the earliest civilizations of Mesopotamia and Iran. It was fused with the art of the great Hellenistic centers—Antioch, Alexandria, Ephesus and others—themselves imbued with the native Eastern traditions which became so strongly revived during the first centuries of the Christian era. Much actual iconography, such as the so-called Syrian type of the bearded Christ, was, perhaps, evolved in Palestine and Syria and spread abroad by the pilgrimages. Other conceptions originated in Egypt, Asia Minor and its hinterland, and elsewhere. It may be well to say here that we cannot at this time speak of Byzantine influence in a narrow sense as applying definitely to that locality. Byzantium was one of a number of centers busy in formulating an art out of the many diverse elements which it received, and it is not until the sixth century, in the time of Justinian, that it developed what we may call a well defined style.

Granting the great influence of the Near East in the formation of this style, it is well, however, not to deny all credit to the classical tradition of Rome. This classical tradition may be taken to include the heritage which Rome had received from the Etruscans, from Greece, and from the later Hellenistic civilization which, in turn, was also closely in touch with the East. That which we may call Roman art was widely diffused throughout the Empire and returns to influence in some degree the whole of the Middle Ages. Rome and Ravenna were probably great creative centers as well as the cities of the Near East and had their share in fusing together the many elements which go to make up Early Christian art.

In all these discussions about origins of style perhaps too much emphasis has been put upon mere terminology and such words as "Roman", "Hellenistic", and "Eastern" have been used as pivots for much over-polemical writing which has tended to confuse the main facts. The Early-Christian world of the Mediterranean was, after all, fairly compact and had a generally diffused civilization which we may call Græco-Roman if we like, and the art of the period is essentially based upon this culture however much it may be modified at times by the Near-Eastern hinterland.

It is not necessary here to speak of the lavish adornment of the countless churches which sprang up throughout the Empire in the enthusiasm of a new faith. In such splendid interiors, where the cost was not to be considered, it is not strange that mosaics covered the walls in preference to frescoes.

The Gospels [24] were the greatest source for the new iconography; scenes from the Old Testament were developed along the naves of Santa Maria Maggiore, the Lateran, and Old St. Peter's, and New Testament subjects were shown at an early date throughout the East, at Santa Costanza, in Rome, and elsewhere; in the Baptistery at Naples, and at Ravenna. Almost of equal importance were the visions of the Apocalypse. From this source come the figures and symbols which adorn the apses and the triumphal arches of the Roman basilicas; the enthroned Lamb with the book of the Seven Seals, the Seven Candle-Sticks, and the symbols of the Evangelists, which were especially popular in Western art, although not unknown in the Near East. Also, the Twenty-Four Elders who offer their crowns to God or to the Mystic Lamb; the Four Rivers of Paradise, and often the souls of the faithful, who under the form of stags (Psalm XLI) drink from their source. The Twelve Sheep, symbolical of the Apostles, issue from Jerusalem, the city of the *Ecclesia ex Circumcisione,* and Bethlehem, the city of the *Ecclesia ex Gentibus,* the Church of the Gentiles, a favorite subject, especially at Rome, for the lower part of the apse. Sometimes the two cities are represented under the guise of women, as at Santa Sabina. By their opposition they show the parallelism which is one of the fundamental points of all this Early Christian iconography.

God the Father is represented as a symbol in the upper part of the apses where the Divine Hand issues from the clouds, holding the crown of recompense, with the Dove as the Holy Ghost.

In addition to this symbolism and to the other motifs which are retained from catacomb art, we have the more realistic treatment of the historical scenes from the Gospels and the miracles of Christ. Realism is also shown in the fondness for portraiture[25] and the representation of living persons, the founders of churches and other important ecclesiastics, as in the Roman apses; at Ravenna and Parenzo; and at St. Demetrius at Salonika.

Without attempting here to trace the origin and development of individual motifs, we should bear in mind that in all probability the actual portrayals of these themes were largely evolved in Syria, Palestine, Egypt, and Asia Minor, and the flourishing Christian communities of the hinterland, and that they show a combination of late phases of Hellenism with the vigorous artistic revival of the Near East. In Italy and other places where the sway of Rome was strongest these conceptions are more definitely modified by the survivals of Late Roman art, which, as we have seen, was itself a combination of the late aspects of Hellenism, especially those of Alexandria, with a certain native Italo-Etruscan realism. When we speak of Roman art we include that Romanized part of the empire of which the capital was the focal point.

This art was cosmopolitan and imperial in the true sense. Pavements from Syria to Britain show a common origin of style. The core of the Early Christian figure style is always Hellenistic, or classical, however much it may have been modified by Oriental or other influences.

The early mosaics of the churches of the Holy Land, which have all perished, must have had a tremendous influence elsewhere, as they were being constantly seen and admired by the throngs of pilgrims. The subjects of several of these are doubtless reflected in some of the small objects which the pilgrims carried away with them. Thus, an Adoration of the Magi on one of the Monza ampullæ probably copies[26] the mosaic on the façade of the Church of the Nativity at Bethlehem,[27] which the soldiers of Chosroes are said to have spared in the sixth century because the Magi had Persian caps. The Virgin is seated with the Child full-face with a star-like wheel over her head. The shepherds are at the right, and the Magi at the left. We know from early writers that there were mosaics in Constantine's Church of the Holy Sepulchre, both in the atrium, and the dome where Constantine and Helena were shown holding the Cross between them. Probably all of the important churches of the Holy Land and of Syria were decorated with mosaics.

The mosaics of the church of Santa Costanza[28] at Rome mark the transition between those of purely Roman antique tradition and those of the Christian period. This circular domed structure with a surrounding barrel-vault supported on coupled columns, was erected by Constantine as a mausoleum for his daughter, Constantia, according to the *Liber Pontificalis*. It is more probable, however, that it was erected later, at least as late as the middle of the fourth century. Constantine's daughter survived him by seventeen years and it does not seem likely that he would have built her the mausoleum during her lifetime. Then, too, the construction seems to be at least as late as the middle of the century, so that we may consider it to date from the time of the Emperor Constans, 352-360. In the fifth century it was converted into a baptistery.

Formerly, the dome, as well as the ring-vault and the niches cut out of the heavy wall, was covered with mosaics, but now practically all that remain are those of the barrel-vault and the two larger niches, or apses, the dome having fallen a victim to the wave of Baroque enthusiasm in the seventeenth century.

The interesting design of this dome has, however, been preserved to us by old drawings, one of which was engraved and published by Ciampini[29] (12). At the base was a river scene—a Nilotic scene of purely Alexandrian tradition like the famous pavement of Palestrina— with cupids engaged in fishing and swimming, surrounded by dolphins and aquatic birds. Caryatids, standing on acanthus scrolls flanked by panthers, support other scrolls and smaller figures which form a decorative scheme dividing the dome into twelve sections with smaller compartments above. These inter-spaces contained scenes from the Old and the New Testaments, some of which have been identified, and they probably formed a more or less complete Biblical cycle, such as we find at Santa Maria Maggiore.

The ring-vault has been almost entirely preserved and consists of eleven compartments of ornamental motifs, some of which are repeated

(13). These mosaics are composed of marble, not glass cubes, and the nearly white backgrounds, the narrow range of color—dark green, brown, red, and yellow of the natural stone—place them in the antique tradition of the first half of the fourth century, and we may conclude that they were executed soon after the completion of the building.

Perhaps the most interesting panel is the vintage scene (14). Here, a vine treated in a naturalistic manner, doubtless the symbolic vineyard of Our Lord, covers the background. Robust cupids pluck the grapes, and, at intervals, there are birds perched on the vines. The treatment of the vine is strikingly similar to certain late antique pavements, especially the one from the Villa of the Laberii at Uthina which we have already mentioned. In the center, is a bust of a young man whom some have supposed to be the emperor, Crispus. In two of the corners, diagonally opposite each other, cupids carry grapes to the vats, aided by bullock-carts; in the other two corners they rhythmically tramp out the juice. This same composition is repeated in another compartment with the substitution of a female bust in the center, which possibly represents Constantia. It is not strange that archæologists of the eighteenth century thought that these subjects were entirely pagan and probably portrayed a Triumph of Bacchus.

In another section (15), we have a great variety of objects scattered in profusion; branches, flowers, fruit, birds, all so naturalistically treated that they are easily identified. Two doves on a bowl recall the well-known "Doves of the Capitoline" found at Hadrian's Villa. Other compartments show a geometric design of crosses and rosettes, or lozenges forming large stars. Two show, in a series of medallions, birds, rosettes, heads of young men, and dancing figures of Eros and Psyche. In one, we see two sheep—the only Christian symbols in a typically antique composition. Some of these motifs are similar to those in the famous fourth century pavement from Kabr Hiram, now in the Louvre.

The two niches, or apses, form a striking contrast with the vault, both in technique and in subject. The left apse (16) shows the *Traditio Legis,* Our Lord between Peter and Paul, giving the Gospels to the former. Although badly altered by restoration, the heads of the Apostles are already of the types which distinguish them throughout all later Christian art. At the base, four symbolic sheep turn towards the Rivers of Paradise, and at the sides are the two cities, Bethlehem and Jerusalem, the *Ecclesia ex Gentibus* and the *Ecclesia ex Circumcisione,* with the symbolic palm trees—a rather abstract interpretation of a composition which we will find often in later mosaics.

The apse on the right (17), which has also suffered from restoration, shows Christ seated upon the Globe and an advancing figure, who is usually interpreted as St. Peter, receiving the Keys of the Church. The Christ here is already of the "Syrian" bearded type; the beardless St. Peter is doubtless a restoration. Ten palm trees, one much smaller than the others, complete the composition. The light background follows the antique tradition.

The great divergence between these mosaics and those of the ringvault have led certain critics, among them Venturi[30] and Toesca,[31] to consider them later, probably dating from the fifth century when the mausoleum was converted into a baptistery. Others, including de Rossi and Wilpert, think that they date, like the vault, from the foundation of the building. They believe that the subjects were new and more difficult to treat than those more nearly in the contemporary antique manner.

There still exists in one of the smaller niches a fragment of mosaic with stars on a white ground, and above, a portion of a circle which contained the Constantan monogram executed in gold cubes. In the sixteenth century, Ugonio[32] saw in the apse at the end of the rotunda, above the principal altar, a mosaic of Our Lord in the midst of the Apostles, a composition evidently allied to that in Santa Pudenziana, of which it may have been a prototype.

The curious mingling of pagan and Christian subjects which we find at Santa Costanza is also seen in the remains of a mosaic which was recently discovered in a hypogeum at the corner of the Via Po and the Via Livenza in Rome. This hypogeum was constructed in the midst of tombs belonging to an earlier pagan cemetery, and probably dates from the middle of the fourth century. There are frescoes, pagan in origin, showing Diana and other mythological subjects, and above these, are the fragments of the mosaics which include representations of cupids fishing, reminiscent of Santa Costanza, and Moses causing water to gush forth from a rock with a kneeling soldier drinking. The light backgrounds and the classical conception of the figures are in the fourth century tradition of Santa Costanza.

The apse of Santa Pudenziana[33] contains one of the noblest of the early Roman mosaics (18). This little church, between the Viminal and the Esquiline, on the site of the house of the senator, Pudens, is one of the most venerable in Rome, and tradition has it that here Saint Peter said his first mass. With the exception of a portion of the apse it has now been transformed in the style of the Baroque.

In the center of the mosaic, Christ, clothed in a tunic of gold, is seated on a throne. He extends His right arm almost horizontally in a gesture of benediction, in the manner of the ancient orators when they wished to command attention. In His left hand He holds an open book with the words: DOMINUS- CONSER- VATOR- ECCLESIÆ- PUDENTI- ANÆ, "The Lord, Guardian of the Church of Pudens," in accordance with the most ancient texts which give the title of the church to St. Pudens rather than to his daughter, Santa Pudenziana. The cushioned throne is embellished with geometric designs and over the back is draped a brocade. Ten of the twelve Apostles are seated either side of Christ, two having disappeared when the apse was made narrower and the whole composition cut down in consequence. They are clothed in the tunic, in the manner of Roman senators, and most of them stretch their right hands towards Christ in sign of respect. St.

Peter, on the right, and St. Paul, on the left, are in profile, and St. Paul holds an open book with the words: LI- BER-GENERAT-TIONIS-I.X., the opening words of the Book of St. Matthew; but this inscription is a modern restoration. Behind each of these figures, there is a female figure draped in gold, holding a crown of laurel over their heads. It is now generally conceded that these figures represent the *Ecclesia ex Circumcisione* and the *Ecclesia ex Gentibus* rather than the daughters of Pudens—Santa Pudenziana and Santa Prassede. The Jewish Church crowns St. Peter and that of the Gentiles, St. Paul.

In the background stretches a portico in the form of a hemicycle, covered with golden tiles, above which are seen the buildings of a city. These buildings have been variously conjectured to represent an ideal conception of the New Jerusalem, Rome of the fourth century, and the actual Jerusalem of the period. There is good reason to believe that there is an attempt here to reproduce the structures of the Holy Sepulchre as they existed at that time.[34]

On a mount behind the head of Christ rises a great jewelled cross of the so-called Golgotha type, and in the clouds with their tones of red, pale-green, and deep-blue are the winged symbols of the Evangelists, one of their first appearances in art, two of them nearly obliterated by the narrowing of the apse.

This work is now generally regarded as dating from the pontificate of Siricius, 384-398, or possibly from the very beginning of the fifth century under Pope Innocent,[35] executed under the administration of the titulary priests, Ilicius, Leopardus, and Maximus.[36] It was restored and perhaps modified under Hadrian I. at the end of the eighth century. In 1588 it was mutilated by the narrowing of the apse, the erection of the baldachino later removed a portion of the lower part, and in 1831 nearly the whole of the right side was entirely done over. Undoubtedly, at the lower part of the composition, there were originally the Twelve Sheep issuing from Bethlehem and Jerusalem.

In spite of the misfortunes which this mosaic has undergone, it still has an air of solemn grandeur, the symbol of triumphant Christianity. The Christ is no longer the simple figure of the catacombs but a god, majestically enthroned. The Apostles are Roman senators used to command. It was at about this time in Rome that the statue of Victory was removed from the Senate and the Vestal Virgins dispersed.

Some have seen evidences of strong Eastern influence in the type of the Christ and the sumptuous use of gold cubes. The jewelled cross which resembles the one in San Stefano Rotondo seems considerably later in style than the rest of the composition, and may well be an interpolation due to the restoration of Hadrian I at the end of the eighth century; but the fine spatial effect of the mosaic as a whole and the types of the Apostles relate it to the classical tradition.

The old portico of the Lateran Baptistery originally contained two apsidal mosaics.[37] One of these, which represented The Shepherding of the Sheep of the Church has long since been destroyed, but the other, above the altar dedicated to the saints, Rufinus and Secundus, still exists and probably dates from the end of the fourth century (19).

On the deep blue of the background a huge acanthus is developed in scrolls of shimmering green bearing flowers of coral and gold. This decorative composition is probably symbolical in character, the promise of the New Life of the Vine, in line with the conceptions of catacomb art. In the fan-shaped motif at the top, reminiscent of Pompeian design, are the Lamb (Christ) and four doves representing the Evangelists. Below these are six jewelled crosses of the Golgotha type. In the blue band which runs at the base of the composition there are still seven of the original twelve crosses of gold, symbols of the Apostles.

The acanthus scrolls are still treated naturalistically, but they are much more carefully composed and unified than in Santa Costanza, and produce an Oriental richness of effect. It is not necessary, however, to go to the East to discover their direct inspiration. Roman art made use of similar decoration, as on the slabs of the Ara Pacis of the time of Augustus. Vine scrolls continued to be a favorite motif of the later Roman mosaicists in the twelfth and thirteenth centuries in the apses of San Clemente and Santa Maria Maggiore. The East Christian influence comes, rather, from the greater brilliancy of color and the slightly more formalized treatment of a long-familiar theme.

In spite of the fact that it is oppressed by its Baroque entourage, this is one of the most beautiful of the decorative mosaics. The subtle shadings of the blues and the greens, the vivid tones of the flowers, and the skillful use of gold to heighten the effect, show the hand of a master.

The early mosaics of Santa Maria Maggiore[38] (20-27) occupy an almost preponderant position in the history of the art, both on account of the fact that we have here the only nearly complete Biblical cycle preserved to us from the early period, and also because of the difficulty of giving them a precise date. It is known that this great basilica was founded by Pope Liberius, 352-366, who may have converted an already existing private palace into a church. The basilica was restored and perhaps entirely reconstructed by Sixtus III, 432-440, who rededicated it to the Virgin Mary. Sixtus had followed with lively interest the debates of the Council of Ephesus which a short time before had proclaimed the divinity of Mary, Mother of God.

The mosaics in question consist of two series (20): one, the Old Testament scenes above the colonnades of the nave, and secondly, the scenes taken from the *Apocrypha* which adorn the triumphal arch. The problem which has puzzled archæologists for the last half-century is whether to consider both series as dating from the time of Liberius or from the time of Sixtus III, or to give the mosaics in the nave to an early period, probably the time of Liberius, and those of the triumphal arch to the reconstruction of Sixtus III after the Council of Ephesus. Without going further into the intricacies of this discussion, it is perhaps better to examine the mosaics themselves before we pass judgment. An added difficulty comes from the numerous and unfortunate restorations which they have undergone, and from the fact that they are badly seen. The details can probably be better studied from photographs than by standing in the church.

There were originally forty-two separate mosaic pictures in the nave, of which twenty-seven now exist (21-23). With the exception of four, they are all divided into two super-imposed parts, each part containing one or more scenes. The subjects are taken from the books of Genesis, Exodus, Deuteronomy and Joshua, and illustrate episodes from the lives of Abraham, Jacob, Moses and Joshua.

The first scene on the left side of the nave, starting from the choir, represents the Sacrifice of Melchisedec (Genesis, XIV, 18). Melchisedec advances to meet Abraham who arrives on horseback escorted by his following. The high priest is clothed in a white tunic and a white mantle bordered with purple, fastened over the chest by a golden fibula, In his hands he holds a basket with two round loaves of bread, and at his feet is an urn for the wine. The figure of Abraham, except for the right arm and the left hand which holds the horse's bridle, is a restoration. Behind, are soldiers in the costumes of Roman legionaries.

The reliance upon the antique is brought out even more forcibly in the next panel which, in three scenes combined in the Roman manner, illustrates the story of Abraham and the Three Angels (21). In the upper portion, Abraham rushes to meet the angels, exhorting them to rest. The angels are shown without wings according to an early tradition. In the Hebrew text they were described as having the appearance of men, and they were therefore represented without distinguishing attributes. Later, they were associated with the Trinity and were given nimbi or a mandorla. A further development was the singling out of one angel as the *Logos* to whom Abraham addressed his speech, as here, in this mosaic, where he is provided with a mandorla. Below, to the left, Abraham, with the gesture of a Roman orator, orders Sarah to prepare the meal. Finally, at the right, are the angels seated before a table upon which are three conical loaves of bread, and Abraham is about to serve them the veal which has been prepared. This is one of the best preserved of the mosaics, as only the lower portion containing the amphora for the wine and a narrow strip running around the edge of the panel have been redone in stucco. Everything about this composition shows a strong dependence upon the antique: the method of combining several scenes in one, in the manner of the Roman historical reliefs, the types of the figures and their classical draperies, the interest in the picturesque details of the background, and, above all, the boldly impressionistic technique which is a translation in mosaic of the best traditions of what we usually call Pompeian painting. Take, for example, the head of the angel seated at the table on the right. Here, comparatively few cubes are used to give an extraordinary sense of reality. The eyes are achieved, each with only two contrasting cubes of black and white, but with a sureness of touch which is hardly equalled until the painting of the late Renaissance.

These same qualities are apparent in more or less degree in the rest of the series which we may briefly enumerate without examining in detail. One of the most beautiful is the next in order, The Separation of Abraham and Lot (22), with the noble figures of the two brothers. Then follow: Isaac Blessing Jacob; Rachel Announcing to Laban the Arrival of Jacob; the Meeting of Laban and Jacob; Jacob Asking Rachel in Marriage; the Marriage of Jacob; the Compact Between Jacob and Laban; Jacob Ordered by God to Return to His Own Country; the Meeting of Esau and Jacob; Hamor and Sichem Coming to Ask Jacob for the Hand of Dinah; the Brothers of Dinah before Hamor and Sichem. On the right side of the nave: the Adoption of Moses by Pharaoh's Daughter; Moses in the Midst of the Philosophers; the Marriage of Moses and Sephora (23); the Passage of the Red Sea; Murmurings of the People of Israel; Miracle of the Quails; Miracle of the Waters; Amalek Coming to Fight the Israelites; Combat against the

Amalectites; Return of the Spies Sent by Moses; God Protects Moses and His Companions; Moses Giving the Book of the Law to the Israelites and His Death on Mount Nabo; The Ark of the Covenant; Passage of the Jordan; Joshua Sends Two Spies to Jericho; Joshua Meets an Angel; Return of the Spies; the Fall of Jericho; the Siege of Gabaon; Great Battle Near Gabaon; Joshua Stops the Sun and the Moon; the Captured Kings Brought to Joshua. The two panels which terminate the series are paintings of the sixteenth century.

Everywhere throughout this great historical cycle we find the same classical characteristics which have already been noted; the naturalistic and lively, if often crude modelling of the figures which sometimes bear a certain resemblance to those gladiators and pugilists of the well-known mosaic from the Baths of Caracalla, and the emphasis upon light-colored and picturesque backgrounds. The crowded battle scenes spring from the same tradition as those on the column of Trajan. Some of the figures, notably Pharaoh's daughter in the scene of the Adoption of Moses, have a certain Oriental character, especially in the richness of their costumes and the employment of gold cubes, but these details, which seem a little out of harmony with the rest of the work, may be due to an early restoration.

Turning to the triumphal arch (24-27), we no longer have scenes of Biblical narrative but subjects relating to the infancy of Christ. At the center of the arch, in a medallion, is the Jewelled Throne with the Book of the Seven Seals as described in the vision of the Apocalypse, probably the earliest representation of this subject in mosaic. Above, on either side, are the symbols of the Evangelists and figures of St. Peter and St. Paul. These figures have been considerably restored. Below the medallion is the inscription: XYSTVS EPISCPVS PLEBI DEI, "Sixtus, bishop, to the people of God," which has caused this work to be attributed to Sixtus III. This inscription must have been inserted when the mosaics were already in place, as it encroaches upon the composition. It, therefore, only shows that the work cannot be later than the middle of the fifth century.

The top-most scene at the left represents the Annunciation according to the account of the Pseudo-Matthew. The Virgin is seated and dressed in a rich oriental costume, and in accordance with the legend, is spinning the purple for the temple veil. Five angels stand about her, two of them turning towards the irresolute Joseph, as if to reassure him. These angels, unlike those in the scenes of the nave, are provided with wings. All of these figures are placed against a gold background which, above, changes into clouds of red and blue where the Dove and the angel of the Annunciation descend over the Virgin's head. During the recent restoration when the mosaic was removed the design for this scheme was discovered drawn in black on the plaster. The Virgin is shown as actually depicted and also a second flying angel which was never executed, and other minor differences; a precious document showing the artist experimented with two schemes.

As a pendant scene, on the right, is the Presentation in the Temple. Mary, holding the Child, is preceded by Joseph who seems to be in the act of offering the Child to Simeon who rushes to meet them. The draped female figure next to Joseph represents the Prophetess Anna, according to the version of St. Luke, and between them is the figure of an angel. Simeon is followed by a crowd of priests and Levites, and in the background, is a temple with a figure in the tympanum which is usually interpreted as representing the Goddess Roma. The angel in the foreground at the extreme right is probably advising Joseph to flee to Egypt, but the figure of Joseph has been almost entirely removed by the cutting down of the mosaic on this side.

On the left, below the Annunciation, we have the Adoration of the Magi. The infant Christ is seated on a jewelled throne with a red cushion and is clothed in a long white tunic decorated with purple *claves*. His head has a golden nimbus with a little cross. Above, is the star which has guided the Magi, and behind the throne are four angels with blue nimbi. At the left of the throne, is the almost obliterated figure of the Virgin, spoiled by repainting, and at the right, is a nobly draped female figure which may represent the *Ecclesia ex Circumcisione,* or St. Anne, the mother of the Virgin. Two of the Magi, dressed in Persian costume, are seen bringing their gifts; the third has been destroyed. The walled town in the background is, doubtless, Bethlehem.

As a pendant to this, on the right, below the Presentation, we have a curious scene taken from the apocryphal account of the Pseudo-Matthew: Christ in Egypt before King Aphrodosius. According to the legend, the Holy Family sought refuge for the night in a certain Egyptian temple containing three hundred and sixty-five idols. As soon as Mary entered with the Child, the idols were thrown to earth and shattered. When the king, Aphrodosius, discovered this he came to prostrate himself before Jesus and abjured paganism. Thus, the scene here depicted explains itself: on the left, Aphrodosius and his followers have left their city to meet the child Jesus who is accompanied by Mary and Joseph and three angels.

The narrow and crowded composition on the left below the Adoration of the Magi represents the Massacre of the Innocents. The figure of Herod is seen at the extreme left—almost entirely restored—in the midst of the Roman soldiers. The only well preserved portion of the mosaic is the group of mothers holding their children. Below this scene we have the walled city of Jerusalem, adorned with gold and precious stones, and five sheep as symbols of the Apostles, the sixth having disappeared under the adjacent Baroque pilaster.

Opposite, on the right, to complete the scheme, are shown the Magi before Herod and Bethlehem with the symbolic sheep below. The Magi in their Persian costumes, stand before the nearly obliterated figure of Herod seated upon a throne.

In the soffit of the arch there is a floral band with a border of alternating rectangles and ovals which becomes a common motif in later work in Rome, Ravenna and elsewhere.

The subjects of these mosaics are generally considered to be a glorification of the divinity of Mary as Mother of God, the doctrine which had been proclaimed by the Council of Ephesus in 431, and their probable execution under Sixtus III would bear this out. However, it is only fair to point out that the Virgin occupies a prominent position in but one subject, that of the Annunciation, and that the others seem to be more of a glorification of the divinity of the Infant Jesus.

The iconography of these scenes presents a puzzling problem which has never been satisfactorily solved. The Annunciation, and, especially, the Adoration of the Magi, where the Child is enthroned, are not represented in this manner elsewhere in Early Christian art. They belong probably to an Oriental-Hellenistic, and not a Roman tradition, and may have been inspired by miniatures or mural decorations which are now lost. The fact that the purely Egyptian subjects of King Aphrodosius is shown, as well as certain qualities of the style, make it seem probable that the prototypes were evolved in Alexandria.

Now that both series of mosaics have been reviewed, we are in a better position to consider the problem of dating. On the whole, the triumphal arch differs both in conception and in technique from the nave. The figures of the arch have less relief and less light and shade than those of the nave, and the gold backgrounds are in marked contrast to the lighter and more naturalistically treated backgrounds of the Biblical cycle. However, certain close resemblances between the two make it seem by no means certain that a century separates them. Both, apparently, start from the same general Hellenistic traditions, even though the classical element is more prominent in the nave, and much of the variety and differences in quality may be due to different hands rather than to different periods. Compare, for example, the soldiers in the Sacrifice of Melchisedec with those in the Massacre of the Innocents, or even the Virgin as represented on the arch with Pharaoh's daughter in the finding of Moses. It is quite possible that in spite of their strong antique character, we do not have to go back as far as Liberius for the execution of the nave, but that both the nave and the triumphal arch were completed in the time of Sixtus III, or a little earlier. In any case it is difficult to conceive of the arch as having been executed earlier than the fifth century. It has recently been well restored without changing the original position of the tesserae.

Technically, these mosaics are of a very high quality, and they prove that, even in this early period, the art had arrived at a point which, in some ways, was never surpassed. However, judged as a decorative whole, they are more or less of a failure. They are of too small a scale, and most of the compositions are too confused to be well seen at a distance, and they must always have had this defect, even though it is now accentuated by inferior restoration and the inharmonious Baroque surroundings.

The basilica of Santa Sabina[39] was originally entirely covered with mosaics. Now all that remains is the inscription of gold letters on a blue ground which occupies the whole width of the interior wall over the entrance (28). It was executed under the pontificate of Celestine I, 422-432, who founded the church, and it describes this event.

The beautiful proportions of this simple rectangular composition, the perfection of the lettering, and the nobility of the two female figures which enframe the inscription at the left and the right are in the best classical manner. The figures stand out on a gold ground. The one on the left, clothed in a long purple robe, represents the *Ecclesia ex Circumcisione* (29), and the pallium closely fitted over the head and even the type of features are characteristic of the women of Palestine. On the other hand, the figure at the right, the *Ecclesia ex Gentibus,* is shown as a Roman matron and resembles certain figures in Santa Maria Maggiore.

At the time of Ciampini,[40] towards the end of the seventeenth century, additional mosaics were still preserved (30). Above the inscription, at the top of the windows, were the symbols of the Four Evangelists, and below, to the left and the right, St. Peter and St. Paul. On the arch of the tribune, Our Lord with a cruciferous nimbus was represented in a medallion, and at either side were seven similar medallions containing male busts without nimbi. The remainder of the composition showed the two cities, Bethlehem and Jerusalem, with a row of doves across the top.

The basilica of San Paolo-fuori-le-mura,[41] founded by Constantine, was reconstructed after a fire, in 386, by Valentinian II and Theodosius. The work was finished by Honorius, 395-424, and his famous daughter, Galla Placidia, in concert with Pope Leo I, 440-461, covered the triumphal arch with mosaics (31). Earthquakes and fires seriously damaged the building at different times until it was practically destroyed by the fire of 1823. Therefore, the mosaics of the arch are almost entirely a restoration. In fact, the only undisputed piece of original work is the head of an angel, of excellent workmanship, now preserved in the local museum.

In this composition as it now exists there is a complete change of style; a violent break with preceding Roman mosaics and with classical traditions. In the center of the arch is a colossal bust of Our Lord in a medallion. The head is surrounded by a nimbus with nine rays. Christ blesses in the Greek manner, and with His right hand holds over His shoulder a baton, which is undoubtedly the handle of a cross. The hard, stern countenance is far removed from the benign figure of Santa Pudenziana, and already anticipates the severe Byzantine type of the Pantocrator. Above, in the clouds, are the symbols of the Four Evangelists. Below these symbols, on either side, are the Twenty-four Elders of the Apocalypse, their first appearance in mosaic, if we may consider that this work dates from the middle of the fifth century; stiff, badly proportioned, monotonous figures clothed in white robes and bearing their martyrs' crowns. At either side of the medallion of Christ are winged angels holding batons, much smaller in scale than the rest of the figures.

Below this upper portion, and separated from it by bands of inscriptions, are St. Peter holding the keys and St. Paul with the sword, obviously executed in the style of the nineteenth century restorers. The authenticity of the inscriptions is doubtful on account of the numerous restorations.[42]

This abstract and formalized scheme has little in common with Santa Pudenziana or Santa Maria Maggiore. The stiff figures stand out on an opaque gold ground. The Twenty-Four Elders show an inferior kind of Oriental conventionalism. If the composition actually dates from the time of Galla Placidia, the artisans probably came from Ravenna or the East. But the style is quite different from any of the contemporary work at Ravenna, such as the Mausoleum of Galla Placidia or the Baptistery of the Orthodox, just as it is different from the preceding Roman mosaics or those which follow it. It is difficult, therefore, to fit it into the fifth century; in fact, in some respects, it more resembles Roman work of the ninth century; but we must also consider that much of the apparent crudeness and hard quality comes from restoration and that there is no proof as yet that the composition is not the original one.

The little oratory of St. John the Evangelist,[43] connected with the Baptistery of the Lateran, was constructed by Pope Hilarius, 461-468. The vault with its mosaics on a gold ground is still well preserved (32). In the center is the Lamb, surrounded by a garland of flowers, ears of wheat, and olive branches; early symbols of the four seasons and of the Resurrection. The garland is surrounded by a border of blue stones and double spirals and is prolonged in the form of a cross. At the interior angles of this square are four red discs traversed by a cross, and it is surrounded by four festoons of flowers and foliage. There is a similar border at the base of the composition. The groins of the vault have bands of foliage and dolphins which terminate at the angles of the square, but that at the base of the groins is modern. Each of the eight compartments thus formed contains two birds facing a vase of fruit, and in them may be recognized the antique symbols of the four elements: ducks, as emblems of water; partridges representing the earth; pigeons, the air; and parrots, fire. The vases of fruit, like the ancient cornucopia, recall the fertility of the earth.

The story goes that Hilarius, while still a deacon, was sent by Pope Leo the Great to the Council of Ephesus in 449, and not wishing to take part in the demonstrations against Flavian, the patriarch of Constantinople, he escaped and took refuge near the tomb of St. John the Evangelist. He later dedicated this oratory to the saint in sign of gratitude, and there is still an inscription relating to this over the entrance door.

With the sixth century, we come to one of the very finest achievements of the art in Rome, the apse of SS. Cosma e Damiano [44] (33), executed during the pontificate of Felix IV, 526-530. The church was constructed in the old temple of Maxentius, and the original bronze door, flanked by its two columns of porphyry, may still be seen from the Forum. Unfortunately, this mosaic has also suffered from restorations and from the reconstruction of the church. The pavement has been raised, bringing the apse down to a much lower level, and the apse itself, as well as the arch, have both been cut down and provided with Baroque embellishments. But, in spite of its cramped position and the above-mentioned mutilations, it still gives an almost overwhelming impression of solemn splendor, and some critics have not hesitated to pronounce it the most beautiful mosaic in Rome.

In the center is the figure of Christ (34), bearded, and clothed in a tunic and mantle of gold with golden nimbus, standing against a pathway of glowing sun-set clouds which contrast with the somber blue of the background. He holds the *volumen*, or scroll, in the left hand, while the right arm is stretched out in the commanding gesture of an orator. A strip of lighter blue, below, is labelled JORDANES in silver letters, here representing the River of Life. A note of mystic symbolism runs through the whole composition, as the palms at the extreme left and right represent Paradise and the phœnix over the one on the left is the emblem of immortality. At the left and the right of Christ, St. Paul and St. Peter, draped in the classical toga, present the titular saints, Cosmas and Damianus, who carry their martyrs' crowns (35, 36). The figure of Felix IV holding a model of the church, at the extreme left, is entirely a restoration of the sixteenth and the seventeenth centuries and clashes with the rest of the work. On the extreme right, is St. Theodore clad in a yellow chlamys. He also, carries a martyr's crown.

The almost rigid formality and symmetry of this composition and its treatment as a piece of sumptuous decoration is a new note in Roman art and has little to do with the earlier classical tradition. In fact, it is the first great example in Rome of the so-called Eastern, or Byzantine, style. The sturdy, forceful figures still retain something of the antique, but we also find these same qualities in contemporary Eastern art. They also have affinities with the mosaics of Ravenna, especially the Apostles of San Vitale, but it is not necessary to suppose a direct connection between the two. They are both, rather, the result of the interdependence and cosmopolitan character of the art of the period.

Urban VIII cut down the arch and inserted under the soffit the present Baroque archivolt. He also placed a window in the top of the vault of the apse which destroyed the sacred monogram and the Hand of God which held a wreath over the head of Christ.

The lower band of the apse, with a gold background, has, in the center, the Lamb with silver nimbus, standing on a mount from which flow the Four Rivers of Paradise, designated by their names: GEON, FYSON, TIGRIS, EUFRATA. At each side, six sheep, symbols of the Apostles, issue from Bethlehem and Jerusalem. The town and the first three sheep on the left are entirely restored. The nimbus of the Lamb and the word JORDANES are the first examples in Rome of the use of silver cubes, which are occasionally employed in the East, and later, at the end of the thirteenth century, in the apse of Santa Maria Maggiore.

At the base of this frieze, runs an inscription of gold letters on a blue ground, interesting because of the insight it gives as to the point of view of those who were responsible for this kind of decoration:

    AVLA DI CLARIS RADIAT SPECIOSA METALLIS
    IN QUA PLVS FIDEI LUX PRETIOSA MICAT
    MARTYRIBVS MEDICIS POPVLO SPES CERTA SALVTIS
    VENIT ET EX SACRO CREVIT HONORE LOCVS
    OPTVLIT HOC DNO FELIX ANTISTE DIGNUM
    MVNVS VT AETHERIA VIVAT IN ARCE POLI.

"The house of God shines with the brilliancy of the purest metals, and the light of the faith glows there more preciously. The physician martyrs have assured the salvation of the people, and a sacred honor has been attached to this place. The pontiff, Felix, has offered to God this gift worthy of Him so that he may live in the celestial domains."

The arch has beeen abbreviated, but the central part of the scheme may still be well seen, and although damaged, it seems to be less restored than the apse itself. Here, also, is one of the Apocalyptic visions of St. John. In the center there is a golden disc containing the Lamb of God reclining on the jewelled Throne surmounted by a cross with, below, the Book of the Seven Seals. On either side are the Seven Candlesticks, and beyond, pairs of angels with dark wings, clad in white tunics. The heads, which are of great beauty, stand out against blue nimbi. Two of the symbols of the Evangelists remain, the angel and the eagle; the bull and the lion have disappeared. Lower down, at the two extremities, an arm holding a crown may be distinguished—all that remains of two groups of the Twenty-Four Elders which originally occupied the spandrels of the arch. This whole apse composition is the prototype of many of the later examples, especially those of the ninth century, and at Santa Prassede there is a rather inferior repetition of this triumphal arch motif which has been preserved.

Although this work shows undeniable Eastern influence, it has an individuality and a forcefulness which sets it apart from the general current. The colossal size and almost brutal energy of the figures have led some critics to consider them the result of a Northern influence brought in by the Goths who at this time were dominant in Italy and were even holding Rome;[45] but it should be remembered that a good deal, at least, of this impression of a certain barbaric coarseness is due to the fact that the mosaic is always seen at too close a range on account of the raising of the pavement.

Fifty years later than SS. Cosma e Damiano, Pope Pelagius II, 587-590, rebuilt the church of San Lorenzo-fuori-le-mura [46] and provided the triumphal arch with a mosaic (37). Owing to the addition of the actual nave and the reorientation of the church under Honorius III, this mosaic now faces the choir. Above, there is a Latin inscription which was remade in 1860 according to old documents, and which records the work done by Pelagius.

The composition of the triumphal arch is an example of the so-called Byzantine manner carried out in a rather hard and lifeless way. It is, technically, very inferior to the nearly contemporary mosaics of Ravenna or SS. Cosma e Damiano, a fact which may be partly explained by the unfortunate condition of Rome at this period as a result of the Lombard invasions. The figures stand out on a gold background. In the center is Christ, seated on a blue globe, as in San Vitale at Ravenna. This emaciated and ascetic figure with black hair and beard, is clad in violet garments and blesses with the right hand in the Latin manner. The left hand holds a long cross.

At the left and the right are St. Peter and St. Paul clad in the white tunic and the pallium. St. Peter holds a cross and St. Paul, a scroll. Beyond St. Peter is St. Lawrence, dressed in the dalmatic of a deacon, and bearing a cross and an open book with the inscription: DIS PER SIT DEDIT PAV PERI BVS, "He has distributed his wealth with liberality among the poor," a quotation from the CXI psalm which was applied to him in the breviary on account of his having given the wealth of the church to the poor before his persecutors could seize it. St. Lawrence has his hand on the shoulder of Pope Pelagius who holds a model of the church. The head of Pelagius, unlike the others, has no nimbus. It seems to have been little restored, and may almost be considered a portrait. On the other side, next to St. Paul, is the martyr, St. Stephen, usually associated with St. Lawrence, shown as a young man wearing the dalmatic of a deacon as well as the mantle. He holds the Gospel open at the words: A DE SIT A NI MA ME A, "My soul is held to follow you." Beyond, is the figure of St. Hypolitus holding a martyr's crown. He is represented here because he was one of the soldiers ordered to guard St. Lawrence and was converted and baptized by him. Below these figures are the towns of Bethlehem and Jerusalem.

An inscription of gold letters on a blue ground runs around the arch. It is dedicated to St. Lawrence and reads:

MARTYRUM FLAMMIS OLIM LEVVITA SUBISTI
I URE TUIS TEMPLIS LUX BENERANDA REDIT

"You underwent martyrdom by the flames, and it is just, O Levite, that an honorable splendor be given to your temple."

The composition has a border similar to the one in Santa Sabina and in the mausoleum of Galla Placidia at Ravenna, with the addition of the chain of rectangles and ovals which is found in so many of the mosaics.

An engraving of Ciampini[47] shows that in his time the mosaic was in bad condition, the towns of Bethlehem and Jerusalem having almost entirely disappeared, and it has undergone numerous restorations since his day. This may account for some of the stiffness and poor color.

We have now reviewed all of the existing Roman mosaics to the end of the sixth century. That there were a great many more there is ample proof from the references to them in old documents, in the *Liber Pontificalis,* and even from drawings of the sixteenth and the seventeenth centuries, for a number of them were not destroyed until they were swept away by the passion for the Baroque.[48]

Old St. Peter's[49] was covered with mosaics; the nave, the apse, and the façade. The nave had a series of Old Testament scenes done under Pope Liberius, 352-366, and restored under Formosus, 891-896. From Grimaldi's drawings they would seem to have been similar to those of Santa Maria Maggiore. The apse which is known by a seventeenth-century drawing, showed Christ enthroned between St. Peter and St. Paul. Below Christ were stags drinking from the Four Rivers of Paradise, and palm-trees enframed the upper zone. At the base was the usual composition of the Lamb on the Mount with the Twelve Sheep issuing from Bethlehem and Jerusalem. The mosaic was restored in the seventh century and again by Innocent III, 1198-1216, who had himself represented by the side of the central Lamb. The head of the figure is still preserved. The façade was first embellished by Leo I, 440-461, and the subjects included the Lamb of God and the Twenty-Four Elders.

The nave of the Lateran had an early series of scenes of the Old and the New Testaments,[50] dating perhaps from the fourth or the fifth century. The subjects of these are used in the present Baroque stucco reliefs of the seventeenth century. The apses of Sant'Agata dei Goti, 455-461, and Sant'Andrea Catabarbara[51], 471-483, contained mosaics, which are known only by late and inferior drawings.

The earliest Roman mosaics; Santa Costanza, Santa Pudenziana and Santa Maria Maggiore, show an art still largely dominated by the spirit of the antique, even though many details may point to an East Christian influence, and the little oratory of Pope Hilarius reverts to the purest traditions of catacomb art. But the arch of Galla Placidia at St. Paul's is a complete break with this tradition, and by the sixth century, the so-called Syro-Palestinian or Eastern style which develops into the Byzantine, is well established in SS. Cosma e Damiano and San Lorenzo.

THE MOSAICS OF RAVENNA

THE MOSAICS OF RAVENNA

In the 5th and 6th centuries Ravenna the most important city in Italy and in the development of mosaics.—Three great personalities, Galla Placidia, Theodoric and Justinian.—The Mausoleum of Galla Placidia.—The Baptistery of the Orthodox.—Sant'Apollinare Nuovo.—San Vitale.—The Archiepiscopal Palace.—Sant' Apollinare in Classe.—The Arian Baptistery.—San Michele in Affrisco.—Lost mosaics.—The salient points of the style and their probable origin.—The influence of the style elsewhere.

V.

THE MOSAICS OF RAVENNA[52]

The art of Ravenna is associated with three great personalities; Galla Placidia, d. 450, Theodoric, 493-526; and Justinian, 526-561. During the fifth and the sixth centuries the city was virtually the capital of Italy, and a center for the extraordinarily varied artistic impulses of the Christian world. The monuments which have been preserved give us, perhaps, the most complete and vivid impression we have of the art of this period, and the mosaics constitute their chief glory.

The so-called Mausoleum and the Baptistery of the Orthodox belong to the time of Galla Placidia; to Theodoric, most of the work in Sant'Apollinare Nuovo and the Arian Baptistery; to Justinian, Sant'Apollinare in Classe, San Vitale, and the Archiepiscopal Palace. The later work in Sant'Apollinare in Classe and the apse of San Michele in Affricisco are of the more decadent period of the Exarchate.

The little building which goes by the name of the Mausoleum of Galla Placidia[53] (38) was, in reality, probably a chapel or an oratory erected in honor of SS. Nazarius and Celsus, attached to the church of that name. It may be dated towards the middle of the fifth century. It is of Greek cross plan with equal arms, constructed of brick, with a small cupola curiously formed of hollow amphoræ, one embedded in the other. Originally, the interior walls were covered by an incrustation of precious marbles, and above this, the barrel vaults of the arms of the cross with the lunettes at the ends, the drum and the cupola are still entirely covered with their embellishment of mosaic (39).

The mosaics of the vaults are all on a blue ground. In the center of the cupola is a Latin cross of gold standing out on a field of gold stars, and at the four angles are the winged symbols of the Evangelists coming out of little clouds. On the four sides of the drum, on the same blue ground, are eight Apostles, two by two, separated by the four windows. Above each group there is a shell with festoons of pearls, and between the figures, in each case, there are two doves drinking from a cantharus. The Apostles are clad in white tunics and mantles, and St. Peter and St. Paul are in profile, an unusual feature, as the heads in the early mosaics are usually shown full face or three-quarters. St. Peter carries the key for almost the first time in monumental art.

The vaults of the transepts have, as a central motif, the monogram of Christ with the Alpha and the Omega in the midst of scrolls, and at either side of these monograms are little figures which may represent the four Apostles, who did not find a place on the drum. At the end of the vaults, there is a formal scheme of acanthus scrolls with two harts drinking from a spring, illustrating Psalm XLII (40).

Opposite the entrance, at the end of the north arm of the chapel, there is a scene of quite different character from the rest of the work (41). Below the window, in the center, is a flaming gridiron. At the left, in an open cupboard, are the four books of the Gospels, and, at the right, a bearded figure in a white mantle, with a nimbus, and carrying a cross and a book, rushes violently towards the center. This figure is usually considered to represent St. Lawrence on account of the presence of the instrument of his martyrdom. In addition, St. Lawrence, as a deacon, would have charge of the Gospels and would carry a cross. This is one of the earliest examples of that realistic, historical style which was transforming Christian art.

On the opposite wall is the famous mosaic of the Good Shepherd (42). Christ is shown seated against a background of rocks and shrubs, surrounded by six sheep. This majestic, beardless figure, clad in purple, with golden nimbus, and holding a long cross, is the early symbolic type of the third and the fourth centuries, suggesting the classical Apollo. In fact, the symbolism of the whole scene goes back to the traditions of Early Christian art, but the richness of Christ's garments and the schematic treatment of the landscape show a strong Eastern influence.

Many may agree with Diehl that the interior of this little chapel is the most exquisite thing which early Christian art has left us. It is undoubtedly, the most complete and the most perfectly preserved mosaic decoration of a small building that exists. Technically, it is of the very highest quality, both in the skillful use of color, and in the manner in which the design is adapted to the space. The effect is well described by John Addington Symonds who speaks of the dim light from the narrow windows which "serves to harmonize the brilliant hues and make a gorgeous gloom."

The style shows a good deal of classical feeling in the naturalism of the figures, the movement, and the treatment of light and shade, but this does not necessarily mean that it shows a native Italian influence as some critics would have us believe. These so-called classical characteristics were common to most of the art of the Near East and were a part of the general Hellenistic tradition. Moreover, here, there is a decided Eastern influence in the use of brilliant color, in the jewelled cross of the cupola, in the schematic treatment of the landscape in the Good Shepherd mosaic, and in the conventional character of much of the detail.

The cupola of the Baptistery of the Orthodox,[54] (43) or, more officially, San Giovanni in Fonte, is considered to have been decorated under Archbishop Neon, 449-452, and it is, therefore, nearly contemporary with the Mausoleum of Galla Placidia.

The central medallion of the dome represents the Baptism of Christ (44). The nude figure of Our Lord stands in the water up to the waist. At the left, John the Baptist, holding a long jewelled cross, pours water on His head, while the Dove descends from above, and at the right, the river Jordan, "JORDANN," is personified in pagan fashion as an old man. A line may be easily distinguished on the gold background surrounding the head and the neck of Christ and the head and the left arm of John the Baptist. This marks the restoration undertaken by Kibel between 1860 and 1880.

Two concentric zones complete the decorations of the cupola; the first showing the Twelve Apostles, and the second, altars and thrones in an architectural setting. The Apostles form a double procession headed by St. Peter and St. Paul and their names are indicated by inscriptions. They are dressed in tunics and pallia, a gold tunic and a white pallium alternating with a white tunic and a gold pallium, thus giving an interesting rhythm to the design. Above their heads, are festoons of drapery, and between each figure, there is a conventionalized acanthus plant as a symbol of Paradise.

The lower, narrower zone is divided into eight equal compartments of colonnades with niches, the niches occupied alternately by four thrones and four altars. The thrones are embellished with jewels and have cushions surmounted by a cross, and at either side are chancel-screens with flowers behind. The altars are each flanked by two chairs, and on each altar, there is a book of the Gospel with an inscription.

There has been much discussion over the symbolism of this scheme. The empty throne would seem to be the *Etimasia*, or the preparation of the throne for the Last Judgment, as on the triumphal arch of Santa Maria Maggiore, but this explanation does not fit the four thrones. The empty chairs have been supposed to represent a council. Perhaps the most plausible theory is that the whole scheme symbolizes the Church with its principal centers.

The eight angles of the drum contain figures of Prophets enframed by volutes of foliage (45). The foliage has been almost entirely restored by Kibel. Lower down, on the arches of the three lower apses, are mutilated inscriptions relating to the rite of baptism.

In style, these mosaics show the same characteristics found in the Mausoleum of Galla Placidia, a little less fine in conception and in the sense of color. The Apostles are treated realistically, much in the late Roman manner, but the tendency to isolate the figures and, at the same time, give them a uniform movement or rhythm, is typically Eastern.

There is the same combination of elements from the Hellenistic Orient here that there is in the Mausoleum of Galla Placidia.

The basilica now known as Sant'Apollinare Nuovo[55] was erected by Theodoric and dedicated to the Saviour under the Arian cult. When it was returned to the Orthodox Church by Bishop Agnellus, 556-569, it received the name of San Martino in Cielo d'Oro, because of its mosaics. Later, probably in the tenth century, it was rededicated and received its present name on account of the translation of the relics of the saint from Sant'Apollinare in Classe.

This basilica has one of the most complete ensembles of mosaics in existence (46-56). Those of the apse have disappeared, but both walls of the nave have retained their decoration complete from the arcades to the ceiling.

These mosaics are divided into three zones. The upper zone, above the windows, consists of twenty-six compositions, thirteen on each side, from the life of Christ. Each of these scenes is separated from the other by a shell surmounted by a cross between two doves. The intermediate zone contains thirty-two figures, sixteen on each side, representing Prophets and authors of the Bible in all probability, although there is no direct evidence for this. These figures occupy the spaces between the windows. The lower zone consists of two processions; at the left, twenty-two virgin saints, preceded by the three Magi (46), leave the town of Classis and approach the Virgin Mary; at the right, twenty-six martyrs, male saints, leave Ravenna and approach Christ (47).

The scenes of the life of Christ, contrary to the processions lower down, begin at the altar and end at the entrance. On the left, are the Miracles and Parables, and on the right, are the scenes from the Passion. Their order is probably in accordance with the reading of the Gospels, as it took place in the old liturgy of Ravenna from the beginning of Lent to Easter Sunday. These episodes are presented with a concentration and clarity, and with a sense of revealing gesture and dramatic conception of the event which we will not find again in Western Art until the frescoes of Giotto.

Beginning with the miracles, we have, in order: The Miracle of Cana; the Multiplication of Loaves (50); the Vocation of Peter and Andrew; the Curing of the Two Blind Men; the Curing of the Woman with Dropsy; the Woman of Samaria; the Resurrection of Lazarus; the Pharisee and the Publican; the Widow's Mite; the Sheep and the Goats (51); the Curing of a Paralytic; the Curing of the One Possessed; the Curing of the Paralytic of Bethesda.

In all these scenes, Christ is shown as young and beardless, while in the scenes of the Passion He is represented as much older and bearded, but there is no reason to separate the two series on this account, as they seem to be similar in style. In both, Christ wears violet robes and has a cruciferous nimbus, and other details show a similar connection between the two. The Miracle of Cana has been three-quarters restored but the upper part of the body of Christ is original. Others of the series show minor restorations, but are, on the whole, in good condition. The subjects are well and simply treated with never more than four or five figures in a scene. They bear certain resemblances to some of the early miniatures, for the most part of Eastern origin, and they are among the very earliest representations we have of New Testament subjects.

The scenes from the Passion are as follows: The Last Supper (52); Christ on the Mount of Olives; the Betrayal (53); Christ Led to Judgment; Christ before Caiphus; Christ's Prediction to Peter; Denial of Peter; Repentance of Judas; Christ before Pilate; Christ Led to Calvary; the Holy Women at the Tomb; the Disciples of Emmaus; Christ Appearing to the Apostles.

These subjects are treated with a dramatic intensity which we do not find in the more symbolic scenes of the Miracles. Throughout, there is a combination of Eastern and Hellenistic elements which relates the style to that of the Rossano Gospels and other early miniatures and points to an East-Christian heritage. In the Last Supper, the type of the round table is of Asiatic origin. In Christ Before Pilate, or Christ Led to Calvary, and in other scenes, we have the best of the realistic, historical style of the sixth century, subjects which have, perhaps, never been more successfully treated in later art.

The Prophets between the windows (48, 49) are related in style to the mosaics above and are probably of the time of Theodoric. They are tall, majestic figures, well diversified in gesture, and carry books or scrolls. Over the heads of the windows are pairs of birds.

On the twelfth of February, 1915, an Austrian bomb fell on the left angle of the façade of the basilica, detaching the first three Prophets, two of the shells above, and the scene of the Paralytic. These mosaics have now been replaced without any serious changes.

The procession of virgin saints issues from the port of Classis (46); Kibel's restoration of the upper portion of the architecture of the town is easily distinguished by its hard regularity. Each saint is provided with a nimbus and wears a rich dalmatic of gold and a white tunic. A fringed veil is carried on the left shoulder and is draped over the left arm, and in the left hand is borne a martyr's crown. The figures are separated by palms with flowering plants at the base. There seems to be an almost rigid monotony in the scheme, but the veils alternate in height, the palms are alternately light green and dark green, and the flowers white and red, giving rhythm to the design. St. Agnes, the only saint who is distinguished by an attribute, has the lamb at her feet. The richness of the coloring, and the frankness of the repetition without dead monotony, make this procession one of the most impressive in art.

At the head are the three Magi bearing gifts and the Virgin and Child seated on a jewelled throne with two angels on either side (54). The entire upper portion of the figures of the Magi is a restoration, but the group of the Virgin and the angels does not appear to have been changed in any essential part. This symmetrical and stylized composition of the Virgin and Child is one of the so-called Byzantine formulæ which were common in Eastern art from the sixth century on.

On the other wall is depicted the palace of Theodoric, with a panorama of Ravenna beyond. The twenty-five martyrs (47) are headed by St. Martin, the patron saint of the basilica of Agnellus, who, alone, is clad in a purple mantle. The rest wear white tunics and mantles and carry their martyrs' crowns. It is interesting to note that all the male saints represented are Roman, corresponding with the female saints where all are Roman with the exception of two.

The figure of Christ, as a pendant to the Virgin on the other wall, is seated on a jewelled throne, surrounded by four angels (55). The whole right side of the figure, as well as the two angels on the right, have been badly remade on too large a scale. This is due to the fact that during the seventeenth century an organ was erected here which was removed early in the following century when the restoration took place.

The figures of the Virgin and of Christ with the surrounding angels seem to be of the same style as the mosaics of the two upper zones, and it is quite probable that they, too, date from the time of Theodoric. The space occupied by the processions of saints may have contained subjects which were distasteful to the Byzantine rulers, so that they were removed to make way for the present mosaics.

These mosaics as a whole show a new iconographical conception, as here the narrative subjects are high and are relegated to second place, while they occupy the most prominent position at Santa Maria Maggiore. The Oriental tendency towards abstraction and stylization, already apparent in the mosaics of Theodoric's time, is fully developed in the processions of the saints, where the forms are flatter and show very little modelling. The female saints are, on the whole, more subtly varied and modelled than the male.

Formerly there were portraits of both Justinian and the Archbishop Agnellus at the entrance to the basilica. These were already in a ruinous condition in the sixteenth century, and now all that remains is the much restored bust of Justinian, IVSTINIAN (56). The emperor's diadem, the nimbus, and the buckle holding the mantle are elaborately adorned with mother-of-pearl, like the mosaics in the choir of San Vitale.

The choir of San Vitale[56] (57-65), the only portion of the church which is adorned with mosaics, shows the early Byzantine style in its full splendor with a brilliant and carefully thought-out scheme.

In the apse, the beardless figure of Christ with cruciferous nimbus, is seated on a blue globe (57). With His right hand, He offers a crown to San Vitale, and in His left hand He holds the Book of the Seven Seals. On either side, are two angels, clad in white, holding long batons. On the left, is San Vitale in a costume of rich Byzantine brocade, and on the right, the bishop, Ecclesius (ECLESIVS EPIS), offers a model of the church. The presence of the bishop without a nimbus would date this mosaic, in all probability, between the years 521 and 534.

On the apsidal arch, two flying angels hold a disk of blue with the letter "A" in the center, from which radiate eight white and red rays. At the sides, are Bethlehem and Jerusalem, designated by inscriptions, and palm trees.

The vault of the choir (58) has for a central motif a medallion, surrounded by a wreath of foliage and fruit, which contains the Divine Lamb on a background of stars. Four winged angels support this medallion. The groins of the vault have pyramidal garlands of foliage and fruit descending to the corners where there are peacocks with spreading tails, standing on globes. The field between the garlands is filled with blue and red volutes, in the midst of which may be distinguished various birds and other animals; peacocks, partridges, herons, doves, gazelles, antelope and so on. The head of the Lamb always seems to face the spectator from any angle, a fact which impressed an early historian of Ravenna, Girolamo Rossi, in the sixteenth century.

A part of the vault fell in the eighteenth century and was replaced by a painted imitation and it has undergone a number of restorations since that time. Even in quite recent years it has been again repaired and cleaned. But in spite of all these changes it remains one of the most beautiful of mosaics, superb in composition and glorious in color.

The subjects on the walls symbolize the evangelical doctrine and the mystery of the altar. At either side of the trifora are represented the Four Evangelists; St. John and St. Luke on the left and St. Mark and St. Matthew on the right (59). These figures are seated in a rocky landscape and above each one is his respective symbol. They have a certain hardness and awkwardness which is perhaps due to restoration. The arches of the trifora are decorated with vine scrolls and vases with doves.

The lower wall on the right shows the sacrifices of Abel and Melchisedec interpreted as a symbol of the eucharistic sacrifice (60). Melchisedec offers the loaf of bread and Abel, the lamb. Above the arch, two flying angels hold a medallion with a jewelled cross, and at either side are Moses and the Prophet Isaiah, the former guarding the flocks of Jethro.

On the opposite wall is the sacrifice of Abraham. Abraham is twice represented (61); at the left we see him serving the three angels, and at the right, he is about to sacrifice Isaac. Above we have a scene similar to the one on the opposite wall. At the left is the Prophet Jeremiah and at the right Moses is shown on the Mount with the Hebrews below.

In the soffit of the arch of the choir (62) there are fifteen medallions in a beautiful enframement of interlaced dolphins and other motifs.

The medallions contain the busts of Christ (restored), the Twelve Apostles, and the two sons of San Vitale, Gervasius and Protasius.

On the nineteenth of April in 547 Maximian solemnly consecrated the church in the presence of Justinian and Theodora. Two famous mosaics in the choir (63-65) commemorate this event and give a more vivid picture of the pomp and the splendor of the Byzantine court than anything else which has come down to us. The panel on the left shows the emperor and his suite with the bishop, Maximian, who is accompanied by two deacons (63). The realistic portrait heads form a marked contrast with the rigid attitudes of the bodies in their stiff garments, but this bold, schematic treatment, thoroughly Oriental in conception, creates a profound impression of dignity.

The second panel, showing Theodora and her suite, is even more striking (64). The gorgeous head-dress of the empress gleams with gold and mother-of-pearl (65) and on the hem of her embroidered robe is represented the Adoration of the Magi. The women of her suite wear the sumptuous Byzantine brocades of the period. Here, there is less stiffness in the attitudes than in the preceding mosaic. At the left is the cantharus, or fountain, in which the faithful made their ablutions according to the early ritual before entering the church. These two panels are doubly precious on account of the almost complete destruction of secular mosaics. They are the only early examples we have which are not of a purely religious character, and perhaps they give a faint suggestion of the vanished glories of the Byzantine palaces.

The chapel of San Pietro Chrysologo in the Archbishop's Palace is now known to have been founded by Pietro II whose monogram occurs on one of the arches. The bishop died in 519 and the mosaics probably date from the first half of the sixth century, and their style, which is similar to those of San Vitale, would bear this out. In both there is the same broad indication with firm, dark outlines combined with many gradations.

In the vault (66-68), four angels, recalling those of San Vitale, support a medallion with the monogram of Christ, and between them, are the symbols of the Evangelists holding jewelled books. The bull is not provided with a nimbus, but this was doubtless left out in one of the restorations. The lion's head and the angel on the right have also been badly restored.

The soffits of the arches which support this vault contain a series of busts in medallions. In the center of two of them the beardless Christ is represented and the other two have the sacred monogram. The remaining medallions show the Twelve Apostles, six male saints and six female saints (69). These are very similar in style to those of the arch of San Vitale.

On the wall of the neighboring presbytery there is a figure of the Militant Christ (70). He is represented as a beardless young man with cruciferous nimbus, bearing a jewelled cross on His shoulder, and holding an open book with the inscription: EGO SUM VIA VERI TAS ET VITA, "I am the Way, the Truth, and Life." The lower part of the figure was at one time badly restored with draperies. It is now generally considered that the Christ was originally represented as a soldier with bare legs, largely on account of Wilpert's comparison with a stucco figure in the Baptistery of the Orthodox. Accordingly, it has been recently thus restored temporarily in paint.

Saint'Apollinare in Classe[57] is nearly contemporary with San Vitale. The mosaics, which are confined to the apse and the arch (71) are, however, probably later than San Vitale, although the work in the apse itself is almost certainly of the sixth century. These mosaics have often been spoken of as decadent, but it does not seem fair to apply this term to the central composition. The surrounding panels are, of course, later and somewhat inferior in style. On the whole, this is one of the most satisfying examples of apse decoration in existence as it is complete and homogeneous with no disturbing elements of later periods.

THE MOSAICS OF RAVENNA

In the apse itself we have a symbolic representation of the Transfiguration, a subject which was rarely shown in mosaic. Our Lord is not represented in person but by a great jewelled cross in a medallion with a background of stars. In the very center of the cross there is a small bust of the bearded Christ in a medallion. To the right and the left of this central theme, Moses and Elias emerge from clouds of brilliant blue and red, and above, is the Hand of God. Below is a pasture with trees and rocks. The three sheep, two on the right and one on the left, complete the scene of the Transfiguration as they represent the three Apostles chosen by Our Lord to be witnesses of His glorification; Peter, James and John. At the base of the composition are twelve sheep, the traditional way of representing the Apostles; but in the center where we should expect the Divine Lamb, we have Sant'Apollinare shown as an orant. This has led some authorities to think that this figure is a later interpolation, but if so, it was done before the twelfth century, as it is mentioned in a document of that time.

On the face of the arch, there is an upper band with the medallion of Christ blessing and the symbols of the Evangelists; below, the Twelve Sheep issuing from Bethlehem and Jerusalem, and at the base, the sacred palms. Still lower, on the right, is the Archangel Gabriel, and on the left, the Archangel Michael. These impressive figures are represented in full Byzantine regalia, and technically they are among the best of the mosaics here, in contrast to the badly restored busts of St. Matthew and St. Luke which fill the remaining space below. The two remaining Evangelists, if they were once represented, have now disappeared.[58]

The remaining work occupies the lower band of the apse itself. In the center, between the windows, are the figures of four archbishops of Ravenna; ECLESIVS SCS; SEVERVS SCS; VRSVS (72); VRSICINVS, according to the inscriptions. These panels are almost identical except for the more or less portrait heads and the treatment of the pilasters at the sides. The shells above, the draped curtains with the crowns suspended over the heads of the figures are in the best sixth century tradition. It is quite possible that the head of Ursicinus, d.536, which seems more individualized than the others, is a contemporary portrait.

Two larger compositions on either side of these figures complete the series. That on the left (73), of historical character, represents the Archbishop Reparatus receiving the privileges of the Church of Ravenna; the one on the right shows the mystical subjects of the sacrifices of Abel, Abraham and Melchisedec (74). It will be noticed that the backgrounds of both these scenes are similar in style to those of the four archbishops and it is probable that these mosaics once commemorated events relative to the consecration of the basilica. However that may be, in the seventh century they were refashioned to represent the subjects we see today. In the first, may be distinguished the archbishop, Reparatus and the emperor, Constantine IV, with his sons, Heraclius and Tiberius. The arrangement is very similar to the mosaic of Justinian in San Vitale, but feebler, and a recent authority has discovered that the heads seem to have been cut out and replaced, so that we may suppose that the earlier scene was refashioned by Reparatus to suit his own ends. This would help to explain various anomalies, such as the scroll of privileges which seems to float in mid air. It must be said, further, that frequent and unfortunate restorations from the seventeenth century on have sadly defaced it and do not permit us to judge it fairly.

The second mosaic, representing the sacrifices is obviously imitated from San Vitale but the execution is very inferior. The lower portion has been much restored.

On the whole there is no great divergence in style between the mosaics of the arch and the apse. The flowers in the panels of the two Archangels are similar to those surrounding Sant'Apollinare, and the twelve lambs and the Archangels, the four archbishops and the figure of the saint seem related to one another. We may conclude that the whole scheme was started in the first half of the sixth century and that about a century later it was completed and modified in an inferior style.

The splendid mosaics of the Baptistery of the Orthodox evidently inspired the similar decoration of the Arian Baptistery (75), a circular structure which originally formed part of the Roman baths, and was consecrated to the Catholic cult in 558. Here, in the Baptism, the figures are transposed, John the Baptist being on the right instead of the left. The personification of the Jordan is a typically classical figure with claws on his head in the manner of ancient marine deities. The Christ, who is beardless here, seems to have been less retouched than the Christ of the Baptistery of the Orthodox. Above, is the Dove, with the two eyes naïvely placed in the top of its head. The pose of the Baptist is evidently copied from the earlier composition, but the artist has omitted to place the rock under the raised foot.

The procession of Apostles is a simplified and stiffer version of the earlier series. The draperies, the very conventionalized palms, and the rather crudely designed throne show few traces of classical influence and point to a later date.

Like so many of the Ravenna mosaics, this, too, has suffered from restorations,[59] but it must always have been a feebler copy of the Baptistery of the Orthodox; even the color is more broken up, varied, and less fine. It is usually dated about the middle of the sixth century, and was probably executed soon after the reconsecration of the building in 558.

Even if the mosaics which we have examined so far have suffered from the vicissitudes of time and at the hands of the restorers, they are, at least, *in situ* and have retained, after all, a good deal of their former glory. The same cannot be said of the unfortunate apse of San Michele in Affricisco or, "ad Frigiselo"[60] (76) which was bought by Frederick William IV of Prussia. Detached from the walls in 1844, it reposed for a while in Venice. Then, the cubes were broken up and sent in cases to Berlin where they were stored for half a century—until 1904, to be exact—when the apse was finally reconstructed in the Kaiser Friedrich Museum. Suffice it to say that the mosaic retains no trace of the original style and bears all the ear-marks of nineteenth century archæology. It is only the composition that can interest us here.

In the center is Christ with a cruciferous nimbus, holding the Book and a jewelled cross. At His right hand is the Archangel Michael, and at His left, the Archangel Gabriel, and the whole is enframed by a border of doves in profile. On the arch above is a bearded figure of Christ seated on a throne and holding the Book, surrounded by angels, and below, are the medical saints, Cosmas and Damianus. According to drawings made before the mosaic was removed, the present reconstruction follows the original composition faithfully enough. In all probability it dates from the sixth century.

The mosaics of Ravenna show us today the greatest extant examples of the sixth century. Nowhere else do we get such a vivid or extended picture of the work of this period. But even here we have only the remains of what once existed. In the early writers, especially Agnellus, there are many allusions to destroyed mosaics.[61] The Cathedral, or Basilica of Ursus, was covered with them, but we do not even know their subjects. Santa Maria Maggiore, among others, had a celebrated image of the Mother of God. The marbles and mosaics of the palace of Theodoric were carried away by Charlemagne to adorn the imperial residence at Aix-la-Chapelle and no traces remain. In the apse of the church of Sant'Agata, was a figure of Christ seated on a throne between two angels, and holding a scroll with the Seven Seals. This was destroyed by an earthquake in 1688 but has been reproduced by Ciampini[62]. It probably dated from the sixth century.

There has been much discussion about the origin of the style of Ravenna. A number of authorities, perhaps inspired by a kind of patriotism, see in it a native product following the antique Roman tradition with little or no outside influence. Others feel that the entire inspiration comes from the Near East and that what it owes to Rome is negligible. Without going into this too deeply, it would seem that an impartial critic would have to take a less dogmatic attitude until we are sure of the actual origin of many characteristics and motifs which are now definitely labelled as Eastern, or even more specifically, as coming from Syria, Palestine, Egypt or elsewhere. The present extent of our knowledge makes many such statements only hypotheses. The rich backgrounds of blue or gold are apparently Eastern, not Roman, and so are, as well, the ceremonial processions, the costumes, and the realistic portraiture. It has also been pointed out that the curious effect some of the figures have of appearing to walk upon their toes, as in the Baptistery of the Orthodox, is an Eastern characteristic.

There are, however, certain typically Western, or Roman traits, such as the frequent representation of the symbols of the Evangelists, although these are by no means unknown in the East. It is also a remarkable fact that the inscriptions, even in mosaics which are purely Byzantine in character, are always in Latin; but this can perhaps be explained on political grounds, and does not necessarily have much to do with the actual style of the work. Certainly, the intimate relations between Ravenna and the Eastern Empire, from the time of Galla Placidia on, would tend to bring influences from that direction. Ravenna, like Venice at a later day, faced the East with her back to Italy. The earlier work of Galla Placidia and Theodoric does show affinities with the late Roman style, as we have seen, but by the time that the Byzantines have established themselves at Ravenna much of the antique tradition dies out. In general, the mosaics show the transition from antique naturalism and impressionism to the more formal mediæval abstraction and conventionalism which practically all the art of the period was undergoing.

Although these works have their own local characteristics which differentiate them from others of the period, we feel that Ravenna itself was not a sufficiently great center to have actually originated the style. Such a style, with its combination of so many early and long-developing traditions, could have only been evolved in one or a combination of the converging points of the Near East. At the end of the next chapter we will consider the possibility of a radiating center from Antioch [63] being responsible for a large part of these Oriental elements. The bold hypothesis brought forward by Dütschke that these mosaics were executed by artists from Northern Africa has little foundation if we compare them with the pavements and the few tomb mosaics from those provinces. Certain general resemblances between them point, rather, to a common ancestry.

The school of Ravenna undoubtedly exerted its influence elsewhere. Local workmen were probably trained with the Byzantine or other Eastern artists and spread themselves in all directions. It is a question whether the mosaics of San Giovanni in Fonte at Naples or those of San Prisco near Capua were influenced from here. It is, perhaps, better to consider them the result of a similar East Christian influence which came by way of the sea. The same may also be said of the Roman mosaics of SS. Cosma e Damiano, nearly contemporary with San Vitale, and of San Lorenzo-fuori-le-mura. The splendid mosaics of Parenzo, across the Adriatic, have, as we shall see, much in common with those of Ravenna and belong to the same school. If they do not show a direct inspiration from the latter, they are, in any case, a result of the same tradition.

OTHER EARLY MOSAICS TO THE SEVENTH CENTURY

OTHER EARLY MOSAICS TO THE SEVENTH CENTURY

Salonika the second city of the Byzantine Empire and its mosaics: St. George, St. Demetrius, the Eski-Djouma, and the recently discovered mosaic in St. David.—Constantinople: the problem of St. Sophia, the mosaics of the Narthex.—The Church of the Holy Apostles.—Mount Sinai: the Monastery of St. Catherine.—Parenzo. —Pola: Santa Maria del Canneto.—Milan: San Lorenzo and the Chapel of St. Victor in Sant'Ambrogio.—Albenga: the Baptistery. —Casaranello.—Naples: San Giovanni in Fonte.—The lost mosaics of Nola.—Capua: San Prisco.—North Africa and Spain. —Summary of the Early Christian style in general.—Antioch as a radiating center?

VI.
OTHER EARLY MOSAICS TO THE SEVENTH CENTURY

In this chapter we shall survey a wide geographical area including the whole of the Near East, and Italy with the exception of Rome and Ravenna. The great flourishing communities in the Near East; Syria with Antioch and the Holy Land, Asia Minor, and Byzantium itself, have very little left to show us, but we must remember that here, throughout this period, there were important centers of radiating influence and that the style of these lost mosaics is, without doubt, reflected in the mosaics of Rome and Ravenna which we have already described.

Salonika,[64] the second city of the Eastern Empire strategically placed to receive all the varied artistic impulses of the Byzantine world, still retains a number of splendid works which are among the best that have come down to us.

The church of St. George is a late Roman domed edifice consecrated to Christianity early in the fifth century. Three of the eight interior niches still have a mosaic decoration of medallions with birds and baskets of fruit, *rosaces* adorned with swastikas, or birds and stars and fleurons on a silver ground, in the same tradition as the vaults of Santa Costanza (77). The cupola had much the same scheme as that of the Baptistery of the Orthodox at Ravenna. There was a central medallion with the figure of Our Lord, but only a fragment of the border, a garland of fruit and flowers, remains. The zone corresponding to the Apostles of Ravenna has also been destroyed, but a second zone, corresponding to the altars and thrones of the Baptistery, has been preserved and is one of the finest decorative ensembles of the fifth century (78). Here there are eight compartments, seven of which are well preserved, with elaborate architectural backgrounds, against which stand pairs of saints in the attitude of orants.⁶⁵ The architecture is in the more ornate Pompeian or Alexandrian tradition and stands out on a gold ground, and the artist has shown a much greater interest in this setting than in the figures themselves, which are here relegated to a rather minor rôle and are small in scale. The compositions are typically late Hellenistic in conception, but the figures of the saints themselves are treated in the more abstract monumental manner with an attempt at portraiture which we associate with East Christian influences.

This use of fantastic architecture, treated in symmetrical parallel perspective, as an ornamental background has an interesting history.⁶⁶ Its origins probably lie in the painted scenery of the Hellenistic theatre. Such motifs were undoubtedly well known at Alexandria, at Antioch and in the various centers of Asia Minor. The so-called Fourth Style of wall painting at Pompeii is derived from it; a fine example is the Villa from Boscoreale in the Metropolitan Museum. In addition to the use of these motifs in St. George and the Baptistery of the Orthodox, and in the Great Mosque at Damascus, we find them in a number of the early illuminated manuscripts. The Council scenes in the Church of the Nativity at Bethlehem, although of the twelfth century, go back to these earlier prototypes, and even in the fourteenth century we have a certain revival of them in the mosaics of Kahrie Djami at Constantinople. By way of Pompeii they spring up again to influence the Adam style in England towards the end of the eighteenth century.

The beautiful mosaics of St. Demetrius (Hagia Paraskevi) ⁶⁷ which were uncovered in 1907, were, unfortunately, very seriously damaged by fire in 1917; but four panels, at least, on the pillars preceding the entrance to the transept, have escaped destruction. One of these represents St. Demetrius, clad in rich brocaded robes, standing with two children (79). It is undoubtedly a votive mosaic referring to some miraculous cure. Probably it is contemporary with the work in San Vitale at Ravenna, although it may be a little earlier, and it is remarkable for its coloring and the skillful placing of the tesseræ to produce varied reflections of light.

On the same pillar there is a damaged panel representing the Virgin and a saint standing against an architectural background. According to Ainaloff, it portrays the well-known Byzantine conception of the Virgin praying for the universe. It is quite different in style from the rest of the mosaics, and probably dates from the tenth or the eleventh century.

The figure of St. Sergius as an orant, clad in a white chlamys adorned with red circles, resembles the St. Demetrius in style and probably dates from the sixth century. This is the third of the four panels which have escaped destruction.

By far the finest of these panels (80) is the one which represents St. Demetrius standing between two bearded personages; usually referred to as the "Founders", from the fact that one of them probably represents Leontius, prefect of Illyrium who founded the church, and the other, one of the early bishops. If this hypothesis is correct, the square nimbi would show that these men were living at the time the mosaic was executed and this would date it in the early fifth century. Although it may be possible to place it as early as this, it is so similar in style to the first panel of St. Demetrius that it would seem to be contemporary with it, and it perhaps shows a sixth century restoration of an earlier original. It seems much more probable, however, that the nimbi are not nimbi at all, but merely crenelations on top of the wall in front of which the figures are standing. If this is the case we do not have to consider that these figures represent living personages and we are quite free to date the work at least as late as the sixth century.

The mosaics above the arcades of the colonnades showing St. Demetrius as an orant, the Virgin and Child with two angels, and medallions of Christ and various saints, all dating from the sixth or the seventh centuries, were destroyed in the fire. On the whole, the work in St. Demetrius is in that historical, monumental style which we find in Sant'-

Apollinare Nuovo or in the contemporary mosaics of Parenzo. An interesting feature of these mosaics is, that unlike those of Ravenna and elsewhere, they do not form a part of any thought-out scheme, but consist almost entirely of ex-voto panels, given by various donors and extending over a considerable period of time.

Of about this period,—the sixth century,—are the mosaics on the soffits of the arches of the Eski-Djouma (Hagia Paraskeoi). Here, there are formal Eastern designs of birds and flowers, vases of lotus or papyrus upon which stand birds, diapers of silver lattice with flowers on a blue ground in the openings, in fact, a whole gamut of Early Christian motifs. The cubes are of rich blues, greens, reds, and silver and gold, and as pure decoration these mosaics are among the best that have come down to us.

The work in St. Sophia at Salonika all seems to be of a later period and we shall not take it up here, but a recently discovered mosaic in the apse of the church of St. David should be mentioned. This represents the vision of Ezekiel (81); a beardless Christ seated on a rainbow within a circular glory and surrounded by the symbols of the Evangelists. Below, are the Prophets Ezekiel and Habakuk. It may date from the sixth century, but it does not compare in quality with those of St. Demetrius.

Of the early mosaics in Constantinople very little remains. Some have been described by the early historians, but as here we are primarily interested in what actually exists, it is not worth our while to attempt to reconstruct them from purely documentary evidence. Those of St. Sophia ("Divine Wisdom," Turkish, *Aya Sofia*)[68], now almost entirely covered with white-wash or paint, are partially known by the drawings which Salzenburg and Fossati made in 1847, but these drawings do not give a clear idea of the style, so that there is a good deal of doubt as to what may date from the time of Justinian and what may be due to subsequent restoration. This was the extent of our knowledge of these mosaics until a couple of years ago. Now this great gap in the history of the art is disappearing. The Turkish Government has permitted Thomas Whittemore on behalf of the Byzantine Institute to uncover and clean these mosaics and St. Sophia itself is being converted into a museum. Mr. Whittemore has already cleaned and restored the vaults of the narthex and revealed to us the splendid decorative mosaics of the time of Justinian (82, 83), as well as the great lunettes over the Royal Entrance to the church and the South Portal which date from a later period.

The narthex is divided into nine bays with groined vaults. The ribs of the vaults are covered with a geometric pattern and center on a roundel containing an eight-armed cross. Each compartment of the vaults has an elaborate floriated design on a gold ground (82). On the broad transverse arches which separate the nine vaults there are alternate squares and roundels filled with geometrical patterns. Each of the eight lunettes opposite the windows contains a cross (83) of the Golgotha type on a gold ground. In the soffit of each arch of the window openings on the west side of the narthex are two crosses and a star of silver on a blue ground, and in the jambs are vine scrolls.

The geometric and floral designs are so similar to those on carvings inside the church that they must be contemporary, that is, of the time of the building of the church by Justinian. There are also similar designs in mosaic in the soffits of some of the arches of the interior. They may be compared with patterns in Coptic textiles. The prevalence of the cross is perhaps due to Justinian's desire to reconcile the Monophysites to the official church.

The mosaic which was originally in the central lunette over the Royal Door to the church, probably a cross as in the other lunettes, was removed to make way for the wonderful Christ Enthroned, but as this is a work of the late ninth or early tenth century we will consider it with the later Byzantine mosaics.

The Church of the Holy Apostles, which was destroyed by Mohammed II, the Conqueror, to make way for his great mosque the Mehmet

Fatih, had a famous series of episodes of the life of Christ which have been described by Constantine the Rhodian and Mesarites. It is interesting to note that these scenes were arranged in chronological order, as at Sant'Apollinare Nuovo, and not according to a fixed iconographical scheme following the order of the great festivals of the Church, such as became the general rule by the tenth century, and which was employed at Hosios Lucas in Phocis, at Daphni, at St. Mark's in Venice and elsewhere. In the scene of the Holy Women at the Tomb, the artist portrayed himself as one of the soldiers, quite in the spirit of the Italian Renaissance. These mosaics were evidently one of the great examples of the more realistic Byzantine style. The vaults of the church of SS. Sergius and Bacchus (Kutchuk Aya Sofia), erected by Justinian and Theodora, once gleamed with mosaics. Procopius writes: "By the sheen of its marbles it was more resplendent than the sun, and everywhere it was filled profusely with gold." Some of these mosaics may still exist under the Turkish plaster. Choricius of Gaza describes mosaics of that city in the churches of St. Sergius and St. Stephen and there are other scattered references to them throughout the empire.

However, one other early mosaic actually remains in Constantinople, that in the apse of the church of St. Irene.[69] This church was rebuilt by Justinian but all of the upper portion including the apse and the dome was restored by Leo the Isaurian about the middle of the eighth century and the mosaic probably dates from this time. The subject is typical of the Iconoclastic period—a large cross outlined in black upon a pale gold ground. There are even some silver tesseræ mixed with the gold. At the base of the semi-dome there are three steps set upon a double band of green and a geometrical border with an inscription in Greek from Psalm LXV. On the face of the arch are other geometrical patterns with a broad wreath of foliage and another inscription in Greek. The upper part of the dome has been restored in paint and gilt as well as the inscription at the base. We may note here that the apses

OTHER MOSAICS TO THE SEVENTH CENTURY 113

of both the Church of the Dormition at Nicæa and St. Sophia at Salonika had similar crosses which were replaced by later mosaics.

The vaults of the narthex of St. Irene originally had mosaics of a geometrical pattern of which two fragments remain in the soffits of the arches. These are not unlike those in the narthex of St. Sophia and are probably of the time of Justinian.

Although some of the recently destroyed mosaics in the Church of the Dormition at Nicæa may have been as early as the seventh century, we will describe this work as a whole under the eleventh century examples in Chapter IX.

In the monastery of St. Catherine on Mount Sinai [70] there is a work of the sixth or the seventh century representing the Transfiguration (84). This is a subject which has been rarely treated in mosaic, the only other early examples being the symbolical rendering in the apse of Sant'Apollinare in Classe, and the one in SS. Nereo ed Achille in Rome which dates from the ninth century. The Christ stands in a mandorla of three shades of blue. He is provided with a silver nimbus with an inscribed gold cross, and six rays issue from the body. He holds a scroll in His left hand and blesses with the right. In the foreground, St. John lies prone, covering his face, while St. James and St. Peter kneel. There is a surrounding border of busts of Prophets and Apostles in medallions with silver backgrounds. Above, and at the side of the apse, are Moses and the Burning Bush and Moses Receiving the Law. On the center of the arch is a dove in a mandorla and at either side, in the spandrels, is a flying angel holding a globe and a baton or torch. Below the angels are two heads in medallions, on the left a bearded man without the nimbus, and on the right a woman. These heads may represent Justinian and Theodora, or more probably, the unknown donors of the mosaic. One of the most striking features of this mosaic is the blue mandorla which may be compared with the one at Cyprus in the Panagia Kanakaria. We should also note the use of the silver backgrounds. Most authorities now agree in dating this work in the sixth century, perhaps contemporary with Justinian who restored the church.

Turning westward, we come to Parenzo,[71] on the shore of the Adriatic nearly opposite Ravenna. The basilica was erected by the bishop, Euphrasius, 535-543, and the beautiful mosaics (86-89), comparable to those of San Vitale, date from his time. The Seven Candlesticks of the Apocalypse still exist between the windows of the façade (85), but they are a modern restoration and the rest of the exterior mosaics have disappeared. The apse (86), however, is finely preserved and is one of the glories of the sixth century. In the center, are the Virgin and Child enthroned, similar to the same subject in Sant'Apollinare Nuovo. Unfortunately, nineteenth-century restoration has somewhat tampered with the original design. On either side are two angels, very similar to those in the apse of San Vitale. Beyond, on the left (87), are St. Maurus holding a crown, the bishop Euphrasius offering a model of the church, and the archdeacon Claudius, all designated by inscriptions; and on the other side, are three anonymous saints, one holding a book, and the other two, their crowns. The Latin inscription below alludes to the foundation of the basilica. Within the arch, is a series of medallions containing the busts of saints. These medallions are alternately of light and dark blue and the saints have gold nimbi. Above the arch, is Christ on the globe surrounded by the Twelve Apostles. About twenty years ago this frieze was freed from a coat of stucco and restored and only the upper portions of the figures are original.

The inscription at the base of the apse reads:
HOC FUIT IN PRIMIS TEMPLVM QVASSANTE RVINA
TERRIBILIS LABSV NEC CERTO ROBORE FIRMVM
EXIGVVM MAGNOQVE CARENS TVNC FVRMA METALLO
SED MERITIS TANTVM PENDEBANT PVTRIA TECTA
VT VIDIT SVBITO LABSVRAM PONDERE SEDEM
PROVIDVS ET FIDEI FERVENS ARDORE SACERDVS
EVFRASIVS SCA PRECESSIT MENTE RVINAM
    LABENTES MELIVS SEDITVRAS DERVIT AEDES

FVNDAMENTA LOCANS EREXIT CVLMINA TEMPLI
QVAS CERNIS NVPER VARIO FVLGERE METALLO
PERFICIENS COEPTVM DECORAVIT MVNERE MAGNO
AEC CLESIAM VOCITA NS SIGNAVIT NOMINE X̄P̄Ī
CONGA VDENS OPERI SIC FELIX VOTA PEREGIT

In the center of the apse, between the windows, three figures are represented, an Archangel, Zacharius, and St. John the Baptist. Zacharius is clad in a rich cape, or chasuble, and tunic, and carries a censor and a coffer, both of which are adorned with little figures. The Archangel bears a globe upon which is represented a cross with twelve rays. John the Baptist, recognizable by the skin which he wears, carries a long-handled cross. The badly adjusted tunic which seems a bit irrelevant in connection with the skin, is probably a later restoration. These three figures resemble closely in style the figures in the upper part of the apse.

The space between the window and the apsidal arch on the left is occupied by the Annunciation (88). Above the scene are three shells of the type found in Ravenna, the middle one being reversed. The Virgin is seated upon a throne in front of a building which probably represents the basilica erected on the site of her house at Nazareth.

As a pendant to this scene on the other side we have the Visitation (89). Behind St. Elizabeth, at the entrance to the house, stands the servant with her finger on her chin. Both of these scenes are enframed by the characteristic border formed of alternate rectangles and lozenges found on a number of the early mosaics, notably the arch of Santa Maria Maggiore at Rome. The style of these last two compositions does not correspond with the rest of the work in the apse, and they may well be of a later date, perhaps of the seventh or the eighth century.

The two smaller lateral apses have retained the upper part of their decoration, in both cases a bust of the beardless Christ Emmanuel who in one, blesses two saints, and in the other, two bishops. The Christs are very similar in style to the one in the apse of San Vitale, and the work here is surely of the sixth century and contemporary with that of the central apse. Moreover, what does remain has been very little restored.

On the whole, the central apse of Parenzo gives one of the loveliest and most complete impressions we have of Early Christian art. The mosaics are complete, even if restored, and below, is the beautiful facing of colored marbles and mother-of-pearl together with the altar and the baldachino.

At Pola,[72] not far from Parenzo on the Adriatic coast, there is a much damaged mosaic in the apse of the little church of Santa Maria del Canneto. The subject was probably the *Traditio Legis* and the head of Our Lord and another head, which without much doubt is that of St. Peter, are fairly well preserved. This work dates from the middle of the sixth century, contemporary with Parenzo and San Vitale at Ravenna, and it was carried out under the same bishop, Maximian, a native of Pola, who was responsible for the mosaics in the latter church. The execution is very fine, extremely small tesseræ being employed, and as we would suppose, it is very similar to San Vitale in style.

In Italy, we have already described the early mosaics of the great centers of Rome and Ravenna, and we must now take up the all too few examples which have escaped destruction in other parts of the peninsula. Going westward from Ravenna, we come to the only two early mosaics which remain at Milan, one in the church of San Lorenzo and the other in Sant'Ambrogio.

The mosaics of San Lorenzo[73] are in the upper part of the two apses of the little chapel of St. Aquilinus. This chapel to the right of the basilica is older than the church itself which was founded in 451. The apse on the right (90) shows Christ on the globe surrounded by the Twelve Apostles. The Christ is of the youthful antique type, and the Apostles, in spite of a certain stiffness, retain much of the classical feeling. In fact, the general effect of the scene is strikingly like that of some of the earlier catacomb frescoes, especially that of the apse of the

Cemetery of Domitilla where we have the same composition, although the Apostles are standing instead of being seated. A careful cleaning of the mosaic has revealed a *scrinium* at the feet of Christ containing a collection of manuscript rolls similar to the one in the fresco. Christ is shown here in the guise of the teacher, or philosopher of antiquity. The figures still show individuality and an impressionistic technique, but the background is of gold. Both apses are in bad repair and have been considerably restored by paint.

In the second apse (91) we have a pastoral scene; four shepherds tending sheep in the midst of a rocky landscape. The two central figures and the head of one of the sheep are quite obviously modern, but the rest is in moderately good preservation. The two other shepherds wear a costume similar to those in one of the mosaics of Santa Maria Maggiore. This scene has given rise to several interpretations. Garrucci[74] thought that it represented Jacob with his flocks; others, the Annunciation to the Shepherds. Traces of horse's hoofs have been discovered in the sky and this has led Wilpert[75] and Toesca[76] to consider it either a symbol of the Innocence of Souls or The Shepherds Disturbed by the Heat of the Sun. Wilpert has attempted a restoration showing the Sun with his chariot and four horses above. Here, even more than in the other mosaic, there is a Hellenistic picturesqueness and realism, especially in the background, and it shows an almost pure late-antique inspiration.

However, in spite of the reliance upon the antique, it seems doubtful if these mosaics date from the fourth century, as some authorities believe. They are more probably of the end of the fifth century, very likely of about 495 when Theodoric restored the church. There is a certain stiffness and clumsiness in the figures which does not seem to point to any direct classical influence, even though they are derived from the classical type. The ornamental bands below are similar to those in some of the Ravenna mosaics.

The chapel of St. Victor, [77] annexed to the church of Sant'Ambrogio, still retains the decoration of the dome and the walls (92, 93). The apse originally had an early mosaic but this has been replaced by a modern one which is without interest. In the center of the dome is the bust of St. Victor (92), similar to the medallion portraits of Ravenna, in a wreath symbolical of the four seasons; roses and lilies, wheat, grapes, and olives. On the two monogrammatic crosses are the names of the donors of the mosaic, and the name VICTOR on the open book identifies the saint. This medallion stands out on a gold ground, and, in fact, the chapel was originally designated as "in Cielo d'Oro," just as the church of Sant'Apollinare Nuovo at Ravenna was originally called San Martino in Cielo d'Oro, which shows that at this period the use of gold backgrounds was unusual. In the corners are the symbols of the Evangelists, and below, on the lateral walls, are six figures of saints on a blue ground; Ambrose (93), Gervasius, Protasius, Materus, Nabor and Felix, according to their inscriptions. These are all saints who were buried in the basilica or its immediate vicinity. They have many traits in common with the male saints of Sant'Apollinare Nuovo, and Toesca would date them midway between the two series of mosaics there. They stand out on the uniform blue with very little modelling or relief. On stylistic grounds, therefore, these mosaics may be placed at the end of the fifth century, contemporary with those of the chapel of St. Aquilinus, or, possibly, in the early sixth century.

Still further westward, on the Ligurian coast, the Baptistery of Albenga [78] has preserved fragments of its early mosaics (94). The principal feature is a Constantinian monogram of white on a background of three concentric circles of different shades of blue. This is inscribed in a square of darker blue and surrounded by twelve white doves symbolizing the Apostles. The borders have green foliage on a white ground, recalling the work in Santa Costanza. In a tympanum are two lambs adoring a jewelled cross. The work here is usually considered to show the radiating influence of Ravenna, but the symbolism, the light backgrounds and the absence of gold cubes have more affinity with the early work in Rome and in Campania. It may be earlier than the end of the fifth century which is the date generally given for it.

At Casaranello,[79] in the heel of Southern Italy, near Taranto, there are also some mosaics (95). The little basilica there was originally much like the Mausoleum of Galla Placidia in form. In the dome there is a gold cross on a circular ground of light blue covered with stars, and beyond, another band of dark blue with larger stars, an Oriental conception of the Universe. Beyond the circular ground are vine scrolls with flowers and bunches of grapes. In one arm of the barrel vaults are bands, interlacing circles, and other motifs which all seem to be Eastern in origin. The use of silver as well as gold cubes in the stars has led Wilpert to date the work in the sixth century, perhaps contemporary with SS. Cosma e Damiano in Rome where silver cubes are also employed, but Haseloff, who first studied it, puts it in the fifth century.

Among the finest of the early mosaics are those of the Baptistery of Soter at Naples[80] in spite of the fact that they are in poor condition (96, 97). This baptistery is attached to the Cathedral and it is entirely Eastern in its square form with a cupola on squinches. The mosaics with their combination of genre and decorative elements with the monumental show a certain relationship with early Ravenna, such as the Baptistery of the Orthodox, or the Mausoleum of Galla Placidia. However, in an illuminating article, Muñoz has pointed out that there is probably no direct connection between the two.

In the center of the vault is a medallion with the monogram of Christ on a blue ground covered with white and gold stars. Above the monogram the Hand of God holds a golden crown. The medallion is surrounded by a border of fruit and flowers, vases, and birds, among which is the phœnix with a nimbus as a symbol of the Resurrection.

Radiating bands of foliage, fruits, and flowers, with birds, ribbons and other motifs, and growing out of urns below, divide the vault into eight trapezoidal compartments, of which, four and a fragment of another are fairly well preserved. The compartments thus formed have, in the upper part, a blue drapery shot with gold and a vase with two birds facing each other, and below, Biblical scenes in more or less complete fragments: The *Traditio Legis* (96), Christ and the Woman of Samaria, the Marriage of Cana, the Calling of Peter and Andrew, and the Holy Women at the Tomb. The *Traditio Legis* and the Marriage of Cana are the best preserved. The four squinches contained the symbols of the Evangelists (97), each with six wings and stars above, but only two of these, the angel and the lion, are preserved, although there are still traces of the bull. The head of the angel is of great beauty, as fine as anything at Ravenna. In the spandrels above the squinches are pastoral scenes, two with shepherds and two sheep alternating with two shepherds and two harts drinking. Each of these compositions is terminated by palm trees and birds. On the walls between these little apses, or squinches, were pairs of martyrs, or perhaps, Apostles on a blue ground, clothed in white and bearing wreaths, and of these, four remain.

The pastoral scenes have lively, impressionistic color and may be compared with the Mausoleum of Galla Placidia. They probably date from about the middle of the fifth century, from the time of Bishop Soter, 465-492. The same may be said of the central medallion with its radiating garlands. Some of the Biblical scenes, however, seem weaker both in coloring and in modelling and these may be later, perhaps about the end of the century. These subjects have a good deal of iconographical importance. The only other representations of the Holy Women at the Tomb, for example, before the sixth century, are on two ivories, and this scene and that of the Samaritan are thoroughly Oriental in conception. The technique, as Muñoz has shown, is a kind of mingling of the manner of the Roman pavements

OTHER MOSAICS TO THE SEVENTH CENTURY

with their graded passages from light to shade and the true mediæval manner with its sharp contrasts from light to dark. The dominant tonality of turquoise-blue and green, enlivened with gold, and the richness and variety of the garlands and other motifs give an effect of beauty which is rare, even in the fifth century.

The fine quality of the mosaics of San Giovanni in Fonte make us regret other early examples in Campania which have perished. St. Paulinus describes the famous apse of the basilica of St. Felix at Nola, a profoundly symbolical composition which must have contrasted with the hunting and fighting scenes shown on the walls of the nave.[81]

Fortunately, a part of the decoration at San Prisco,[82] near Capua, has been preserved (98, 99). The mosaics which were in the church itself have perished and are only known from rather poor drawings. Those in the dome were in the so-called catacomb style with a central medallion from which radiated bands dividing the surface into equal compartments. The medallion contained a throne on a sphere surrounded by stars, and in the compartments were saints carrying wreaths, who were divided from each other by vases flanked by birds. Around the base there was a broad band of leaves and fruit with small figures of winged genii. In the apse, were processions of saints.

The actually existing mosaics are in the adjoining chapel of Santa Matrona. The vault had a central medallion which has disappeared. It is divided into four compartments by palm trees, and the compartments are filled with beautiful vine scrolls issuing from vases; two doves face each vase (98).

Three of the lunettes still retain their decoration. In the one over the entrance, is a bust of Christ in a medallion between the Alpha and Omega (99). That on the left contains the Throne with the Dove and the Book of the Seven Seals between two of the symbols of the Evangelists, the bull and the eagle. The third has an angel, the symbol of St. Matthew (the lion, symbol of St. Mark, has disappeared) and a representation of Bethlehem. The fourth lunette, known by a seventeenth-century engraving, contained a jewelled cross with the Four Rivers of Paradise and the twelve apostolic doves, precisely the scheme which St. Paulinus adopted for the neighboring basilica of Nola at the beginning of the fifth century.

Affinities with the early mosaics of Ravenna and San Giovanni in Fonte would place these in the second half of the fifth century or, possibly, as Bertaux suggested, in the early sixth.

Tombal mosaics [83] which have been discovered in Northern Africa and Spain, dating for the most part from the fifth century, and showing a relationship with the early work at Ravenna, the Naples Baptistery and certain Palestinian pavements bear witness to the wide diffusion of these mosaic workers along the shores of the Mediterranean. At Tabarka (Thabraca) in Morocco a number of lids of sarcophagi have figures of *orans,* vases with affronted birds and vine scrolls executed with cubes of colored marbles and blue glass but with little or no gold. Similar in style are the two recently discovered tombal mosaics at Tarragona which are probably of the fifth century but executed upon sarcophagi of an earlier date. One (100) represents a male figure in a white toga holding a scroll with an inscription above, the whole enclosed in a guilloche border. The other has a Lamb in the center with a vase with naturalistic branches and an inscription, surrounded by a border of foliage. A similar mosaic, although less well preserved, was found at Huesca in Northern Spain and there is a fragment of one in the museum at Valencia which shows that there was probably a wide diffusion of such work throughout the peninsula during these early centuries. There were also scanty remains of fifth-century mosaics in a little church at Constanti near Tarragona.

Summing up the work of the first six centuries, we may say, broadly speaking, that there is an ever increasing influence, which is usually considered Eastern, apparent both in the striving for rich and gorgeous effects of color and in abstract and conventionalized design. The fountainheads of inspiration may well have been in the Near East, in Syria, Asia Minor, and, later, in Constantinople itself, but this is difficult to prove on account of the almost complete destruction of the work in these regions. The Hellenistic tradition, however, lasted on throughout the period, and at times is strongly felt, especially in Italy itself, where it was reinforced by the native classical tradition of Rome. Rome and Ravenna, which have more to show us than any of the other centers, even if they did not originate and give the great creative impulses, fused many diverse elements into styles which may properly be called their own.

An interesting hypothesis, formulated by Diehl and others, is to consider a great part of the Eastern influence in these mosaics as the result of the spreading out of a flourishing creative center in Syria, especially in Antioch. Ravenna, Parenzo, St. Demetrius, San Giovanni in Fonte, San Prisco and others resemble each other strongly in a broad way, however much they may differ in minor and, apparently, more local characteristics. Antioch, a great cosmopolitan port, midway between Egypt and the Hinterland of Asia Minor and Mesopotamia, was one of the most important centers for the development and the diffusion of Early Christian iconography. Little of its mosaics and nothing, even of its architecture, survive, and we only surmise an Antiochene style from certain minor objects; illustrated manuscripts, ivories, silver and other articles of luxury which possibly had their common place of origin here.

We have only this, as yet, uncertain foundation upon which to base a definite style. Nevertheless, many of the characteristics of these mosaics, which must have had a common source, are those which we would expect to find in Syria. Palestine, the center of the Faith, provided ideas, and, no doubt, much of the iconography, but in the earliest times it was without a well-established artistic tradition and this may have been supplied by artists from the flourishing schools of

Antioch and Alexandria which stood on either side. As we shall see, the mosaics of the Dome of the Rock at Jerusalem and in the Great Mosque of Damascus of the late seventh and early eighth centuries, were very likely executed by Syrian artists. We may hope that further research and, especially, the excavations now going on at Antioch itself will clear up some of these very interesting and still baffling points.

Italian mosaics as widely separated as those of Ravenna, Albenga on the Ligurian coast, Campania and Casaranello, and others in the Mediterranean from Salonika to Spain and Northern Africa, as well as pavements from Palestine, however they may have developed locally into distinctive styles, have sufficient characteristics in common to infer that they go back ultimately to a common source. The art relied upon a special material and highly trained craftsmen, and we may suppose that the centers where it first flourished were at or near those localities which were noted for the production of glass, such as Egypt and Syria, and later, possibly Constantinople itself. Mosaicists from such centers would spread out to supply the demand, bringing the material with them, and would largely control the character of the work, until certain places, such as Ravenna or Rome became strong enough to establish schools and traditions and develop a more or less independent style. All this would have been facilitated by the manifold maritime contacts between important centers which flourished throughout the whole of the Early Christian period.

THE SEVENTH AND EIGHTH CENTURIES

The Seventh and Eighth Centuries

Jerusalem: the "Dome of the Rock".—Damascus: the Great Mosque.—Spain: the Sanctuary of the Mosque at Cordova.—The Roman group: reasons for the strong Eastern influence.—Sant'Agnese.—Oratory of St. Venantius.—Santo Stefano Rotondo.—San Pietro in Vincoli.—Oratory of John VII.—San Teodoro.—St. Sophia, Salonika.

VII.

THE SEVENTH AND EIGHTH CENTURIES

During the seventh and the eighth centuries, the vital centers of mosaic production must have still been in the Near East, but practically all traces of the work there have disappeared. It is, on the whole, an interlude between two great periods—the time of the Arab invasions and the iconoclastic controversy. The Eastern Empire was at a low ebb, awaiting the revival under the Macedonian emperors of the tenth century. Two series stand out, however, in the midst of this general barrenness, one in the mosque at Jerusalem known as "The Dome of the Rock," and the other in the Great Mosque at Damascus.

The Dome of the Rock, the "Mosque of Omar" of the Crusaders, and sometimes called the Blue Mosque from the colored tiles of the exterior, was built by the Caliph Abd al Melek in 691. It is a dome structure of centralized plan. An octagonal outer arcade and an inner circular arcade lead to the central space which is covered by a cupola on a high drum. The rich marbles of the walls and columns, the gilded cornices, the colored glass of the windows and the mosaics combine to form an interior "surpassed in gorgeousness of color and mystery of lighting by no other shrine, not even St. Mark's itself. A series of circular enclosures are set one within the other, so disposed that the columns and piers do not conceal one another but permit you a view of the whole from almost any part of the building." [84]

The mosaics are in three groups. The first [85] (101) is on the spandrels of the octagonal arcade and is dated by a Kufic inscription 691-2. The second group (102) is on the spandrels of the arches of the circular arcade, on the outer face only, and although it bears no inscription it is contemporary with the first group. The third series (103) is seen on the two registers of the drum and has an inscription referring to the restoration of 1028.

These three groups form a vast homogeneous scheme although they differ distinctly in style from each other. Those of the octagonal arcade which are, perhaps, the most striking are largely composed of bold floral motifs (101) which fit into the triangular spaces of the spandrels. Each motif is similar to the others in its general construction but varies infinitely in detail. The soffits of the arches are adorned with garlands, bands, and rosettes.

The mosaics of the circular arcade are composed of a more continuous pattern of sumptuous acanthus scrolls (102) developing out of the plant itself, or vases at the base, and running over the arches. The same motif is repeated on the four great piers of the dome which break the continuity of the arches.

Lastly, on the lower part of the drum we have a band of acanthus scrolls growing out of elaborate vases crowned by diadems and the so-called Sassanian winged motif. A similar scheme is repeated in the rectangular panels between the windows in the upper register of the drum. These scrolls are stiffer and more stylized (103) than those of the circular arcade but this was probably done consciously as being more in keeping with a continuous band of decoration which should emphasize the horizontal feeling. This group is probably contemporary with the others, and some of the more mechanical effects may be due to the eleventh century restoration. The panels of the upper register have suffered more than any other part of the work and are badly restored.

The vault of the east porch has a mosaic of checkerboard pattern composed of small squares.

These are perhaps the finest purely decorative mosaics in existance. No figures appear, in accordance with the precepts of the Koran, and the designs are entirely derived from plant forms, vases, and so on. The whole scheme is perfectly unified in its broader lines and adapted to the architecture, but at the same time, the individual motifs are subtly diversified, so that we get an infinite variety of form within prescribed limits.

The method is no less admirable than the design. Simple, strong colors are employed, shades of blue, of green, touches of red and orange, emphasized by spots of mother-of-pearl, silver, and gold against a plain gold ground, but the dominant tones are always green, blue and gold. Where the gold is used in the designs and not in the background, the cubes are tilted to get stronger reflections of light and are often contrasted with silver cubes. The mother-of-pearl is always placed where the light may strike from the side to get the full value of tone. In short, a consummate technique where nearly every tessera seems to have been manipulated to get the full æsthetic effect.

This work was probably done by Christians, for the Mohammedans had no school of their own capable of producing it. The style resolves itself into the early Hellenistic tradition of naturalism modified by Oriental conventionalism and abstraction. It is probably not Byzantine in origin but may well be a product of that Syro-Palestinian school with Antioch as a center, which, at an earlier period may have influenced the art of Ravenna. Some of the motifs go back to the early art of Mesopotamia and Persia.

Early in the eighth century the Caliph Walid I, d. 706, transformed the Byzantine church of St. John into what has since been known as the Great Mosque of Damascus, and caused it to be embellished with mosaics [86] (104, 105). Those on the arches of the west portico and a great panel over one hundred and fifty feet long within the portico have been uncovered by Eustache de Lorey, and the extraordinary architectural compositions in which no figures appear, like the work in the Dome of the Rock, but in which are interspersed naturalistic trees and foliage, give us, perhaps, more than a hint of the glories of a great vanished secular art like that of the Byzantine palaces or of Bagdad. The mosque became, perhaps, the most famous in Islam and the Arab writers sang its praises. Muquaddasi, writing at the end of the tenth century says "The mosque is the most beautiful thing that the Muslims possess today."[87] On the exterior of the adjacent Dome of the Treasury there are other later mosaics resembling those of Jerusalem but less good in execution.

Here, in the Great Panel, we find groups of buildings with foliage similar to those in the backgrounds of early illuminated manuscripts of Alexandrian or Syrian origin (104). There are superimposed structures like the fanciful theatrical decoration of the so-called fourth Pompeian style, as in the Villa from Boscoreale or the House of Livia at Primaporta, reflections, probably, of a once flourishing secular art derived from both Hellenistic and Oriental sources, as opposed to the purely religious. We have already noted the same influences in St. George and in St. Demetrius at Salonika and in the Baptistery of the Orthodox at Ravenna and we shall find them continuing until the fourteenth century mosaics of the Kahrie Djami at Constantinople. But in these examples, however much the backgrounds may predominate, they are always considered a setting for a religious theme, while here, the buildings and trees are portrayed for themselves alone in sheer love of sumptuous decorative effect (105). It has been thought that the Great Panel represents an actual scene. The river would be the Barada, flowing through Damascus which is shown in the group with the bridge, and beyond would be the villages of the far-famed oasis of the Ghuta. It was but natural that the Moslems with little or no developed art of their own, and with their antipathy for the religion of those whom they had conquered, should turn to this purely secular phase of East Christian art, of which Syria had undoubtedly been a flourishing center.

This work, like that in the Dome of the Rock, was done by Christians, and technically it is admirable. In the gold backgrounds the tesseræ are often tilted forward to catch the light. Silver is employed for the reflections of water and other high-lights, and there is frequent use of mother-of-pearl. The colors are comparatively simple: green, blue, violet, yellow, red, and black. Tesseræ of white, pink, brown and red limestone are used in addition to those of glass. "Some of the finest trees, with their shadows in mauve and light pink, curiously anticipate, as do those at the Villa Livia at Rome, the paintings of Cézanne!"[88]

Muqaddasi's description of the Great Mosque, written about 985 and translated by Miss Van Berchem, is worth quoting. He says: "Then it [the sahn] is entirely paved with white marble and the walls are faced with variegated (*mujazza'*) marble up to the height of two fathoms and thence to the ceiling with polychrome mosaic (*fusāfisā*), in the gilt parts of which are pictured trees, cities, and inscriptions of the greatest beauty and delicacy, of exquisite workmanship. There is hardly a tree or a notable town which has not been pictured on these walls. The capitals of the columns are gilt, and all the arches (*qanātir*) of the porticoes (*arwiqa* pl. of *riwāq*) were decorated with mosaics. All the columns of [*i.e.*, next] the sahn are of white marble; the surrounding walls, the arches, and the little arches (*firākh*) above them are decorated with mosaics forming inscriptions and decorative motives (*turūh*). The whole roof is covered with sheets of lead, the cresting (*sharrāfīyāt*) is decorated with mosaic on both faces. In the court, to the right, stands a Treasury on eight columns, the walls of which are encrusted with mosaics.

Al-Walid, they say, gathered together for its construction skilful artisans of Persia, India, the Maghreb, and Rum. He devoted to it the proceeds of the Land Tax of Syria for seven years, employing also eighteen shiploads of gold and silver which sailed for Cyprus, without counting the tolls (*ālāt*) and the mosaics which were sent to him by the King of Rum. . . ." And the commentator adds in a note: "Mosaic is composed of [little pieces of] glass, like the two-drachm [glass] weights, of yellow, dust grey, black, red, black and white, and gilt. [For the last named] are made by placing gold on their surface, covered by another layer of thin glass. Then the plaster is worked up into a paste with gum-arabic, and spread on the wall, and this mosaic is embedded in it and figures and inscriptions are formed. Some parts are entirely encrusted with gold mosaic, so that the wall appears to be a blaze of gold".

The Moslems, throughout their history, employed mosaic to some extent, although they were always more interested in various kinds of inlays which should be properly classed as intarsia, and in tile. Whatever may have existed at Bagdad has disappeared. Later fragments of the tomb of the Sultan Baybars at Damascus of 1285 are much inferior to those of the Great Mosque. Baybars also restored the mosaics of the Great Mosque. The art was still practiced at Damascus in the fourteenth century as the Mausoleum of Tankiz has a rather crudely executed scroll decoration which attempts to imitate the earlier style.

We may take up here the only other important work done under Mohammedan influence. This is the sanctuary of the Mosque at Cordova, dating from the early tenth century (106). The caliph, El-Hakim, wrote to the Byzantine emperor, Nicephoras Phocas, for mosaic workers, such was their fame at this time, and the emperor sent a mosaicist and a present of cubes. These mosaics consist of ornamental bands and Arabic inscriptions on the façade of the mihrab and around the three doors, and also in the cupola of the Capilla del Zancarron, which forms a sort of vestibule to the mihrab. There are floral designs on a gold ground, more conventionalized than those of Damascus or the Dome of the Rock. Great richness and harmony are obtained with the use of but a few colors; dark blues, reds, and greens. The cupola with its penetrating arches and small central dome with eight melon compartments is especially fine on account of the way in which the patterns are fitted to the varied surfaces. There is a delicacy of treatment both in design and in the use of tesserae which are much smaller than the average, and this blends extremely well with the surrounding decoration of intricately carved marble which has taken on the tone of old ivory.

Returning to the Christian mosaics, we find the only extant examples surely of the seventh century in Rome.[89] It is not surprising that these are all strongly Eastern, or Byzantine in character. The popes under whom they were produced were for the most part from the eastern provinces. Greeks, Syrians and other orientals came in great numbers to Rome and Southern Italy. Their churches and monasteries were rich and influential. A strong impetus was given these migrations by the conquests of the Arabs and the dissensions caused in the empire itself by the iconoclastic controversy. The close ties which were thus brought about between Rome and the Near East are naturally very apparent in contemporary mosaics and painting.

The apse of Sant'Agnese (107) was executed under Honorius I, 625-640. This composition in its simplicity, the placing of the three figures against the plain gold background, is one of the most impressive in all mosaic. In the center is the saint in the sumptuous costume of a Byzantine empress, with spots of red on her cheeks. Above, the Hand of God is stretched forth to place the wreath upon her head; at her feet lies the sword of the executioner; flames break forth at either side. On the left, the pope, Honorius, presents a model of the church; on the right, we have either Sylvester I under whom the basilica was constructed, or Innocent I who restored it, each wearing a brown chasuble and a white pallium. These stiff, elongated figures show little relief or modelling; the bodies are hardly realized beneath the rigid garments. They have the effect of decorative images and are perhaps even more impressive for this reason. Venturi has pointed out that they seem "woven in" as if they were more brilliant spots on the brilliant brocade of the background, and, in fact, they anticipate the Roman work of the ninth century which treats the surface almost as if it were a gorgeous textile. The almost isolated figure of St. Agnes foreshadows the apse of Torcello, and in the twelfth century a similar composition with three figures is used in the apse of the Cappella San Giusto in the cathedral of Trieste.

The inscription below [90]—gold letters on a blue ground—is worth translating to give an idea of the spirit in which the work was conceived: "The cut (shaped) metals produce a painting of gold and the light of day seems to be compressed and enclosed in it. One would think that the dawn, assembling the clouds from liquid sources, burns and spreads life to the fields. Such a light, the rainbow produces among the stars; such a purple brilliance, are the colors of the peacock. Chaos, which was able to put an end to night as well as day, has brought the martyr from the tomb. By a sign from on high which is seen by all, the pontiff, Honorius, has proclaimed these vows. His vestments and his acts define him; his visage lets one perceive a pure heart."

The ancient church of San Teodoro (108), a little circular structure of unknown origin at the foot of the Palatine, contains an apsidal mosaic which has been so much restored that it is difficult to place. Opinion, generally, would give it to the early seventh century, but Wilpert puts it at the time of Felix IV, contemporary with SS. Cosma e Damiano. In the center, is Christ seated on a globe, blessing, and holding a staff surmounted by a cross. We may compare this with the figure in the apse of San Vitale or that in San Lorenzo fuori-le-mura. On either side are St. Peter and St. Paul who each present a martyr, the one on the right probably being St. Theodore, and the other, possibly Cleonicus. The gold background is almost entirely modern, the head of Christ and the hand of St. Paul are remade, and the saint next to St. Paul is a late restoration, but the main outlines of the composition have been kept. Much of the restoration was done by the Barberini in the middle of the seventeenth century. The best preserved figures are St. Peter and the following saint, and here the heads have a good deal of resemblance to the medallions of San Vitale.

Adjoined to the Lateran Baptistery is the oratory of St. Venantius (109-111), containing mosaics of the time of John IV, 640-642, called Dalmata from his place of origin. Venantius had been a Dalmatian bishop, and the Istrian schism now being ended, the pope thought that by doing honor to the national saint of the province he would unite it more closely to Rome. With Venantius and the bishop, Domnius, eight canonized Slavonian warriors were also represented. Thus, the mosaic has a certain political character.

In the upper part of the apse (109), on the background of red and blue clouds, there is a rather magnified bust of Christ blessing, flanked by two angels. Below, in the center, is the figure of the Virgin as an orant, and at either side (110, 111), are eight saints, four in the apse itself and four on the adjacent walls. These include St. Peter and St. Paul, St. John the Baptist and St. John the Evangelist, the Pope with a model of the church, and the eight martyrs. Four panels above show the symbols of the Evangelists in pairs and the towns of Bethlehem and Jerusalem.

The bust of Christ blessing is one of the first examples in mosaic of the type of the Byzantine Pantocrator which in the course of the centuries assumes colossal proportions, fills the apses of Hosios Lucas and Daphni, and comes to a climax in the marvellous figures of Cefalù and Monreale.

Two hands seem to have worked here. The figures in the apse are thick-set with large heads, but those on the walls are more elongated, stiffer, with smaller heads more in the manner of Byzantine elegance. There is some attempt at portraiture, not unlike San Vitale which was a century earlier. The color is rich and brilliant with repeated touches of coral and gold. It is no longer fused, as at Sant'Agnese, but more vivid and spotty, somewhat like the later ninth-century Roman work.

Here, too, like Sant'Agnese, the inscription [91] below the apse, in gold letters on a blue ground, speaks of the "metallic brilliance equal to the sacred waters," showing that these early mosaicists were fully alive to the purely æsthetic appeal of their work.

In a chapel in Santo Stefano Rotondo, on the Cœlian, there is a mosaic (112) which is usually attributed to Pope Theodore, 642-649, although there is no documentary evidence to corroborate this. According to the *Liber Pontificalis*, the pope had the bodies of the two martyrs transported from the Via Nomentana, where they were buried, to this spot, and the mosaic probably commemorates this event. In the center of the niche, is a jewelled cross surmounted by a bust of Christ in a medallion. Above, in a semi-circle of blue, studded with stars, the Hand of God holds a martyr's crown. On either side are the two martyrs, Primus and Felicianus, designated by inscriptions. Each wears a purple tunic with a white chlamys. Below, red flowers spring from the soil which is indicated by a strip of green.

This mosaic is in very bad condition. The heads of the two saints as well as the bust of Christ are wholly restored, the garments have been much done over, and a part of the gold background has been frankly indicated in paint. The central motif of the cross and the medallion is, perhaps, derived from early Palestinian iconography; it should be compared with the apse of St. Irene at Constantinople and the early apse of Santa Sophia at Salonika. Where there has been no restoration the tesseræ are more irregular in shape than in preceding work, and, especially in the background, they are arranged to give a good deal of variety of texture to the surface. As Venturi says, they give almost the impression of the strokes of a brush.

The church of San Pietro in Vincoli contains a very interesting panel representing St. Sebastian (113), not as the beautiful adolescent familiar in later art, but as an old and bearded man holding a martyr's crown. A late inscription on the altar would give the mosaic to the time of Pope Agathon, 678-681, and there is no good reason to dispute this. According to the old writer, Paulus Diaconus, the pestilence of 680 almost depopulated Rome, and even the rest of Italy, and we have here, probably, one of the first of those plague offerings which were so common later in the Middle Ages and the Renaissance. The background is blue, not gold, and this has led some to suppose that the work is earlier than the seventh century, but the style of the figure makes 680 seem a reasonable date. The cubes are placed rather far apart so that the cement between them is very apparent. This gives a certain softness, but without detracting from the clearness of the design.

The demolition in 1609 of the oratory of John VII,[92] 705-707, in consequence of the rebuilding of St. Peter's, destroyed one of the most important and probably one of the finest of the early Roman mosaic ensembles. There are still fragments of the mosaics which were preserved and carried away, and we can gain an idea of the arrangement of the scheme from the drawings which were made by Grimaldi, the architect, towards the end of the sixteenth century, now in the Vatican Library,[93] by the engraving of Ciampini[94] (114) and by a seventeenth century fresco. On one wall was a central panel of the Virgin as an orant with a smaller figure of the Pope below at one side. This was surrounded by scenes from the life of Christ in seven compartments, arranged in the manner of a Byzantine retable. Several of the compartments contained two or more episodes grouped together, the scheme followed by Ghiberti in his doors for the Florentine Baptistery. On another wall were scenes from the life of St. Peter in six compartments. The striking innovation in composition here—smaller panels grouped about a great central figure in the later mediæval manner—has led some to suppose that the smaller scenes were added afterwards, and that only the figure of the Virgin as an orant is of the time of John VII; but there is no proof of this.

This Virgin (115), now in the church of San Marco at Florence, is a noble figure, clad in the costly garments of a Byzantine empress. Her robe is of a rich red and is adorned with pearls. On her head is a jewelled diadem. Her features are regular and impressive, and the color in the cheeks is indicated by red lines recalling the red spots on the cheeks of St. Agnes. The upper part of the figure of John VII has also been preserved (116), and is now in the new Museo Petriano at St. Peter's. This is of much smaller scale than the Virgin and, as we know, it was placed in the lower left-hand part of the panel. The Pope, who carries a model of the chapel has a square nimbus and wears a yellow tunic with reddish folds. The main lines of the composition are indicated in black. This fragment has probably been a good deal restored.

Other fragments which are now in the Museo Petriano are the much restored bust of St. Peter Preaching (117), from the scenes of his life; and, from the life of Christ, the Washing of the Child (118), the head of Christ from the Entry into Jerusalem, and the badly restored Virgin and Longinus from the Crucifixion. The head of Christ is well preserved; it is excellent in technique, with widely spaced tesseræ and fine in color. The fragment of the Washing of the Child, which formed a part of the scene of the Nativity occupying the space above the central panel, is also in very good condition and shows an almost impressionistic treatment. The iconography of this scene showing the midwife, Salome, is purely Eastern in origin. Also from the Nativity is the fine bust of the Virgin, draped in a blue mantle on a gold ground, now in the cathedral of Orte. As in most of the other work, the tesseræ here are irregular in shape and vary in size, permitting the cement to be very apparent, and fusing the brilliant colors together.

The finest bit which has come down to us is, undoubtedly, the central portion of the Adoration of the Magi (119), now in the sacristy of Santa Maria in Cosmedin. The Virgin is seated on a jewelled throne with a green cushion and wears a violet robe and a blue mantle. The infant Jesus, on her knees, holds a *volumen,* or scroll, in the left hand and stretches out His right hand towards a coffer filled with gold offered to Him by one of the Magi. Of the latter figure there remains only the hand and the arm, clad in green. Above, at the right, is an angel, robed in white, with blue and green wings and a blue nimbus, and Joseph is standing behind the throne with lowered head. The cubes here are widely spaced and vary in size. Marble cubes, as well as glass, are used, especially in the flesh tones. Perhaps no mosaic in Rome is more worthy of careful study than this, on account of the excellence of the technique and the skill with which vibrating spots of jewel-like color are obtained. It is now so placed that it may be examined at close range and in a good light. The rich chromatic fusion and the texture of the surface, as well as the decorative line, are, perhaps, Byzantine, but there is an undercurrent of classicism in the well-rounded, noble figures and in the sweep of the draperies.

It is not until the very end of the eighth century that we find other mosaics in Rome, and, as these properly belong to the ninth-century group we will take them up in the next chapter.

Although this group of seventh and eighth century Roman mosaics show an ever-increasing Byzantine influence which is prevalent in the whole of the eastern Mediterranean, they have an individuality which is sufficient to set them apart as a definite school within the general development. Very few traces of the earlier classical impressionism or naturalism remain and we find the usual Eastern stylization, neglect of the third dimension and use of broad masses of color to fill in the contours, common to all work of the period. But it is especially the treatment of color that sets these mosaics apart. The masses are enlivened and broken up chromatically within themselves by spots of often vividly contrasting tones which give a warmth and vitality quite apart from the design itself. These tendencies may be seen, of course, in earlier mosaics, at Ravenna or Campania, or elsewhere, but no where outside of Rome are they so strongly developed. The style is already well marked in the apse of Sant'-Agnese and even more so in the Oratory of St. Venantius and the Chapel of John VII, anticipating the work of the ninth century, which, as we shall see, in some respects merely follows and elaborates to the extent of mannerisms, an already well-established tradition.

There are few extant mosaics in the Near East between the eighth and the eleventh centuries. The work at Nicæa was probably as late as the eleventh century, and it is very doubtful if the two apses at Cyprus which have been placed as early as the sixth century, are earlier than the second great period of Byzantine development.

However, some of the mosaics in Santa Sophia at Salonika [95] are undoubtedly much earlier than the eleventh century Ascension of the dome, and the evidence deduced from the inscriptions and the style would place them in the last quarter of the eighth century at the close of the iconoclastic period.

In the center of the vault before the apse, on a gold ground, is a circle with a silver ground containing a cross. The rest of the vault is covered with a design of gold squares, alternately containing silver crosses and vine leaves. In the apse is a seated figure of the Virgin holding the Child upon her knees (120). On the gold background of the apse there may still be distinguished a cross, now of gold, but which may have been originally of color and similar to the cross of Saint Irene at Constantinople and others which have disappeared. This cross may have been as early as the sixth century. Similar in style to the apse is the central medallion of the dome with the figure of Our Lord in the mandorla supported by angels. The medallion itself is enclosed in a border of foliage.

These mosaics are inferior in quality to sixth and seventh century work. The figures are heavy and clumsy, there is less richness of color, and the technique is much cruder than that of the earlier work at Salonika, at Ravenna or elsewhere. They obviously belong to a period of decadence, and it seems logical to place them at the end of the eighth or in the ninth century.

THE ROMAN SCHOOL OF THE NINTH CENTURY

THE ROMAN SCHOOL OF THE NINTH CENTURY

Peculiarities of the style: Eastern and Western influences.—SS. Nereo ed Achille.—The Triclinium of the Lateran.—The Christ from the Vatican crypt.—Santa Maria in Domnica.—Santa Cecilia.—Santa Prassede.—San Marco.—Influence of the Roman School elsewhere; Germigny-des-Près, Aix-la-Chapelle.

VIII.

THE ROMAN SCHOOL OF THE NINTH CENTURY

This group of mosaics [96] which we shall now consider, is, in certain respects, one of the most interesting, and it has given rise to a good deal of discussion. In general, the style seems to be purely Byzantine in origin, especially in regard to the technique, in the conventionalization and the sacrifice of reality to sumptuous ornamental effects. But the figures of these apses have a peculiar character of their own which is quite unlike anything we know in actual Byzantine art. It has been suggested that they show a Northern influence in the types of the heads and in a certain crudeness and coarseness of execution, which came in on account of the close relations existing between Rome and the empire of Charlemagne at this time. It is, however, difficult to prove this by any actual comparisons. The Northern ivories and other objects which are brought forward to substantiate this claim have their own peculiar characteristics which do not, to my mind, bear any close resemblance to the Roman mosaics.

Whatever the reason may be, this Roman style has much originality. When one has once seen these strange haunting figures woven into their gold backgrounds they are not easily forgotten. Until recently it has been the fashion to define this style as decadent. This is largely on account of the almost complete absence of modelling in the figures and the incorrect drawing; the over-large heads with their great, staring eyes giving a neurotic and almost sinister expression to the faces. At present, a more catholic taste has modified this point of view. We realize that the aim was the antithesis of naturalism. The figures are thought of as images, or icons, almost as symbols, to produce a direct religious appeal, further enhanced by brilliant effects of color. Abstraction may at times be carried too far, resulting in mere awkwardness, and the figures may not always be well adapted to the space, but on the whole they achieve a certain solemn grandeur, and as mere decoration and color they are superb.

Near the Scala Santa in the piazza of the Lateran there is an imposing eighteenth-century hemicycle containing an apsidal mosaic (121). Its history has been varied. Originally in the Triclinium of Leo III, 795-816, it was entirely restored in 1625 by Cardinal Barberini.[97] Under Clement XII, 1730-1740, it was removed to the Scala Santa, broken up and entirely remade, and placed in its present position by Benedict XIV in 1743. The reason for thus honoring this mosaic is that it commemorated a great political event, the accord between Leo III and Charlemagne and the foundation of the Empire of the West. It therefore dates from about 800.

Actually, we have here an eighteenth century copy which gives no idea of the original style, but the old lines of the composition have been followed fairly accurately. On the arch to the right is Christ, enthroned, giving the keys to St. Peter and the banner to Constantine. The corresponding scene on the left shows St. Peter giving a pallium, symbolical of spiritual power, to Leo III and a banner to Charlemagne. The Latin inscription below refers to this: "Holy Peter! Thou givest life to Leo, the Pope, and victory to Charles, the king." In the apse we have the Apparition of Jesus to the Apostles. Our Lord stands on a mount from which issue the Four Rivers of Paradise. He holds a book with the words: PA X VO BI S, "Peace be with you." On either side are the Eleven Apostles. The inscription below refers to this scene.

Two Apostles' heads, saved from the old mosaic and now in the Vatican Library, give some idea of the style and they are not typical of the ninth century. The faces are elongated and emphasized by dark lines, but they show strength and a certain plastic quality.

The lost mosaic of the apse of Santa Susanna was also executed under Leo III. Ciampini's engraving of it[98] shows Christ and the Virgin with various saints, as well as the Pope and Charlemagne.

THE ROMAN SCHOOL OF THE NINTH CENTURY

A niche in the *confessio* below the main altar of St. Peter's contains a mosaic (122) representing Christ blessing, and holding a book with the inscription: EGO SUM VIA VERITAS ET VITA QUI CREDIT IN ME VIVET,"I am the Path, the Truth, and Life, he who believes in Me shall live." There are signs of a good deal of restoration. In Ciampini's reproduction there is a globe surmounted by a cross in place of the open book; a drawing made by Grimaldi in the early seventeenth century shows the book, but with the inscription differently placed. A passage in the *Liber Pontificalis* would tend to attribute it to the time of Leo III, and, as far as the style is concerned, there is no reason to suppose that it is not of the early ninth century, although some would place it as early as the seventh.

In the church of SS. Nereo ed Achille there is an original mosaic of the time of Leo (123). This mosaic, which is on the triumphal arch, is a very abstract rendering of the Transfiguration, a subject rare in Early Christian iconography. In the center is Christ in a mandorla, with Moses and Elias at either side, while Peter, James, and John are prostrated on the ground. At the left is the Annunciation, and corresponding to it on the right, is the Virgin holding the Child before her in the stiff attitude of a Byzantine icon, accompanied by an angel. According to Venturi [99] this scene represents an Adoration of the Magi in a reduced form. The Virgin wears a red robe in both scenes.

It is rather lifeless in character and one of the less successful works of the period but it has decorative value and is well adapted to the space. The forms have no substance and appear to be woven into the background. There is a certain pleasing vertical rhythm in the composition, and harmony of color. The apse was, doubtless, also adorned with a mosaic, but of this we have no record.

Pascal I, 817-824, is responsible for three important works; Santa Prassede (124-129), Santa Maria in Domnica (130), and Santa Cecilia (131). Of these, the ensemble in Santa Prassede is the most notable, and, next to Santa Maria Maggiore, it is the most extensive and complete series of mosaics in Rome.[100]

On the triumphal arch (124) we have a subject hitherto not seen; the New Jerusalem according to the vision of St. John. In the golden enclosure which is studded with jewels stands Christ accompanied by two angels and various saints (125). At the left is Santa Prassede and at the right is the Virgin, not Santa Pudenziana as some have supposed. Beyond the Virgin are St. John the Baptist, St. Paul, and St. John the Evangelist, and beyond Santa Prassede is St. Peter. The figures of an old man and a youth behind the others at both ends of the row are either Isaiah and Jeremiah, or Moses and Elias. The open gates of the city are guarded by angels, and beyond are the groups of the Elect, the one on the right preceded by St. Peter and the other, by St. Paul. The blue sky of the background is covered with small white clouds, and below there is a green meadow with flowers. Still lower in the spandrels are the multitudes spoken of in the Apocalypse, clad in white and carrying palms.

Here, we have a complicated subject admirably treated from the point of view of composition. The individual figures are of the usual style of the time, stiff, with little or no modelling, and expressionless faces. They seem almost like decorative spots in a design. The color is not as brilliant as in some others of the period, but the whites, reds, greens, and dark slate-blues are fused together by the irregular tesseræ, and are impressive if only from their sheer mass.

The apsidal arch (124) is clearly a copy of the earlier one at SS. Cosma e Damiano of which so little remains. In a blue medallion are the Lamb, the Cross, and the Throne below with the Book of the Seven Seals. The seven Candlesticks, the angels and the symbols of the Evangelists, together with the Twenty-Four Elders offering their crowns, complete the Apocalyptic vision (126). The background is gold and the whole composition is surrounded by one of the usual borders of the time, a band of alternating rectangles and ovals. The figures here are stiff and uninteresting, especially the groups of the Elders, which are monotonous and uninspired even from a purely decorative point of view. It is interesting chiefly from the fact that it is a complete version of the much finer one of SS. Cosma e Damiano which has been so sadly mutilated.

The scheme of the apse also follows the precedent set by SS. Cosma e Damiano. In the center, against a background of clouds, a colossal Christ raises His right hand in proclamation and holds a *volumen* with the other. On either side are three figures; on the left, Santa Pudenziana between St. Paul and Pascal I, on the right, Santa Prassede between St. Peter and a deacon. At the extremities are the two palm-trees, and on the one on the right, is perched the symbolic phœnix. Above, is the Hand of God holding a laurel crown, and below the feet of the Savior is the Jordan. The whole stands out on a blue ground.

The lower zone has the usual subject of the Pascal Lamb standing on the Mount with the Four Rivers of Paradise, and at either side the Twelve Sheep, white on a gold ground, issuing from Bethlehem and Jerusalem. The inscription, gold letters on a blue ground, speaks of the "brilliancy of the varied metals" and refers to the translation of the relics of martyrs to the church.

Compared with SS. Cosma e Damiano the figures seem stiff and lifeless, but instead of emphasizing these so-called decadent qualities, let us, rather, admire the beauty of the scheme as mere design, the fine, vibrant color effects, like a rich brocade. One should remember that these are religious mosaics, seen in the dim light of a sanctuary, and from this point of view the uncompromising stylization strengthens the emotional and æsthetic appeal.

The chapel of San Zeno (127-129), also at Santa Prassede and the work of Pascal I, is unique in Rome. Even the form of this little structure with its cupola on a square plan, is Byzantine. It was erected by the pope as a tomb for his mother, Theodora Episcopa, and dedicated to the martyr, Zeno, whose relics were transferred here from the catacombs on the Appian Way. The interior is completely covered with mosaics on a gold ground and the impression they produce is almost comparable in its way to that of the mausoleum of Galla Placidia.

On the exterior wall over the door, are two superimposed series of busts in medallions (127). Those of the upper series are blue on a gold ground, those of the lower, gold on a blue ground, giving an interesting rhythm to the design. In the center of the upper row is a medallion of Christ, twice the size of the others, backed by a cross, and on either side are six Apostles. In the lower series are the Virgin and Child, the saints, Zeno and Valentinian, and eight female martyrs. Below are two later portraits of popes in rectangular panels.

In the center of the vault (128) there is a medallion containing the bust of Christ upheld by four angels, recalling the similar scheme of the vault of the Archiepiscopal Palace at Ravenna. In the lunette over the entrance are busts of the Virgin, SS. Prassede and Pudenziana, and Theodora, the mother of Pope Pascal, the latter being provided with a square nimbus. Above is the Pascal Lamb surrounded by four stags. On the wall above the altar are the Virgin and St. John the Baptist, and in the lunette below, Christ surrounded by four personages, one of whom is probably St. Peter. It is thought that this scene represents the Transfiguration, and, if so, the other two figures would be Moses and Elias. The little niche over the altar contains a twelfth or thirteenth century mosaic of the Virgin and Child, a later interpolation having no connection with the rest of the work. On the right wall there are three saints, James, John and Andrew, and below, Christ between two other saints, probably Zeno and Valentinian; on the opposite wall are three female saints (129), Praxed, Pudentia and Agnes. In the small lunette below is the Lamb on the Mount with the Four Rivers and four stags. The wall opposite the altar shows St. Peter and St. Paul at either side of the jewelled throne.

When one becomes used to the dim light, the strongest impression is the wonderful, dull glow produced by the free and varied arrangement of the tesserae. Both figures and background seem fused together into a gorgeous fabric. This is emphasized by the very irregular wall surfaces and the rounded edges of the vault and the lunettes. There is a soft, almost powdery quality like a butterfly's wing of colossal scale, a strange and beautiful texture quite equal to anything ever achieved in paint.

Another of Pascal I's productions is the apse of Santa Maria in Domnica (130), or "della Navicella," on the Cœlian which was provided with a mosaic when he reconstructed the ancient basilica. On the arch above, Christ is represented in a mandorla, seated on a rainbow. On either side is an angel heading a procession of six Apostles. There is a good deal of rhythm in these fourteen almost identical figures with the repeated notes of the flying draperies. They stand out against the blue of the sky, and at their feet is a green meadow with red and white flowers. Lower down, in each spandrel, is the figure of a Prophet, either Isaiah and Jeremiah, or Moses and Elias. In the apse itself, we have the Virgin and Child enthroned, surrounded by groups of angels, and Pascal I, who is shown with a square nimbus, holding the Virgin's foot. This composition, which shows the Virgin alone and surrounded by a choir of angels, foreshadows the type developed by the *Trecento,* by Duccio and the Sienese, and the early Florentines.

The figures are typical of the work of this period and do not call for especial comment, but as an ornamental scheme, this mosaic is one of the best, and there are splendid harmonies of color. Here the tones are not fused and graduated in the Byzantine manner of Santa Prassede but are more detached in the older Roman tradition. But we have the same broken-up surface reflecting a shimmering light. The numerous restorations are easily detected by their smooth hardness. There are wonderful harmonies of silvery grays, dark blues, yellows and veridian green. The nimbi of the angels surrounding the Madonna in the apse are a veridian green edged with white, and not blue, as usually described.

The inscription below is similar to the others of the period and states in quite pagan fashion that the glory of this work "shines like that of Phœbus in the universe when he frees himself from the dark veils of the obscure night."

In the church of Santa Cecilia we find the third of Pope Pascal's apses (131). This mosaic is almost identical with the one in Santa Prassede and belongs to the group which is derived from SS. Cosma e Damiano. Christ, larger than the other figures, holds the *volumen* and blesses with His right hand. Above His head is the Hand of God holding a wreath. At the right are St. Peter, St. Valerian, and St. Agnes; at the left, St. Paul, St. Cecilia, and Pascal I who holds a model of the church. The usual palm trees close the composition. Below, is the band of the Lamb on the Mount with the Twelve Sheep issuing from Bethlehem and Jerusalem, and the inscription extolling the work of the pope. The floral border contains, just above the head of Christ, the monogram of Pascal.

The mosaics of the arch disappeared during the restorations of the early eighteenth century but the subjects are known from the engravings of Ciampini;[101] the Virgin and Child on a throne with female saints, and the Twenty-Four Elders below.

This apse shows the peculiarities of the apse of Santa Prassede in a more exaggerated form. The head of Christ is unusually large with emaciated cheeks and enormous, staring eyes. All of the other figures are elongated, rigid, lifeless, with expressionless faces; but their rather weird and uncanny character is not without fascination from a modern point of view and they have a good deal of decorative value. The same may be said for the amusing procession of lambs below. In the past these mosaics have been sufficiently criticized for their bad qualities. Stranger and more decadent works are produced and admired every day. No one will dispute, I think, the value of this work as mere design and color. The color here is more vivid, and, perhaps, more barbaric than in Santa Prassede. The yellows of the robes of St. Cecilia and St. Agnes give a striking and individual note.

Before leaving Santa Cecilia we may notice the bit of frieze on the loggia of the atrium, gold scrolls with lilies and leaves on a dark blue ground, and little medallions with crosses and busts. The "L" in the decoration may refer to Leo III, and if so, the mosaic was probably executed under him.

The last of the mosaics of this school is in the apse of San Marco (132) and was produced under Gregory IV, 827-844. The composition is similar to that of the earlier apses; Christ in the center, with St. Mark the Pope, St. Agapetus and St. Agnes on the right, and, on the left St. Felicissimus, St. Mark the Evangelist and Gregory IV. In place of the two palm trees at the extremities there are two flowering plants. The figures are even stiffer and more lifeless than those of the earlier apses and they are less well adapted to the space. The curious idea of placing them on plinths was perhaps derived from Byzantine ivories and it accentuates their already complete divorce from reality, giving them the effect of equally spaced icons with their names inscribed on the bases below. This custom of placing the figures upon a base was followed later in the twelfth-century apses of Trieste, Torcello, and SS. Maria e Donato at Murano. Christ holds an open book with the words: EGO SVM LVX EGO SVM VITA EGO SVM RE SVRRECTIO. "I am Light, I am Life, I am the Resurrection."

The scheme is completed by the usual subject of the Lamb on the Mount and the Twelve Sheep issuing from Bethlehem and Jerusalem, and, below, is the inscription of gold letters on a blue ground, a dedication of Gregory IV to St. Mark asking his intercession with God in return for the temple which he has erected to him.

VASTA THOLI PRIMO SISTVNT FVNDAMINE PVLCHRA
QUAE SALOMONIACO FVLGENT SVB SIDERE RITV
HAEC TIBI PROQVE TVO PERFECIT PRAESVL HONORE
GREGORIVS MARCE EXIMIO CVI NOMINE QVARTVS
TV QVOQVE POSCE DEVM VIVENDI TEMPORA LONGA
DONET ET AD CAELI POST FVNVS SIDERA DVCAT

G-B. de Rossi called this "the most barbarous of Roman mosaics" and this opinion has been followed more or less ever since. Here again, however, recent criticism tends to reverse this judgment and finds great decorative value and even æsthetic appeal in this highly formalized scheme. The very frankness of treating the figures as isolated images has something to recommend it. The color here strikes a new note in which browns and whites predominate, varied by yellows and greens, and instead of being gloomy and lifeless it is often impressive. In certain lights there is a deep, rich lustre suggesting the patina of old bronze. Also, there is apparently less restoration here than in most of the other Roman apses.

We also have the greater part of the composition of the arch. In the center is a medallion with the bust of Christ and at either side are the symbols of the Evangelists in medallions. Below, are St. Peter and St. Paul. The style here seems a little less hard than that of the apse, but there is no reason to suppose that this work is earlier. It has all the characteristics of the ninth century. The mosaic of San Marco is the last expression of this school. For more than two hundred and fifty years, until the time of Pascal II, 1099-1118, there are no extant mosaics in Rome.

In France there is an interesting reflection of the Roman school in the little church of Germigny-des-Près [102] (133), south of Orleans, near the great abbey of St. Benoit. When Charlemagne was embellishing his palace at Aix-la-Chapelle with the mosaics of Ravenna, Théodulfe, abbot of Fleury-sur-Loire and bishop of Orleans, was a great admirer of the work and sang its praises in verse. He it was who adorned this church with mosaics and stucco, but all that now remains is the apse and a few minor fragments. Much was destroyed by fire as early as the ninth century and successive restorations have removed the rest. Even the apse itself underwent several unfortunate restorations during the nineteenth century, but enough remains of the old work to determine its character.

THE ROMAN SCHOOL OF THE NINTH CENTURY 153

The subject is unusual, the Ark of the Covenant between two Archangels. The ark conforms almost exactly to the description in Exodus, 25, 11-20, even to the two golden Cherubim on the top. The two Archangels lean over the ark in identical attitudes. Between them is the blue sky studded with stars and the Hand of God may be distinguished above. The inscription of silver letters on blue is as follows: "Regard the holy oracle and the Cherubim, contemplate the splendor of the ark of God, and, at this sight, be advised to touch by thy prayers the master of the thunder, and join, I pray thee, the name of Théodulfe to thy vows."

The Latin reads:
ORACLVM SCM ET CERVBIN ASPICE SPETANS
ET TESTAMENTI EN MICAT ARCA DEI
HAEC CERNENS PRECIBVSQVE STVDENS PVLSARE
   TONANTEM
THEODVLFVM VOTIS IVNGITO QVOESO TVIS

In style, this mosaic is nearer to the Roman school than to Ravenna but it is inferior, both in composition and in technique. The composition is dull and uninteresting in its rigid symmetry, and the Archangels are not well adapted to the space. The best of the color is in the robes of the Archangels where there is a harmonious combination of silver and gold, blue, red, and green.

This is the only mosaic existing in France but chroniclers mention others as early as the fifth century. Gregory of Tours used them in the church of St. Martin, and the church of La Dourade at Tours still testifies by its name to the splendor of the mosaics there. Others of the seventh century are mentioned at Autun, Auxerre and elsewhere, and there were many more, but this art was always foreign to the French traditions and never gained a real foot-hold. We would not expect those who produced the marvellous colored glass of the Gothic period to have a great interest in this medium. In fact, after the Romanesque period it is not a type of decoration at all suited to their architecture.[103]

We have already mentioned Charlemagne's great interest in mosaics.

Nothing, of course, remains of the work in his palace at Aix-la-Chapelle, but in the dome of the Cathedral we have what purports to be a modern copy of the original mosaic. The only idea we can form of this great cupola—the vision of St. John—is the mediocre and probably inaccurate design of Ciampini (134). The actual mosaic was executed after 1881, and although it pretends to copy the style of the early centuries it is hard and mechanical, with all the faults of the period. In the center is Christ on a gold ground with the Twenty-Four Elders below. On the walls are the Twelve Apostles, the Archangels, Michael and Gabriel, Mary, John the Baptist, Charlemagne and Pope Leo III. It is thought that the original was executed largely by native workmen with material brought from Ravenna.

THE ELEVENTH CENTURY IN THE NEAR EAST

THE ELEVENTH CENTURY IN THE NEAR EAST

The great revival in Byzantine art and the impetus given to mosaics.—The new style and its iconography defined.—Constantinople: the New Church of Basil I. and the Church of the Holy Apostles.—Cyprus: the Panagia Angelokistos, the Panagia Kanakaria.—The Lunette of Leo VI in St. Sophia.—Hosios Lucas in Phocis.—Kiev: St. Sophia and St. Michael.—Nicæa: the Church of the Dormition.—Salonika: St. Sophia.—Chios: Nea Moni.—Macedonia: Seres.—Vatopedi; the Catholicon.—Grottaferrata.—Daphni.—Bethlehem: the Church of the Nativity.—Jerusalem: the "Dome of the Rock" and the Mosque of El-Aksa.—Byzantine miniature, or portative mosaics.

IX.

THE ELEVENTH CENTURY IN THE NEAR EAST

With the tenth and eleventh centuries we come to the second great period of mosaics, comparable to the work at Ravenna of the sixth and seventh centuries. During this so-called Second Golden Age of Byzantine art the empire was the seat of the most brilliant civilization of the Middle Ages. The new strength of the government under the Macedonian emperors with its increased wealth and luxury gave great impetus to the arts, and the capital became once more a radiating center whose products were the envy of Europe and the Near East. Through her ivories, her miniatures, her enamels, her stuffs, Byzantium became, in a way, the great teacher of Europe, and her prestige continued unabated until the thirteenth century and the time of the Fourth Crusade.

Mosaics with their possibilities of rich and splendid effects were never more in favor than during this period and their fame caused Byzantine artisans to be called to the churches of Kiev in South Russia, to St. Mark's at Venice, and to the Norman kingdom of Sicily. Unfortunately, the mosaics of Constantinople itself, done at this time, have nearly all perished, but those in Greece at Hosios Lucas in Phocis and at Daphni, those of Nicæa and of Kiev, are great cycles still in fairly good preservation, showing the development of the style, and the final phase may be seen at St. Mark's and in the churches of Palermo.

The school of mosaicists in the capital itself must have been tremendously flourishing to have enabled so many workmen and artists to spread out to Russia, Sicily, Venice and elsewhere. We may say that until the time of the Fourth Crusade the Byzantine style dominated the art of mosaic, except, perhaps, with the exception of the more native school of Rome.

At first glance these mosaics may not seem to be very different from the earlier examples. The technique remains much the same—cupolas, vaults and the upper portions of the walls are covered with figures standing out on a plain gold ground—but if we study the composition themselves we will find that there has been a very radical change in iconography.[104] Each scene has now a dogmatic and liturgical significance inspired by the theologians, its treatment tends to become fixed as well as its special position in the church. The order of the compositions is no longer chronological, as in the Biblical scenes of Sant'Apollinare at Ravenna; each scene plays a definite symbolic rôle in the conception that the Church, according to the words of an eighth century theologian, "is Heaven on earth, the place in which God lives and dies."

In the cupolas, is Heaven, where Christ, no longer the tender savior of mankind, but the Pantocrator, or judge and ruler of the world, is represented, guarded by Archangels. Below, are often the Prophets or Apostles bearing witness to the All-Powerful and announcing the coming of His reign. The Virgin occupies the apse of the sanctuary, sometimes as an orant symbolizing the Church in prayer, as at Torcello, but more often seated and holding the Child. Usually on the vault before the sanctuary is the symbolic throne of the Last Judgment, the *Hetimasia*, and in the sanctuary itself the subjects relate to the mystery of the Eucharist, the celebration of the mass, predecessors and figures of Christ, Abraham, Aaron, Melchisedec. Also, the great doctors of the early Church, and bishops and deacons to reinforce and illustrate the celebration of the divine mystery. We are far from the time when profane subjects, such as the emperor Justinian and his court, find a place almost in the very sanctuary as they do at San Vitale.

In the body of the church—the nave, the aisles, the narthex—we have the terrestrial Church. Here are the saints, their positions fixed according to an exact hierarchy determined by their importance, and above all, the Twelve Great Feasts of the Church as an expression of dogma—the Annunciation, the Nativity, the Presentation, the Baptism, the Raising of Lazarus, the Transfiguration, the Entry into Jerusalem, the Crucifixion, the Descent into Hell, or *Anastasis*, the Ascension, the

Pentecost, the Death, or Dormition of the Virgin. Two of these scenes, the Crucifixion and the Descent into Hell, were given a special importance as symbolizing the mystic signification of the Church. The iconographical treatment of a number of the subjects was fixed as early as the fifth or sixth century, but others, such as the Descent into Hell and the Dormition, seem to have been evolved at this time.

Other accessory scenes sometimes accompany the Twelve Feasts, as at Hosios Lucas and Daphni, where the Washing of the Feet and the Incredulity of Thomas are shown with the Crucifixion and the Descent into Hell. The west wall was reserved for the Last Judgment, a vast composition which receives its final development during this period. Torcello and the Baptistery of Florence have the only extant examples of this subject in mosaic.

A cycle which takes on an extraordinary importance at this time is the life of the Virgin, drawn from the *Apocrypha*. We find it at Kiev and at Daphni, and in its most beautiful and final development in the much later mosaics of the Kahrie Djami. The Old Testament cycle which was so important in the fifth and the sixth centuries tends to disappear in the East, but we find it in the West in the narthex of St. Mark's, the Cappella Palatina, and Monreale.

Although, as we have seen, the whole scheme was more or less rigidly fixed according to the liturgy and the dogmas handed down by the theologians, there were, nevertheless, many minor variations in the treatment; but in general, all the important mosaics from St. Luke to St. Mark's and the Sicilian churches were planned on these general principles.

The researches of Diehl, Millet, Heisenburg and others have shown that this new iconographic system must have been pretty well established by the ninth or the tenth centuries. The lost mosaics of the New Church and of the Church of the Holy Apostles at Constantinople, executed under Basil I, 867-886, probably followed the new arrangement, if we interpret correctly the contemporary accounts of Constantine the Rhodian and Mesarites.[105]

Perhaps there has never been a time when the artist has been so controlled from without as he was during this period and throughout the subsequent history of Byzantine art, although we must say that from the tenth to the twelfth centuries at least, the rules were not so fixed and stereotyped as to become empty formulæ tending to deaden real artistic expression. They rather guided and directed the whole scheme and within their limits the artist was free to exercise his best abilities in composition, in the balancing and massing of color and the treatment of form. It has been said that the figures tend to become monotonous and stereotyped and totally lacking in individuality, and although this is in part true, especially for the later work at St. Mark's and at Monreale, it is by no means true for the period as a whole. In the Crucifixion, the Dormition, and other work at Daphni the human figure is treated with great beauty, even in the nude, and there is a grace of line and a subtlety and variety in the drapery which is comparable to the art of classic Greece or the painting of the early Renaissance.

Before taking up typical examples of the eleventh and the twelfth centuries we may mention here two mosaics on the Island of Cyprus[106] which are rather difficult to place. One is in the apse of the church of the Panagia Angelokistos at Kiti on the southern coast of the island, near Larnaca, and the other is in the church of the Panagia Kanakaria, near the village of Lithrankomé, on the southern slope of the ridge forming the backbone of the Karpass. Both mosaics are in very poor condition.

The Panagia Angelokistos shows a standing Virgin and Child, the so-called *Hodegetria* type, with the Archangels Michael and Gabriel at either side holding orbs and sceptres. All the figures have nimbi which are very dark in the center and are framed in bands of a dark and a light blue. The Virgin stands on a plinth and wears a tunic and a dark mantle. The Archangels have peacock's wings with "eyes"—a kind of wing which is seen in representations of Seraphim, but uncommon elsewhere, the only other instance being in the Sinai mosaics. The figures have Greek inscriptions and the Virgin is called "Saint Mary" instead of the usual *Theotokos* or "Mother of God," which has influenced some in giving the mosaic an early date.

The apse of the Panagia Kanakaria recalls such compositions as the apses of San Vitale or Parenzo. Here we have the Virgin represented as Queen of Heaven, seated on a throne between two angels, and surrounded by an oval mandorla, or glory, of dark blue, between two palm trees. The Virgin wears a purple tunic and a blue mantle, and the Child, a blue tunic, a white mantle, and a golden cruciferous nimbus. The whole is enclosed in a border containing a series of medallions of the Twelve Apostles, in ruinous condition, which may be compared with the medallions in Ravenna on the arch of San Vitale, in the chapel of the Archiepiscopal Palace, and others.

Smirnoff and Dalton have dated these mosaics as early as the fifth or the sixth centuries, and Schmidt would put them in the ninth century. The Arabs occupied Cyprus from 650 to 964, and the architecture of the two churches is later than the Arab invasion. It seems impossible to date the mosaics before the Arab conquest and certain analogies with early work at Ravenna and Salonika may be explained by conservatism or the fact that they are provincial. Moreover, the technique, as far as one can judge from the illustrations, seems to differ considerably from that of the early period, especially in the transition from the light to the dark shades. The compositions seem to show more relationship to later eleventh or twelfth century work, such as the apses of Nicæa or San Giusto at Trieste, so that it seems probable that these mosaics are even later than Smirnoff would place them, at least as late as the eleventh century.

Fortunately we have now one important work in Constantinople itself to illustrate this period, the recently uncovered lunette over the

Royal Door in the narthex of St. Sophia (135). It dates from the time of Leo VI, 886-912, and is therefore, only a few years later than the lost work of Basil I in the church of the Holy Apostles.

In the center is Christ seated upon a lyre-backed throne richly studded with jewels. He has a cruciferous nimbus and wears the tunic and mantle. In His left hand He holds a book with the inscription in Greek: "Peace be with you. I am the Light of the World", and He blesses with His right hand. At His feet is the prostrate figure of an emperor with a nimbus who can be recognized from coins as Leo VI. Above, on either side of Christ are medallions, the one on the right containing the head of the Virgin, and that on the left, an Archangel. These may represent the Mother of God and the Archangel Gabriel, the personages of the Annunciation, or, perhaps, the three figures are attributes of Divine Wisdom (*Hagia Sophia*); Faith (Christ Enthroned), Hope (Angel of the Annunciation), and Charity (the Virgin). The background is in three bands; the lowest, green to symbolize the earth, the second blue, for the sky, and the top-most and by far the largest, gold, for the celestial firmament. The cubes of the gold background are set closely together in wavy horizontal lines with the width of a tessera left between each line. This gives a striking difference in texture between the background and the figures themselves.

The figure of Christ and the heads of the medallions are of great majesty and beauty and altogether worthy of a sumptuous imperial art at its fountain head. The lyre-backed throne is found on coins of the period, in Byzantine miniatures, and in later Italian mosaics and frescoes, becoming a common feature in twelfth century art.

Within the past year Whittemore has uncovered the splendid lunette over the South Portal (136) representing the Virgin and Child enthroned between the Emperor Constantine who offers the City of Constantinople and the Emperor Justinian who offers the Church. The majesty of the composition, the striking portraiture, and the sumptuous detail reveal

Byzantine art of the Golden Age at its height. The work probably dates from the end of the tenth century, ordered by Nicephorus Phocas, 963-969, or John Zimisces, 969-975.

So far these are the only extant examples we have in Constantinople itself of the great mosaic art of the Macedonians and the Comnenes and for the present we must rely upon the more or less provincial works of Greece, South Russia and Italy to complete our knowledge of the period.

This Byzantine style was particularly well suited to the various types of cruciform-domed or single-domed churches which achieved their greatest development during this period. The unification of the interior on a centralized plan culminating in the dome, gave each subject portrayed its own architectural enframement and permitted it to be subordinated, if necessary, to other subjects of greater significance. Thus the architecture and decoration are interrelated and complementary to each other. The number of comparatively small and curving wall surfaces, with constantly varied perspectives, provide an ever-changing reflection of light which is the very essence of mosaic. We shall see that when this style is carried into Sicily and used in churches of basilican plan, such as the Cappella Palatina or Monreale, the long, flat expanses of the nave walls present a much greater difficulty. The multitude of narrative scenes, especially in Monreale, separated only by ornamental borders, tend to become confused and give an over-crowded effect with a complete absence of rhythm in the design, and it is only in the apses that the happiest results are obtained.

The larger of the two churches of the monastery of Hosios Lucas in Phocis,[107] dedicated to St. Luke, is one of the most interesting examples of the later Byzantine style, and still contains nearly the whole of its interior decoration intact, including the magnificent pavement of porphyry and jasper, the marble covering of the walls, and, above all, the mosaics. It is a fine example of the systematized and schematic treatment of the period, and the mosaics are probably the earliest extant which follow the iconographic rules we have already described. The monastery was founded in the second half of the tenth century by the emperor Romanos II, d. 963, and the mosaics probably date from the first half of the eleventh century.

In the center of the cupola is the Pantocrator (137)—surrounded by Archangels, St. John the Baptist, and the Virgin. Unfortunately this is largely a restoration in paint of about the seventeenth century. A lower zone of sixteen Prophets was still seen by Didron in 1839 but this has now almost entirely disappeared.

In the apse the Madonna (138) is seated upon a throne, holding the Child, clad in a golden tunic, and in the small dome over the sanctuary there is a representation of the Pentecost (139), the Apostles receiving the spirit of the Holy Ghost, which is here symbolized by the Dove placed on the throne of the *Hetimasia*. In the pendentives are men in variegated costumes representing the Tribes and Languages. On the sides of the bema are shown the great doctors of the Church, and in the little lateral apse at the left are the two Biblical episodes of Daniel and the Lions and the Three Children in the Fiery Furnace.

On the walls, vaults and pendentives of the Church are Gospel scenes corresponding to the great ecclesiastical Feasts, and an array of saints and martyrs arranged in order of their importance; at the west, monks and ascetics and martyrs; near the altar, bishops and deacons; in the arms of the cross, warrior saints in attendance on the Christ of the dome above. On the whole, the figures of saints are treated with a certain monotony but a few stand out in striking contrast with the individuality of portraits, especially the young St. Luke the Gourniot.

Four of the great Feasts were placed in the squinches below the dome; the Annunciation (destroyed), the Nativity, the Presentation, and the Baptism; and they are continued in the narthex by the Crucifixion and the *Anastasis*, with the Washing of the Feet and the Incredulity of Thomas in the lateral apses. One of the finest of the surviving mosaics is the Pantocrator over the central door of the narthex.

This ensemble is rather uneven in quality. There is a certain monotony in the types combined with stiffness and awkward gestures; but here and there, are figures of real beauty and nobility which foreshadow the work at Daphni. The color, also, is brilliant and harmonious, and the whole scheme is tied together by the warm gold of the backgrounds.

Diehl justly compares these mosaics with the miniatures from the famous Menology of Basil II in the Vatican. In both we find the same two opposed traditions, the monastic, with its stiff ascetic saints, and the antique, with its striving for nobility of gesture and elegance in the draperies, shown particularly in the Gospel scenes. Thus, we have here in this ensemble the work of at least two different schools. We should guard against considering the great series of saints as necessarily a less well realized and more primitive aspect of the Byzantine evolution. There has always been a tendency to consider them as an earlier phase of the development which produced the work at Daphni. However, as Diez has pointed out, they represent, rather, another school, that of the purely religious, hieratic art of the monasteries whose roots go back to the earliest traditions of the East. The subjects and figures depicted are conceived solely as symbols of profound religious beliefs and dogmas, and the historical and narrative element is entirely subordinated. Much that may seem stiff, or crude, or over-austere is not the result of archaism or imperfectly understood anatomy, but, as in the case of the Roman mosaics of the ninth century, the expression of a different viewpoint in which spiritual significance is paramount, even though, from the very nature of things, it may be only partially successful. Daphni, on the other hand, represents the other tradition which contends for supremacy at this time, that of the imperial court with its sympathy for Hellenic traditions of grace, beauty, and greater naturalism.

With the conversion of Vladimir, prince of Kiev, in 989, South Russia came under the jurisdiction of the Orthodox Church and the influence of the Byzantine civilization.[108] Jaroslav, 1015-1054, the son of Vladimir, wished to make his capital the rival of Constantinople, and filled the city with churches, monasteries and palaces. The church of St. Sophia with its mosaics dates from his time.

St. Sophia[109] bears no resemblance to its namesake in Constantinople, as it is of rather small dimensions with eight small aisles parallel to the nave; but the mosaics are purely Byzantine. They have been much damaged by fire and pillage; for a long time they were covered with whitewash and only a part of them were rediscovered in 1885. They have also suffered to some extent from restorations, but in spite of this they are still splendid examples of eleventh-century Byzantine art.

In the dome Christ was represented as the Pantocrator (140), surrounded by angels and the Twelve Apostles, with the Four Evangelists in the pendentives. At present, the figure of Christ remains, one of the Archangels, and the upper portion of the figure of St. Paul. On the inner surface of the triumphal arch is Aaron in high-priest's robes, carrying a censor.

On the two piers of the triumphal arch are the Angel and Virgin of the Annunciation, and in the lower zone of the bema are standing figures of saints with admirably executed portrait-like heads. Above the saints is the scene of the Communion of the Apostles (141), and in the upper part of the apse is a colossal standing figure of the Virgin as an orant, draped in purple and wearing the red shoes denoting royal rank, a personification of the Church on Earth for which she intercedes.

In the four arches beneath the dome there were originally forty medallion busts of martyrs, but of these only fifteen now remain. There are three medallions at the top of the triumphal arch containing the three persons of the *Deesis*. There are also, above the eastern and western arches of the dome, the remains of figures of Christ Emmanuel with a scroll and of the Virgin. Of the Four Evangelists once in the pendentives, only St. Mark remains; he is seated before his desk, writing his Gospel.

Other episodes of the Passion which once adorned the north and south arms of the cross have also disappeared.

In the monastery church of St. Michael at Kiev there are a few mosaics of which the Communion of the Apostles is the most important. It has been thought that this work was probably later than St. Sophia and that it was largely executed by native workmen, but it follows closely Byzantine models and Ainaloff has shown that a group of Byzantine craftsmen from the monastery of the Blachernae came to Kiev in 1073, and among other buildings, were responsible for the monastery of Michael. An earlier group from this famous monastery of the capital may have executed the work in Santa Sophia. The mosaics of Hosios Lucas and Kiev are in the same tradition and point to a common center which may well have been the Church of the Blachernae.

In style, the mosaics of St. Sophia stand midway between Hosios Lucas and Daphni. They show some of the stiffness and awkwardness of the earlier work combined with an admirable sense of portraiture and a fine use of color.

Practically nothing remains in the little church of the Dormition at Nicæa (Iznik),[110] the old metropolis of Bithynia, now in a very ruinous condition. In the apse was a standing Madonna (142), holding the Child who blessed with His right hand and held a scroll in His left. The Child is represented as if seated on the Madonna's lap, although she is standing, an anomaly which has never been satisfactorily explained, as there were no indications in the mosaic that the Madonna was originally shown as a seated figure. Above the head of the Virgin was the Hand of God from which three rays issued, and she was standing upon a plinth, reminding one of the Virgins in the apses of Torcello and Santa Maria e Donato at Murano and the Christ of the apse of San Giusto at Trieste, all probably of the twelfth century. In fact, the composition of this apse was very similar to that of the great apse at Torcello.

This apse originally contained a cross in place of the Virgin and

Child, probably similar to the one in St. Irene at Constantinople and to the one which once existed in St. Sophia at Salonika.

A medallion on the vault in front of the apse contained the *Hetimasia*, with the cushioned throne, the Book, and above, the dove with a nimbus of seven rays. The *Hetimasia* occupied the same position as at Daphni, the Cappella Palatina and elsewhere—a typical Byzantine arrangement from the eleventh century on. The *Hetimasia* was flanked by two pairs of Archangels (143), each holding a *labarum* and a globe and clad in richly jewelled robes according to the later Byzantine formula. These Archangels may be compared with those at Torcello and Trieste.

The style of these mosaics would date them from about the middle of the eleventh century, but it has been sometimes supposed that they were earlier, perhaps contemporary with the building of the church at the beginning of the ninth century.[111]

The mosaics of the narthex, a little inferior in quality to these last, were certainly of the eleventh century. In the low dome was a gold cross of eight branches inscribed in a medallion with a border. Between each arm of the cross were two stars. Surrounding this medallion were four medallion busts of Christ, the Baptist, St. Joachim, and St. Anna. In the pendentives were the Four Evangelists seated before their desks, figures conceived with great dignity and comparable to the work at Hosios Lucas or Daphni. Above the tympanum of the door, was a half-figure of the Virgin as an orant (144), draped in a violet mantle bordered with gold. This beautiful figure bore a striking resemblance to the Madonna in the apse of Torcello, and was of a much finer execution than the decoration of the dome.

The decorative motifs in the borders of the Nicæa mosaics are typical of the eleventh century and later, and have analogies with those at Hosios Lucas, Trieste, and Torcello.

We have already mentioned the panel in St. Demetrius at Salonika representing the Virgin and a saint in connection with the earlier work there. It is probably of this period, at least not later than the eleventh century.

The Ascension in the dome of St. Sophia at Salonika [112] (145) probably dates from about this period; that is, the middle of the eleventh century. In the center is the Pantocrator seated on a rainbow in a medallion upheld by two angels. Below, is the Virgin as an orant, flanked by two angels and accompanied by the Twelve Apostles; the figures are separated by trees. This is a skillfully arranged composition. The figures of the Virgin and the Apostles are well handled, showing a good knowledge of anatomy, and some variety of movement, and they are cleverly designed to appear correctly proportioned when viewed from below. The color-scheme is rather subdued; the violet robe of the Madonna alone standing out from the grayish-white draperies of the rest of the figures.

As we have already observed elsewhere, the style of the central medallion is in marked contrast to the lower band and it is probably part of an older composition dating from as early as the ninth century. It does not seem possible that it can be contemporary with the rest of the mosaic. The lower band, however, with its emphasis on movement, and its striking resemblance to the same scene of the Ascension in one of the domes of St. Mark's, is undoubtedly of the eleventh century.

The extensive decoration of the Nea Moni [113] on the island of Chios would have borne comparison with Hosios Lucas or Daphni had it not suffered such severe damage. This monastery church was built by Constantine IX Monomachus, 1042-1054, and like Hosios Lucas and Kiev it is a reflection of the art of Constantinople of the eleventh century. The earthquake of 1881 destroyed practically the whole of the dome as well as injuring the rest of the mosaics. The dome showed the Pantocrator surrounded by nine angels, and, at a lower level, the Twelve Apostles— a typical eleventh-century conception.

Turning to the surviving mosaics, we have in the main apse a standing figure of the Virgin as an orant, and in the two smaller lateral apses, busts of the Archangels Michael and Gabriel. Of the eight scenes of the life of Christ in the church, seven are still fairly well preserved: The Annunciation, Presentation in the Temple, Baptism (146), Transfiguration, Crucifixion, Deposition, and *Anastasis* (147); the Nativity having been lost. In the narthex there are other scenes from the life of Christ which are in rather bad condition: the Raising of Lazarus, the Washing of Peter's Feet, the Ascension, the Pentecost, and another scene which may represent Christ Preaching. There are also several isolated figures in the narthex. Above the entrance are the remains of a colossal bust of Christ, and in a little cupola in front of this door, there is a Virgin as an orant in a medallion, surrounded by eight warrior saints. Finally, on the west wall are the Prophets Daniel and Isaiah and busts of other saints.

These mosaics show an advance even over those of Kiev in richness and variety of color and a certain ease and grace, both in composition and in the rendering of the human form.

Before turning to the culmination of this school at Daphni, there are a few other examples to consider, all in a more or less fragmentary state.

In the Metropolitan Church of Seres [114] in Macedonia there is a Communion of the Apostles (148) represented in the lower part of the apse, as at St. Sophia, Kiev. This mosaic suffered greatly from a fire in 1849 and has been badly restored in paint. As usual in this subject, Christ is portrayed twice, standing beneath a ciborium, and giving bread and wine to the two groups of Apostles who approach from the right and left. The artist has taken great pains to give variety to the figures, in movement, in the treatment of the drapery, and in the facial types. On the whole it compares favorably with the best work of the period and should probably be dated towards the end of the eleventh century.

The monasteries of Mount Athos once had a considerable number of mosaics but these have almost entirely perished. A few are still to be seen at Vatopedi and at Xenophon.

In the tympanum of the royal door of the Catholicon at Vatopedi [115] there is the usual Byzantine representation of the *Deesis*—Christ enthroned between the Virgin and St. John the Baptist—and on either side of the door are the Virgin and the Angel Gabriel representing an Annunciation, while the same subject is again shown upon spandrels in the interior. There is also a damaged figure of St. Nicholas in the tympanum of one of the lateral doors leading to the first inner narthex.

The *Deesis* and the Annunciation are usually considered to be of the end of the eleventh century, but they are inferior in quality to most of the other work of the period. The fragments of other mosaics are probably later.

The mosaics in the new Catholicon of Xenophon were originally in the old church. There are two panels, one of St. George, and the other, of St. Demetrius, the figures standing out on a gold ground. These are typically good works of the period of Daphni, or a little later.

We will now leave the Near East for the moment to consider two mosaics in the Basilian abbey of Grottaferrata near Rome,[116] which clearly belong to this school. The abbey was founded by St. Nilus the Younger at the beginning of the eleventh century, and, as might be expected in a community of Greek monks, although so near Rome, the work shows a purely Byzantine inspiration.

Over the triumphal arch, consecrated in 1025, there is a Pentecost (149) showing two equal groups of the Apostles enthroned with the rays of light descending upon their heads. This mosaic was probably executed in the eleventh century soon after the consecration of the church. The clear and brilliant color and the variety in the draperies, and the modelling are in the best Byzantine tradition.

Above the entrance door is the *Deesis*, Christ enthroned between the Virgin and St. John (150). Here, the workmanship is less good; the figures are elongated and stiff and the color opaque. This has led Venturi and others to consider it later and probably by a native artist who did not understand his Byzantine models so well.

With Daphni [117] (151-156) we reach the culmination of the school. It is only in a few places—the Mausoleum of Galla Placidia, San Vitale, Parenzo, the Cappella Palatina—that we find as extensive and complete work of such high quality. As Millet has so well said: "Daphni is distinguished by a very pronounced superiority, by the variety, the suppleness, the elegance of design, the finesse of modelling, the richness of color, finally, in the compositions, by a veritable invention, both in gesture as well as in the interpretation of the theme and the disposition of the lines and masses. The real beauty of these mosaics is a surprising phenomenon."

This little monastic church is charmingly situated near the old road which leads from Athens to Eleusis. It dates from the middle of the eleventh century and probably received its decoration soon afterwards. It was long neglected and numerous earthquakes have seriously damaged the mosaics. Restorations undertaken between 1889 and 1894, although necessary, were carried out with the archæological zeal characteristic of the last century, and have not improved the present appearance of the work. The isolated figures of saints have suffered less than the principal scenes.

The arrangement is that typical Byzantine scheme which we have already seen at Hosios Lucas, at Kiev, and at Chios. In the dome, is a colossal bust of the Pantocrator (151), and below, in the spaces between the windows of the drum, stand sixteen Prophets. The Pantocrator, with a cruciferous nimbus, holding the Book and blessing with His right hand, is one of the great achievements of the art of this period. Seldom have latent energy and power been better expressed. The schematized and yet intensely vital countenance and the extraordinary hands are the work of a master. Its prototype was probably in the New Church of

Basil I, and it leads in its turn to the great figures of the Sicilian apses. The splendid figures of the Prophets with their scrolls show the more classical Byzantine style at its best and point the way to the domes of St. Mark's at Venice. A brief summary of the rest of the work will have to suffice here.

The *Hetimasia* is represented in the vault of the sanctuary and in the two lateral niches are the Archangels Michael and Gabriel. In the apse itself there is a seated Virgin, now almost entirely destroyed.

In the apses below the *Hetimasia* are personages relating to the eucharistic cycle: Aaron and Zacharius, doctors of the church, bishops, deacons; John the Baptist as the Prodromos, and shown with wings, occupies the niche of the left absidiole.

In the transepts north and south of the central dome are groups of martyrs commemorated in the *Menelogia,* and above the two side doors leading into the narthex are busts of St. Sergius and St. Bacchus, while the rest of the western portion of the church contains busts or standing figures of other saints.

The most essential part of the scheme is, however, the series of the great Feasts of the Church, occupying the transepts, the pendentives of the dome, and the narthex. In the church itself are: the Birth of the Virgin, the Salutation, the Adoration of the Magi, the Baptism, the Transfiguration (152), the Raising of Lazarus, the Entry into Jerusalem (153), the Crucifixion (154), the *Anastasis* (155), the Incredulity of Thomas, and the Death of the Virgin. The Presentation in the Temple has been destroyed. The Crucifixion and the *Anastasis* are given positions of especial importance at either side of the choir, and the Death of the Virgin is above the entrance door. It is interesting to note that the important subjects of the Ascension and the Pentecost are lacking, while other episodes, not usually included in the cycle, are added, such as the Birth of the Virgin, the Adoration of the Magi and the Incredulity of Thomas.

In the narthex, in two distinct groups are: at the left, the Last Supper, the Washing of Feet, and the Betrayal, all scenes relating to the Passion; and, on the right, episodes from the life of the Virgin: the prayer of Joachim and Anna (156), the Blessing of the Virgin by the Priests, and the Presentation.

All of this work, with the exception perhaps of a few secondary isolated figures, seems to show a common inspiration and dates from the same period. It is of a consistently high quality, and scenes such as the Crucifixion, the *Anastasis,* and the Death of the Virgin are among the great achievements of Byzantine art.

In the following chapters we shall trace the further developments of the Byzantine school in Venice, Torcello and Trieste, and in Sicily. In the Byzantine empire itself there are no surviving mosaics of importance until we reach those of the Kahrie Djami at Constantinople, dating from the early fourteenth century.

There are a few other surviving mosaics in the Near East, to be more exact, in the Holy Land, executed by Byzantine masters, both for the Saracen rulers and for the Crusaders during their occupation of Jerusalem.

The Church of the Nativity at Bethlehem [118] once had a complete and splendid series of mosaics, of which now only fragments remain. The greater part was still in existence at the close of the sixteenth century when it was described by Quaresimus. According to an inscription in the choir, the work was carried out by one Ephraim, probably in 1169, under the reign of King Amaury of Jerusalem, in the time of the emperor, Manuel Comnenus.

At the west end of the church was a vast representation of the Tree of Jesse, now entirely destroyed. Above the architrave in the nave were long rows of medallion busts of the ancestors of Christ, and above these, between conventionalized "tree" designs which seem to show a Persian influence, were churches and tables with Greek inscriptions relating to the œcumenical and provincial Councils, subjects which strikingly recall the fifth-century mosaics of St. George at Salonika, or the Baptistery of the Orthodox. Still higher, between the windows, was a procession of angels advancing towards the choir. All that have survived are seven of the Councils, three of them very incomplete, six angels, and seven of the medallion busts.

In the choir and the transepts were scenes from the Life of Christ, three of which are fairly well preserved; the Entry into Jerusalem, Incredulity of Thomas, and the Ascension, together with a fragment of the Transfiguration. There was a Nativity in the crypt which has now disappeared.

It is possible that this decoration replaces a much earlier one, for it would be strange if the church had not received mosaics in the interior at an early time, when those of the façade were already celebrated in the sixth century. Furthermore, the conventionalized architecture of the Council scenes goes back to the fifth century. However, in actual technique and details the work seems to be of the twelfth century, and the iconography of the scenes from the life of Our Lord is typical of the Byzantine style of the later period. De Vogüé pointed out very justly, years ago, that the work has a certain political aspect which fits in very well with the times. The Councils and the other subjects illustrate a doctrine which was common to both the Greek and the Latin Churches, and bear witness to the amicable relations existing towards the end of the twelfth century between the Latin Kingdom of Jerusalem and the Eastern Empire. Much of the ornamental detail, as in the Dome of the Rock, is very Eastern in character, going back ultimately to Mesopotamian and Persian sources, and the color-scheme, with its prominent use of green, is somewhat different from typical Byzantine work.

There are mosaics in the Mosque of El-Aksa at Jerusalem which date from a restoration under Saladin in 1187.[119] In the dome is a diaper pattern of conventional floral scrolls, and in the drum, conventionalized "trees" inferior to those of Bethlehem or the Dome of the Rock. Both mother-of-pearl and silvered cubes are employed to render the high lights. At Damascus we have already noted the rather unimportant restorations and later work of the thirteenth and fourteenth centuries.

There remains to be considered a branch of the art which seems to have developed in the Empire about the twelfth century and continued to be very popular for two hundred years—miniature, or portative mosaics (157-159).[120] These mosaic pictures, usually small in scale, were the objects of great veneration, and were exposed in the churches, in the oratories of the palaces, and carried about from one place to another.

The idea is a very old one, going back at least as far as the *emblemæ* of the Romans which were also sometimes carried about. Suetonius says that Cæsar took pavements with him upon his campaigns. Most of the surviving Byzantine examples are of the thirteenth or fourteenth centuries, but a few are earlier. The art of mosaic does not lend itself readily to work on such a small scale, as all its own special effects are derived from its size and the surrounding space. Here, the cubes employed are very minute; it is often difficult to detect their joining. They are placed upon a specially prepared ground of wax, and gold and silver are used to bring out the high lights and details.

Among the best of these miniature mosaics are the two panels of the Twelve Feasts of the Church (157) in the Opera del Duomo at Florence (thirteenth or early fourteenth century), the bust of Our Lord in the Bargello (158), the Transfiguration (159) and the circular medallion of St. George in the Louvre (thirteenth century), the St. Theodore in the Vatican (twelfth century), an Annunciation at South Kensington (thirteenth century), the St. John the Baptist in the treasury of St. Mark's (thirteenth century), and a number which are still preserved in the monasteries of Mount Athos, especially the early Crucifixion at Vatopedi.

SICILIAN MOSAICS

SICILIAN MOSAICS
Saracenic and Byzantine influences under the Normans which produced the mosaics.—Cefalù.—The Martorana.—The Cappella Palatina.—Secular decoration: La Zisa and the *Camera di Ruggero*.—Monreale, etc.— Messina: the Cathedral; San Gregorio.—Sicilian influence on the mainland: Salerno; Capua; Santa Restituta at Naples.

X.

SICILIAN MOSAICS

The Sicilian mosaics of the twelfth century,[121] on the whole, are the greatest surviving manifestation of the mediæval Byzantine school. Nowhere else is there so much of such a high quality. It is also fortunate that, in general, they have suffered much less from restoration than those of Venice and elsewhere.

An island in the center of the Mediterranean, Sicily has always been the meeting-place of a variety of races—Phœnicians, Greeks, Carthaginians and Romans, Byzantines and Arabs, Normans, French and Spaniards. When the Normans conquered the island in the eleventh century, they were wise enough to build upon the Saracenic culture which had preceded them, and, for a century and a half, they made Palermo the most brilliant and cosmopolitan capital of Europe. Their extreme toleration caused them to accept, as a rule, the best that was brought to them. Modified Gothic buildings were adorned with Byzantine and Saracenic splendor, the result being the most beautiful hybrid art which the Middle Ages produced; and the mosaics of Cefalù, the Martorana, the Cappella Palatina and Monreale are the chief glory of this art.

The great apse of the Cathedral of Cefalù (160) is dated 1148 by an inscription, and it was executed by Greek artists brought over by Roger II. High in the apse is a colossal bust of the Pantocrator blessing, according to the usual scheme of Byzantine iconography, and placed here because of the absence of a dome. Below is the Madonna as an orant, flanked by four Archangels, and still lower, on either side of the window, are the Twelve Apostles arranged in two superimposed groups. On the lateral walls are figures of saints, bishops, deacons, warriors and Prophets in four parallel zones. All of the secondary personages are provided with Greek inscriptions. The upper rows of these figures, as well as the

Cherubim and Seraphim of the vault of the choir (161), are later in date than the apse, probably of about the middle of the thirteenth century.

The great scale of the apse is magnificent. We feel that here is a composition that could not be treated as well in any other medium. The Christ is the best example of this Sicilian type of the Pantocrator, finer than the contemporary one in the Cappella Palatina, which is now largely a restoration, and much finer than the almost identical one in the apse of Monreale. Here an expression of great strength is combined with benignity, and there is none of that hardness which we find in other Byzantine examples, even at Daphni, or at Hosios Lucas, and at Monreale. The other figures—the Virgin, the Apostles—are admirably conceived; there is grace and dignity in the poses, sufficient knowledge of anatomy, well-studied drapery, and a consummate knowledge of color.

The upper rows of figures in the choir and the angels of the vault do not equal the work we have just described; they are much more weakly conceived, but, in the vault especially, they follow the best traditions of color. The peacock's wings of the Cherubim are in graded shades of blue resplendent with gold, the whites showing gradations of transparent greens which finally reach the most intense blues, and there is a remarkable variety and richness in the tones.

The church of the Martorana,[122] (162-167) or Santa Maria dell' Ammiraglio, was embellished about 1143 by the munificence of the admiral, George of Antioch. It is a typical Byzantine edifice of Greek cross plan, with a marble covering on the wall and mosaics above. A considerable part of the mosaics is still preserved. In the center of the dome (163) is the Pantocrator blessing, surrounded by four Archangels, and lower, in the drum, are eight Prophets, with the Four Evangelists in the squinches completing the composition. In the soffits of the arches are medallions of warrior and bishop saints, and in the north and south arms of the cross, the Apostles.

All that remains in the apse are the Archangels Michael and Gabriel, and the majority of the Feasts of the Church have also disappeared. The Annunciation and the Presentation still exist on the walls of the central square, and, on the vault of the west arm of the cross are the Nativity (164) and the Dormition (165), these last two being, perhaps, the finest of the surviving mosaics. Finally, near the west end of the church are two mosaic pictures of great historic interest which were probably once on the façade. One portrays the founder, George of Antioch, at the feet of the Virgin bearing a scroll with an inscription in Greek containing a supplication on behalf of the admiral to Christ, who appears in the upper corner emerging from the heavens. The upper picture shows Christ crowning King Roger II (166). These two very interesting works have been much marred by excessive repairing.

The best of the work, however, such as the Nativity and the Dormition and certain individual figures of saints (167), is of the highest quality and may be compared with Daphni. In fact, perhaps these scenes give one a better idea of the technical perfection of the fully developed Byzantine style than do those of Daphni, as they are still in excellent condition. Repeated visits to Daphni only tend to confirm the impression of how much vitality those admirable works have lost through mechanical restoration. The exquisite blending of color in the Martorana is only equalled at Cefalù and in the best of the mosaics of the Cappella Palatina.

The Cappella Palatina [123] (168-174) which was finished by Roger II, according to the Greek inscription at the base of the dome, is the most extraordinary monument of the art of the Normans in Sicily on account of its jewel-like perfection and its combination, on a small scale, of the diverse elements which went to make up this civilization. The nave and the aisles (168), divided by antique columns, are those of a Western basilica, the sanctuary with its dome on squinches is that of a Byzantine church, and the intricate interlacings of the pavement of porphyry, serpentine, and mosaics, and the stalactite ceiling with its polychrome decoration are Saracenic.

Some of the mosaics have disappeared and others have been renewed. Those on the west wall were changed in the fourteenth century by the Aragonese and nothing remains of the original work. Those of the principal apse and those of the apse on the left were renewed in the sixteenth and eighteenth centuries, and, finally, in 1798, some of the mosaics which covered the north wall of the sanctuary were destroyed. However, we are fortunate in having the greater part of the old work intact, and these brilliant pictures on a gold ground, together with the rich marble facing of the lower part of the walls, and the stalactite ceiling with its painted figures, animals and monsters, produce an impression of extraordinary splendor.

The mosaics of the choir and sanctuary, and, in part, those of the nave are purely Byzantine with Greek inscriptions, and are of the time of Roger II. Those of the nave, showing Old Testament subjects (171) and scenes from the lives of St. Peter and St. Paul (173), have Latin inscriptions and were done by native workmen under William I, 1154-1166, and already betray the more careless execution of the later work at Monreale.

The older work conforms to the Byzantine iconographical scheme. In the center of the dome is a medallion of the Pantocrator surrounded by eight Archangels (169) and, below, in the squinches, are the Four Evangelists writing at their desks, with the Prophets David, Solomon, Zachariah, and St. John the Baptist in the drum. Eight busts of Old Testament Prophets in the spandrels between the larger figures complete this part of the decoration. There is a Greek inscription around the base of the dome in which Roger II dedicates the church to St. Peter in the year 1143.

In the upper part of the apse is a colossal bust of Christ (170), and below the Virgin is seated with SS. Mary Magdalene, John the Baptist, James and Peter. All of these are almost a complete restoration of the eighteenth century. On the triumphal arch is the *Hetimasia* with the Archangels Michael and Gabriel below. The two lateral apses contain busts of Christ and the Virgin, the Nativity and the Adoration, and busts of St. Peter and St. Paul.

The Twelve Feasts of the Church were represented on the walls of the sanctuary. Those on the right, from the Nativity to the Entry into Jerusalem are still preserved, but no trace remains of the later scenes of the Passion which undoubtedly once existed on the left wall; the cycle ends with the Ascension and the Pentecost in the vaults of the north and south arms of the sanctuary.

These mosaics in the sanctuary are the finest in the church and show the Sicilian style at its best. One of the most remarkable is the Entry into Jerusalem (172). It is interesting to compare this with the same subject at Daphni. At Daphni we find, perhaps, slightly more robust forms, more breadth and dignity; but in the Cappella Palatina there is more movement, along with an equal skill in drawing, more interest in the background and in genre details, as in the naked child in the foreground who struggles to pull off his garment.

The vast decoration of the Cathedral of Monreale [124] (175-179) is impressive from its very size and from the effect of splendor which it produces, and perhaps too much has been said about the comparatively poor quality of the work, even if it does illustrate the decline of the Sicilian school. However, in detail, the work is much less fine than that at Cefalù, the Martorana, or the Cappella Palatina. There is more dryness and stiffness, and the color is colder. The technique also is more mechanical. Perhaps a good deal of this inferiority can be explained from the fact that the work was done too quickly; mere artisans were employed and many of them used the old formulæ without much inspiration. The mosaics of the apse and the main body of the church are much better than those of the aisles which are more careless in execution.

The apse (175) copies the scheme of Cefalù (160): there is the same colossal bust of the Pantocrator, but harder in expression, the Virgin with two Archangels and the Apostles below, and finally, a row of fourteen saints. On the triumphal arch is the *Hetimasia* with Archangels and Seraphim; in the lateral apses are St. Peter and St. Paul and scenes from their lives. As in the Cappella Palatina, the nave has a series of Old Testament scenes (176, 177), and in the aisles are scenes from the Gospels, while the vaults and walls of the transepts have the Feasts of the Church. Even the soffits of the arches have busts of saints in medallions, and in the spaces between the larger subjects are standing figures of saints and the Apostles. The inscriptions in the apse are in Greek, but elsewhere they are in Latin.

On the lower part of the first two piers of the choir there are two historical subjects somewhat similar to those in the Martorana. That on the right (178) represents William II offering a model of the church to the Virgin, who is seated, with two angels, and the Hand of God above. On the left (179), we have Christ enthroned, laying His hand upon the head of the king, who is represented as a smaller figure standing at His side. There seems to be some attempt at portraiture in the features of the king.

This great series of mosaics was completed in the incredibly short space of eight years, and it has great merit, if only for the carefully thought-out scheme, which in spite of its complexity does not disturb the lines of the architecture, and produces an effect of dazzling richness.

Another Sicilian mosaic of the greatest interest is in a chamber of the palace of the Zisa (180, 181),[125] erected by William I, 1154-1166, at one end of the old royal park. Here, above a lovely stepped fountain which is adorned with mosaics in conventional designs, are three connected medallions on a background of floral scrolls, reminding one of a sumptuous Byzantine brocade. The medallions contain conventionalized trees; those at the end are flanked by peacocks, the central one, by archers shooting at birds. This should be compared with similar work in the chamber of King Roger in the Royal Palace where hunting scenes and other subjects are represented (182, 183). This last mosaic, especially, has been much restored, but the work must have originally been of fine quality, probably executed by those artists who were employed on the royal palace. These mosaics are doubly precious on account of the fact that almost nothing remains of profane work. The splendors of the Byzantine palaces are known only by the inadequate descriptions of the early texts, and it is easy to forget that the art of mosaic was not entirely the monopoly of religion but that it probably played an almost equally important part in the great secular decorations of the time.

The Cathedral of Palermo has lost all of its old mosaics with the exception of an Enthroned Madonna and Child over one of the doors. This has been much tampered with, so that much of its original character has been lost, but it seems to have belonged to the Norman period.

Before leaving Sicily there are a few examples to be noticed at Messina.[126] Little of the original work in the three apses of the Cathedral remains. It was carried out under Roger II, about 1130, but it had already suffered much from fire and earthquake even before the disaster of 1908. There was much restoration in the thirteenth century after the earthquake of 1232.

The principal apse (184) showed Christ enthroned between the Archangels Michael and Raphael, the Virgin, and St. John. At His feet, three small figures, added in the thirteenth century, showed the later kings, Frederick and Peter and the Archbishop Guidotto. The whole of the central portion has been replaced by paint. In the left apse was a seated Virgin and Child between two angels, and beyond the angels on the right and left were Eleanor, the wife of Frederick, and Elizabeth, the wife of Peter. In the right apse the central figure was St. John with his Gospel seated between St. Nicholas and the Bishop, Mino, with small interpolated figures of the young King Louis and his tutor, John of Randazzo, Duke of Athens. Venturi is enthusiastic over the high quality of these mosaics, but what little remains is now in process of restoration and they are seen with great difficulty.

The church of the former monastery of San Gregorio at Messina had a mosaic in the apse of a seated Virgin and Child with St. Gregory kneeling with a scroll (185). This mosaic has now been removed to the Messina Museum. Although restored, this is a fine work in the best Sicilian manner of the Cappella Palatina and Cefalù.

Before leaving the Sicilian mosaics we may mention two ikons which seem to belong to the school. One, which shows a Virgin of the *Hodegetria* type, is in the Museo Nazionale at Palermo, and the other, a Crucifixion, is in the Kaiser-Friedrich Museum, Berlin.

This flourishing Sicilian school spread to the Norman possessions on the mainland but most of the work has disappeared. However, the cathedral of Salerno [127] still contains mosaics of interest. In a lunette over the central doorway on the interior of the façade, there is a half figure of St. Matthew holding a book with the first words of his Gospel in Latin (186). The background is blue with a green band and a green and gold border. The head of the saint has a gold nimbus, the tunic is of blue and white, and the mantle of reddish brown and gold. The fine quality of this work is in the best Byzantine tradition of the eleventh century, and it is possible that it dates from the reconstruction of the church by Robert Guiscard, 1076-1085, but this would place it earlier than the Sicilian work. It was more probably done under the later Normans about the middle of the twelfth century, and contemporary with Cefalù or the Cappella Palatina.

The mosaics in the lateral apses of Salerno are at least a century later. That in the right apse was dedicated by Giovanni di Procida, the friend of King Manfred and one of the originators of the Sicilian Vespers, and may therefore be dated about 1260. Here, we have the Archangel Michael holding the globe and *labarum*, with a seated St. Matthew below, holding an open book. On the left are Saints Fortunatus and John, and on the right, Saints James and Lawrence. Below St. Matthew is the small kneeling figure of Giovanni di Procida and an inscription in Gothic letters relating to the dedication. The style seems to continue the traditions of the Sicilian school, but this mosaic, although complete, was badly restored under Pius IX in 1873.

The apse on the left contained a Baptism but only a fragment of the upper portion remains. This shows a semicircle with the stars and the sun and moon, and rays issuing from the Hand of God; below, are two concentric rows of busts of angels. In style these angels seem to be later than the work in the other apse, and recall the Sienese painters who were working in Naples in the fourteenth century. The Baptism itself and the lower aquatic scene were replaced in fresco during the fifteenth or sixteenth centuries. The river scene with its birds and animals, if it reproduces the subject of the original mosaic, recalls the apses of the Lateran and Santa Maria Maggiore in Rome.

The central apse was also once covered with mosaics and a recent clearing away of the eighteenth century stucco has revealed fragments of a wide border composed of a garland of leaves and fruit. Also, on the wall above, other fragments have come to light, among them the symbols of the Evangelists, especially a very fine representation of the eagle in the best Sicilian tradition.

At the entrance to the Cathedral of Capua [128] there is a much damaged representation of the Virgin and Child with St. John the Evangelist. It is of little value on account of its ruined condition but seems to follow in the Byzantine-Sicilian style of the twelfth century.

In a Gothic apse in the church of Santa Restituta,[129] adjacent to the Cathedral of Naples, there is a Madonna (187) holding the Child on her lap, and seated upon an elaborate Cosmatesque throne between Sta. Restituta and St. Januarius. This work of the early fourteenth century is almost Gothic in feeling, and according to the inscription, was executed by a Florentine, Lello, in 1322. The style is similar to some of the work in the Florentine Baptistery and the Coronation in the Cathedral, but the throne is in the Roman tradition and a certain roundness and fullness in the forms suggest the influence of Cavallini. There is a profuse, but skillful use of gold cubes in the draperies of the figures which blends them into the background and gives a glowing tone to the whole composition. This work is undoubtedly by a master who was familiar with the best which had been produced in both Rome and Florence and it shows little or no influence of the Sicilian school.

Nearly contemporary with this mosaic in Santa Restituta is one of the last works of that school of decorators and sculptors—the Cosmati and the Vassalletti—which was at its height a century or so earlier. This is the central portal of the cathedral at Teramo in the Abruzzi which was signed by Diodato in 1332. The portal with its colonettes and statuettes in niches, surmounted by a rose window, is one of the finest achievements of the Cosmati school. The bands of mosaic which are combined with intarsia in elaborately worked out geometrical motifs are in the usual mediæval Roman tradition.

VENETIAN AND FLORENTINE MOSAICS

VENETIAN AND FLORENTINE MOSAICS

The Venetian School—The early work in St. Mark's.—The Genesis cycle of the narthex.—The influence of Venice elsewhere.—Torcello.—Murano.—SS. Maria e Donato.—Ravenna: the Madonna now in the Archiepiscopal Palace.—Trieste. Venetian influence in Milan: the apse of Sant'Ambrogio.—Venetian influence in Tuscany: the Florentine Baptistery; the Duomo; San Miniato; San Frediano at Lucca; the apse of the Cathedral of Pisa.—Genoa: San Matteo.

XI.

VENETIAN AND FLORENTINE MOSAICS

In the eleventh century, Venice, with her rapidly growing Eastern trade and her intimate relations with the Byzantine Empire, was in a better position than any of the other Italian states to appreciate the splendor of the great mosaics of the Second Golden Age at Constantinople, at Salonika and elsewhere. Never showing any marked originality in her art until nearly the time of the Renaissance, it was natural that she should turn to Constantinople, and to the Church of the Holy Apostles for the plan of the new St. Mark's, and to the Byzantine mosaicists for its embellishment.

The first church of St. Mark [130] which was built about 830 was destroyed by fire in 976, and the present church was begun in 1063 under the Doge, Domenico Contarini. At the time of Contarini's death in 1070 it was practically finished, and his successor, Domenico Selvo, began to adorn it. According to the Chronicle of Bembo the decoration of the interior was finished by 1094. It would be natural to suppose that the mosaics (188-204) began at the apse, spread to the vaults and ended in the narthex and on the façade. Some of the oldest work may date from the end of the eleventh century, but the greater part of the early work is probably not before the middle of the twelfth century.

Although even the earlier mosaics have undergone countless restorations, and the greater part of them have been replaced by supposed copies or adaptations of the old work in the declamatory and florid style of the sixteenth and seventeenth centuries, out of scale and clashing with the architectural lines of the building; nevertheless, the vast extent of the output, the fact that the entire vaults and the upper part of the walls of a great church are completely covered, together with the wonderful marble incrustation of the lower part of the walls, makes of St. Mark's one of the most beautiful of all Byzantine interiors. The softly-glowing gold of the backgrounds, broken by the richer color of the figures, with the ever-changing perspectives and reflections make a profound impression. Only a closer study reveals the fact that even the early work is, for the most part, on a lower level than the best work of Daphni or Cefalù.

All of this earlier work was probably done by Byzantines, aided, no doubt, by native craftsmen; a document of 1153 mentions a Greek artist, Marco Greco Indriomeni. In fact, it is not until the fourteenth century that a purely native Venetian manner can be distinguished.

The general scheme (188) followed the theological conception which we have already seen at Hosios Lucas and Daphni. The Heavenly Church occupies the domes; the Church of Christ announced by the Prophets, made triumphant by the Savior ascending to Heaven, and revealed to the world by the Apostles. On the central vaults is the cycle of the great Feasts, and on the adjacent walls, the Miracles of Christ and the Life of the Virgin. A patriotic motive led to the life of St. Mark being represented in the sanctuary. In the less important portions of the nave are Prophets, scenes from the lives of the Apostles and other minor figures, and, on the west wall, the Revelation. Thus, the interior in its entirety represents a great affirmation of the Faith, while in the narthex is the prelude—the story of the Creation.

Without giving a detailed description of all these subjects, we may divide them into two groups; those of the late eleventh or the twelfth century in the church, and the Genesis group of the thirteenth century in the narthex.

The early work in the church (189-196) includes Christ Between the Virgin and St. Mark *(Deesis)* in the tympanum over the entrance door; the Pentecost of the west dome; the Ascension of the central dome; the Christ Emmanuel Surrounded by Prophets of the east dome; the Feasts of the Church and the Life and Miracles of Christ on the adjacent vaults and the upper portion of the walls; the Life of St. Mark in the sanctuary.

Except for minor details, the iconography is typically Byzantine. In the Ascension of the central cupola (189, 190), Christ is seated on the rainbow in a starry circle, surrounded by four angels. Below, are the Virgin with two angels, and the Apostles, as in the dome of St. Sophia at Salonika; and between the windows of the drum are the personifications of sixteen Virtues bearing scrolls with Scriptural texts. In the spandrels are the Four Evangelists represented as writing the Gospels, and beneath them, the Four Rivers of Paradise shown as river-gods with urns, according to the antique tradition. St. Matthew and St. Mark are modern.

The Pentecost of the west dome (191) bears a good deal of resemblance to the one in Hosios Lucas. In the center is the symbolic representation of the Throne with the Dove in a nimbus, and below are the Twelve Apostles, seated, with the rays coming down from the Throne on to their heads. Lower down, are the Sixteen Nations, in pairs, male and female, as described in the *Acts,* and in the pendentives are four angels with *labara.* This Pentecost and the Ascension seem to be among the earliest mosaics in the church. They are better executed and less stiff than the early scenes of the life of Christ, for example, and they may possibly date from the end of the eleventh century, or, in any case, from the first half of the twelfth.

The Christ Emmanuel of the east dome (192, 193) is shown surrounded by the Old Testament Prophets bearing scrolls with their prophecies, and in the pendentives are the symbols of the Four Evangelists. This is one of the early mosaics, but it seems to me to be later than the Pentecost or the Ascension, most likely sometime after the middle of the twelfth century.

Although, in general, the style of all these early works is typically Byzantine, there are numerous minor features which seem to be peculiar to the Venetian school, and which differentiate them for those at Hosios Lucas, Daphni and elsewhere in the Near East. Some of these features are survivals from the fifth or sixth centuries; such as the representation of martyrs in the sanctuary, as at Ravenna and Parenzo; the personifications of the rivers in the Ascension dome, which go back to classical precedents; and also the allegorical figures of the Virtues in this last dome. Then, too, there are very few Greek inscriptions, the majority being in metrical Latin.

The mosaics of this early group are by no means uniform in quality or in treatment; they were executed by many hands, and at different times, and the task of analyzing them is made doubly difficult by the great amount of restoration. However, as Toesca[131] has pointed out, we may distinguish at least two different aspects of the Byzantine style. The more classical manner with its delicate gradations of tone, simplicity of composition and a certain calmness in the attitudes, is seen in the Christ Between the Virgin and St. Mark over the main portal on the west wall (194), and in the scenes of the Temptation and the Entry into Jerusalem (195). But in other mosaics there is the more lively Byzantine conception, the tendency to exaggerate expressions and gestures, and contrasts of color and of light and shade, as in the Virtues of the Ascension, the Apostles of the Pentecost, and in certain scenes of the Passion on the arches below. This is well brought out, for example, by comparing the *Anastasis* (196) with the above-mentioned Entry into Jerusalem. Certain groups of scenes are undoubtedly by the same hand and show identical facial types, as in the Entry into Jerusalem, the Cleansing of the Temple and the Washing of Feet. The scenes from the life of St. Mark in the sanctuary (197) are in the more lively and picturesque manner, and probably date from the end of the twelfth century.[132]

Even more interesting in some respects than the mosaics of the interior is the Genesis cycle of the narthex (199-202), covering the six shallow domes and the vaults in front of the principal entrance to the church between the first and second domes. In the first dome is the story of Creation and Adam (199, 200), and in the adjacent vaults, Cain and Abel, Noah, and the Tower of Babel, followed by the story of Abraham

(201) in the second dome, that of Joseph in the next three, and finally the history of Moses (202). The Creation is portrayed in three concentric zones with the story of Cain and Abel in the three adjacent lunettes. The subjects of the other domes are arranged in a single border, the center being filled with a decorative motif on a gold ground.

The Genesis subjects go back to the traditions of Early Christian art; we have already found them in Santa Maria Maggiore and elsewhere. They rarely find a place in the later Byzantine art of the East, but, for some reason, in the West they were popular during the twelfth and thirteenth centuries. We find them in mosaic in the Cappella Palatina, in Monreale and in the Florentine Baptistery, and there are several series of frescoes; San Giovanni in Porta Latina, at Rome; Ferentillo; and Assisi. All of these are derived from early prototypes of at least the fifth or the sixth centuries, but this narthex series has an especial interest from the fact that the Finnish archæologist Tikkanen[133] has shown that it is evolved from a different early tradition than the others, a tradition practically identical with the fragments of the famous Cotton Bible. Judging from the few surviving examples of the miniatures, the imitation is faithful, with the exception of the introduction of architectural backgrounds where none originally existed.

The subjects are treated with great liveliness and animation and a fondness for genre details; at times with a true mediæval sense of humor. The date is about the middle of the thirteenth century. Some think that the mosaics of the western or entrance section of the vestibule are entirely by Byzantine masters and are earlier than those of the northern part, where there seem to be certain Romanesque characteristics and where the work may have been done by Italians. In fact, all of the work has a certain linear quality which we do not find in other strictly Byzantine mosaics, and it is possible that it was executed entirely by Italian pupils of the early Byzantine masters.

The mosaics of the adjacent Cappella Zeno (203), portraying a second series of scenes from the life of St. Mark, have enough similarity with the style of the narthex to be dated in the thirteenth century. They have unfortunately suffered from excessive restoration. Some of the mosaics in the church seem, also, to have been restored or redone at this time.

Finally, the adornment of the façade was probably finished at this period, if we may suppose that the work began in the interior and gradually progressed outward. In any case, the Translation of the Body of St. Mark, over the left entrance, the only surviving old mosaic of the façade (204), which was certainly finished before 1275, is similar in style to those of the narthex.

The fourteenth-century work in the Baptistery we will leave until a later chapter.

In Venice itself there are no other early examples which survive, and in fact there are few records of any, but on the neighboring island of Torcello,[134] the fine old Cathedral is famous on account of its lovely Byzantine choir-screens and its admirable mosaics. The extraordinary contrast between the apse with its single figure on a luminous gold ground and the opposite wall with its crowded Last Judgment creates a profound and lasting impression. The church was founded in the seventh century, altered later, and again partly reconstructed and restored in 1008 by Bishop Orso Orseolo, son of the Doge of Venice. The mosaics (205-208) are, for the most part, probably the work of the Byzantine masters who were called to Venice which would make them contemporary with the early work in St. Mark's of the twelfth century, or even before.

We will first consider the vault (205) in front of the right lateral apse where we find a central medallion containing the Lamb, supported by four angels, two of them standing and the other two kneeling upon globes. The ribs of the vault have a plant motif and the background is filled by acanthus scrolls containing animals and birds. This composition was evidently inspired by the vault of the choir of San Vitale at Ravenna which it resembles so strikingly. We may also recall the vault in the Archiepiscopal Palace at Ravenna of the time of Theodoric and the ninth century vault of the Cappella di San Zenone at Santa Prassede in Rome.

The style and execution are not early although there are reminiscences of the early work at Ravenna, but it seems probable that the composition itself repeats that of a mosaic of the seventh century, the time of the foundation of the church, and which was almost completely done over in the twelfth century.

In the central apse (206) is a standing figure of the Madonna holding the Child, with the Twelve Apostles below; on the arch are the two figures of the Annunciation. The figure of the Virgin, draped in blue, isolated against the gold background, is very impressive in its stark simplicity. The group of the Apostles, monotonous in gesture and severe in expression, remind Diehl of the work at Hosios Lucas. In fact this mosaic appears to be earlier than any of those now existing in St. Mark's, and it is possible that it is as early as the middle of the eleventh century.

In the apse to the right (207), the Cappella del Sacramento, Christ is seated on a throne holding a book of the Gospels, with Michael and Gabriel at either side. Below, are standing figures of Saints Nicholas, Ambrose, Augustine and Martin. The Christ is similar to the Christ in the tympanum over the entrance door in St. Mark's, perhaps a little earlier, which would place it in the first half of the twelfth century.

The vast Last Judgment (208) occupies the whole of the west wall. For the study of Eastern iconography it is of the utmost importance.[135] At the top is the Crucifixion with the Virgin and St. John, and below are five zones diminishing in breadth from top to bottom, the two lowest broken by the door, in the tympanum of which there is a bust of the Virgin. The zone below the Crucifixion shows the *Anastasis,* or Descent into Hell, flanked by colossal figures of the Archangels Michael and Gabriel. In the next scene Christ is seen in a mandorla between the

Virgin and John the Baptist, forming the *Deesis,* with two angels behind. On either side, are groups of the Apostles, seated, who act as judges, and in the background is a crowd of heads with nimbi—the Blessed. From the mandorla a stream of fire descends to the right through the lower zones until it reaches the Damned in the lower right-hand corner. Supporting the mandorla are Cherubim with eyes in their wings, and on the top of each wing appear one of the symbols of the Evangelists.

The following zone contains the empty throne *(Hetimasia)* with the Bible, and behind it, the instruments of the Passion guarded by two angels. Two kneeling figures, male and female, adore the book—the Apocalyptic Book of Life. On either side, angels are blowing curved horns, and beasts vomit out bodies and fragments of bodies; land animals appear on the left and sea monsters on the right. An angel on the right carries a starry scroll and scatters stars with his other hand. In the middle of the next zone an angel holds a balance which flying devils attempt to push down with spears—the Weighing of Souls; on the left are the Elect; on the right, angels thrust the Damned into Hell. In the corner, Lucifer is seated on a two-headed dragon holding a small figure of Anti-Christ.

In the lowest zone, on the right, are the sinners undergoing their various punishments; the sensual, up to the waist in flames, the violent, walking naked in darkness, the lazy, seated in a bog, those who sinned by sight, with serpents entering the orbits of their skulls, those who sinned with their ears, scorched by fiery ear-rings; and lastly, those who sinned by touch, as masses of skulls and bones. On the left, is the Garden of Eden, with St. Peter and an angel at the gate, and a figure holding a two-armed cross—the repentant thief. Beyond are the Virgin and Abraham holding the souls in his bosom.

This detailed description of the theme, aside from its interest as one of the great theological conceptions of the Middle Ages, shows how extraordinarily complicated the subject was which the artists were forced

VENETIAN AND FLORENTINE MOSAICS 199

to represent, and how well, on the whole, they succeeded in arriving at a certain unity and balance in the composition.

It will be interesting to compare this Last Judgment with the one in the Florentine Baptistery (219-222) which was probably executed about a century later, and which is the only other complete representation of the subject in mosaic.

In the apse of the church of SS. Maria e Donato at Murano, the island midway between Venice and Torcello, there is a standing figure of the Virgin alone, without the Child (209) on a platform similar to the one in the apse of Torcello. Although it bears some resemblance to the early work in St. Mark's, it is paler in tone and of a more minute technique, and it probably dates from the early part of the twelfth century.

Another much restored mosaic, which was formerly in the apse of San Cypriano at Murano, is now in the Friedenskirche at Berlin. It shows Our Lord enthroned, with the Virgin, St. Peter, St. John the Baptist, St. Cyprian and two Archangels which are similar to those in the Cappella del Sacramento at Torcello and those in the north apse of the Cathedral of Trieste.

Closely related to the work at Torcello are the two apses in the two churches which together form the Cathedral of Trieste.[136] In the north church in the Cappella del Sacramento are the Virgin and Child flanked by the Archangels Michael and Gabriel (210), and below are the Apostles (211) divided into two groups by a palm tree. The work seems to be early, probably from the end of the eleventh century, and it is thoroughly Byzantine in style, although the inscriptions are in Latin. The types of the Apostles are early, as St. Peter and St. Paul have no attributes, and this may mean that the work is an eleventh century restoration of a much earlier mosaic. A thorough modern restoration was carried out in 1863.

In the second apse (212), in San Giusto, Christ is shown treading upon the asp and the basilisk, with San Giusto and San Servolo on either side. The style is similar to that of the other apse. The ornamental borders in both apses are identical with those of the lateral apse at Torcello, and both works may well be by the same hands. The throne of the Virgin here at Trieste has the same decoration as that of Christ's throne in the Cappella del Sacramento at Torcello, and in the second apse, the Cappella di San Giusto, Christ stands on a platform which is identical with those below the Virgins of the apses of Torcello and Murano.

In 1112, the apse and the triumphal arch of the Basilica Ursiana At Ravenna [137] were completely covered with mosaics which must have constituted one of the most extensive decorations of the period. This work was demolished in 1741 together with the rest of the basilica, but we may gain an idea of the rather complicated scheme from an eighteenth century engraving. Fortunately we have a few fragments of the actual mosaics, now in the Archiepiscopal Palace; the full length figure of the Madonna as an orant (213), the heads of the Apostles Peter and John (214), the busts of San Barbaziano and Santo Ursicano, and another unidentified head.

The Madonna recalls the similar figure from SS. Maria e Donato at Murano, and the heads may be compared with the Apostles of the apses of Torcello and Trieste, and in general, with the early work in St. Mark's. Some, however, do not group these mosaics with the Byzantine tradition of Venice, but see in them characteristics allied to the early work at Ravenna and consider them to be the final manifestation of that school.

In the twelfth century, the fame of the Venetian mosaicists spread to other parts of Italy, again to Milan and a little later to Rome and Florence. In 1218, the pope, Honorius III wrote to the Doge, thanking him for sending a master mosaicist to Rome to embellish the apse of St. Paul's, and asking for two more. We will take up this Roman apse under the Roman mosaics of the twelfth and the thirteenth centuries.

The apse of Sant'Ambrogio at Milan [138] (215), in spite of many changes brought about by restoration, is without doubt a Venetian work of the twelfth century. This is clearly shown by the general character of the composition and by what is left of the original style, although it has been variously dated from the ninth to the thirteenth centuries. In the center, Christ is enthroned with angels and the saints, Gervasius and Protasius. He blesses in the Eastern manner and holds a book in His left hand with the inscription: EGO SUM LUX MUNDI. At the sides are two episodes portraying the miraculous intervention of St. Ambrose at the funeral of St. Martin.

Throughout the Middle Ages waves of Byzantine influence had spread over Tuscany at different times, and this influence was never stronger than in the thirteenth century, especially in the schools of painting, where it was responsible, among other things, for the rise of Cimabue and Duccio. It is undoubtedly this sympathy for the Byzantine style which caused the Florentine Baptistery [139] to receive, early in the century, the most extensive series of mosaics to be found in Italy outside of Venice and Sicily (216-225). Venice was probably the source of direct inspiration, as all of the earlier work is very like the various phases of the Eastern style as practiced at St. Mark's, and it is only later that this is modified by native masters.

The oldest work in the Baptistery is the vault of the rectangular apse, or "scarsella" (216) which, according to the inscription, was carried out in 1225 by a certain Fra Jacopo Fracescano.[140] Fra Jacopo may well have been a Venetian. In any case his style is purely Byzantine and seems to have been derived from the followers of the early workers in St. Mark's, of the period just before the narthex mosaics.

The center of the vault is filled by a large medallion, in the middle of which, within a smaller medallion, is the Lamb with a nimbus. The space between this central medallion and the outer border is subdivided into eight compartments, each containing a Prophet. The motifs in these borders—foliage, urns with birds facing each other and stags—

show the same kind of inspiration from early Christian art that we find in St. Mark's. The whole medallion is upheld by four kneeling figures, placed on Corinthianesque capitals, which may well have offered suggestions to the sculptors of the Renaissance. Below, on one side are the Madonna and Child (217), seated on a cushioned throne, and on the other, St. John the Baptist (218). The scheme is both original and interesting, and the artist has sought striking contrasts of light and shade and rich chromatic effects. The work is among the best produced in the thirteenth century.

Also related to these apse mosaics are the Prophets standing under arches on the intrados of the arch and the two borders on the exterior of the arch. The outer border consists of a scroll with bunches of grapes and a bust of Christ in the center. At the base of the scrolls are nude figures seated upon animals. The inner band contains busts of Christ, the Apostles and other saints.

The vast scheme of the dome (219), an octagonal cloister vault, shows the work of many different hands, difficult to distinguish on account of the numerous and confusing restorations. They are all more or less closely related to Venetian workers of the thirteenth century, and show as well reminiscences of certain Giottesque artists of the fourteenth century.

In the middle of the vault there is an ornamental border around the opening for the lantern (220). In the top zone are Christ between four Seraphim, together with angels, Archangels, Principalities, and Powers. Below Christ and the Seraphim, in the west compartment, is another colossal Christ in a medallion (221), seated on the rainbow, and forming the center of a Last Judgment which fills three of the eight sections of the dome. The other five sections contain scenes arranged in four superimposed zones, including Old Testament subjects from the Creation to the Deluge, the life of Joseph, the life of Christ, and the life of John the Baptist. The individual scenes are divided from each other by decorative columns.

The work probably began at the top, possibly under the direction of Fra Jacopo, for the border bears a good deal of similarity to those in the "scarsella." There is no valid reason for supposing that the work was executed by Andrea Tafi,[141] who, according to Vasari, went to Venice and bribed a Greek mosaicist, Apollonius, to return with him to Florence. The angels and other figures of the top zones show those violent contrasts of color and exaggerated movement which we have already seen at St. Mark's. The Last Judgment is typically Byzantine with no traces of a native manner, and, on the whole, the style is inferior to the best work in Venice, betraying a certain clumsiness in the figures, especially in the seated Apostles. The colossal Christ is rather weak in conception and lacks the majesty of the best Byzantine examples. However, the artist who depicted the scene of Hell was a real master of the grotesque, and even of the horrible (222). The complicated, writhing, twisting forms have great vitality. A certain sardonic humor is combined with gifts for caricature, and the extraordinary bluish-green Satan is not unworthy of one of the later Florentines.

In fact, as others have already noted, Giotto was directly inspired by this mosaic when he painted his Last Judgment in the Arena Chapel at Padua.[142] Giotto's Lucifer is almost identical with the Lucifer of the Baptistery, and a comparison of the fresco with the mosaic will bring out many other similarities. As the largest and most important early mural in Florence it naturally created a great impression, and it is probable that it influenced Dante[143] in some of the conceptions of his *Inferno*.

Although this Florentine Last Judgment follows the Byzantine tradition, it differs considerably from the earlier version of the subject at Torcello. The whole of the central part is taken up by the colossal Christ in the tondo, so that we no longer have the typical representation of the *Anastasis* with the *Hetimasia* and the River of Fire below. On the other hand, the conventional rendering of Hades which we find at Torcello is here elaborated into a realistic and picturesque scene of genre more in line with the later Italo-Byzantine style of the nearly contemporary narthex mosaics of St. Mark's.

The rest of the work, the scenes from the Old and the New Testaments, is not of the highest quality. It often seems careless and clumsy and it has been marred by successive retouching. In some of the scenes from the life of Christ, Toesca sees the hand of the master, possibly Gaddo Gaddi, who did the Coronation of the Virgin in the lunette over the portal in the Cathedral. More interesting are certain scenes from the life of the Baptist where the Byzantine manner disappears and we may clearly distinguish the hand of native artists. In the Birth of John (223), especially, one head (224), beautiful in its strong characterization, stands out far above the level of the surrounding work, so strikingly in the manner of Cimabue, that, by comparing it with the head of St. John (230) in the apse of the Cathedral of Pisa, it seems safe to attribute some of this series to him and his assistants. In rectangular panels on the parapet of the gallery there are thirty-six busts of Prophets [144] ascribed by Vasari to Gaddo Gaddi. These nobly conceived heads (225) are contemporary or a little later than the work in the cupola. The busts of bishops just below the cupola are much later, most of them dating from the time of the Renaissance.

It is difficult to over-emphasize the beauty of the interior of the Baptistery. The mosaics seem to gradually develop out of the architecture. The friezes in the architraves of the two orders, and the series of Prophets on the parapet tie in with the gilded capitals and the busts of the bishops above, all leading by degrees to the climax of the cupola whose tone is thus in proper relation to the walls below. Although there is much restoration in the Last Judgment and many of the other scenes, and several styles may be distinguished in the work, the general effect is one of great harmony; a rich golden brown shot through with dull whites, blues, and a curious bluish green. A work conceived as grandly and completely as this must have influenced the early Tuscan painters, and have helped to give them their sense of scale and breadth of treatment and, perhaps, a certain fondness for somewhat restrained and sombre color.

The above-mentioned Coronation of the Virgin (226) over the central portal in the Cathedral [145] is attributed to Gaddo Gaddi by Vasari. It is much less Byzantine in style than the earlier mosaics of the Baptistery; it is, in fact, Gothic in feeling. If not by the hand of Gaddi, it is at least a contemporary work of the very end of the thirteenth century.

In the church of San Miniato at Florence [146] there is a mosaic in the apse (227) representing Christ blessing, surrounded by the symbols of the Evangelists, with the Virgin and St. Miniatus at either side. The subject is really a *Deesis* with St. Miniatus in place of the Baptist. The date is 1297, and it is thoroughly Byzantine in style. It is hard in quality and the figures are stiff and lifeless, but this is probably due to the restoration of 1860. There is also a much restored *Deesis* (228), originally of the early thirteenth century, on the façade of the church above the entrance.

On the façade of the church of San Frediano at Lucca [147] there is a mosaic representing the Ascension (229). Our Lord is shown in a mandorla held by two angels and separated from the Apostles by an ornamental band which divides the composition into two parts. It has the usual Byzantine characteristics of the period—the second half of the thirteenth century—and it is probably contemporary with the upper portion of the Last Judgment in the Florentine Baptistery.

Towards the end of the century, Pisa [148] perhaps in imitation of Florence, began a mosaic in the apse of the Cathedral (230); a Christ with the Virgin and St. John the Evangelist on either side. This mosaic was not finished until 1321 and it shows the work of several hands, and it has suffered somewhat from restoration. Fortunately, one head, that of St. John, has escaped the hands of the restorer, and as it is an unquestioned work by Cimabue, it is of the greatest importance as a clue to his style.

The small apses of the transepts also contain mosaics which have been more or less tampered with. In the right transept is an Assumption, and in the left, an Annunciation. These are probably from the designs of the painter Francesco Traini (active about 1320 until after 1364), a follower of the Lorenzetti of Siena, and now generally admitted to be the author of the Triumph of Death frescoes in the Pisan Campo Santo.

By the fourteenth century the renown of the Florentine mosaicists must have been well established, for, in addition to Lucca and Pisa, we find one of them, a certain Lello, working as far away as Naples in 1322 (187).

A possible off-shoot of the Florentine school is a lunette over the central door of the Gothic church of San Matteo in Genoa. This mosaic shows a half figure of St. Matthew. The church was built in 1125 and done over in 1278 and the much restored lunette is later—probably of the fourteenth century.

ROMAN MOSAICS OF THE TWELFTH AND THE THIRTEENTH CENTURIES

Roman Mosaics of the Twelfth and the Thirteenth
Centuries

The revival in Rome.—The combination of early traditions with the Byzantine style.—San Clemente.—Santa Francesca Romana.—Santa Maria in Trastevere.—Christ between St. Peter and St. Paul from the Vatican crypt.—San Bartolomeo all'Isola.—Restoration of the apse of Old St. Peter's.—San Paolo-fuori-le-mura.—San Tommaso in Formis.—Civita Castellana.—Spoleto: the *Deesis* on the façade of the Cathedral.—The vault of the Sancta Sanctorum; the Cosmati and their influence.—Santa Maria sopra Minerva; the tomb of Durande di Mende.—Santa Maria Maggiore; the tomb of Gonsalvo Rodriquez.—Palazzo Colonna: Madonna and Saints.—Santa Maria in Aracœli; the Cappella di Santa Rosa; the Madonna in the lunette.—The Brooklyn Museum Madonna.—Santa Sabina; the tombstone of Munio da Zamora.—San Crisògono; Madonna and Saints.—Jacopo Torriti; the Lateran apse, the apse of Santa Maria Maggiore.—Rusuti and the façade of Santa Maria Maggiore.—Assisi.—Cavallini; his work in Santa Maria in Trastevere.—Giotto; the "Navicella."—Reasons for the abrupt ending of the Roman school in the early fourteenth century.

XII.

ROMAN MOSAICS OF THE TWELFTH AND THE THIRTEENTH CENTURIES[149]

There are no mosaics in Rome between the apse of San Marco of the early ninth century and the apse of San Clemente of the late eleventh, a period of nearly three hundred years. The frescoes which still survive from this interim show that the Eastern influence never died out, that, in fact, it increased and reached its height in the thirteenth century, as it did in Tuscany. It seems as if the great native masters of the end of the thirteenth century, Torriti, Cavallini, Cimabue, and Duccio had first to utilize all the possibilities of the Byzantine style before transcending it.

But the Roman mosaics are never purely Byzantine. They cannot be considered as a direct off-shoot of that school, as those of Venice and of Sicily. Some of the figures seem to show a direct inspiration from classical art in the sturdy forms and in the draperies, and not merely the Byzantine interpretation of classicism; and a curious kind of conservatism causes these Roman masters to go back to the earliest mosaics for their motifs and compositions. Thus, the great acanthus scrolls of San Clemente have their prototype in the apse of the Lateran Baptistery, and the symbolic doves on the cross belong to the conceptions of the fifth century. Torriti at the Lateran and Santa Maria Maggiore retains the fifth-century scheme of the original work. In short, here, the usual strong Byzantine influence, common to all mediæval mosaics, is interpreted through Roman eyes which had looked upon the existing productions of the Early Christian period with sympathy and understanding.

The apse of San Clemente (231)[150] dates from before the reconsecration of 1128, if not from the time of Pascal II, 1099-1118. The background is covered by a series of conventionalized acanthus spirals containing small figures, birds and vases. There is a shell-like ornament above from which the Hand of God descends toward the crucifix. Our Lord is represented as dead on the cross with His head fallen side-ways (232). The twelve doves are symbols of the Apostles. On either side are the Virgin and St. John the Baptist. At the base of the acanthus plant in which the cross is standing, is the old symbolic conception of the stags drinking from the Four Rivers of Paradise. Further on, are peacocks and other birds, shepherds with their flocks, and a woman feeding chickens. Four seated figures with books are the Latin Fathers of the Church; on the right SS. Ambrose and Gregory, on the left, SS. Jerome and Augustine. On a line with the Church Fathers we also have what is apparently a condensed version of the legend of Sisinius, his blindness and subsequent conversion, the same subject which had already been treated with such verve in the eleventh century frescoes of the lower church. On the right, is the blind Sisinius led by a boy with his wife, Theodora, behind, and the figure further on, between SS. Ambrose and Gregory, probably represents the celebration of the Mass. On the left, as a pendant to the first group, we have Sisinius cured of his blindness, accompanied by two other figures. The detached figure beyond is probably Sisinius again, making a votive offering of the Gospel roll. As in the early mosaics, we have, in the band below, the Thirteen Lambs as symbols of Christ and the Apostles, issuing from Bethlehem and Jerusalem.

The spirals of foliage show the old motif of the chapel of Sante Rufina e Seconda treated in a more formal and conventionalized way, characteristic of the twelfth-century Byzantine manner. These, the procession of the Lambs, the shell above, and numerous minor details are so in the Early Christian spirit that some critics have considered the mosaic to be the copy of an early one, originally in the old church.[151] In fact, the central scene of the Crucifixion is in contrast to the rest of the scheme, being more in line with the conceptions of the twelfth century.

As mere decoration this apse is superb, a splendid example of fused and brilliant color; the varied greens of the foliage, accented with more brilliant tones, merge into the gold of the background.

The composition of the triumphal arch is more characteristic of the period, resembling that of San Paolo-fuori-le-mura carried out a century later. In the center is a bust of Christ in a medallion with the symbols of the Evangelists at either side in the midst of conventional clouds. On the left are seated figures of St. Paul and St. Lawrence with the Prophet Isaiah below, and balancing these on the right, are St. Peter and St. Clement with the Prophet Jeremiah. The figures of the saints and Prophets are typical of the Roman Byzantine style of the twelfth century.

The apsidal mosaic of Santa Francesca Romana (233), or Santa Maria Nuova, in the Forum, was probably executed about 1161 at the time when Alexander III reconstructed the church which had received rich gifts from the powerful Frangipani. In the center, the Virgin and Child are seated upon an elaborate Byzantine throne, with St. John and St. James on the left, and St. Peter and St. Andrew on the right. The figures are all shown under arches, a curious composition which is not found elsewhere, and the Virgin wears a peculiar diadem. The dry outlines, the minute folds of the draperies, and the linear technique seem to have been inspired by Byzantine miniatures, and the same sources, or possibly Early Christian sarcophagi, are responsible for the background of arches.

This is one of the strangest of the Roman mosaics. The general scheme is interesting, but it seems to have been carelessly done and is provincial in execution. The figures are inclined to be heavy and awkward, and the color is opaque when compared with other examples of the period, such as we find in San Clemente or Santa Maria in Trastevere. The tesseræ are more regular and more closely placed than in other work of the time or in earlier examples, and they are much smaller in the faces and in the garments than in the background. Thus the surface tends to be smooth and hard, and there is little of that vibration of color and woven-together texture that we get in the best work.

The mosaics of the triumphal arch have been lost, but according to Ciampini's engravings and to old drawings,[152] the composition was typical of twelfth-century Rome. In the center was the monogram of Christ with the Seven Candlesticks and the symbols of the Evangelists, and below, the Prophets Baruch and Isaiah. This composition is almost identical with the one on the triumphal arch of Santa Maria in Trastevere, which it probably copied.

The mosaic of the apse of Santa Maria in Trastevere (234)[153] is of fine quality and one of the most impressive in Rome. The subject is the Coronation of the Virgin who is represented as seated with Christ upon an elaborately carved Byzantine throne. Both figures, rather heavy in proportions, but well-modelled and impressive, are clad in the richest of Eastern brocades; the Virgin wears a jewelled diadem. On the left are three standing figures, SS. Calixtus and Lawrence, and Pope Innocent II with a model of the church; on the right, SS. Peter, Cornelius, Julius and Calepodius. Above, is one of those shell-like ornaments which we have already seen at San Clemente, and in the band below are the Lambs issuing from Bethlehem and Jerusalem. The whole is enclosed by an ornamental border in the older Roman tradition—foliage growing out of urns with the sacred monogram in the center. As in San Clemente, the technique is largely Byzantine, but the composition and the decorative motifs are traditionally Roman. There is a sombre richness of color; deep browns, a variety of blues and reds, with the high lights brought out in gold.

The scheme of the triumphal arch is the same as that which formerly existed in Santa Francesca Romana; the Cross with Alpha and Omega in the center, the symbols of the Evangelists, and Isaiah and Jeremiah below (235), with scrolls. Just above the Prophets are birds in cages.

The seven scenes from the life of the Virgin below the procession of Lambs are the work of Cavallini and will be described later.

Santa Maria in Trastevere is the only church in Rome which still retains a portion of the decoration of its façade—the Virgin and Child seated on a throne with two small figures of worshippers below, and, at either side, five female figures in rich Byzantine costume with lighted lamps, the Wise and the Foolish Virgins (236). The work must have originally been thoroughly Byzantine in character but frequent restorations make it difficult to determine the style with any accuracy. It is usually considered as contemporary with the apse, but it is possible that it dates from the time of Innocent III, 1198-1216, who had a good deal of work carried out on the church. According to Venturi, three of the Wise Virgins on the left, with full, rounded forms which contrast with the stiffness of the others, are due to a renovation by Cavallini, but if this is so, it would seem that they must have received additional restoration at least as late as the seventeenth century. On this façade the artists evidently felt that an absolutely flat surface was not suitable for mosaics, which, to be properly seen, need reflected light, since we find that the upper portion of the wall has been projected in a flat curve.

Near the top of the campanile, facing the façade, under a canopy, there is a bust of the Madonna and Child on a gold ground. This has probably been a good deal restored, but it seems to be of the same period as the façade itself.

In San Bartolommeo all'Isola[154] there still remains a fragment from the façade, a bust of Christ which is so similar in style to the Christ of the apse of Santa Maria in Trastevere that it may be by the same hand.

Christ is shown with the cruciform nimbus, blessing and holding the Book. The whole façade was originally covered with mosaics which were ruined during the flood of 1557. A Baroque portico was added to the church in the rebuilding, so that this half-figure of Christ is now in the choir of the Cappuccini, surrounded by modern construction, but it probably occupies its original position on the old façade. It is interesting to note that the surface curves outward in the same manner as the façade of Santa Maria in Trastevere.

There is a much worked-over mosaic which was formerly in the atrium of the old basilica in St. Peter's but is now in the crypt. The subject is Christ blessing, between St. Peter and St. Paul. The close resemblance of the Christ to the one in the apse of Santa Maria in Trastevere justifies us in placing the work in this period, although it has been considered to be of the time of the Emperor Otto II, towards the end of the tenth century. In any case, the work has been so much repaired that it does not at present have much intrinsic merit.

Innocent III, 1198-1216, restored the apse of Old St. Peter's[155] (237) which we have already described in an earlier chapter. Fragments of this work—the heads of Innocent III (238) and Gregory VIII and a phœnix—have been preserved in the Cappella dei Conti at Poli. The head of Innocent III is in better condition than the rest and shows some attempt at portraiture.

In 1218, as we know, Honorius III was employing Venetian mosaicists to restore the apse of San Paolo fuori-le-mura. This mosaic was almost entirely destroyed in the fire of 1823, and the modern reconstruction (239) can retain little of the original style; the central figures are wholly modern. In the upper portion Christ is enthroned, blessing and holding the Book, on the left are St. Paul and St. Luke, and on the right, St. Peter and St. Andrew, while beyond the figures are palms. In the lower band is the empty Throne with the instruments of the Passion, a jewelled cross, guarded by two angels, and the Twelve Apostles separated by palm-trees. The diminutive figure of Honorius is seen kissing Christ's foot. On the arch, to the left, are the Virgin and Child enthroned, and an angel; to the right, John the Baptist with a small figure of the Pope in adoration, and another angel.

Even in its present state this work seems to be out of the Roman tradition and much more in the contemporary Venetian style, both in the general composition and the scale and the placing of the figures. This is borne out by the fragments of the old mosaic which are now in the sacristy. These include three fine heads of the Apostles (240) strongly individualized and purely Byzantine in character. There are also fragments of the beautiful frieze; conventionalized birds and leaves of rose and silver on a blue and gold ground.

Coming within the sphere of Roman influence is the mosaic on the façade of the Cathedral of Spoleto,[156] signed and dated 1207 by a certain "Doctor Solsternus." The subject is the *Deesis,* treated in the usual Byzantine manner. In fact, the work is much more purely Byzantine in style than the usual Roman work, and bears a good deal of resemblance to the mosaics of Grottaferrata. It is beautifully composed in the Gothic lunette and has great decorative value.

The thirteenth century witnessed the rise of the important school of architectural decorators known as the Cosmati.[157] It is beyond our province to describe their work; pavements of geometric design with an intarsia of porphyry, serpentine and colored marbles; church furniture, choir-screens, ciboria, and candle-sticks in which glass mosaic was combined with carved marble for polychrome effects; and the more purely architectural use of intarsia in the cloisters of St. Paul's and the Lateran. A number of the Cosmati were mosaicists in the stricter sense of the term, and it is in this connection that they interest us here.

Above the portal of San Tommaso in Formis, beautifully placed in a simple architectural enframement, there is a small tondo representing Christ enthroned (241), stretching out one hand to a black slave and the other to a white slave who carries a cross. The inscription: SIGNUM ORDINIS SANCTÆ FRATERNITATIS CAPTIORUM refers to a papal decree of 1220 regarding the treatment of slaves. Innocent III gave this church to the order founded by John of Malta to abolish slavery, and freed slaves were formerly lodged in the monastery of San Tommaso. This is a finely balanced little composition, classical in its restraint. An inscription on the archivolt: MAGISTER JACOBUS CUM FILIO SUO COSMATO FECIT OHC *(sic)* OPUS tells us that the work in by Mæstro Jacopo, the father of Cosmas.

This same Jacopo signed a half-figure of Christ in the narthex of the Cathedral of Civita Castellana (242), dated 1210. The chief value of this mosaic, which is rather archaic and very Byzantine in style, is its skillful adaptation to its architectural setting.

About 1275, Nicholas III rebuilt the Sancta Sanctorum,[158] the private chapel of the Popes near the Lateran, and it was probably at this time that the mosaics there (243) were executed. These are productions of the Cosmati is a rather dry Byzantine manner. The vault of the vestibule has a Virgin and Child with SS. Lawrence and Stephen, two angels and two kneeling Popes; and in the elliptical vault of the apse, is a medallion with the bust of Christ supported by four angels.

The attractive and very Byzantine Madonna and Child in a niche in the Cappella San Zeno in Santa Prassede (244) is a work, or, at least, a restoration of the thirteenth century, although it is sometimes attributed to the ninth century, probably on account of the fact that all the surrounding mosaics are of that period.

Another work of the Cosmati is a little Annunciation in mosaic on the spandrels of the baldachino in Santa Maria in Cosmedin.

There is a group of minor works in Rome executed by various members of the Cosmati school and dating from the end of the thirteenth century. It was the fashion at this time to provide the lunettes of Gothic wall-tombs, and occasionally the portals of churches, with mosaics of the Madonna and Child, sometimes accompanied by various saints, and figures of the donors or the deceased in adoration.

Two of these tomb mosaics are signed by a certain Giovanni Cosmas; one on the tomb of Durande de Mende, d. 1296, in Santa Maria sopra Minerva (245), and the other on the tomb of Gonsalvo Rodriguez, d. 1299, in Santa Maria Maggiore (246). In both, the Madonna and Child are seated upon an elaborate Cosmatesque throne, accompanied by saints. The attenuated forms and the rather weak but graceful line already show a Gothic influence. In both these mosaics the defunct prelate kneels at the Virgin's feet; Bishop Durande accompanied by St. Privat, bishop of Mende and St. Dominic; and Bishop Gonsalvo, by St. Matthew and St. Jerome. This Giovanni who signs his work, "Johns Filius Magri Cosmati Fec (it) Hoc opus," was one of the several sons or pupils of Cosmas II, the head of the second family of the Cosmati, active in the last quarter of the century. It is probably Cosmas II's signature, "Magister Cosmaties fexit hoc opus" that we find on a pillar to the left of the entrance to the Sancta Sanctorum.

Another funerary mosaic which is very similar in style to the tomb of Durande is in the Cappella di Santa Rosa at Santa Maria in Aracœli.[159] Here, the Virgin and Child are seated on a throne without a back which was probably taken away during a restoration. On either side are St. Francis and St. John the Baptist. A kneeling figure wearing the robes of a senator has never been certainly identified; Giovanni Colonna and Pandolfo Savelli have been suggested.

Santa Maria in Aracœli has still another of these works, which in the seventeenth century was taken to the Palazzo Colonna where it is still preserved. This work has undoubtedly been rearranged, and a good deal of it has been lost, for the half-figures which remain are all on the same level; the Virgin and Child accompanied by two small angels, St. John the Evangelist and St. Francis, and between them, the small kneeling figure of Giovanni Colonna. At the extreme left is the Colonna coat-of-arms.

There were several other examples of this type. A fragment of one of them, a head of the Madonna, is now in the Brooklyn Museum (247).

Still another funerary mosaic of a different type is on the slab which covers the tomb of Munio da Zamora, d. 1300, the Spanish general of the Dominicans, in the church of Santa Sabina (248). The somewhat rigid figure is represented as dead, and clad in the robes of the Dominican order. The simple tonality of black and white is rather impressive.

Finally, in San Crisògono there is a Madonna and Child between St. James and St. Chrysògono (249) which has often been ascribed to

Cavallini. The forms are fuller and show more modelling than those of the Cosmati, but they are much weaker than those of Cavallini, and the work, at the most, may be ascribed to one of his followers.

Much better is the Madonna and Child in the lunette of the lateral portal of Santa Maria in Aracœli (250). The rounded well-modelled forms are like Cavallini, but there is more gold in the draperies, and the lines are more minute and calligraphic in quality. It is undoubtedly by a master who was familiar with both the work of Cavallini and Torriti, and Toesca ascribes it to the latter.[160]

Jacopo Torriti,[161] at the end of the century, signed the apses of the Lateran and Santa Maria Maggiore. In the first (251), which dates from 1290, nothing remains of Torriti's actual work, and we only have a copy of the nineteenth century which is chiefly valuable for its composition and iconography; but in Santa Maria Maggiore, which was completed five years later, Torriti shows himself to be a superb decorator and colorist who interpreted the Byzantine style in an intensely personal way.

In both cases, earlier compositions of the fifth century were utilized with certain additions. In the Lateran,[162] at the top of the apse, the head of Christ is seen in the clouds, surrounded by angels. Just below the Christ, the Dove descends to a jewelled cross on a mound from which issue the Four Rivers of Paradise. Two stags and six lambs are quenching their thirst at the divine source. On the left are the Virgin and SS. Francis, Peter and Paul, with the smaller figure of the kneeling Pope, Nicholas IV; on the right, we have SS. John the Baptist, Anthony, John the Evangelist and Andrew. The figures stand in a flowery field adorned with birds and cupids, and below, is a Nilotic scene with aquatic birds and animals and cupids fishing. In the frieze between the windows are the Apostles separated by trees. On the left there is a small figure of a Franciscan monk, kneeling at the feet of St. James, drawing with a compass. This is probably a portrait of the artist himself, although in his signature, "Jacobus Torriti pict(or) (h)oc op(us) fecit," he does not mention the fact that he is a monk. Another small figure on the right, who is wielding a hammer, is, according to the inscription, "Frater Jacobus de Camerino," Torriti's assistant.

The Christ in the clouds, the Golgotha cross, and the Nilotic scene are all parts of the original fifth-century scheme. The figures, even in their present state, are nobly conceived in the best classical Byzantine style, modified by Roman traditions.

The apse of Santa Maria Maggiore (252, 253) contains one of the most beautiful mosaics in existence. The subject is the Coronation of the Virgin. Against a background of acanthus scrolls filled with birds, Our Lord and the Virgin are seated upon an elaborate Cosmatesque throne, enclosed in a tondo upheld by groups of adoring angels. On the left are SS. Peter, Paul and Francis with the smaller kneeling figure of Pope Nicholas IV; on the right, SS. John the Baptist, John the Evangelist, and Anthony of Padua with Cardinal James Colonna as a pendant to the Pope on the other side. Below is the River Jordan in which dolphins and birds are swimming among tiny ships, and at the extremities are bearded river-gods after the classical manner.

Below this principal composition are five scenes from the life of the Virgin; the Annunciation, the Nativity, the Dormition (254), the Adoration of the Magi, and the Presentation.

As in the Lateran we have a typical fifth-century scheme with the introduction of later motifs—the tondo of the Coronation and the attendant saints. In fact, the river scene is so thoroughly early in spirit that some have thought that it and the garlands were actually a part of the original mosaic and contemporary with those of the triumphal arch. However, this is not possible, as the apse was reconstructed at a later period, and however much Torriti may have been inspired by an earlier model, the actual work is his. The Coronation is also typical of the later period, a development from the earlier one at Santa Maria in Trastevere. The scenes from the life of the Virgin are treated in typical Byzantine fashion as far as the iconography is concerned, but perhaps they have never been better rendered than here, in grace of line and refinements of composition.

Torriti was a master trained in the conventional Byzantine formulæ, both in iconography and technique, but he employs them with a consummate taste and knowledge which gives individuality to his work. His types take on a new suaveness and serenity, as in the Christ of the tondo, or the surrounding angels, or in the Virgin of the Nativity. His draperies with their delicately clinging folds are less conventional. Above all, he is a superb colorist; seldom have more iridescent tones been produced in mosaic. The tesseræ are used as spots in a kind of impressionism; soft greens, grays, powdery blues blend into one another in a luminous haze. The high-lights of the draperies are picked out with gold but never in too sharp a contrast, and there is intense color in the shadows.

The mosaics of the façade of Santa Maria Maggiore [163] are of about this time, and a part of them still exist, in a much restored condition, incorporated in the present upper loggia. Above, we have Christ seated on an elaborate throne with a curved back, in a star-studded tondo which resembles Torriti's Coronation motif in the apse (255). The signature, "Phillip' Rusiti fecit hoc opus," is on the lower edge of tondo, which is surrounded by four angels holding candle-sticks and censers. On the left are standing figures of the Virgin and St. Paul, and on the right SS. John, Peter and Andrew. The central motif shows Rusuti to have been a follower of Torriti, from whom he borrowed the decorative scheme and the type of the Christ. The types of the angels, and their draperies, have analogies with the work of Cavallini, placing Rusuti somewhere between the two artists.

In the lower zone are four scenes relating to the founding of the basilica; the Virgin ordering Pope Liberius to found a church in a place indicated by a fall of snow (256), the Virgin commanding the Patrician Giovanni to build her a church on this spot, the Patrician referring his vision to the Pope, and the Pope tracing the plan of the new basilica upon the snow. According to Vasari, these mosaics are by Gaddo Gaddi. The work has been much tampered with; the types of the Virgin almost seem to be of the fifteenth century, but, on the whole, the work may be assigned to the school of Cavallini. There is a striving for perspective and an over-emphasis upon details, and the execution is much inferior to that of Torriti and Cavallini, although it is difficult to judge it in its present condition.

We may mention here a little mosaic at Assisi, a bust of St. Francis, which is undoubtedly a product of the Roman school of the late thirteenth century. It is in the spandrel between the twin doors of the Lower Church. The work is in the broad, impressionistic style of Torriti and Cavallini but more careless in execution, and Mather [164] has ascribed it to Gaddo Gaddi.

The Roman school culminates with the work of Pietro Cavallini,[165] who, about 1291, completed the lower part of the apse in Santa Maria in Trastevere with seven scenes from the Life of the Virgin. This work was ordered by Bertoldo di Pietro, the brother of Cardinal Stefaneschi. He is shown in the central mosaic, kneeling and being presented to the Virgin by St. Peter.

The scenes from the Life of the Virgin include the Birth of the Virgin (257), the Annunciation, the Nativity (258), the Adoration of the Magi, the Presentation, the Dormition (259), and the Assumption. Cavallini shows himself to have been trained in the Byzantine traditions, as he follows the usual scheme of iconography, and even the conventional types, but he transcends these even more than does Torriti, simplifying and ennobling the older themes. He obtains depth and perspective without stepping over the true limitations of mosaic into the sphere of painting.

Much has been written upon Cavallini's feeling for form, and upon the great part he played in the revival of painting, especially in connection with his famous frescoes of Santa Cecilia. His nobly-rounded figures and his modelling in relief were partly derived, no doubt, from a study of the antique, and partly because he was especially sympathetic to the more classical aspects of the Byzantine style. Comparing the Annunciation, the Nativity, the Dormition with the similar scenes in Santa Maria Maggiore, we are struck by the greater feeling for space, for broader modelling and light and shade, and by the tendency which Cavallini shows to break away from stereotyped treatment, as in the rapid movement of the Angel of the Annunciation and the natural pose of the Virgin seated upon the elaborate Cosmatesque throne. Even more striking, however, is the way in which Cavallini models in color, doing away with hard outlines and fusing the figures into the background to obtain atmosphere. He employs gold for the high-lights of the drapery, but only enough to render the more natural reflections of light, so that its use ceases to be a mere convention; and in the same manner, he achieves a real depth and richness of color in the shadows. He seems to have thought and modelled in tones, rather than to have filled in spaces defined by lines.

With Cavallini the Roman school comes to an end, as a few years later the papal court was removed to Avignon, and artistic activities in Rome were practically brought to a close, not to be revived again until the time of the Renaissance.

Ghiberti attributes to Cavallini the mosaics of the old façade of San Paolo fuori-le-mura. According to a sixteenth century drawing in the Vatican the composition showed Christ in a mandorla, and below, the Virgin, St. Paul, St. John the Baptist with the donor, Pope John XXII at his feet, and St. Peter. A part of this composition was reconstructed behind the triumphal arch but only the head of the angel to the right of Christ seems to be original in part, and here we already find the influence of Giotto.

A work of the very end of the period which only survives in a sorry adaptation of the eighteenth century, was the famous "Navicella" executed by Giotto [166] for St. Peter's (260). The mosaic was ordered by

Cardinal Giacomo Stefaneschi and was probably completed by 1298. The subject was the familiar one from the Gospel of St. Matthew of Christ Walking Upon the Waves, a theme full of dramatic possibilities, and it enjoyed great fame throughout Italy, so that there are numerous more or less faithful copies of it in fresco and drawings. The seventeenth-century copy done by the painter Cosimo Bartoli for the church of the Cappuccini and now in the Museo Petriano shows the original composition before the restorations of the later seventeenth century. The work can, in fact, be best studied in this painting and in several old drawings. The present mosaic is in the portico of St. Peter's over the entrance. It is in the theatrical style of the period and does not even preserve the original arrangement except superficially.

Two heads of angels have been saved which probably belonged to the original work. One, formerly in the Vatican crypt, is now in the Museo Petriano, and the other (261) is in the little church of San Pietro Ispano at Boville Ernica (Bauco), south of Rome near Frosinone, where it was taken in 1610 when the old mosaic was taken down on account of the rebuilding of St. Peter's.

The original mosaic was in the form of a lunette like the present one, and the old drawings and frescoes show no place in the composition for two busts of angels. However, it is generally considered that these two busts were placed in the spandrels above the lunette, but they may have been either side of the inscription below the mosaic itself. The angel from Boville Ernica has little or no restoration and it is in remarkably good condition. The head, surrounded by a gold nimbus, stands out on a blue ground. Greens and yellows predominate in the wings; the hair is green, red, and orange; the flesh tones are rose with greenish shadows, and the tunic is dark blue with high-lights of white and gold. The use of gold in the garment, the impressionistic treatment of the hair and wings, and the greenish shadows combined with the flesh tones are typical of the late thirteenth century, as in the work of Torriti or Cavallini, but the full, rounded forms and a certain majesty of conception are strikingly like the early works of Giotto, and the mosaic may be safely attributed to him.

The other head in the Museo Petriano has not fared so well. In 1727 it was completely done over in the style of the period. Recently, it has again been entirely remade in order to have it resemble as closely as possible its companion at Boville Ernica.

With Giotto, we come to the end of the Roman mosaics in the mediæval tradition. There are no extant mosaics in Rome between the *Navicella* and the late fifteenth century vault of Santa Croce in Gerusalemme and Raphael's dome of the Chigi Chapel in Santa Maria del Popolo. Roman mosaics from Santa Costanza to those of Cavallini and Giotto give us the most complete picture we have of the evolution and diversity of styles for a period of a thousand years.

THE FOURTEENTH CENTURY

THE FOURTEENTH CENTURY

The Byzantine Renaissance; character of the new style.—Constantinople: the Kahrie Djami.—Arta: Church of the Parigoritissa.—The Fetiye Djami.—The changing character of mosaics and the influence of painting, etc.—St. Mark's: the Baptistery and the Chapel of St. Isidore.—The façades of the cathedrals of Orvieto and Siena.—Mosaics in Northern Europe: Prague; Marienwerder; Marienburg.

XIII.
THE FOURTEENTH CENTURY[167]

The Byzantine Empire, after the disasters of the Crusades and the sack of Constantinople, never recovered its former prestige, but the Latins were driven out in 1254, and under the new dynasty of the Palæologi, it continued to exist for another two hundred years. Too many writers, following a rather biological point of view in regard to the development of art, have treated this period as one of complete decadence. This gives a very false impression of actual conditions. It was a time of experiments, of innovations, and of new developments which only ceased with the conquests of the Turks. The best of the frescoes at Mistra, at Mount Athos and in Macedonia need not fear comparison with contemporary work in Italy; they are not of the stereotyped and lifeless tradition into which Byzantine art always tends to fall, but which is not characteristic of it, as a whole, except in the survivals after the fifteenth century. The masterpieces of this later style are the mosaics of the Kahrie Djami[168] at Constantinople (262-267).

This mosque was formerly the church of the monastery of Chora, one of the most ancient foundations in the city. It was rebuilt for the second time at the beginning of the twelfth century by Maria Ducas, a princess of the imperial family. After the return of the Greek princes, it was restored and embellished between 1310 and 1320 by Theodore Metochites, minister of the Emperor Andronicus Palæologus, 1282-1328.

The mosaics are in the inner and outer narthexes. In the outer narthex are scenes from the life of Christ, while in the second narthex, is the cycle of the life of the Virgin, taken from the *Protevangelium* of St. James, which it follows almost scene for scene. The church itself was originally adorned with mosaics but these have been destroyed or covered with white-wash, although a few fragments have been recently brought to light.

In the two cupolas of the second narthex there is, as it were, an introduction to the scenes below. One (262) shows Christ in the center with figures of the patriarchs from Adam to Methuselah and representatives of the Twelve Tribes of Israel; the other shows the Virgin surrounded by sixteen Kings of Israel; and eleven Prophets. Over the tympanum leading from the inner narthex into the church (263), Theodore Metochites in a high white turban striped with red, a gold tunic, and flowered green mantle, is represented as offering a model of the church to the enthroned Christ. In addition to these mosaics, there are, over the entrance door, a bust of Christ, and opposite, the Virgin between two Archangels, beside a number of individual figures of saints and Apostles. A fine Dormition of the Virgin (264) has been recently discovered over the central door in the church.

Kondakoff's theory that the majority of these mosaics are of the twelfth century, and that they were only restored by Theodore, is not at all borne out by the style. A comparison of them with others which are surely of the twelfth century, such as those of Daphni, will bring this out clearly, and it would seem that Diehl, Millet, and others have conclusively proved that the work must be contemporary with the rebuilding of the church in the early fourteenth century. We also have the proof of Nicephoras Gregoras in his *History,* who states that Theodore Metochites redecorated the whole interior; and, finally, the mosaics are too homogeneous to be mere patch-work.

We are at once struck by the great differences from the earlier Byzantine style. The compositions are much freer, with more interest in elaborate architectural backgrounds and representations of nature. There is a fondness for intimate and familiar details, an interest in perspective and movement, and an almost complete breaking away from the traditional rendering of old themes. Note the life and movement of the prancing horses in the scene of the Wise Men Before Herod (265), and the animation and details of genre in the Birth of Christ and the Adoration of the Shepherds. Above all, the scenes from the apocryphal life of the

Virgin afforded an opportunity to indulge a taste for variety in composition, picturesque backgrounds inspired, no doubt, by the great humanistic revival of the period, and for the introduction of contemporary types and costumes. The almost Baroque attitude of the Virgin in the Annunciation (266) is unlike anything in earlier Byzantine art, and in the scene where the Virgin receives the wool for the temple veil from the high-priest (267), the artist shows more interest in the grouping of the elongated figures against a background which might almost be a stage setting, than in the subject itself. The variety and delicacy of the color, and the desire to obtain new tonal effects probably shows the influence of contemporary fresco painting.

These mosaics have, as a matter of fact, many characteristics in common with the frescoes of the period at Mistra and Mount Athos, and the later Byzantine school in general. In its varied compositions, its sense of the picturesque and fondness for familiar detail, this school has analogies with the Gothic art of western Europe, and, especially, with Italian painting of the *Trecento*. The question arises as to what extent this Byzantine Renaissance is indigenous and original, and how much it may have been influenced by the West. Aïnalof comparing the mosaics of the Kahrie Djami with those of the narthex of St. Mark's, and both with the Gothic art of the West and with the Italian painting of the *Trecento*, comes to the conclusion that this Byzantine work of the fourteenth century is due rather to the mingling of the styles of the West with the older Byzantine tradition than to any great creative originality. It is true that there was a good deal of intercourse between the court of the Palæologi and the rest of Europe, especially Italy, throughout this period; but it seems too much to say that the Byzantine work shows a direct Italian influence. The two styles are, rather, the results of general tendencies which were common to both. There are no details in the mosaics of the Kahrie Djami which point to a direct inspiration from anything Italian, and I think that we may conclude with Millet that

Constantinople herself played the predominating rôle in the development of the Byzantine Renaissance.

At Arta,[169] in the church of the Paregoritissa, the dome has a colossal bust of Christ, with Prophets bearing scrolls, between the windows of the drum. The church was erected by the despots of Epiros at the beginning of the thirteenth century and craftsmen were probably imported from Constantinople to execute the mosaic. This mosaic follows the older tradition rather than the newer style of the Kahrie Diami, and may be dated in the thirteenth century.

The dome of the Fetiye Djami (268, 269),[170] at Constantinople, originally the church of St. Mary Pammakaristos, shows, however, the newer tendencies of the early fourteenth century. There is a medallion of Christ in the center, surrounded by twelve Prophets. The Christ is of a much milder, sweeter type than the severe Pantocrator of the twelfth century, and there is a striving for variety and liveliness in the poses of the Prophets. It is one of the most attractive of the smaller Byzantine dome decorations, both in composition and color.

This marks the end of the Byzantine mosaics—a glorious tradition which had lasted for a thousand years. The Near East which had seen the rise and development of the art, was already in the hands of the Turks, soon to take Constantinople itself. Henceforth, its practice is confined to Italy, except for the sporadic attempts to revive it in Northern Europe during the nineteenth century.

Turning again to Venice, we find two series of mosaics of this period at St. Mark's, in the Baptistery and the Cappella di Sant'Isidoro,[171] both carried out about the middle of the century under the Doge, Andrea Dandolo, 1342-1354.

In the Baptistery, are thirteen scenes from the life of the saint, and a lesser number of scenes from the life of Christ. The dome above the altar (270) shows Christ enthroned in a starry disk, surrounded by nine angels and the Nine Intelligences, according to St. Paul. In the pendentives are the Four Latin Fathers of the Church; Augustine, Jerome, Gregory and Ambrose. The cupola over the font shows the Sending Forth of the Apostles. In the center, is Christ with a scroll and banner, seated on a double rainbow. Below, are the Apostles, each baptizing a convert accompanied by a sponsor in native costume. A tower behind each group suggests a city, the place of the baptism, and the name of the Apostle. Here, in the pendentives are the Four Greek Fathers; Gregory of Nazianzus, Basil, Athanasius, and John Chrysostom.

These mosaics, even more than those of the Kahrie Djami, show the characteristics of this last phase of the Byzantine school in their liveliness and movement, their love of accessory detail, in costumes, architecture, even in furniture and the appointments of the table, as in Herod's Feast (271). There is a certain lightness and gaiety, an unconcern with the seriousness of the subject, and a fondness for pageantry, which makes one think of Flemish miniatures, and of the North Italian painting which developed a little later with the so-called International School. In fact, here there is undoubtedly a direct influence from contemporary Italian painting, as, for example, in the angels in the dome surrounding Christ; but, in general, here again, the execution, the iconography, even the types are Byzantine, and the work must, at least, have been superintended by Greek artists. Whatever the work may lack in seriousness is more than balanced by its decorative quality and its striking and brilliant color.

The Cappella di Sant'Isidoro with scenes from the life of that saint is less interesting than the Baptistery. The work is of the same general style as the latter. The adventurous career of St. Isidore gave an opportunity for the portrayal of lively, anecdotal scenes of genre; but the execution is inclined to be dry and hard, and the color is opaque, perhaps in part due to the effects of bad restoration.

During the fourteenth century, we are safe in supposing that Venice had a trained school of mosaicists, independent of the Byzantine masters, and that she provided her own materials from the glass factories of Murano. From this time on the work is essentially Venetian, or native, in character and shows little or no Eastern influence. A small mosaic of the Crucifixion on the Gothic wall-tomb of the Doge, Michele Morosini, d. 1382, in the church of SS. Giovanni e Paolo, is quite in the style of contemporary North Italian painting.

In the rest of Italy there is little fourteenth-century work of importance. The cupola of the Florentine Baptistery was practically completed, although there is evidence that restorations were carried out even at this early date. Rome lay neglected on account of the Babylonian Captivity.

The most significant work, outside of Venice, is the embellishment of the Gothic façades of the cathedrals of Orvieto and Siena. The Cathedral of Orvieto was begun in the last decade of the thirteenth century, and the façade was probably originated by the Sienese, Lorenzo Maitani, in the early fourteenth century, and continued by Andrea Pisano in 1347, Andrea Orcagna in 1354 and others. Here, the marble base and the piers with their pinnacles and crockets, form a sort of gigantic Gothic tryptich for a series of pictures in mosaic. The marble has now toned to a warm ivory and the glittering mosaics give an extraordinary polychrome effect, which would be finer if they were not, for the most part, rather garish intrusions of the seventeenth and eighteenth centuries. The scenes have to do with the life of the Virgin and her glorification.

They are above the doors and in the three pointed gables and include the Annunciation, the Marriage of the Virgin, the Baptism of Christ and the Coronation of the Virgin. Two monks, Cecco Vanni and a certain Francesco, may have been responsible for the early mosaics and at least one member of the Cosmati family of Rome—Jacopo— worked here. The most important scene—the Coronation of the Virgin —is in the central gable over the rose window.

A much refashioned mosaic in the South Kensington Museum representing the Nativity of the Virgin with two Prophets in the spandrels was long looked upon as the work of Orcagna, but although it may once have formed a part of the decoration at Orvieto, the signature, "Andreas Cionis," and the date, "MCCC Sexagesima" have been proved to be forgeries.[172]

The façade of Siena employed mosaics to a much smaller extent, reserving them for the three gables. Here, as at Orvieto, they are inferior works of a late period, and are interesting only for their general polychrome effect.

Northern Europe, as we have seen, did not take kindly to this art. It was not adapted to Gothic architecture with its absence of wall spaces and strongly vertical lines; here, its place was taken by stained glass. However, before the full development of Gothic, in the later Romanesque period, we hear of mosaics in France and Germany, and even in Spain, although nothing of this work now remains. The Abbot Suger, 1082-1152, covered with mosaics the pavement and the arch of the lateral portal of St. Denis. These were apparently formed of marble, enamel and gold tesseræ, and some figures were represented together with fantastic beasts and decorative patterns. There were a number of early pavements, including one in the church at Ainay, near Lyon, which was consecrated in 1152 by Pope Pascal II.

In Germany, mosaics are mentioned at various places, especially at Hildesheim, where the famous Bishop Bernward ordered scenes of the Sacrifice of Abraham, and the Trinity; but these were doubtless pavements.

In the fourteenth century, however, there was a final attempt to acclimate the art in the North.[173] Mosaicists from Venice were called to Bohemia by the emperor Charles IV, and in 1371 executed a Christ in Glory and a Last Judgment on the exterior of the Cathedral of Prague in which the emperor and empress and the six patron saints of Bohemia figured. This was entirely done over in 1837. About 1380, these same masters proceeded to North Prussia where at Marienwerder, a town on the Liebe founded by the Teutonic Order, they did a Martyrdom of St.

John the Evangelist. This last mosaic, which is in the Dom-Kirche, still exists in a much altered state. Also, at Marienburg, another Baltic town founded by the Teutonic Order, then at the zenith of its power, they executed a Virgin and Child (272). This colossal figure in relief, twenty-six feet in height, is in a niche on the exterior of the Marien-Kirche. It is in a late Gothic style and has been much restored.

This attempt to carry the art across the Alps bore no more fruit than did Charlemagne's efforts six centuries earlier. These are the only wall mosaics we have in Northern Europe from the apse of Germigny-des-Prés until the modern work which begins about the middle of the nineteenth century.

FROM THE RENAISSANCE TO THE NINETEENTH CENTURY

From the Renaissance to the Nineteenth Century
The increasing influence of painting and the relationship of the painters of Venice and Rome to the mosaicists.—St. Mark's: the Chapel of the Mascoli; Giambono.—Florence: Baldovinetti and Ghirlandaio.—Rome: Santa Croce in Gerusalemme, the Cappella di Sant'Elena.—Santa Maria del Popolo: the Chigi Chapel; Raphael and Luigi de Pace. Venice; the influence of Titian, Tintoretto and others.—The trial of 1563; the Bianchini and the Zuccati.—The lowest ebb of the art.—Revival under Leopoldo dal Pozzo.—The Vatican Studio: Muziano da Brescia.—Decoration of St. Peter's; the altars.

XIV.
FROM THE RENAISSANCE TO THE NINETEENTH CENTURY

With the Renaissance [174] begins a new phase in the history of mosaic. This period, which brought about such brilliant changes in architecture, in sculpture and in painting, gives the death-blow to it as an independent art. To survive at all, mosaic had to finally become the slave of painting. When we look at the early examples, those of Ravenna, Parenzo, or Rome, we feel that the artists who produced them were, first of all, mosaicists, men who thought and expressed themselves in that medium. These mosaicists understood perfectly the possibilities as well as the limitations of their own special technique, and it never occurred to them to imitate any other. With the help of assistants they undoubtedly both designed and executed their work. Far from imitating the art of painting, their prestige was so high that the painters frequently copied them, as, for example, in such apses as those of Foro Claudio in Southern Italy, San Bastianello at Rome, San Silvestro at Tivoli and elsewhere—frank transcriptions, both in composition and technique, of mosaics.

In the mosaics of Daphni, or those of Sicily, and in the early work in Venice it is the same. Even Torriti and Cavallini, when they worked in mosaic, expressed themselves as mosaicists and not as painters. But even Cavallini with his chromatic color effects, his fusing of the outlines with the background, and his feeling for spatial and plastic effects, shows that he was alive to the new influences which were beginning to revolutionize painting. We have already noted the pictorial quality in the Kahrie Djami and the Baptistery of St. Mark's. The next steps are the translation of the designs of painters into mosaics, the constantly increasing efforts to imitate the actual gradations of tone and light and shade which were a result of the more naturalistic modes of painting. Comparatively few colors were used in the early work, but now the tones are vastly multiplied to compete with pigments. The tesseræ are fitted more closely together, and even polished smooth, doing away with that texture which is the very essence of good mosaic. The mosaicists tend to become mere artisans, mechanically filling spaces, matching colors to the cartoons spread out before them, and their product degenerates into an imitative and completely unsuitable medium of expression. It is only in our own day that there has been some recovery from this complete subjugation to another art.

The work in the Chapel of the Mascoli in the north transept of St. Mark's stands midway between the old and the new.[175] It is quite in the style of contemporary painting, especially of the Paduan school and Jacopo Bellini, with the possible influence of such Florentines as Andrea del Castagno. It shows the same fondness for perspective in the elaborate architectural backgrounds exhibiting the new Renaissance detail, and in the wiry figures with their tormented and rather metallic draperies. But it is also broadly treated in a manner which does not overstep the boundaries of good mosaic.

The subjects are five scenes from the life of the Virgin, and the Virgin and Child between the Prophets, David and Isaiah. The Birth of the Virgin and the Presentation (273) were signed by Michele Giambono in 1444, and Giambono is probably responsible for the execution of the rest, although the cartoons may have been provided by others. Giambono, in painting, was a follower of Jacobello del Fiore, and influenced by Gentile da Fabriano and Pisanello. In the Death of the Virgin (274), a noble composition, worthy of Mantegna, some see the hand of Andrea del Castagno. It is more probable, however, that this composition was originally executed by Giambono and later modified by an artist trained in the Mantegnesque tradition. The central part with the figure of the Virgin and the two Apostles each side of the bier recalls Mantegna's wonderful painting in the Prado, and these figures, together with the Christ and the medallion heads in the frieze above, are strongly reminiscent of Mantegna and quite different in style from the rest of the work. The end of a scroll with the word FECIT in the lower right-hand corner is similar to the other inscriptions and would show that the work was originally carried out by Giambono. The Visitation is also similar in style to this mosaic and was probably largely executed by the same artist. No more work of importance was done in St. Mark's during the rest of the century, and the mosaics of Giambono are the last which have any connection with the older traditions.

In 1506 the enthroned Christ of the central apse was executed by one Petrus according to the inscription, PETRUS.F. MCCCCCVI. The figure has a certain dignity and does not as yet show the influence of the High Renaissance and the group of painters headed by Titian. It replaces an earlier composition which was destroyed in the fire of 1419. There are several other minor works by Petrus in the basilica.

Florence was much too occupied with painting to give more than a passing interest to mosaics, but at least two artists of note devoted a part of their time to this medium. Alesso Baldovinetti, 1425-1499, according to Vasari, studied the processes and technique and wrote a book about it. In 1455, he did a head of Christ supported by angels over one of the doors in the interior of the Baptistery, and he also repaired the mosaics of the dome, which were already in disrepair, as well as those of San Miniato.

His pupil, Domenico Ghirlandaio, began a mosaic in the Chapel of St. Zenobius in the Duomo, of which only fragments remain, and undertook a few other works. The Annunciation (275) over the north portal of the Cathedral is probably from his cartoons. The Madonna, seated under a Renaissance portico, the kneeling angel with flying draperies, and the balustrade with the trees in the background form a typical Ghirlandaio composition. Gold is used for the background and also with good effect for the high-lights in the pavement and on the draperies. Also in Florence there is a similar Annunciation in the central lunette of the portico of the Annunziata. It is in rather poor condition but seems to be of this same school.

Ghirlandaio's brother, David, worked on the façades of Orvieto and Siena. David also did a Madonna and Child which was carried to France by the Président Jean de Ganai, who had accompanied Charles VIII into Italy. This, a poor and much retouched work, is now in the Musée Cluny. In fact, what little remains of this fifteenth-century work in Florence is in a rather minute and dry manner and is not of great interest. We may mention the half length figure of St. Zenobius (276) by Monte di Giovanni di Miniato, 1505, now in the Opera del Duomo. As Vasari says in his Life of Titian: "In truth it is deplorable that mosaic, that art which is equally precious by reason of its beauty as by reason of the permanency of its materials, should not be more cultivated by artists and more encouraged by Princes."

There is one fifteenth-century example in Rome in the church of Santa Croce in Gerusalemme,[176] the vault of the Cappella di Sant'Elena (277), executed about 1480. This is a rather banal and complicated rendering of the type of decorative scheme made popular by Pinturicchio, Antoniazzo Romano, and the fifteenth-century painters of the Sistine Chapel—interlacing circles and ellipses, figures in niches, and the interspaces filled with garlands and arabesques. The actual design has been attributed to the architect Baldassare Peruzzi. In the central tondo is a bust of Christ surrounded by cherubs, a composition obviously inspired by Melozzo's frescoes in Santi Apostoli. In the four adjacent ellipses are the Evangelists with their symbols—Peruginesque figures— and between, are four small scenes from the legend of the True Cross. In the soffit of one arch are St. Sylvester in papal garb, and St. Helen with the Cross, with the symbols of the Passion in the tondo; in the other, St. Peter and St. Paul with the Lamb of God. In spite of a rather weak and complicated composition this mosaic has a good ornamental effect on account of its well arranged and brilliant color.

Raphael had used cornices of imitation mosaic in his first "Stanza" of the Vatican; he also provided cartoons for the mosaics which formed part of the decoration of the cupola in the chapel which he designed for

Agostino Chigi at Santa Maria del Popolo.[177] The mosaics (278) represent the creation of the world according to the theories of Aristotle and Ptolemy, and associate gods and angels in the true Renaissance spirit. There is a central medallion with the Creator, surrounded by eight compartments containing the planets in their mythological form; Jupiter, Saturn, Diana, Mercury, Venus, Apollo, Mars, all represented as half-figures and with guardian angels above; the eighth compartment is reserved for the fixed stars, represented on a sphere. By the side of Venus is the date, 1516, and a cupid holding a torch which contains the monogram of the mosaicist, Luigi di Pace, whom Agostino Chigi had obtained expressly from Venice. The work was badly damaged during the sack of Rome in 1527, and in the following century, in 1651, it was repaired by order of the pope, Alexander VII, of the Chigi family.

This is the only product we have of the High Renaissance. The design shows Raphael's characteristic elegance and restraint, and the individual compartments are beautifully proportioned to the space, although, as Gerspach has pointed out, the figures are, perhaps, too small. As a mosaic, it is excellent in execution, unusually so, for the period. The color is clear and brilliant with dominating tones of blue and gold.

In Venice,[178] during the first quarter of the sixteenth century, begins that tremendous activity of mosaicists controlled by painters, which destroyed so much of the early work at least partially existing at this time, and which even threatened to do away entirely with the old output. It is true that many of the old mosaics in St. Mark's were in very bad condition. The basilica had settled, the coating of cement used to attach the work to the walls was sometimes of poor quality and did not hold, the fires of 1419 and 1429 had done much damage. But we may be sure that the artists of the time rejoiced in the opportunity to replace the old. To the men of the Renaissance the Byzantine mosaics seemed uncouth and barbarous. Vasari represents the average taste of the time in his contempt for these and his excessive admiration for the work of his contemporaries, which, he says, "seems painted in oils."

Titian proposed to do away completely with the old work and to replace it by mosaics executed from the cartoons of contemporary painters. This proposal was adopted about 1530, and twenty years later, the vaults of the atrium between the two main entrances were covered with new mosaics from the designs of Titian, Pordenone and others. A reaction came in 1610,[179] and the Government forbade the destruction of the old mosaics, and decreed that in case it was necessary to replace them, a careful design should be taken so that they might be restored to their original condition. This praiseworthy attitude did not bear much fruit, for whenever the mosaics were restored it was always in the style of the period when the work was done; in times of creative art it is next to impossible for the artist to adapt himself to the style of other days. However, at least the decree of 1610 probably preserved such Byzantine mosaics as still exist.

It would be tedious to enumerate all these productions of the sixteenth and seventeenth centuries carried out by the Zuccati, Bianchini, and others famous in their day. Some were mere artisans who copied the cartoons of Titian, Tintoretto and other less well-known painters. A few furnished the designs for some of the lesser mosaics themselves. Although the mosaic workers of the later period did not have the status of the great painters, they were, nevertheless, held in honor, and the Republic constantly tried to keep the quality of the output on a high level. Each artist was required to produce a "masterpiece" to be passed upon by a committee of competent judges before he was admitted to regular employment, and he was also required to train two assistants in order that the supply of craftsmen should not give out. Thus, in 1563,[180] there was a competition in order to give each artist his proper place by order of merit. Each was required to do a figure of St. Jerome from a single model. The judges were Jacopo Sansovino, Tintoretto, and Paolo Veronese, and the first place was assigned to Francesco Zuccato, who was not without guile, as he is said to have had his model secretly improved by the hand of his friend Titian.

In spite of the interest of the State, the work became more and more of a mere craft. Until the seventeenth century, the cartoons were usually on paper. These were applied to the plaster surface and the design of the mosaic was pricked through. In many cases these cartoons were probably only outline drawings and the mosaicist worked out the color scheme. In the seventeenth century and later, when there was a complete dependence upon painting, elaborate colored cartoons were provided, carefully worked out on canvas, and some of these are still preserved.

One of the most famous of the sixteenth-century mosaics in St. Mark's is the great Apocalypse in five compartments on the vault preceding the first cupola (279), the work of the brothers Zuccati. The Angels Guarding the Seven Churches of Asia, a part of this scheme, was the subject of the so-called "Trial of 1573" which throws an interesting side-light on the conditions of the art at this time. The Bianchini brought suit against the Zuccati who were charged, among other things, with having used paint on their mosaics to produce the effects. The case was referred to a celebrated tribunal of artists; Titian, Tintoretto, Veronese and others. The Zuccati were warmly defended by Titian, who had provided cartoons for them, but they were forced to do over at their own expense those mosaics which showed traces of paint.

The principal reason for a disparaging attitude towards all of these productions is the fact that they are so completely out of harmony with their surroundings. Mosaics are primarily architectural decoration, and, as such, they should be in scale and in character with the building. These colossal figures with their often violent attitudes, flying draperies, and over-dramatic qualities are always out of proportion and at discord with the setting. They not only destroy the effect of the earlier work, but the masses and perspectives of the church itself. In a proper environment of Baroque character, of sufficient scale and spaciousness, the best of them would probably have a certain grandiose quality. Venetian mosaics never reached the low level of dull, servile copying of paintings, such as the altar-pieces of St. Peter's. Even if they were dominated by painting, they sought to interpret that art in their own medium, rather than to exactly reproduce it.

The art was at its lowest ebb from the middle of the seventeenth century to the arrival of the Roman, Leopoldo dal Pozzo in 1715. During this period the work lacks almost all inspiration—an empty copying of the cartoons of secondary painters. Technique declines to the point where the cubes are often touched up with paint after they are in place, although, as we have seen, this process was not unknown even in the sixteenth century. The general inferiority of the artists employed on St. Mark's was fully realized, even by the authorities of the time, and various attempts were made to obtain mosaic workers from Rome, a reversal of the days when under Honorius III, Rome herself had sought help from Venice.

Leopoldo dal Pozzo,[181] a Roman who worked at Venice from 1715 to 1745, may be said to have raised mosaic again, for a time, to the level of an art. The rich, glowing color of his lunette (280) over the north door of the façade of St. Mark's, representing the Doge with the Nobility and Clergy receiving the body of St. Mark, is unique in the eighteenth century. It was executed from a cartoon by Sebastiano Ricci, a typically pompous and rather theatrical conception of the time, but dal Pozzo's gorgeous effects of vibrating color have no precedent until we go back to the work of Giambono or the fourteenth-century mosaics of the Baptistery. The fact that the brilliancy of this work is out of harmony with its surroundings should not prevent us from giving due credit to its intrinsic merits, especially in a period where there is so little to admire.

In 1516, as we have seen, the Venetian Luigi de Pace worked in Rome at Santa Maria del Popolo. For the next sixty years there are no more mosaics in Rome of any importance, for it is not until 1576 that the work in connection with the new basilica of St. Peter's begins. This continues through the seventeenth and the eighteenth centuries and sums up the output of the period. At first there was no official studio in connection with the Vatican; the artisans were recruited from the various private workshops of Venice and Rome, under the direction of a master mosaicist, and were employed from time to time as the occasion required. This was more or less the state of affairs under Muziano da Brescia, 1528-1592, Provenzale da Cento, 1575-1639, G. Calendra, 1509-1648, Fabius Cristofari, and de Gessi. In 1727, under Pietro Paolo Cristofari, who was named superintendent of the pontifical studio by Benedict XIII, it had a more regular existence. After being installed in various localities, it was finally established in the Vatican itself, in the Cortile di San Damaso, by Leo XII, where it remains today.

We are now concerned with the work of the seventeenth and eighteenth centuries.[182] As in Venice, the designs and cartoons were provided by painters. A good deal of favoritism seems to have been shown in the choosing of these men, popular artists whose work was not considered to be on the highest level even in their own day; the names of most of them have been all but forgotten, except by the curious, and it is sufficient to mention the Cavaliere d'Arpino and Pietro da Cortona. The architect and sculptor, Bernini, also directed the designs for a time.

Thus, the great central dome (281) and the domes and vaults of the aisles and chapels were covered with mosaics done, for the most part, during the seventeenth century. The compositions are, of course, in a Baroque style and of a scale and character to harmonize with the architecture. Although the subjects run the gamut of sacred history, we think of them primarily, together with the profusion of colored marbles, gilding, sculptured saints and putti, as architectural decoration, and, as such, they are good in scale while the very brilliancy of the material is more suited to this high-keyed, grandiose scheme than fresco would be. In fact, most of them are at such a distance from the eye that they seem like highly varnished paintings. As mosaics, most of them are inferior to those of St. Mark's, both in design and in execution. In the first place, the cartoons provided were usually by secondary masters and show the defects rather than the good qualities of the Baroque. The compositions are commonplace and repeat *ad infinitum* the same overstrained attitudes; the draperies are voluminous and contorted without reason; the drawing is facile, careless, even incorrect. Then, too, the mosaicists must have worked hastily and merely copied the suggestions of the painters without much initiative of their own, for the color is light in tone and monotonous, taking even less advantage than usual of the possibilities of the medium.

Perhaps the best of this rather dull production is in the central dome where, on account of the vastness of the space, the problem of obtaining sufficient scale, has been very successfully solved. The mosaics are in the lantern, in compartments between the sixteen ribs, and in the pendentives. At the highest point, is God the Father, surrounded by Cherubim. In each compartment in five superimposed rows, are, commencing at the top, angels in adoration, heads of Cherubim in medallions, angels with the instruments of the Passion; Christ, the Virgin, John the Baptist, and the Twelve Apostles—all in the fourth row—and in the lunettes below, half-figures of various saints and pontiffs. The frieze under the drum has an inscription in blue letters six feet high, on a gold ground: TV ES PETRVS ET SVPER HANC PETRAM EDIFICABO ECCLESIAM MEAM ET TIBI DABO CLAVES REGI CŒLORVM.

This design is the work of the Cavaliere d'Arpino, and the mosaic in the lantern was executed by Provenzale da Cento, 1575-1639. The Four Evangelists in the pendentives from cartoons of Giovanni de Vecchi and Cesare Nebbia were carried out by Provenzale and his pupils. The work was begun under Clement VIII, 1592-1605.

It is unnecessary to describe the mosaics of the aisles and chapels or those of the altar-frontals which are on the whole of an inferior quality; whatever interest they may have is derived from their being a part of the general decorative scheme. Neither should we linger over the few other examples of this period in Rome in Santa Maria di Loreto, San Cesareo, or Santa Maria Scala Cœli at the Tre Fontane.

We must, however, notice one, perhaps, unfortunate phase in the development of the art which began under the pontificate of Urban VIII, 1623-1644, and continues to our day; the actual copying of well-known paintings in order to preserve them. Urban VIII was not noted for his æsthetic sensibilities; it was he who stripped the Pantheon of its bronze tiles to provide material for the famous throne and baldichino of St. Peter's. He had the practical idea of replacing the altar-pieces in St. Peter's by imperishable copies in mosaic, largely as a precaution against fire. The idea of copying paintings was not entirely a new one; we find it prevalent under the Romans in the famous "Doves" of the Capitoline Museum, the mosaic of the so-called Battle of Issus from Pompeii, and in many others, but such unimaginative and rather vulgar conceptions had, of course, entirely disappeared in the great periods of the art.

Now we have the laborious copying of a painting line for line and tone for tone. The thousands of cubes which go to make up such a picture are so carefully joined and so carefully polished that they are no longer apparent, the aim of deceiving the eye is achieved, the tedious processes are hidden, and the effect is that of some brightly-colored surface, such as linoleum. The matching of tones was carried to such lengths that the Vatican workshop claims to have tesseræ in over twenty-eight thousand different colors—some of the most beautiful of the old mosaics were produced with less than twenty. A considerable number of the works of painters, some famous, some forgotten, have been preserved in this petrified form—Raphael, Caravaggio, Guido Reni, Domenichino, without mentioning others. They may be seen above the altars in St. Peter's and elsewhere, Raphael's Transfiguration was enlarged four times so that it might be used as a pendant to Domenichino's Communion of St. Jerome.

Portraits in this mode became popular. There is one of Paul V, now in the Borghese Gallery, by Provenzale, which is said to contain seven hundred thousand tesseræ. Never, perhaps, has human labor been put to more futile uses. The typical attitude of the eighteenth century in regard to mosaic is that of Charles de Brosses who visited the Vatican Studio in 1739. After extolling the work there he speaks of the early Venetian mosaics as "tous fort vilains ... sans goût, sans dessin, et même d'un coloris plat, tranchant et désagréable."

Throughout the eighteenth century the only workshops for mosaic are those of Venice and Rome. It is interesting to note that the revival of the Roman school of decorators in the seventeenth century had given Sir Christopher Wren the idea of employing mosaics in St. Paul's, but this was never accomplished, although the idea has been revived and partially carried out in recent times.

NINETEENTH CENTURY AND MODERN MOSAICS

NINETEENTH CENTURY AND MODERN MOSAICS

The Romantic Movement and the new interest in the Middle Ages; the influence upon mosaics.—Mosaics and archæology; restorations.—Venice: the Salviati.—The Vatican Workshop; the Restoration of St. Paul's, etc.—Other nineteenth century restorations in Italy.—The revival of interest in mosaics in Northern Europe.—Russia.—France; Belloni and the "Pompeian School"; Charles Garnier and the Paris Opèra.—Later mosaics.—Germany. —England.—America.—The revival of mosaic as an independent art; influences from the past; its relation to modern painting.— Recent work in Germany, Denmark, Norway and Sweden.— England.—Recent work in America.—The future of mosaic as architectural decoration.

XV.

NINETEENTH CENTURY AND MODERN MOSAICS[183]

At the beginning of the nineteenth century the workshops at Venice and the Vatican continue their usual routine. The general artistic movements of the first half of the century, Neo-Classicism and Romanticism in their various phases, had little or no direct bearing upon the art. But the enthusiasm for the art of the Middle Ages, and the new archæological spirit of the times had a great deal of influence. This almost passionate interest in a long-neglected period led, naturally, to a desire to preserve those things that had survived and prevent further destruction. But the exuberant archæologists of what we may call the old-fashioned school did not stop there; they not only wished to preserve, but, often, to complete what was missing.

When repairing was necessary, or thought necessary, whole blocks of mosaics were removed, the outlines carelessly taken, and then mechanically replaced in the pseudo-mediæval manner. Giovanni Moro, 1822-1858,[184] carried out a good deal of this work in St. Mark's and executed some original mosaics in the atrium, including a Madonna in the lunette on the end wall. His original compositions differ little from his restorations. Both are in a hard, desiccated, lifeless style which attempts unsuccessfully to copy the types and schemes of the twelfth and thirteenth centuries. Until the nineteenth century, restorations are always in the prevailing style of the period and are easily detected, as, for instance, in the flagrant example of the figure of Pope Felix IV in the apse of SS. Cosma e Damiano. In the nineteenth century they are more insidious and work themselves into the general scheme, tending always to give a hard, smooth, mechanical look. This is well brought out at Monreale where the renovations have given a certain dead character to the whole which could not originally have been there. It is only in very recent years that restorations have been accomplished which can be called worthy of the name. In such cases the mosaics are removed carefully in blocks and then replaced without disturbing the original position of the tesseræ, as recently, for example, in St. Mark's and in Santa Maria Maggiore.

The output in Venice continues to be of the same character as that of Del Moro. A Last Judgment over the main portal of St. Mark's, done by Liborio Salandri in 1836, is a cold, dull accomplishment, in greatest contrast to the glowing mosaic of Leopoldo dal Pozzo nearby. One of the most unfortunate periods began in 1867 when the *Società Limited Salviati* had the exclusive right to "restore" the mosaics of the Basilica. The work was poor in quality, even for the time, paint even being employed. After 1880 a more intelligent period of true conservation began.

The workshops of Venice continued throughout the nineteenth century, as they still do, to be the center for the actual manufacture of mosaic, and the glass factories of Murano had, practically, a monopoly for the production of the material used. In accordance with the ideas in regard to technique which still largely prevail, the artist or designer having nothing to do with the actual execution, cartoons or designs were sent here to be "made up," so to speak, and then exported. Most of the mosaics of Europe and the United States have been produced in this way which accounts, in large part, for their generally inferior quality.

In Rome, the Vatican *atelier* had a great opportunity when the disastrous fire of 1823 at San Paolo fuori-le-mura necessitated the complete renewal of the old mosaics of the apse and the triumphal arch. The work at least follows the lines of the old compositions but the execution is in the usual mechanical manner of the time. Pius IX ordered the series of medallions of his predecessors which now adorn the nave, and the decoration of the façade (282), a composition in the early Christian manner, also dates from this period.

The special Vatican industry of the copying of painting went on in the same way throughout the whole of the century. It is almost impossible to distinguish, even if one so desired, between those done in the seventeenth century and those of today. The unhappy copy of Leonardo's Last Supper in the Church of the Minorites at Vienna was executed by a similar group of workmen in Milan about 1803. Recently the Vatican has taken an interest in original work more in harmony with the possibilities of the medium and it has carried out at least one admirable scheme of restoration in Santa Maria Maggiore which may well serve as a model for future efforts of this kind. Its most ambitious undertaking at the present time is the adornment of the Ottolenghi Mausoleum at Acqui.

Russia [185] would seem to be a country peculiarly adapted for the development of the art, but nothing of importance has been done there since the days of St. Sophia at Kiev. There was a tentative revival in the eighteenth century which led to nothing. In 1839 the mosaics of St. Sophia at Kiev were rediscovered under the coating of whitewash and soon afterwards, restored. Perhaps the interest thus created inspired the Emperor Nicholas in 1846 to found a studio in Rome for the instruction of Russian mosaicists. This studio was transferred to St. Petersburg (Leningrad) in 1850 and placed under the supervision of the Academy of Fine Arts, another instance of mosaics being treated as merely an adjunct of painting. The result was a number of rather insignificant productions in the Cathedral of St. Isaac, and elsewhere, the work of craftsmen completely dominated by the ideals of pictorial art peculiar to the more conventional and academic schools of the period.

In France,[186] interest begins with the establishment of a workshop, in the early years of the century, by Belloni, an Italian from the school of the Vatican. He founded an *atelier* at Paris which was subsidized by the government and had a lingering existence until 1831. Completely dominated by the neo-classic ideas of the Empire, and by the painter, **David**, this *atelier* naturally had little interest in wall mosaics, but produced pavements in the Pompeian style. The best example is in the Salle de Melpomène in the Louvre.

Charles Garnier, the great architect of the Second Empire, was enthusiastic over the possibilities of mosaic as architectural decoration and planned to use it extensively in the new Opéra. It was actually employed in the vestibule and on the ceiling of the exterior loggia, where there are medallions after cartoons by Garnier himself and M. de Curzon, executed by the Salviati at Venice. The new interest thus created caused the government to establish a school of mosaics which lasted for about ten years, and was responsible for the apse of the Panthéon and other work. This *atelier* was organized under the direction of Edouard Gerspach whose little book, *La Mosaïque*, had done so much to stimulate a new interest in the art. He was sent to Rome to choose materials and the craftsmen from the Vatican workshop whom Pope Pius IX authorized to go to Paris. Since that time there have been a number of private workshops in France.

The apse of the Panthéon has the rather grandiose subject of Christ Revealing to the Angel of France the Destinies of Her People; figures on a gold ground, inspired by the old Ravenna or Roman apses, hard and mechanical in execution like the other mosaics of the period. Other examples include the apse of the Madeleine, the vaulting of the main stair-case of the Louvre, and the work in the New Cathedral of Marseilles, where Revoil, the architect, who also designed the mosaics, was especially inspired by the Mausoleum of Galla Placidia. Only the mosaics of the portico were completed. The work was executed by the Salviati.

Additional mosaics which, in a way, form a transition from mid-nineteenth century to modern work, are those on the tomb of Pasteur by Luc-Olivier Merson, those in Nôtre-Dame de Fourvières at Lyons and the Basilica at Lourdes, not to mention the rather uninspired work at Sacré-Cœur in Paris. At Sacré-Cœur we have Christ in Glory surrounded by St. Michael, the Virgin, and Joan of Arc; to the left, three scenes from the history of France. The work was begun in 1912 by Henri-Marcel Magne and Luc-Olivier Merson and finished in 1923. The frieze of the Grand Palais was designed and installed by Fournier in 1900, a not unsuccessful scheme, using only three tones against a uniform background of red.

In Germany during the Romantic period, interest was revived in mosaic along with the rest of the art of the Middle Ages. We have already seen that in 1844, Frederick William IV of Prussia bought the apse of San Michele in Affricisco in Ravenna. Although Venice was almost the sole source for material, beginning with the last quarter of the nineteenth century, Germany became an important center.

Nineteenth-century German work was, perhaps, even more archæological in character than elsewhere. The actual execution was, as a rule, done by Italians in the usual routine way, and the subjects, religious themes inspired by earlier Italian mosaics, or by national history. The subjects are treated in the rather cold, naturalistic manner characteristic of the general run of academic painting of the time, and show the influence of the Nazarene school. We have already noted Schaper's work in the dome of Aix-la-Chapelle, restored in 1869, in our discussion of ninth-century mosaics. The Kaiser Wilhelm Memorial Church in Berlin has a vast ensemble which compares in area with St. Mark's or Monreale, dull in conception and execution. It would be tedious to describe the work in the Erlöserkirche at Homburg, in the Schlosskapelle at Posen, in the Wartburg, and elsewhere. On the west façade of the Cathedral of Erfurt there is a colossal figure of the Virgin on a gold ground, executed in 1870. The historical scenes on the façade of the Maximilianeum at Munich, from paintings by K. von Piloty, were not done until 1902, but they have all the worst faults of the nineteenth century and are out of character with the architecture. The same may be said for the mosaics, 1894, of the pediments of the National Theatre of Munich, which replace frescoes by Schwanthaler.

England fares no better than the other countries of Northern Europe. A studio was installed for a time in the South Kensington Museum and was responsible for a series of portraits copied from paintings by British artists. L. J. Poynter did the cartoons for the St. George of the Houses of Parliament, Clayton and Bell those of the Guard's Chapel in St. James Park, and also a series of mosaic pictures in the Cathedral of Chester. They exhibit the usual failings of "revival mosaics" —smoothly polished surfaces with the tesseræ so close together that the joints cannot be distinguished, and designs which are conceived with no feeling for the medium, but only suggest the pictorial qualities suitable to painting. The work is no better or no worse than contemporary productions in France or Germany. With the exception of the work at South Kensington, it was all executed away from the spot, on paper, by foreign firms. In this respect, the mosaics of the chapel for the school at Giggleswick, by T. G. Jackson, are better, as they were done *in situ*, and are treated more broadly in true mosaic fashion.

Sir Christopher Wren, as we know, had once thought of embellishing St. Paul's with mosaics. From 1863 to 1892 this idea was partially carried out. The eight spandrels of the dome contain the Four Evangelists, designed by Watts, and Four Apostles by Alfred Stevens. The apse, the sanctuary bay, and the choir also have mosaics, so that this ensemble is one of the most pretentious of the nineteenth century. It may be said that the designs are more successful than other contemporary works in England, but the technical execution leaves much to be desired.

In the first two decades after the Civil War, American culture turned back to its European sources. This was the period of the adaptation or even mere copying of the various European styles of architecture, Romanesque, Gothic, and Renaissance, together with their characteristic decorative forms. Artists like John La Farge, of wide sympathies and thorough training in the modes of expression of the Old World, helped to create a new interest in a more lavish decoration and possibilities of color in keeping with the more sumptuous character of the buildings which were then being erected, especially in regard to mural painting and stained glass. Mosaics were also introduced during this period of a general borrowing from Europe, but it must be said that nineteenth-century America showed even less interest in this medium than contemporary Europe, and the work has the usual faults which we have already discussed—a mechanical technique, inspiration and execution completely divorced, designs of painters carried out by workmen, not craftsmen. In fact, most of the actual work was executed in Italy from American cartoons and this is, generally speaking, true of all but the most recent output.

The Library of Congress at Washington has the well-known Minerva of Peace designed by Elihu Vedder, and the panels of History and Law by Frederick Dielman, which do not lack a certain inspiration but are marred by an indifferent execution. We may include with these American mosaics those (283) in the apse of the American Church of St. Paul in Rome, designed by Sir Edward Burne-Jones—Pre-Raphaelite in style and rather lifelessly carried out. The more or less conventional and older religious forms inspired Edwin H. Blashfield in his work in St. Matthews Church, also in Washington, and we find this same influence in the work of the son of John La Farge in the National Catholic Cathedral. Bancel La Farge also designed the apse of Trinity College Chapel at Washington. Other religious mosaics in this same category are those in All-Saints Church at Richmond, Virginia, and in the two Presbyterian churches at Rochester, New York. In the Baptistery of the Church of the Holy Redeemer at Detroit there are mosaics (284) designed by Rudolf Scheffler which are reminiscent of the style of the early Venetians. The New Cathedral at St. Louis is in process of receiving the most extensive series of mosaics which have been attempted in America up to the present time. The church is Byzantine in style and the mosaics (285) cover the dome, the pendentives and the vaults, and in general, both in scheme and manner, they follow the vast Sicilian decorations of the twelfth century. Other recent religious mosaics are those of St. Bartholomew's in New York (286), and the more purely decorative work in the Temple Emmanuel in the same city, both designed by Hildreth Meiere.[187]

A number of public buildings in America besides the Library of Congress have received a certain amount of mosaic decoration along conventional lines, such as the State Capitols at St. Paul and at Des Moines, and Leland Stanford University in California. More recently the frontal colonnade of the Detroit Public Library[188] has been embellished with a series representing the Seven Ages according to Shakespeare, designed by F. J. Wiley in the style of the Italian Renaissance. It is interesting to note that they are composed of cubes of baked enamelled pottery instead of the usual glass or marble tesseræ.

The naturalism of nineteenth-century art was not suited to the peculiarities of the processes of mosaic, and this, combined with the prevalent mechanical execution, accounts for much of its poor quality. All sense of the material quality of the medium has been lost. The revolutionary artistic movements of the latter part of the century, Impressionism, Post Impressionism, the work of Cézanne, Gaugin, Van Gogh, the breaking away from mere naturalism and the new interest in abstract form, study of the basic principles of design, the reaction against mechanical processes and interest in the inherent qualities of special mediums—all these factors have had a far-reaching influence upon mosaic. Some of the most recent work shows a sincere attempt to revive it as an independent art, to rediscover the secret of its success in the past. This has led in some cases to examples of more or less successful archaism, work in which the spirit as well as the technique of the older mosaics has been well understood and reproduced; others have gone farther and used this knowledge as the basis for real inspiration and originality. There is, perhaps, a tendency for a too direct reversion to the past; for merely scientific copying of even the best work leads to barren results.

On the whole the public has shown little interest in the art, and its possibilities as architectural decoration have hardly been touched upon.

This may be partly due to what M. Dordoré calls an "archaism" in taste, the habit of associating certain techniques entirely with the periods in which they had their greatest development. Thus, mosaics are considered Byzantine, just as pastels are often thought of as typically of the eighteenth century, or stained glass as being typically mediæval. This point of view prevents the adaptation of interesting processes to new needs. There is no technique which is not independent of a style or a period. Mosaics are not necessarily Early Christian or mediæval, nor need their use be confined exclusively to ecclesiastical decoration.

Discussing contemporary mosaics in an inclusive way, in a general review of this kind, one runs the risk of omitting works that have not been brought to one's attention, or, of perhaps overemphasizing or underrating others. Here, an attempt is made to describe briefly certain examples in regard to their importance as contributions to a living art, and without pretending that the list is complete.

The best of the recent work in France [189] seems to show the beginnings of a true renascence. There have been interesting experiments with new materials and processes, especially the combination of tesseræ with flat expanses of gilded or colored cement, in place of the older method of covering the entire surface with cubes. Subjects show a stylization and simplification suitable to the material without servile, archaistic copying. We may mention the baptismal fonts of Maurice Denis in the church of St. Paul at Geneva, as well as his work in the Cathedral of Quimper. Also, the work of Decôte, Gaudin, Labouret, Guilbert-Martin, Louis Bouquet, and the Swiss artist, Alexandre Cingria in a number of churches and oratories. The Stations of the Cross by the Brothers Mauméjean in the Sanctuaire de Sainte-Thérèse de l'Enfant Jesus at Paris (287) show originality and a good understanding of the medium.

Germany,[190] especially Munich, has been the center of an interesting group of artists in this modern revival. Johan Thorn Prikker has been inspired by the work of the first centuries, especially Early Christian symbolism which he has treated as abstract decoration in the Altkatholischen Kirche at Essen, the Hague, and elsewhere (288); Emile Nolde and Prince Max von Hohenlohe also use the principles of Early Christian art in a modernistic way. Others are Karl Caspar, Max Pechstein, Ewald Duellberg (289) and César Klein. On the tower of the Frauen-Friedenskirche at Frankfurt am Main there is a colossal figure of the Virgin in high relief covered with mosaic (290). It was probably inspired by the mediæval work at Marienwerder.

In Germany a good deal of interest has also been shown in the use of mosaic as secular decoration in private houses, in hotels and office buildings. One example, of modernistic design, is the work of César Klein in the circular Roman bath of the Excelsior Hotel, Berlin. Even ocean liners have not been immune and the panels of aquatic life on a silver ground (291), designed by Maria May for the ball-room of the S. S. Bremen, are among the most striking of modern mosaics. The Swedish liner "Kungsholm" also has interesting mosaics.

In Denmark, Joakim Skovgaard has designed church mosaics in Copenhagen in a more conventional manner, executed by Italian workmen. In the Town Hall of Stockholm, Einar Forseth has portrayed scenes from Swedish history (292). In these, he attempts to create an historical, native style by going back to earlier examples of national art. They are treated broadly and simply in a manner not unlike the twelfth-century mosaics of Venice and Sicily, but unfortunately the execution is rather hard and mechanical. Emanuel Vigeland, the noted Norwegian sculptor, has done mosaics which show a good deal of personal religious feeling, in a style not unlike that of the Kahrie Djami. In Holland, Molkenboer's mosaics for the church of St. Antonius at Schevenigen show the influence of modern French work.

In Serbia there has been a notable revival, especially in the Cathedral of Topola, near Belgrade. This work is largely archæological in character, going back to the earlier native traditions when the predominating influences were Byzantine, and the Cathedral shows a complete Byzantine scheme of the eleventh century, influenced by the style of the native frescoes.

In England, a Russian, Boris Anrep [191] has done some very interesting mosaics showing a thorough knowledge of the principles of the technique which he uses in a personal way. A pavement (293) done by him for a private house in London portrays in a series of scenes, the very modern theme of the life of a lady of fashion in the year 1922—medallions on a ground of dark green marble. Treated in a very modernistic manner, he combines great inventiveness with an excellent sense of style. Other works by Anrep include pavements in the Tate Gallery and in the National Gallery (294) and an apse at the Military College, Sandhurst. The most extensive work now going on in England is that in Westminster Cathedral, London. The apse, the sanctuary of the Lady Chapel and the triumphal arch of the nave have already been finished. The style may be described as pseudo-mediæval and does not show any great distinction.

We have already touched upon the religious mosaics in America. Secular work[192] has, on the whole, been less hampered by convention, and if it is not always eminently successful, it at least shows a striving to adapt itself to its modern architectural setting. Some of the work, moreover, is excellent both in design and execution. In our present-day buildings of concrete mosaic is especially appropriate as, like the old work, it becomes a part of the actual structure. Among the ever-increasing number of contemporary examples we may mention by way of illustration the panels of *chinoiserie* design in the Oriental Theatre at Chicago by Rudolph Scheffler, and the modernistic panels for the Avalon Theatre in the same city, designed by Charles L. Morgan. The Fisher Building and the MacCabees Building at Detroit, the Rochester Savings Bank at Rochester, New York (295), the International Telephone and Telegraph Building in New York (296), and a number of others have used mosaics successfully either in wall panels or on the vaults.

Perhaps Canada may boast of one of the finest achievements to date on this continent, the vaults (297) of the entrance lobby of the Metropolitan Life Insurance Building in Ottawa, designed by Barry Faulkner.

In the portico of the Currier Gallery of Art at Manchester, New Hampshire, there are mosaics which were designed and executed by Salvatore Lascari in 1928. Here we have a series of figures symbolic of different epochs of civilization. The design follows the older traditions but the execution shows an understanding of the inherent qualities of the medium which raises it well above the usual American product.

Among the more recent notable American mosaics are the murals in the Union Terminal Station at Cincinnati (298), the ceilings in the Ohio State Office Building at Columbus, the reception room in the Irving Trust Building, New York (299) and Barry Faulkner's murals at Rockefeller Center (300).

Modern architecture, especially in Northern Europe and America, has entered upon a new development, emerging from the slough of servile copying and the often unintelligent adoption of outward forms ill-suited to the present day. Science, the strides made by engineering, have made possible our soaring sky-scrapers of steel and concrete and are revolutionizing all construction. There is an emphasis upon fundamentals, upon planes and masses, which has often the quality of great art in its dynamic simplicity, and together with this, a decoration is evolving which is not merely a veneer of historical detail, but the logical culmination of the structure itself, just as it was in the creative periods of the past. If mosaics are to play a part in this regeneration, few will stop to consider whether they are archæologically correct or not. They will look, rather, for a rebirth of the spirit of the enduring work of the great periods, of that happy combination of living design with rich, brilliant, and harmonious color which will always impress us at Ravenna or Cefalù.

NOTES

In these notes are given specific reference to all the important sources and supplementary information as well as many inscriptions and quotations.

NOTES

The word Mosaic is probably derived from the Greek Μουσειος (belonging to the Muses), Latin *Musivum*.

[1] Professor Hamlin in the *Encyclopædia Britannica* (14th ed., vol. 15, p. 833) defines mosaic as an outgrowth of inlay. "When the area of such inlays is greater than the exposed area of the original material, which thus becomes merely a base and frame to hold the pieces of inlay, the result may be called mosaic".

On the origin of mosaic see Gauckler, article *Opus Musivum*, in Daremberg et Saglio, *Dictionnaire des antiquités*, vol. III, Paris, 1877 *et. seq.*, and O. M. Dalton, *Byzantine Art and Archæology*, Oxford, 1911, p. 325ff.

"La première fois qu'un homme se divertit, sur la terre ou la sable, à disposer des cailloux, des coquillages, des noyaux de fruits, en suivant un ordre préconçu, la mosaïque naquit." Léon Dordoré, in *L'Amour de l'Art*, April, 1928.

For Sumerian mosaics see C. Leonard Woolley, *The Development of Sumerian Art*, London, 1935, pp. 41 ff., 68, 72, 89. The buildings at Warka are published in the *Abhandlungen der Preussischen Akademie der Wissenschaften, Phil.-Hist. Klasse (Ausgraben in Uruk-Warka)*, Nos. 4, 6, 7, 1929-1934. The temple of A-anni-padda is described in *Ur Excavations*, vol. I, *al 'Ubaid*, publ. by the British Museum and the Philadelphia Museum.

For Mexican mosaics see M. H. Saville, *Turquois Mosaic Art in Ancient Mexico*, Contribution from the Museum of the American Indian, Heye Foundation, vol. VI, New York, 1922, with excellent illustrations and a good bibliography. Also, J. A. Mason, *Turquoise Mosaic from Northern Mexico*, Bibliography from the Pennsylvania Museum, Jan., 1929, pp. 157-175; for the mosaic from Chichen Itzá see E. H. Morris, *The Temple of the Warriors at Chichen Itzá*, Carnegie Institute, Washington, D. C., 1931 (colored plate). Mexican mosaics may be seen in the Museum of the American Indian, New York; the Peabody Museum, Cambridge, Mass.; the State Natural History Museum, Vienna; the Ethnographic Museum, Rome and the British Museum.

[2] *Burlington Magazine*, 1923, p. 272.

L. March Phillips in his *Form and Colour* (London, 1915) makes interesting and stimulating comments in regard to the æsthetic qualities of mosaic. He considers that the inherent quality—color—is essentially sensuous, mystical and Eastern while form and structure are essentially Western (Greek).

Where mosaic has been used most successfully as, for example, in St. Mark's, it has been used structurally and controls the architecture. "Domes, vaults, and apses combine to display the richness and softness of the material." They are purposely heavy with blunt edges and "they are there because they have been chosen by the mosaic as its own fitting vehicle."

[3]*Liber Pontificalis Ecclesiae Ravennatis*, in *Monumenta Germaniae Historica*, Hanover, 1878, I, p. 289.

[4]Article *Mosaic in Encycl. Brit.*, XIV ed.; Gerspach, *La Mosaïque*, Paris, 1891, p.238 ff., and in *Gazette des B-Arts*, 1880, p.145 ff.; Saccardo, *Les Mosaïques de Saint-Marc à Venise*, Venice, 1897, p.175 ff.; Rioli, *Dell'artifici o pratico dei mosaici antichi e moderni*, Palermo, 1870; G. Antonelli, *Sul modo di tagliare ed applicare il mosaico*, Venice, 1858; Milanesi, *Del arte del vetro pel mosaico* (XVI century), reprinted Bologna, 1864; Marg. Van Berchem and E. Clouzot, *Mosaïques chrétiennes,* Geneva, 1924, p.LIX ff.; A. Agazzi, *Il mosaico in Italia*, Milan, 1926, p.81 ff.; G. A. Wagner, *Mosaic, Its Material and Technique*, in *The Western Architect*, April, 1927.

For the restoration and conservation of mosaics see: Mrs. R. E. M. Wheeler, *Experiment in Removing a Fragment of a Roman Pavement*, in *Museums Journal*, July, 1933; and W. E. Mayes, *Removing a Roman Pavement*, in *ibid.*, August, 1933; E. H. Swift, *Byzantine Gold Mosaic*, in *Am. Journal of Archæol.*, 1934; Biagio Biagetti, *Splendori di arte antica nella Basilica Liberiana rinnovelati dal Sommo Pontefice Pio XI*, in *L'Illustrazione Vaticana,* nos. 5 and 6, 1931.

[5]Saccardo, *op.cit.*, p.77.

[6]G. Boni, *Il Duomo di Parenzo e suoi mosaici*, in *Archivio storico dell'arte*, 1894, pp.110-130; Walter S. George, *The Church of Saint Eirene at Constantinople*, London, 1912, p.52; Marg. van Berchem, *The Mosaics of the Dome of the Rock at Jerusalem and of the Great Mosque at Damascus,* (reprinted from K. A. C. Creswell, *Early Muslim Architecture*, Oxford, 1932) pp. 219 and 245.

[7]Barbet de Jouy, *Les mosaïques chrétiennes des basiliques et églises de Rome*, Paris, 1857, p.IX.

[8]Published by Prof. D. M. Robinson in the *A. C. L. S. Bulletin*, 1932.
Pebble mosaics were used by the Romans. A pavement from a house on the Palatine, probably of Republican times, was "not composed of marble but of pebbles from the Umbrian confluents of the Tiber, red, yellow, green and black limestones, grouped so as to produce a polychromatic effect. . . ." (Quoted from a report by Boni in E. Strong, *Art in Ancient Rome*, London, 1929, vol.II, p.33 ff.)

[9]Gauckler, *op.cit.*; Berchem and Clouzot, *op.cit.*, p.LIX; C. Cecchelli, *Roman Mosaics*, (transl. by E. Savinio) in *Formes,* 1930; R. Hinks, *Roman Carpets,* in *Architectural Review,* 1931.

The Romans also had a coarser and simpler kind of pavement than the one to which they gave the name *opus tessellatum,* called *opus signium,* because it was supposed to have been first used at Signia. It was composed of a base of powdered brick, or tile, and chalk, upon which simple geometric designs were formed by inserting pebbles or white marble tesseræ. Some beautiful examples have been recently uncovered at Herculaneum.

[10]B. Nogara, *I mosaici antichi conservati nel palazzi del Vaticano e del Laterano,* Milan, 1910.

[11]See A. Kisa, *Das Glas im Altertume,* Leipzig, 1908.

[12]*Inventaire des mosaïques de la Gaule et de l'Afrique,* Paris, 1909; Dalton, *op.cit.,* p.424 ff.; Cabrol, *Dictionnaire d'archéologie chrétienne,* article *Afrique,* section xxv; Gauckler, *op.cit.*; A. Blanchet, *La mosaïque,* Paris, 1928, p.28 ff. and bibliography.

Other references for pavement mosaics in general will be found in the bibliography at the end of this volume.

[13]Dalton, *op.cit.*, p.421 ff.

For a list of pavements in Palestine see A. Baumstark, *Palestinensia,* in *Römische Quartalshrift,* XXa, 1906, pp.139-141. For the mosaic found at Kabr Hiram, near Tyre, and now in the Louvre see Renan, *Mission de Phénecie,* Paris, 1864. For the map mosaic at Madaba see A. Schulten, *Die Mosaikkarte von Madaba,* Berlin, 1900 and A. Jacoby, *Das geographische Mosaik von Madaba,* Leipzig, 1905.

Interesting pavements have been recently uncovered at Jerash in Transjordania under the auspices of the British School of Architecture at Jerusalem, and Yale University. These include one with a border of bold scrolls interspersed with animals, within which there is a river scene and bird's-eye views of towns. Another pavement from a synagogue shows the Ark with many small figures of animals in processions. More recently (1933) two pavements have been discovered by Princeton University at Daphne, the suburb of ancient Antioch, one of which, dating from the third or the fourth century, shows an elaborate landscape bordered by a frieze which is "virtually a pictorial atlas of Daphne."

For the sixth century mosaics at Jerash see: *Bulletin of the American Schools of Oriental Research,* 1930, pp.13 ff., and J. W. Crowfoot, *Churches at Jerash,* Jerusalem, 1931; M. S. Briggs, *Newly Discovered Syrian Mosaics,* in *Burlington Mag.,* 1931.

For the mosaics of Antioch see C. R. Morey, *Excavation of Antioch-on-the-Orontes*, in *Parnassus*, May, 1935. The excavations here which are still in progress are undertaken jointly by the University of Princeton, the Museums of Baltimore and Worcester and the Musées Nationales de France. Most of the mosaics are still *in situ* but a few have been removed to the museums. There is a Judgement of Paris in the Louvre, a Venus and Adonis at Princeton, a Bacchus and Hercules at Worcester and two dancing figures at Baltimore.

[14] P. Gauckler, *Le domaine des Laberii à Uthina*, in *Mon.Piot.*, III (1896), p.177 ff., Pls. XX-XXIII.

[15] A. Ballu, *Les ruines de Timgad*, Paris, 1911.

[16] S. Aurigemma, *I mosaici di Zliten*, Rome-Milan, 1926; *ibid*, "In a Roman Villa at Zliten," in *Art and Archæology*, 23, 1927, pp.161-169, also articles in *Dedalo*, 1924, pp.197-219, 333-361, 397-414.

[17] Toesca, *op.cit.*, I, p.61 and note 61, p.78; O. Fasiolo, *I Mosaici di Aquileia*, Rome, 1915.

[18] Dalton, *op.cit.*, p.328, note 2.

[19] C. Ricci, *Appunti per la storia di mosaico*, in *Bollettino d'Arte*, 1914, p.273 ff. See, also, C. Ceccheli, *Origine del mosaico parietale Cristiano*, in *Architettura e Arti decorative*, 1922.

Fragments of what were probably wall mosaics have been found at Zliten (Aurigemma, *op.cit.*, p.42 ff.) showing scrolls and animals, and also in the Terme of Leptis Magna where we find geometric designs, festoons and bunches of grapes (P. Romanelli, *Leptis Magna*, Rome, 1925). The vault of the Mithræum below the church of San Clemente at Rome, probably dating from the third century, shows traces of mosaics.

[20] Van Berchem and Clouzot, *op.cit.*, p.XIX.

[21] E. Müntz, *Bulletin et Memoires de la Soc. Nat. des Antiquaries de France*, VI série, ii,1891, pp.294-321; J. B. de Rossi, *Roma sotteranea*, iii, pp.582, 592-3; Gerspach, *op.cit.*, pp.36 and 43; Dalton, *op.cit.*, p.331.

[22] The Roman mosaics have been well photographed by Alinari, Anderson, Brogi and others. General works covering all the mosaics through the ninth century are: J. B. de Rossi, *Musaici cristiani e saggi dei pavimenti delle chiese di Roma anteriori al Secolo XV*, Rome, 1870-1893; J. Wilpert, *Die römischen Mosaiken und Malereien der Christlichen Bauten vom IV bis XIII Jahrhundert*, Freiburg, 1917 (contains the only complete series of colored reproductions); M. Van Berchem and E. Clouzot, *op.cit.* (fully illustrated); A. Venturi, *Musaici cristiani in Roma*, Rome, 1925.

Briefer references in A. Venturi, *Storia dell'arte italiana*, Milan, 1904 *et seq.*; Dalton, *op.cit.* p.332 ff.; Diehl, Manuel, I, p.347 ff.; Pératé in Michel, *Histoire de l'art*, vol.I, Paris, 1905. Gerspach, *op.cit.*; F. X. Kraus, *Geschichte der christlichen Kunst*, Freiburg, 1896; O. Wulff, *Altchristliche und byzan-*

tinische Kunst, 2 vols., Berlin, 1914-1918, I, p.313 ff.; K. M. Kaufmann, *Handbuch der christlichen Archaologie,* 3d ed., Paderborn, 1922; A. L. Frothingham, *The Monuments of Christian Rome,* new ed. New York, 1925; W. Lowrie, *Monuments of the Early Church,* New York, 1923; P. Toesca, *Storia dell'arte italiana,* Turin, 1915 *et seq.;* R. Van Marle, *La peinture romaine au moyen-age,* Strassburg, 1921; *ibid, The Development of the Italian Schools of Painting,* The Hague, vol 1, 1923.

The engravings in Ciampini's *Vetera Monimenta* etc., Rome 1690, 1697, although sometimes inaccurate, are valuable as showing the condition of the mosaics in the seventeenth century and for reproductions of a number of examples which have been since lost.

[23]For the Eastern elements in Early Christian art see: Strzygowski, *Orient oder Rom,* Leipzig, 1901, *ibid., Ursprung der Christlichen Kunst,* Leipzig, 1920 (translated with notes by Dalton under the title, *East Christian Art,* Oxford, 1925); Ainaloff, *Hellenistic Origins of Byzantine Art* (Russian), Leningrad, 1900; De Vogüé, *La Syrie Centrale,* Paris, 1860-61 (a pioneer in this field but still of value). Among the more general summaries are: *L'art byzantin* by G. Millet in Michel,, *op.cit.,* vol.I.; Diehl, *Manuel d'art byzantin,* 2d ed., Paris, 1925, vol.I, p.15 ff., and *ibid, Les origines orientales de l'art byzantin,* in *L'Amour de l'Art,* 1924; Dalton, *op.cit.,* pp.46-74; Toesca, *op.cit.,* I, p.156 ff; W. Neuss, *Die Kunst der alten Christen,* Augsburg, 1926; G. Duthuit, *Byzance et l'art du XII siècle,* Paris, 1926. Emphasizing the Western or Roman elements are: Wickhoff, *Die Wiener Genisis,* Vienna,1895; Riegl, *Die spätrömische Kunstindustrie,* Vienna (new edition, 1927), 1901; *ibid., Stilfragen,* Berlin, 1893; Rivoira, *Le origini dell'archittetura lombarda,* Rome, 1901 (translated by G. McN. Rushforth under title, *Lombardic Architecture: its origin and development,* London, 1910); G. Galassi, *Roma o Bisanzio,* Rome, 1930.

See also the stimulating essay by C. R. Morey, *The Sources of Mediæval Style,* in *The Art Bulletin,* 1924.

For a protest against an over-emphasis upon Oriental influences see L. Bréhier, *Orient ou Byzance?,* in *Revue archéologigque,* V, 1907, pp. 396 ff.; and G. Millet, *Byzance et non l'Orient,* in *ibid.* XI, 1908, pp.171 ff.

[24]G. Millet, *Recherches sur l'iconographie de l'Évangile,* Paris, 1916.

[25]W. de Gruneisen, *Le portrait. Traditions hellenistiques et influences orientales,* Rome, 1911; G. Millet, *Portraits bizantins,* in *Rev. de l'art chrétien,* 1911.

[26]Dalton, *op.cit.,* p.623; Garrucci, *Storia dell'arte cristiana,* etc., Prato, 1872-80, Vol. VI, Pl. 433-5.

[27]Weir Schultz, *The Church of the Nativity at Bethlehem,* London, 1910.

[28]Venturi, *Storia,* vol.I; *ibid, Musaici cristiani,* p.7 ff.; Van Berchem and Clouzot, *op.cit.,* p.1 ff.; Michel (Pératé), *op.cit.,* vol.I, p.39 ff.; Wilpert, *op.cit.* I,

p.272 ff.; Toesca, *op.cit.*, I, p.166; Van Marle, *Italian Schools*, etc., I, p.7 ff.; Dalton, *op.cit.*, p.332; A. Schmarzow, *Der Kuppelraum von S. C. in Rom*, Leipzig, 1904; G. B. de Rossi, *Della decorazione interna del Mausoleo Constantiniano della via Nomentana, appellato Sta. Costanza*, in *Bollett. dell'Instit. di Corresp. Archeol.*, 1889, p. 79 ff.; C. B. Kunstle, *Das Mausoleum von Sta. C. und seine Mosaiken nach De Rossi*, in *Rom. Quartalschrift*, 1890, p.12; F. Jubaru, *La decorazione bacchica del mausoleo di Santa Costanza*, in *l'Arte*, 1904, p.467 ff.; R. Michel, *Die Mosaiken von Santa Costanza*, Leipzig, 1912.

[29] *Op.cit.*, vol.I. Francesco d'Ollanda, a Dutch artist, made a drawing in the sixteenth century, now in the Escurial, which was engraved by Bartoli, and the lower part reproduced by Ciampini. There are sketches of about the same date in the Library of St. Mark at Venice, and descriptions and sketches by Pompeo Ugonio in the Library of Ferrara. (See Müntz, *Revue archéologique*, XXXV, 1878, p.357.)

[30] *Op.cit.*

[31] *Op.cit.*

[32] Müntz, *art.cit.*, in *Rev. archéol.*

[33] General references as for Santa Costanza and G.B.de Rossi, *op.cit.*, pp.13 and 14; L. Lefort, *La mosaïque de Ste. Pudentienne à Rome*, in *Rev. archéol.* II, series XXVII, 1874, p.96; *ibid* in *Nuovo Bollet. d'archeol. crist.*, 1896, p.174 ff.; P. Crostarosa in *idem*, 1895, p.58; H. Grisar in *Civiltá Cattolica*, vol. III, 1895, p.272 and vol. XII, 1897, p.473. A drawing by Ciaconio (*Bibl. Vat.; cod.vat.*, 5407) made in 1595 before the apse was cut down shows the lower part of the composition. This is reproduced by Van Berchem and Clouzot (*op.cit.*, p.64).

[34] De Rossi, *op.cit.*; Ainaloff, *Hellenistic Origins*, p.282 ff.; Toesca, *op.cit.*, I, p.168.

[35] Wilpert, *op.cit.*

[36] De Rossi, *op.cit.*

[37] Venturi, *Storia*, II, p.243, and *Musaici cristiani*, p.18; Dalton, *op.cit.*, p.341; Wilpert, *op.cit.*, I, p.247 ff.; Michel, *op.cit.*, I, p.46; Toesca, *op.cit.*, I, p.167 ff.; Van Berchem and Clouzot, *op.cit.*, p.9 fl. and p.103 ff.

[38] General references as before. For the extensive early bibliography which has been largely superseded or incorporated in later works see Dalton, *op.cit.*, p.338, note 1.
Ainaloff (*Journal* etc., 1895, p.94 ff.), Venturi (*Storia*, I, p.266), and Richter, (J. P. Richter and A. C. Taylor, *The Golden Age of Classical Christian Art*, London, 1904) consider the mosaics of the nave and the triumphal arch contemporary, rejecting De Rossi's theory that the nave was done under Liberius and the arch under Sixtus III. Ainaloff considers that all the work was executed for Sixtus (fifth century), but Richter would place it in the second or the beginning of the third century, claiming that work of such high

quality and direct classical inspiration is beyond the powers of fifth-century decadence. Details of later character he considers due to restoration. Wilpert (*op.cit.*, vol.I, p.414 ff.) gives the nave to Liberius and the arch to Sixtus III. Toesca (*op.cit.*, vol.I, p.175) considers that all the mosaics are of the time of Sixtus III or a little earlier.

The mosaics are fully illustrated in the works cited by Richter and Taylor, Van Berchem and Clouzot, and in the admirable colored plates of Wilpert. There is an excellent summary of Ainaloff's article in Richter and Taylor, *op.cit.*, pp.415-419. In addition to the above references see: F. Blanchino, *De Sacris immaginibus musivi operis a S. Syxto Papa III* etc., Rome, 1727; O. Tozzi, *Storia della basilica di Santa Maria Maggiore*, Rome, 1904; S. Scaglia, *I musaici antiche della basilica di Santa Maria Maggiore*, Rome, 1910; G. Biasiotti in *Bollet.d'Arte*, 1914 p.73 ff.; B. Biagetti, *art.cit.*; Paolo Muratoff, *La pittura bizantina*, Rome, (no date), p.56 *seq.* and p.61 *seq.* The triumphal arch has been admirably restored by Commendatore Biagetti.

[39] General references as before and Van Marle, *La peinture romaine*, p.14; Venturi, *Musaici cristiani*, p.17; Van Berchem and Clouzot, *op.cit.*, p.79 ff.

[40] *Op.cit.*, vol.I, p.191, Pls.XLVII and XLVIII.

[41] General references as before and E. Müntz in *Revue de l'art chrétien*, vol.IX, 1898, pp.1 and 108; Van Berchem and Clouzot, *op.cit.*, p.87 ff.

[42] For these inscriptions see Van Berchem and Clouzot, *op.cit.*

The one at the top reads:

    TEODOSIVS CEPIT PERFECIT ONORIVS AVLAM
    DOCTORIS MVNDI SACRATVM CORPORE PAVLI.

"Theodosius began, Honorius completed the temple, sanctified by the body of Paul, the doctor of the world."

On the curve of the arch we have:

    PLACIDÆ PIA MENS OPERIS DECVS HOMNE PATERNI
    GAVDET PONTIFICIS STUDIO SPLENDERE LEONIS.

"The pious soul of Placidia rejoices in the splendor which the interest of the pontif Leo adds to the work of her father."

Below St. Paul, at the left:

    PERSEQVITVR DVM VASA DEI FIT PAVLUS HONORIS
    VAS SE DELECTVM GENTIBVS ESSE PROBAT.

"While he pursues the elect of God, Paul becomes a vessel of election and proves to the Gentiles that God has chosen him as such."

Below St. Peter:

    VOCE DEI FIS PETRE DEI PETRA CULMEN HONORIS
    AVLE CELESTIS SPLENDOR ET HOMNE DECVS.

"Peter! Be to the voice of God, the rock of God, the culmination of honor, all splendor and glory of the celestial court."

[43] Wilpert, *op.cit.*, I, p.247, ff; Van Berchem and Clouzot, *op.cit.*, p.9 and p.103 ff.; Michel, *op.cit.*, I, p.46; Venturi, *Storia*, I, p.246, and *Musaici cristiani*, p.18; Toesca, *op.cit.*, I, p.167; Clausse, *Basiliques et mosaïques chrétiennes*, Paris, 1893, p.184. In the tympana below the vault there were standing figures of the Evangelists with their symbols above. These were destroyed in the seventeenth century but are known from an engraving in Ciampini (*op.cit.*, II, tav.LXXV.)

[44] General references as before and Van Marle, *Italian Schools*, I, p.119 ff; C. R. Morey, *Lost Mosaics and Frescoes of Rome of the Mediæval Period*, Princeton-Oxford, 1915, p.35 ff.; Muratoff, *op.cit.*, p.67.

[45] W. Lowrie, *Monuments of the Early Church*, new ed., New York, 1923, p.311; A. L. Frothingham, *The Monuments of Christian Rome*, new ed. New York, 1925, p.74. I find no stylistic evidence for this assumption. See Toesca (*op.cit.*, I, note 92, p.238) who compares these types with the bronze statue of a Byzantine emperor at Barletta.

[46] General references as before, especially Van Berchem and Clouzot, *op.cit.*, p.189 ff.; Toesca, *op.cit.*, I, p.221.

[47] *Op.cit.*, II, Pl.XXVIII.

[48] C. R. Morey, *op.cit.*; E. Müntz, *The Lost Mosaics of Rome*, in *American Journal of Archæology*, 1886, p.295 ff.; de Rossi *op.cit.*, *Notizie bibliografiche dei musaici perduti*, in the *Introduction*.

[49] Michel, *op.cit.*, I, p.42; Wilpert, *op.cit.*, I, p.362 and Fig. 114.
The composition of the apse is typical of early Roman work from the apse of SS. Cosma e Damiano onward, the figures of Innocent III and the Roman Church on either side of the Lamb in the lower band being, clearly, interpolations of the twelfth or thirteenth centuries. The whole apse may have been redone under Innocent III, preserving the older composition as in the cases of the apses of the Lateran and Santa Maria Maggiore a century later (see note 133).

[50] Wilpert, *op.cit.*, I, p.213, and *ibid*, *La decorazione della Basilica Lateranense*, in *Riv. di Archeol. Christiana*, 1921.

[51] Drawings, *Bibl.Vat.*, *Codex 5407*; reproductions in Ciampini, *op.cit.*, Pl. LXXVII; Garrucci, *op.cit.*, IV, Pl.240; H. Grisar, *Roma alla fine del mondo antico*, Rome, 1908, p.89; G.B.de Rossi in *Bollet. di archeol. crist.*, series II, vol.II, 1871, pp.5 and 41; A. Muñoz, *Sant'Agata dei Goti*, Rome, 1923.

[52] The mosaics of Ravenna have been well photographed by Alinari, Anderson, Corrado Ricci and others. General descriptions of all the mosaics may be found in A. Venturi, *Storia, I*; Dalton, *op.cit.*, Wulff, *op.cit.*, Diehl, *Manuel*, and *ibid*, *Ravenne*, Paris, 1927. The results of the latest researches and criticism are summarized in Toesca, *Storia*, I, p.181 *et seq.*, and Van Berchem and Clouzot, *op.cit.* Works devoted entirely to the mosaics are J. P. Richter,

Die Mosaiken von Ravenna, Vienna, 1878; Ainaloff, *Mosaics of the Fourth and the Fifth Centuries*, Petrograd, 1895 (Russian); Barbier de Montault, *Les mosaïques des églises de Ravenne*, Paris, 1897; Riedin, *The Mosaics of the Churches of Ravenna*, Petrograd, 1896 (Russian), analyzed by Dobbert in *Repertorium für Kunstwissenschaft*, 1898, vol.XXI, p.98 ff; Corrado Ricci, *Ravenna*, Bergamo, 1902; H. Dütschke, *Ravennatische Studien*, Leipzig, 1909; J. Kurth, *Die Wandmosaiken von Ravenna*, Munich 1912; G. Galassi, *La cosìdetta decadenza nell'arte musiva ravennate*, in *Felix Ravenna*, fasc.16, 1914, and *ibid.*, *Roma o Bisanzio*, Rome, 1930 (profusely illustrated).

For an account of the restorations see Ricci, *Ravenna e i lavori fatti dalla Sovrintendenza dei monumenti nel 1898*, Bergamo, 1899 and *ibid.* in *Arte italiana decorativa e industriale*, XIII, 1904, pp.21-5.

For early sources see Agnellus, *Liber Pontificalis sive Vitæ Ravennatum* (IX) century published in Muratori, *Rerum italicarum scriptores*, II, Milan, 1723, and also in *Monumenta Germaniæ Historica*, Hanover, 1878 and re-edited by A. Testi Rasponi in *Raccolta degli Storici italiani*, Milan, 1924 *et seq;* Rubeus, *Historiarum Ravennatum libri decem.*, Venice, 1589; Ciampini, *op.cit.*

[53] Sac. Sante Ghigi, *Il Mausoleo di Galla Placidia*, Bergamo, 1910; C. Ricci, *Il sepolcro di Galla Placidia*, in *Bolletino d'Arte*, 1913 and *ibid.*, *Il Mausoleo di Galla Placidia in Ravenna*, Rome, 1914; Muratoff, *op.cit.*, p.63 *seq.*

[54] Sangiorgo, *Il battistero della basilica Ursiana di Ravenna*, Rome, 1900; C. Ricci, *Il battistero della Cattedrale*, Rome, 1932; Muratoff, *op.cit.*, p.65.

[55] *A Muñoz* in *L'Arte*, 1905, p.55 ff.; A. Baumstark, *I mosaici di S. Apollinare nuovo* in *Rassegna Gregoriana*, 1910, p.33 ff.

The procession of female saints strangely recalls frescoes in certain of the cave-temples of Khotan, although in these the iconography is typically Chinese. Cf. Sir Aurel Stein, *Ancient Khotan*, London, 1907.

[56] Quitt, *Der Mosaikencyclus von San Vitale*, in *Byz.Denkmaler*, III, Vienna, 1903; Toesca, *op.cit.*, I, p.193 and notes 56-60, p.234.

[57] Santi Muratori in *L'Arte*, 1910, p.60 ff.; Toesca, *op.cit.*, I, p.200 ff.; Van Berchem and Clouzot, *op.cit.*, p.159 ff.; Muratoff, *op.cit.*, p.78.

[58] Galassi (*op.cit.*, p.198 ff.) comparing these mosaics with the ninth century Roman mosaics of Pascal I and Gregory IV, with which, in fact, they have many points in common, thinks that they are a restoration of the tenth century.

[59] For the extent of these and other restorations see the plates in Van Berchem and Clouzot, *op.cit.*; Muratoff, *op.cit.*, p.74. Galassi (*op.cit.*, p. 194 ff.) considers that the whole medallion of the Baptism is a restoration of the eighth century and that the Apostles Peter and Paul together with the young Apostle by the side of Paul were also done over at this time.

[60] O. Wulff, *Das Ravennatische Mosaik von S. Michele in Affricisco im Kaiser Friedrich-Museum*, in *Jahrbuch der Königlich preuszischen Kunstsammlungen*, vol.25, 1904, pp.374-401, with colored plate; C. Ricci, *La chiesa di S. Michele "ad Frigiselo"*, in *Rassegna d'arte*, 1905, pp.136-142. A watercolor copy of the mosaic in the Museum of Ravenna probably gives a better idea of the style of the original than the work which now exists in Berlin.

[61] For the lost mosaics of Ravenna see E. Müntz, *The Lost Mosaics of Ravenna*, in *American Journal of Archæology*, 1885, pp.115-130.

[62] *Op.cit.*, I, Pl. XLVI.

[63] Strzygowski, *Antiochenische Kunst*, in *Oriens Christianus*, 1902 and *ibid*, *Ravenna als Vorort aramäischer Kunst*, in *Oriens Christianus*, 1915.

[64] For the mosaics of Salonika see Dalton, *op.cit.*, p.374 ff.; Diehl, *Manuel*, I, p.132 ff.; Van Berchem and Clouzot, *op.cit.*, p.66 ff.; Diehl, Le Tourneau and Saladin, *Les Monuments chrétiens de Salonique*, Paris, 1918; Ch. Diehl, *La Peinture Byzantine*, Paris, 1933. For historical sources see O. Tafrali, *Thessalonique, des Origines au XIV Siècle*, Paris, 1919.

[65] The saints are: Romanus, Eucarpion, Ananias, Basiliscus, Priscus, Philippus, Therinus, Leo of Patara, Philemon of Comara, Onesiphorus, Porphyrius, Cosmas, and Damian.

[66] See A. M. Friend Jr., *The Portraits of the Evangelists in Greek and Latin Manuscripts*, Part II, in *Art Studies*, 1929.

[67] P. N. Papageorgiou in *Byzantinische Zeitschrift*, XVII, 1908; Ouspenski, *Recently Discovered Mosaics at St. Demetrius, Salonika*, in *Izvjestija (Bulletin) of the Russian Archæological Institute of Constantinople*, XIV, 1908; O. Tafrali in *Revue archéol.*, II, 1909 and I, 1910; Diehl and Le Tourneau, *Les mosaïques de Saint-Demetrius de Salonique*, in *Monuments Piot*, XVIII, 1911; Dalton, *op.cit.*, p.378, for additional bibliography and mosaics destroyed by the fire of 1917.

[68] The best resumés of the little that is known about these mosaics are those of Dalton (*op.cit.* p.391 ff.) and Diehl (*Manuel*, I, p.163 ff.) See, also, Fossati, *Aya Sofia*, London, 1852; Salzenberg, *Altchristliche Baudenmäler von Konstantinopel*, Berlin, 1854; Lethaby and Swainson, *The Church of Sancta Sophia, Constantinople*, London and New York, 1894, pp.273-289; Ebersolt and Thiers, *Les églises de Constantinople*, Paris, 1913; Muratoff, *op.cit.*, p.72; A. Heisenberg, *Grabeskirche und Apostelkirche; zwei Basiliken Konstantins*, Leipzig, 1908, and *ibid*, *Die alten Mosaiken der Apostelkirche und der Hagia Sophia*, in Ξένια of the National University of Greece, 1912; and especially, Thomas Whittemore, *The Mosaics of St. Sophia at Istanbul*, Paris, 1933; J. Pozzi, *Les mosaïques de Sainte Sophie*, in *Beaux Arts*, 1933; *ibid*, *La réapparition des mosaïques de Sainte Sophie*, in *Rev. archéol.*, 1934; F. Rutter, *Mosaics in the Dome of St. Sophia, Constantinople*, in *International Studio*,

1930; R. Byron, *Hidden Splendour; Mosaics in St. Sophia in Constantinople,* in *Art Digest,* 1932.

Mosaics which have been assigned to the time of Justinian include the Cherubim in the pendentives of the great dome, the angel with orb and sceptre on the south side of the apse, and a number of decorative mosaics in the soffits of the arches and other minor positions. Others known to us are: the Pantocrator of the dome, the enthroned Virgin and Child in the apse, the Pentecost in the western cupola of the gallery, the saints and Prophets along the north and south walls, the *Etimasia* in a medallion flanked by the Virgin and St. John the Baptist on the eastern arch beneath the dome. Below this last is the portrait of John Palæologos. These mosaics may possibly date from the time of Romanos (eleventh century) with restorations of the fifteenth century. On the opposite western arch is a medallion of the Virgin and Child between St. Peter and St. Paul, perhaps of the time of Basil I. The side aisles and the galleries have geometric and floral designs in great variety which may well be from the time of Justinian. Until these mosaics are fully uncovered and studied it is mere speculation to give them a correct dating. It is probable that comparatively little of the work actually dates from the sixth century and that eventually the bulk of it will be assigned to the time of the Macedonians and the Comnenes with restorations as late as the fifteenth century.

For documentary references to these mosaics and other lost mosaics see: J. P. Richter, *Quellen der byzantinischen Kunstgeschichte,* Vienna, 1897, Index s.v.*Mosaiken.* The description of the lost mosaics of the Church of the Apostles by Constantine the Rhodian was edited by E. Legrand (*Revue des études grecques,* IX, 1896, p.32 ff.) For the description by Mesarites (twelfth century) see: A. Heisenberg, *op.cit.,* II, p.3 ff.

[69] Beljajef, D., *Saint Irene,* in *Vizantieski Vremenik* (published by the Imperial Academy of Sciences), Leningrad, 1895; W. S. George, *The Church of Saint Eirene at Constantinople,* London, 1912.

[70] Dalton, *op.cit.* p. 383; Van Berchem and Clouzot, *op.cit.,* p.183 ff.; Benesevic, *Sur la date de la mosaïque de la Transfiguration au Mont Sinai,* in *Byzantion,* I, 1924; *ibid* in *Monumenta Sinaitica,* fasc.I, Leningrad, 1925 (Russian), Pl. 2-7.

See, also, F. M. Abel, *Notes d'archéologie chrétienne sur le Sinaï,* in *Revue biblique,* 1907, pp.105-12 and S. Vailhé, *La mosaïque de la Transfiguration au Sinai est-elle de Justinien?,* in *Revue de l'Orient chrétien,* 2d series, II, pp.96-98.

There has always been some question as to the actual date of this mosaic. Two inscriptions on the beams: "For the salvation of our late monarch Justinian" and "To the memory of our late queen Theodora" (Vailhé, *op.cit.*)

prove that the church was at least roofed over after the death of Theodora (548) and before the death of Justinian (565). A Greek inscription on the mosaic itself below the Transfiguration and above the medallions of the Prophets, tells that the work was done by the abbot, Longinus, who together with his deacon, John, is represented in the row of Apostles at the top of the apse. A second inscription in the right-hand corner of the mosaic reads: "By the care of Theodore priest and prior, indiction XIV." Abel, (*op.cit.*) has shown that this indiction would fall either in 550-51 or in 565-66, just at the death of Justinian and some do not consider either of these dates as plausible for the execution of the mosaic. If the two portrait medallions in the spandrels represent Justinian and Theodora they are shown in a simple fashion which is not consistent with the pomp of the mosaics at San Vitale. It has been suggested that these medallions represent Christ and the Virgin, Moses and St. Catherine, St. John and the Virgin, or what seems more probable, two unknown donors. Miss Van Berchem (*op.cit*.p.188) takes this last point of view and on stylistic grounds dates the mosaic in the seventh or the eighth century, although it is more generally considered to be contemporary with Justinian. In the sixteenth century other mosaics still existed here showing the Virgin and Child between Moses and St. Catherine.

[71]Dalton, *op.cit.*, p.372; Diehl, *op.cit.* I, p.223 ff.; Toesca, *op.cit.*, I, p.202 ff.; Van Berchem and Clouzot, *op.cit.*, p.175 ff.; G. Boni, *Il Duomo di Parenzo*, in *Archivio storico dell'arte*, 1894; P. Deperis, *Il Duomo di Parenzo e i suoi mosaic;* in *Atti e memorie della Soc. istriana di arch. e stor. patr.*, X, 1894; A. Amorosa, *Le basiliche cristiane di Parenzo*, Parenzo, 1895; O. Marucchi, *Le recente scoperte nel Duomo di Parenzo*, in *Nuovo Bull. di arch. crist.*, 1896; Wlha and Niemann, *Der Dom von Parenzo*, Vienna, 1899; F. H. Jackson, *The Shores of the Adriatic, the Austrian Side*, London, 1908, pp.107 seq.; A. Pogatschnig, *Parenzo*, in *Atti e memorie della Soc. istriana di arch. e stor. patr.* XXVI, 1911; Muratoff, *op.cit.*, p.76.

[72]A. Morassi, *La chiesetta di Santa Maria Formosa o del Canneto a Pola*, in *Bolletino d'Arte*, 1924; Galassi, *op.cit.*, p.110 ff.

[73]For this and the following Italian mosaics in this chapter use the general references under note 22.

The Christ and the Apostles follow the same general scheme as the fourth century fresco in the Cemetery of Domitilla (Wilpert, *op.cit.*, Pl.193); Muratoff (*op.cit.*, p.58) would place this in the fourth century.

[74]*Storia dell'arte cristiana nei primi otto secoli della Chiesa*, Prato, 1872-1880, I, p. 224.

[75]*Op.cit.*, II, p.1192 and III, Pl.40.

[76]*Op.cit.*, I, p.208 and note 76, p.235.

NOTES

[77] Dalton, *op.cit.*, p.372; Van Berchem and Clouzot, *op.cit.*, p.III; Toesca, *La pittura* etc., p.14 ff., and *Storia*, p.209 and note 77, p.235; Wilpert, *op.cit.*, III, Pls.83 and 84.

[78] E. Mella, *Il Battistero di Agrate conturbia e di Albenga*, in *Atti della Soc. di Arch. e Bell Arte di Torino*, 1883, p.57; P. Toesca, *La pittura e la miniature nella Lombardia*, Milan, 1912, p.21 ff.; *ibid, Storia*, I, p.208 and note 75, p.235; Ainaloff, *The Mosaics of the Baptistery of Albenga*, in *Vizantieski Vremenik*, VIII, 1901, p.520 ff.

The monogram of Christ enclosed in a halo within two larger concentric halos represents the Trinity and it seems to be similar in iconography to a lost mosaic from Gaza in Palestine. The twelve doves as symbols of the Apostles were, also, probably represented in the fifth century mosaics at Nola (see note 81) and Capua. The style seems to show a direct contact with those Syro-Palestinian influences which were also active in Southern Italy.

[79] A. Haseloff, *I musaici di Casaranello*, in *Bollettino d'Arte*, 1907; W. de Gruneisen in *Archivio della R. Soc. Romana di storia patria*, XXIX, p.518.

[80] E. Bertaux, *L'Art dans l'Italie Méridionale*, Paris, 1901, I, p.43 ff.; A. Filangieri di Candida, *I restauri dei musaici del Battistero di S. Giovanni in Fonte*, in *L'Arte*, 1898; A. Muñoz, *S. Giovanni in Fonte*, in *L'Arte*, 1908; A. Sorrentino, *La basilica di Santa Restituta in Napoli*, in *Bollettino d'Arte*, 1909; A. W. Bijvanck, *Het mozaïek in de doopkerk bij de Kathedral te Napels* (with French summary), in *Nederlandsch Hist. Inst. Rome Med.* vol.10, 1931.

The iconography of these mosaics is directly related to the ritual of baptism. Those worthy to be baptized were instructed in the laws of Christianity (*Traditio Legis*) and in the Gospels (symbols of the Evangelists) and the regenerating effect of the water of baptism is recalled in the miracles of Christ here represented.

[81] Wickhoff, *Der Apsismosaik in der Basilica des H. Felix zu Nola*, in *Römische Quartalschrift*, III, 1889, p.158. Lost mosaics in the early Christian basilica of St. Severus are superficially described by Muratori in his *Rerum Italicarum Scriptores* (I, part II, pp.293-4). They represented Our Lord with the Apostles and four Prophets below.

The basilica of St. Felix contained scenes from the Old and the New Testaments, but it is uncertain whether these were frescoes or mosaics. The mosaic of the apse showed a representation of the Trinity in which a hand symbolized God, a dove, the Holy Ghost, and a cross or a lamb, Our Saviour. The Apostles were also represented as lambs or doves. One of the lost mosaics at Santo Prisco at Capua had this same symbolical treatment (see note 82), and we have already found it at Albenga. The apse of San Clemente in Rome (see note 150), probably copying an earlier composition, is derived from an analogous scheme. The most characteristic elements of this style are not found in any of the existing mosaics of Ravenna, and it seems more probable to suppose a common place of origin in Syria or Palestine, which, during this period were in close contact with Campania and Liguria by way of the sea.

[82] Wilpert, *op.cit.*, III, Pls.74 ff.; Bertaux, *op.cit.*, I, p.50 ff.
The apse had mosaics which were destroyed in 1759. They were described and engraved by Michele Monaco in his *Sanctuarium Capuanum*, Naples, 1630.

[83] Gauckler, *Mosaïques tombales d'une chapelle de martyrs à Thabraca*, in *Mon. Piot*, III, 1897.
Also in southern Italy, a tombal mosaic found at Teano, has a crude representation of the Adoration of the Magi with St. Peter and St. Paul, showing that the custom of thus adorning sarcophagi, common in northern Africa and Spain, was not unknown in Italy itself (Toesca, *op.cit.*, I, p.207 and note 73).

[84] Mary Berenson, *A Modern Pilgrimage*, London and New York, 1933.

[85] Marg. Van Berchem, *The Mosaics of the Dome of the Rock and of the Great Mosque at Damascus* (transl. by K. A. Creswell, reprint from *ibid.*, *Early Muslim Architecture*, Oxford, 1932).
Miss Van Berchem is the first to carefully study these mosaics and publish them with comprehensive and admirable illustrations. The scanty early bibliography is not of much value. The Marquis de Vogüé in his *Temple de Jérusalem* (Paris, 1864) pointed out the great interest of the work. Mention should be made of the discussion which arose between Herzfeld (*Genesis der islamischen Kunst*, in *Der Islam*, I, 1910, pp.27 ff. p.105 ff., and II, p.235 ff.) and Strzygowski (*Felsendom und Aksamochee*, in *Der Islam*, II, p.79 ff.). Herzfeld correctly affirmed that these mosaics were based on Hellenistic traditions while Strzygowski considered them "purely Persian". For a complete analysis of the Arabic texts which mention these mosaics as well as those of Damascus and others which have disappeared see Marg. Van Berchem, *op.cit.*, pp.156-167.
We seem justified in accepting the existence of a Syro-Palestinian school of mosaicists in spite of the scanty remains—pavements excepted—which have come down to us. Mention has already been made in an early chapter of the lost mosaics of Palestine. Arab texts mention mosaics in the churches of Edessa and Lydd (Van Berchem, *op.cit.*, p.558). The Church of Mār Gabriel in the Túr Abdín (Northern Mesopotamia) has a fragment of mural mosaic: vine scrolls on a gold background, springing from a vase and framed in a border of rosettes, similar to motifs in the Dome of the Rock

(Gertrude L. Bell, *Churches and Monasteries of the Túr Abdĭn*, in *Zeitschrift für Geschichte der Architektur*, IX, p.67).

Miss Van Berchem's careful analysis of individual motifs show a predominating influence of Hellenistic and Græco-Roman traditions combined with others which are purely Eastern, such as the Sassanian crescent and the winged motif. The acanthus scrolls, for instance, are of the same type as those of the Ara Pacis from Rome, and other classical examples, and unlike those in the early mosaics of Rome and Ravenna. It is a curious fact that the thirteenth century apse of Santa Maria Maggiore at Rome shows acanthus scrolls more in the tradition of those of the Dome of the Rock.

Until the sixteenth century the outer walls of the Dome of the Rock were also covered with mosaics. These have entirely disappeared and we have only vague indications regarding them (Van Berchem, *op.cit.*, p.153).

Miss Van Berchem considers that the three series of mosaics are of one period and that the drum is not of 1027 but that this group was "more or less remade at the date of the inscription, though preserving at the same time its original composition and certain parts almost intact."

[86]Eustache de Lorey, *Les mosaïques du VIIIe siècle de la mosquée des Omeiyades à Damas,* in *Cahiers d'art,* IV, 1929; *ibid, A Novel Aspect of Byzantine Art of the Eighth Century; ibid, Mosaics in the Mosque of the Omayyads at Damascus,* in *Parnassus,* May, 1930; *ibid, The Mosaics of the Mosque of the Omayyads at Damascus,* in *Syria,* 1931; E. Kühnel, *Die Mosaiken der Omayadenmoschee in Damaskus,* in *Il Cicerone,* November, 1929; *Les ceramiques de la mosquée des Omeiyades,* in *Art et décoration,* Paris, 1929; Marg. van Berchem, *art., Damascus,* in *Mon. Piot,* 1930, and *op.cit.,* p.230; G. Migeon, *Les mosaïques de la grande mosquée de Damas,* in *Rev. archéol.,* 1929; M. Chamot, *Damascus Mosaics,* in Apollo, 1931.

Other fragments of mosaics had already been known before de Lorey's recent discoveries, both in the arcades of the court and in the interior of the mosque. These are enumerated by Miss Van Berchem who studied them in 1927 (*op.cit.*, p.231). In 1893 a disastrous fire severely damaged those which still existed in the interior. One of the most important is the fragment enframing the windows of the north transept which shows trees and buildings in the style of the Barada panel already described.

[87]Marg. van Berchem, *op.cit.*, p.230.

[88]Mary Berenson, *op.cit.*, p.162.

[89]The bibliographical references under note 22 also apply to the following Roman mosaics.

[90]The Latin reads:
    AVREA CONCISIS SVRGIT PICTVRA METALLIS

ET COMPLEXA SIMVL CLAVDITVR IPSA DIES
FONTIBVS E NIVEIS CREDAS AVRORA SVBIRE
CORREPTAS NVBES RORIBVS ARVA RIGANS
VEL QVALEM INTER SIDERA LVCEM PROFERET IRIM
PVRPVREVSQVE PAVO IPSE COLORE NITENS
QVI POTVIT NOCTIS VEL LVCIS REDDERE FINEM
MARTYRVM E BVSTIS HINC REPPVLIT ILLE CHAOS
SVRSVM VERSA QUOD CVNCTIS CERNITVR VNO
PRÆ SVL HONORIVS HÆC VOTA DICATA DEDIT
VESTIBVS ET FACTIS SIGNANTVR ILLIVS ORA
LVCET ET ASPECTV LVCIDA CORDA GERENS

[91] The figures of saints on the walls resemble the figures in the panel of St. Demetrius and the Founders at Salonika which may be a century earlier. The Latin inscription is as follows:

MARTVRIBVS X̄P̄Ī D̄N̄Ī PIA VOTA IOHANNES
REDDIDIT ANTISTES SANCTIFICANTE D̄Ō
AC SACRI FONTIS SIMILI FVLGENTE METALLO
PROVIDVS INSTANTER HOC COPVLAVIT OPVS
QVO QVISQVIS GRADIENS ET X̄P̄M PRONVS ADORANS
EFFVSASQVE PRECES MITTIT AD AETHRA SVAS

[92] E. Müntz, *L'oratoire du pape Jean VII*, in *Revue archéologique*, 1877; A. Bartolo, *Un frammento inedito dei musaici vaticani di Giovanni VII*, in *Bollettino d'arte*, 1907.

[93] *Bibl. vaticane, ms. Barberini*, 50, p.89 and pp.90-91.

[94] *Op.cit.*, III, Pl.XXIII.

[95] For the general bibliography of St. Sophia see note 112. Diehl (*Mon. Piot*, 1909, p.39 ff.) dates the cross as early as the fifth or the sixth century and the Virgin at the close of the eighth. The Greek inscriptions are discussed by Dalton (*op.cit.*, p.376) who also gives additional bibliography. Among the names contained in six cruciform monograms inscribed in circles on the north and south walls of the bema are those of Constantine VI and his mother Irene. The date would thus be not far from 785, and the Virgin in the apse would have replaced the cross upon the downfall of the iconoclasts.

[96] See general references under note 22. The most recent and authoritative criticism is that of Toesca, *op.cit.*, I, p.394 ff.

[97] Alemanni, *De Lateranensibus Parientinis restitutis*, Rome, 1625, with an appendix, Rome, 1756.

Below the scene on the right is the inscription:

BEATE PETRE DONAS̄ VITA LEON. PP. ET BICTO̅
RIA CAROLO REGI DON̄AS.

At the base of the apse is:
>   DOCETE OMNES GENTSE VAPIZANTES EOS IN NOMINE
> PATRIS ET FILII ET SPIRITVS SCS ET ECCE EGO VOBISCVM
> SVM OMNIBVS DIEBVS VSQVE AD CONSVMATIONEM SECVLI

On the arch is another inscription:
>   GLORIA IN EXCELSIS DEO ET IN TERRA PAX OMNIBVS
>   BONE BOLNVTATIS

[98] *Op.cit.*, II, Pl.XL. This is also reproduced in Alemani, *op.cit.*, p.10. On the left of Our Lord were the Virgin, St. Peter, St. Susannah and the Pope, on the right, SS. Paul, Caius, Gubinus and Charlemagne. See, also, article *Charlemagne*, in Cabrol, *Dictionnaire d'archéologie, chrétienne et de liturgie*, Paris, 1909.

For the lost mosaics of San Martino ai Monti see Van Marle, *op.cit.*, I, p.102 for additional references. These were ordered by Pope Sergius II, 844-847, and included a Virgin surrounded by saints and other holy personages carrying their emblems.

[99] *Musaici cristiani*, p.28.

[100] E. Müntz in *Revue archéol.*, XXVIII, 1874, p. 172 ff.; Baldoria, *La cappella del Zenone a Santa Prassede in Roma*, in *Archivio storico dell'arte*, IV, 1891.

At the base of the apse is the inscription:
>   EMICAT AVLA PIAE VARIS DECORATA METALLIS
>   PRAXEDIS DNO SVPER AETHRA PLACENTIS HON ORE
>   PONTIFICIS SVMMI STVDIO PASCHALIS ALVMNI
>   SEDIS APOSTOLICAE PASSIM QUI CORPORA CONDENS
>   PLVRIMA SCORVM SVBTER HAEC MOENIA PONIT
>   FRETVS VT HIS LIMEN MEREATVR ADIRE POLORVM

The general references for this and the three following Roman mosaics in Santa Maria in Domnica, Santa Cecilia and San Marco will be found under note 22.

At Santa Maria in Domnica the inscription at the base of the apse reads:
>   ISTA DOMVS PRIDEM FVERAT CONFRACTA RVINIS
>   NVNC RVTILAT IVGITER VARIIS DECORATA METALLIS
>   ETDECVS ECCE SVVS SPLENDET CEN PHOEBVS IN ORBE
>   QVI POST FVRVA FVGANS TETRAE VELAMINA NOCTIS
>   VIRGO MARIA TIBI PASCHALIS PRAESVL HONESTVS
>   CONDIDIT HANC AVLAM LAETVS PER SAECLA MANENDAM

At Santa Cecilia the inscription extolling the work of Paschal is as follows:
>   HAEC DOMVS AMPLA MICAT VARIIS FABRICATA METALLIS
>   OLIM QVAE FVERAT CONFRACTA SVB TEMPORE PRISCO
>   CONDIDIT IN MELIVS PASCHALIS PRAESVL OPIMVS

HANC AVLAM DNI FORMANS FVNDAMINE CLARO
AVREA GEMMATIS RESONANT HAEC DINDIMA TEMPLI
LAETVS AMORE DEI HIC CONIVNXIT CORPORA SANCTA
CAECILAE ET SOCIIS RVTILAT HIC FLORE IVVENTVS
QVAE PRIDEM IN CRYPTIS PAVSABANT MEMBRA BEATA
ROMA RESVLTAT OVANS SEMPER ORNATA PER AEVVM.

[101] *Op.cit.*, II, Pls. 51 and 52.

[102] Prévost, *La basilique de Théodulfe et la paroisse de Germigny-des-Prés*, Orleans, 1889; Van Berchem and Clouzot, *op.cit.*, p.223 ff. For an account of the church before the unfortunate modern restorations see G. Bouet, *L'église de Germigny-des-Prés*, in *Bulletin Monumentale*, 1868.

[103] For bibliography for mediæval French pavements in mosaic see C. Enlart, *Manuel d'archéologie francaise*, Paris, 1919, vol. I, p. CIV. See, also, H. Woodruff, *Iconography and Date of the Mosaics of La Daurade*, in *Art Bulletin*, March, 1931.

[104] Didron, *Manuel d'iconographie chrétienne*, Paris, 1845. For a brilliant resumé of this new iconography see Diehl, *Manuel*, II, p.484 ff. There is a mine of information in Millet's *Recherches sur l'iconographie de l'Évangile*, Paris, 1916. For the importance of Byzantium in the formation of the new style see Bertaux, *La part de Byzance dans l'art byzantin*, in *Journal des Savants*, 1911, pp.164 and 304.

[105] The texts of Mesarites and Constantine the Rhodian may be found in Heisenberg, *Grabeskirche und Apostelkirche; zwei Basiliken Konstantins*, Leipzig, 1908; see, also, Salzenberg, *Altarchristliche Baudenkmaler von Konstantinopel*, Berlin, 1854, and Ebersolt, *Constantinople byzantin et les voyageurs du Levant*, Paris, 1919, and Heisenberg, *Die alten Mosaiken der Apostelkirche und der Hagia Sophia*, in Ξένια of the National University of Greece, 1912.

[106] Dalton, *op. cit.*, p. 384; Smirnof, *Mosaics of Cyprus*, in *Vizantieski Vremenik*, IV, 1897, pp. 1-93; T. I. Schmidt, *Panagia Angelokistos*, in *Izvestia*, XV, 1911, p. 217. The mosaics are reproduced from Smirnof's photographs in Diehl, *Justinien*, Paris, 1901, Figs. 125, 126, 127. It is possible that these mosaics existed as early as the sixth century and that as venerated images they withstood the vicissitudes of the centuries and were incorporated in buildings of a later date. In this case analogies with later mosaics would be explained by restoration.

[107] Dalton, *op.cit.*, p.393; Diehl, *Manuel*, II, p.509 ff.; *ibid*, *L'église et les mosáiques de Saint-Luc en Phocide*, Paris, 1889; *ibid*, in *Monuments Piot*, III, 1897; *ibid*, in *Études byzantines*, Paris, 1905, p.382 ff.; R. W. Schultz and S. H. Barnsley, *The Monastery of St. Luke in Stiris in Phocis*, London, 1901; Th. Schmidt, *The Mosaics of the Monastery of Saint Luke* (in Russian), Kharkof, 1914. Muratoff, *op.cit.*, p.100.

The most recent work on the Grecian mosaics is: Ernst Diez and Otto Demus, *Byzantine Mosaics in Greece, Hosios Lucas and Daphni*, Cambridge, Mass., 1931, which contains colored illustrations of the more important subjects.

[108] See B. Lieb, *Rome, Kiev et Byzance a la fin du XIe siecle*, Paris, 1924.

[109] Dalton, *op.cit.*, p.394 ff.; Diehl, *Manuel*, II, p.513; D. Ainaloff and E. Rieden, *Ancient Monuments of Art in Kiev; the Cathedral of Santa Sophia* (in Russian), Kharkoff, 1899 (illustrated); the same author's earlier work, *The Cathedral of Santa Sophia at Kiev*, Leningrad, 1899, without illustrations serves as text to the fine plates of Th. Solntseff published by the *Imperial Russian Archæological Society of St. Petersburg* between 1871 and 1887 under the title of *Antiquities of the Russian Empire*; Th. Schmidt, *The Basilica of Santa Sophia at Kiev* (in Russian), Moscow, 1914; D. Ainaloff, *Die Mosaiken des Michaelsklosters in Kiew*, in *Belvedere*, 1926, p. I ff.; Diez and Demus, *op.cit.*, p.III.

[110] Dalton, *op.cit.*, p.388; Diehl, *Manuel*, II, p.520; *ibid, Études byzantines*, p.353 ff.; O. Wulff, *Die Komesiskirche in Nicäa und ihre Mosaiken*, Strasbourg, 1903; Th. Schmidt, *Die Koimesis-Kirche von Nikaia*, Berlin and Leipzig, 1927 (thirty-five plates).

These mosaics disappeared either during or after the Greek occupation of a few years ago.

[111] An article by Th. Schmidt in *Izvestia* has not yet appeared but his conclusions are in a note in *Byzantinische Zeitschrift*, XXV, p.260. He gives to the seventh, or possibly the sixth century the two beautiful angels on the curve of the arch preceding the apse, dates the Madonna of the apse after 787, and the narthex in the eleventh century. Schmidt's explorations included the uncovering of two fine mosaic icons of Christ and the Virgin. All of this work was already much damaged in 1921 by the Turks and now practically nothing remains.

[112] Dalton, *op.cit.*, p.374 ff.; Diehl, *Manuel*, II, p.521, and in *Monuments Piot*, XVI, 1909; Diehl, Le Tourneau and Saladin, *op.cit.*, p.117 ff.; J. I. Smirnof, *Mosaics of St. Sophia, Salonika*, in *Viz Vrem.*, V, 1898 (Russian); Muratoff, *op.cit.*, p.96.

[113] Dalton, *op.cit.*, p.396; Diehl, *Manuel*, II, p.518; Strzygowski, *Nea Moni auf Chios*, in *Byzantinische Zeitschrift*, V, 1896, p.145; O. Wulff, *Die Mosaiken der Nea Moni von Chios*, in *ibid*, XXV, 1925, pp. 115-143; Diez and Demus, *op.cit.*; A. C. Orlandos, *Monuments byzantins de Chios*, Athens, 1931.

[114] Dalton, *op.cit.*, p.398; Diehl, *Manuel*, II, 524; Perdrizet and Chesnay, *La metropole de Serres*, in *Monuments Piot*, X, 1904; Diez and Demus, *op.cit.*, p.116, would date this mosaic in the thirteenth century.

[115] See Dalton, *op.cit.*, p.398, for other earlier references.

[116] A. Venturi, *Storia,* II, p.416 ff.; A. L. Frothingham, *Les mosaïques de Grottaferrata,* in *Gazette archéologique,* 1883, p.335 ff.; Baumstark, *Il musaico degli apostoli nella chiesa di Grottaferrata,* in *Oriens Christianus,* IV, 1904. Toesca (*op.cit.*, III, p.927) attributes the mosaic of the Pentecost to the end of the twelfth century.

[117] Dalton, *op.cit.*, p.396; Diehl, *Manuel,* II, p.524 ff., G. Millet, *Les mosaïques de Daphni,* in *Monuments Piot,* III, 1897 and *ibid, Le monastère de Daphni,* Paris, 1899; E. Bertaux, *Les mosaïques de Daphni,* in *Gazette des Beaux-Arts,* 1901; Diez and Demus, *op.cit.;* Muratoff. *op.cit.*, p.101 seq.

[118] According to the description of Quaresimus (*Elucidatio Terrae sanctae,* Rome, 1639, II, p.645 ff.) the Tree of Jesse would seem to have been quite Western in character, showing the inspiration of the Crusaders. It resembled those French conceptions of the middle of the twelfth century, perhaps inspired by the abbot Suger, such as the windows of St. Denis and Chartres (see E. Mâle, *L'Art religieux du XIIe siècle en France*). Ciampini in his *De Sacris Aedeficiis a Constantino mago constructis,* Rome, 1693, Pl. XXXIII, shows an engraving of the north side of the nave with its arrangement. De Vogüé was the pioneer of modern research and gives a detailed description of the mosaics in his *Les Églises de la Terre Sainte,* Paris, 1860. Monographs on the church which also deal with the mosaics are: Weir Schultz, *The Church of the Nativity at Bethlehem,* London, 1910; Wiegand, *Die Gebürtskirche in Bethlehem,* Leipzig, 1911; Vincent and Abel, *Bethlehem,* Paris, 1914; A. Baumstark, *Palestinensia,* in *Römische Quartalschrift,* 1906, pp. 143-149, 157-188.

[119] De Vogüé, *Le temple de Jérusalem,* p.101 ff.; Dalton, *op.cit.*, p.415.

[120] Dalton, *op.cit.*, p.430, gives a nearly complete list of existing portative mosaics. See, also, E. Müntz, *Les mosaïques byzantines portatives,* in *Bulletin monumental,* Caen, 1886, vol.52; D. Talbot Rice, *New Light on Byzantine Portative Mosaics,* in Apollo, 1933.

[121] There are good general accounts of the Sicilian mosaics in the works of Diehl, Dalton, Venturi and Van Marle already cited. The most recent and authoritative account is that of Toesca, *op.cit.*, II, p.940 ff. See, also, Diehl, *L'art byzantin dans l'Italie méridionale,* Paris, 1894, and Salazaro, *Monumenti dell'arte meridionale d'Italia,* Naples, 1882; Muratoff, *op.cit.,* p.111 *seq.*

[122] Tchukareff in *Proceedings of the Russian Imperial Archæological Society,* New Series, IV, pp.50-67 (Russian).

[123] Terzi, Amari, and Cavallari, *La Cappella di S. Pietro nella reggia di Palermo,* Palermo, 1889. A. A. Pavlovsky, *Iconographie de la chapelle palatine,* Paris, 1895 and *ibid,* in *Revue archéologique,* XXV, 1894.

[124]Gravina, *Il Duomo di Monreale,* Palermo, 1859 *et seq.;* Serradifalco, *Il Duomo di Monreale,* Palermo, 1838.

[125]See Venturi, *op.cit.,* II, p.408. A fragment of mosaic now in the Museum of Syracuse, representing a lion under a tree, may possibly have belonged to a similar kind of decoration. This is composed of oblong tesseræ.

[126]Dalton, *op.cit.,* p.406; Toesca, *op.cit.,* III, note 32, p.1031.

[127]Venturi, *op.cit.,* II, p. 414-16 and pp. 429-31; Van Marle, *op.cit.,* I. p. 137; Bertaux, *op.cit.,* p.190. Fragments of mosaics, now under the roof, show symbols of the Evangelists. Toesca (*op.cit.,* III, note 32, p.1032) dates the mosaic on the façade as of the thirteenth century on account of the rather Gothic character of the inscription, but it would seem to be at least as early as the twelfth century.

[128]Venturi, *op.cit.,* II, p.416.

The apse of the Cathedral had a mosaic which was engraved by Ciampini (*op.cit.*) and represented the Madonna with SS. Peter, Stephen, Paul and Agatha, with two Prophets on the spandrels and a medallion containing Our Lord above.

A small ruined mosaic above the portal of Santa Maria Libera at Aquino seems to be of the middle of the twelfth century and in the usual Byzantine style. The church of Santa Lucia at Gaeta had a mosaic of the Virgin and Child long since lost.

[129]Van Marle, *op.cit.,* V, p.316; W. Rolffs, *Geschichte der Malerei Neapels,* Leipzig, 1910, p.41; A. Sorrentino, *art.cit.;* E. Müntz, in *Revue archéol.,* I, 1883, p.20; F. Hermanin, *Gli affreschi di Pietro Cavallini a Santa Cecilia in Trastevere,* in *Gallerie naz.ital.,* V, Rome, 1902; Venturi, *Storia,* V, p.634. Although the decoration of the throne shows that Lello was familiar with Roman work, his style, especially the treatment of the drapery in thin, clinging folds, is typically Florentine of the early fourteenth century.

[130]Much of the extensive early bibliography on St. Mark's has been superseded or incorporated in later criticism. The best general accounts are in O. Wulff, *op.cit.;* Venturi, *op.cit.,* II, p.418 ff.; Dalton, *op.cit.,* p.399; Van Marle, *op.cit.,* I, p.231 ff. The most recent authoritative accounts are in Diehl, *Manuel,* II, p.536 ff. and Toesca, *op.cit.,* II, p.950 ff. P. Saccardo's *Les Mosaïques de Saint-Marc,* Venice, 1897, contains all the material to be found on the mosaics which was incorporated in Ongania's voluminous work, *La basilica di San Marco,* Venice, 1878-1893, and is still the most complete monograph on the subject.

G. and L. Kreutz, *La basilica di San Marco,* Venice, 1843, is an early standard work now largely out of date. See, also, S. Biessel in *Zeitschrift für christlichen Kunst,* 1893, p.231 ff.; C. Neumann, *Die Markuskirche in Venedig,* in *Preussische Jahrbuch,* 1892; L. Testi, *Storia della pittura ven-*

eziana, Bergamo, 1909 (for references to documentary evidence); C. Bricarelli in *Civiltá cattolica,* 1915, p.147 ff. (for the numerous restorations). A. Robertson's *The Bible of St. Mark's,* London, 1898, is a handbook containing a complete list of all the subjects and their arrangement but with no critical analysis.

There is a forthcoming monograph on these mosaics by Otto Demus (*Die Mosaiken von San Marco in Venedig,* Vienna-Leipzig).

See, also, G. Gombosi, *Il più antico ciclo di mosaici di San Marco,* in *Dedalo,* 1933; O. Demus, *Über einige venezianische Mosaiken des 13 jahrhunderts,* in *Belvedere,* 1931; Muratoff, *op.cit.,* p.108 seq.

[131]*Op.cit.*II, p.951. Constant restorations, even earlier than the Renaissance, make it doubly hard to date these mosaics with precision. The Gethsemane scenes from the life of Christ are so similar in style to the Genesis of the narthex that they should be included with the thirteenth-century work of these craftsmen, and with them, others, such as the Finding of the Body of St. Mark in the right arm of the church.

[132]Gombosi (*art.cit.*), contrary to general opinion, considers that the mosaics in the tribune to the right of the organ, representing the legend of St. Mark, are the oldest in the church and that they are far removed from Byzantine canons. He compares them with certain contemporary pavements in Piedmont and with certain miniatures. He thinks that the Byzantine style of the cupolas which culminates in the Passion scenes on the triumphal arch, is later.

[133]J. J. Tikkanen, *Die Genesismosaiken von San Marco in Venedig,* Helsingfors, 1889; *ibid* in *Acta Societatis scientiarum Fennicæ,* Helsingfors, 1889, XVII, p.207 ff. and in *Archivo storico dell'arte,* 1888, fasc. VI, p.212, VII, p.257 and IX, p.348.

The mosaic decoration of the ciborium in the cathedral of Parenzo is so similar in style to these narthex mosaics that it would seem to have been derived from them.

Although it is beyond our scope to describe the purely decorative mosaics of St. Mark's, carried out during the thirteenth and fourteenth centuries when the exterior received its revetment of precious marbles and sculptures, we may take as an example of this very characteristic and exquisite Venetian style, the arch above the portal of Sant' Alipio. Here, there is a combination of sculpture in relief with panels of mosaic. Delicate borders of spiny acanthus leaves are silhouetted against a background of gold tesseræ; typical Byzantine emphasis upon contrasts of light and shade is here developed into an original style.

Outside of St. Mark's the only other early mosaic in Venice is a small

Madonna and Child in the Byzantine manner of the twelfth century, now in a tabernacle in the sacristy of Santa Maria della Salute.

In the Czartoryski Museum at Krakow there is a head of an Apostle which is very Venetian in character. It appears to be of the thirteenth or the fourteenth century and may have originally come from St. Mark's.

[134]Dalton, *op.cit.*, p.401; Diehl, *Manuel*, II, p.544 ff.; Venturi, *op.cit.*, II, p.428 ff.; Saccardo, *op.cit.*, p.19; Toesca, *op.cit.*, II, p.953 ff.; Galassi, *op.cit.*, p.190 ff.; L. Conton, *Torcello*, Venice, 1927; A. Renan in *Gazette des Beaux-Arts*, XXXVIII, 1888, p.407 ff.; B. Schultz, *Die Kirchenbauten auf der Insel Torcello*, Berlin, 1927. Saccardo (*op.cit.*, p.21) dated these in the eighth century. All of the mosaics of Torcello have been frequently and badly restored; the whole upper zone of the Last Judgment was entirely reset and certain fragments scattered, including a head which is now in the Castello at Milan.

An inscripttion found under the altar proves that the Duomo of Torcello was erected by order of Isaac, the Exarch of Ravenna, in 639. (See V. Lazzarini, *Una inscrizione Torcellana del secolo VII*, in *Atti del R. Istituto Veneto di Scienze, Lettere ed Arti*, 1914.) Galassi (*op.cit.*, p.190 ff.) thinks that the vault dates from this period, although it was almost entirely made over in the twelfth century, and that like the work of Parenzo and Pola, it is a direct off-shoot of Ravenna. He also considers that the four Church Fathers in the lateral apse date from the ninth century, showing the influence of Ravenna, but that these, also, were almost entirely restored in the twelfth century.

[135]See P. Jessen, *Die Darstellung des Weltgerichts bis auf Michelangelo*, Berlin, 1883 and G. Voss, *Das jüngste Gericht in der bildenden Kunst des fruhen Mittelalters*, in *Beitrage zur Kunstgeschichte*, VIII, Leipzig, 1884, pp. 48-52.

[136]K. v. Haas, *Die Mosaiken im Dom von Triest*, Vienna, 1859; G. Clausse, *Basiliques et mosaïques chrétiennes*, Paris, 1893.

[137]G. Gerola in *Felix Ravenna*, 1912, V. p.177 ff.; Galassi, *op.cit.*, p.250 ff. The engraving of 1741 is from a now lost drawing by the architect Buonamici and is contained in G. L. Amadesi, *Metropolitana di Ravenna*, Bologna, 1748, and reproduced by Gerola (*art.cit.*), and Galassi (*op.cit.*, Fig. 144). In the apse itself was the Resurrection in three scenes; in the zone below, the Madonna, three saints, and two scenes from the life of Sant'Apollinare; in the lowest zone a row of the early bishops of Ravenna. On the arch was Christ in a mandorla bearing the cross, flanked by two angels, the Virgin, and the Apostles. In the spandrels below were two scenes from the life of Sant'Apollinare, two figures offering lambs, and two palm trees. Galassi (*op.cit.*, p.251 and note 9, p.301) thinks that this work is a direct continuation of the school of Ravenna, but Toesca (*op.cit.*, p.953) con-

siders that it was probably executed by Venetian artists. Another proof of the spread of Venetian influence at this time is the head of a Madonna (about 1135), now in the *sala capitolare* of the Cathedral of Ferrara, a fragment remaining from work carried out in the church. (Cf.Toesca, *op.cit.*, note 21, p.1028.)

[138] Venturi, *op.cit.*, II, p.431; Van Marle, *op.cit.*, I, p.239; Toesca, *op.cit.*, II, p.950; *ibid, La pittura e la miniatura nella Lombardia*, p.128 ff. The throne of Our Lord is very similar in style to the thrones of the Virgin and St. John the Baptist in the "scarsella" of the Florentine Baptistery; both developed from the same Venetian source.

Fragments of this apse which were removed during restorations have been preserved. One, the head of St. Proteus, is now in the Castello Sforzesco at Milan, and the other, a head of St. Martin, is in the Museo Cristiana at Brescia. These heads seem to be earlier than the actual mosaic, perhaps as early as the ninth or tenth century, but the apse as we now have it, allowing for restorations, was probably the work of the eleventh and twelfth century Venetian school.

[139] Venturi, *op.cit.*, V, p.217 ff.; Dalton, *op.cit.*, p.412; Van Marle, *op.cit.*, I, p.262; C. Soulier, *Les influences orientales dans la peinture toscane*, Paris, 1924, pp. 118-147; Toesca, *op.cit.*, II, p.1001 ff.; Pératé in *Les Arts*, Feb., 1908, p.8 ff.; R. Davidsohn, *Forschungen zu Geschichte von Florenz*, Berlin, 1896; A. Cocchi, *Le chiese di Firenze*, Florence, 1903; K. Frey in G. Vasari, *Le Vite*, Munich, 1911, I, p.328 ff. (the last three for documentary evidence and successive restorations).

Toesca, who has had an opportunity to observe the mosaics carefully at close range, classifies them as follows: the decoration at the top of the dome is by Fra Jacopo or a similar master; a part of the angelic hierarchy below is by a master working in the more "violent" style of St. Mark's with strong contrasts of light and shade; other figures, including the Christ, the Seraphim and the Dominations are by a weaker hand. The colossal Christ of the Last Judgment shows a more rigid treatment of the usual Byzantine formula. The angels with symbols of the Passion, to the right of Our Lord are in a more graceful style. The Inferno shows still another artisan who founds his style upon a more popular Byzantine manner with an original use of color. Two different craftsmen may be especially distinguished among a number who must have worked upon the Old and New Testament scenes. One, in the life of Christ, shows a strong sense of color, but confuses and complicates the usual Byzantine scheme with little feeling for form or space, and he may be compared with the supposed Gaddo Gaddi who executed the Coronation of the Virgin over the portal of the Duomo. The other, in certain scenes from the life of the Baptist, shows a strong feeling for line and the portrayal of emotion, and, in fact, exhibits so many of those qualities which we associate with the art of Cimabue, that we may presume that Cimabue actually worked here. The head from the Birth of St. John may well be by his own hand. It seems probable that he must have already had a reputation as a mosaicist at Florence before he was called to work upon the apse at Pisa.

Salmi in a recent article (*I mosaici del "Bel San Giovanni" e la pittura del secolo XIV a Firenze*, in *Dedalo*, February, 1931) points out striking examples of the influence of the mosaics upon contemporary painters, and agrees with Toesca in seeing the hand of Cimabue in scenes from the life of the Baptist and also in the scene of Joseph sold by his brethren.

Alfred Nicholson (*Cimabue*, Princeton, 1931, p.26) does not consider that Cimabue actually worked here, although he thinks that the head of Zacharias "and especially that of the youth in the Birth of John show more than the usual Byzantine approximations of Cimabue's style." F. J. Mather, Jr. (*The Isaac Master etc.*, Princeton, 1932) has attempted to reconstruct the work of Gaddo Gaddi. He sees sufficient stylistic analogies between many of the narrative scenes and the Prophets below the windows of the Baptistery, the Coronation of the Virgin in the Florentine Duomo, the frescoes by the so-called Isaac Master in the Upper Church at Assisi, and the lower series of mosaics on the façade of Santa Maria Maggiore at Rome, to attribute all of these to one hand, and following Vasari's statements in regard to the Baptistery and Santa Maria Maggiore, he gives them all to Gaddo Gaddi.

Berenson (*Italian Pictures of the Renaissance*, Oxford. 1932) in accord with Toesca and Salmi, attributes a part of the Birth of John in the Baptistery to Cimabue.

[140] Milanesi in his edition of *Le Vite di Vasari*, Florence, 1878-85, I, p.339 ff. discusses the difference between this Fra Jacopo of 1225 and Jacopo Torriti who worked in Rome towards the end of the century. See, also, R. Davidsohn, *Das älteste Werk der Franciscaner-Kunst*, in *Repertorium für Kunstwissenschaft*, XXII, 1899, p.315 ff.

[141] For Andrea Tafi see Vasari's life of the same in Milanesi, *op.cit.*, I, p.331 ff. and for the names of other mosaic workers discussed by Milanesi see *ibid*, I, p.343, note 2, and G. Richa, *Notizie istoriche delle chiese fiorentine*, Florence, 1754, V, p.XLII.

[142] E. F. Rothschild and E. H. Wilkins, *Hell in the Florentine Baptistery and in Giotto's Paduan Fresco*, in *Art Studies*, 1928.

[143] E. H. Wilkins, *Dante and the Mosaics of His "bel San Giovanni"*, in *Speculum*, II, 1927. The lively, popular style of these figures, with a tendency to caricature, was not unknown in later Byzantine art and Toesca compares

them with the miniatures of a John Climax manuscript in the Vatican (*Bibl. Vatic., Cod. vat. gr. 394*). It is one phase of the later Byzantine style, which in general, in its fondness for expressive and contrasting line, light and shade, and violent emotion, had much influence upon Cimabue. The right-hand group of figures in Cimabue's great Crucifixion at Assisi have points in common with these figures of the Baptistery Inferno.

[144] Vasari (Milanesi), I, p. 346. Mather (*op.cit.*, p.59) thinks that fifteen of the Prophets are in the style of Andrea Tafi and his school and that the remaining twenty-one are by Gaddo Gaddi, but there does not seem to be any marked stylistic difference between the two groups.

[145] Van Marle, *op.cit.*, I, p.275. As we have already mentioned, we may trace the style of this artist in certain scenes from the life of Christ in the Baptistery, and resemblances between this work and some of the later scenes from the life of the Baptist seem to me to be even more striking, as, for example, the figures of the king and queen in the St. John before Herod. Mather (*op.cit.*, p.46) ascribes this Coronation to Gaddo Gaddi and dates it not later than 1290. He gives the interesting suggestion that it may have been done for the old cathedral of Santa Reparata and moved to its present position in 1357 when the west front of the old cathedral was demolished. He sees fractures where it was carefully broken into four pieces; one for the two heads, one for each body, and one for the four angels at the left.

[146] Van Marle, *op.cit.*, I, pp.262 and 271; L. Dami, *La basilica di S. Miniato al Monte*, in *Bollettino d'arte*, 1915; Soulier, *op.cit.*, p.148. The figure of Christ in the center has suffered less than the work at the sides.

[147] Van Marle, *op.cit.*, I, p.275; Soulier, *op.cit.*, p.149; Salmi (*art.cit.*, p.554 ff.) would date this mosaic soon after the middle of the century, and associates it with the Guelfs who were expelled from Florence in 1247 and settled in the "borgo" of San Frediano where they were responsible for the construction of a portico in front of the church. In any case it may be considered a direct Florentine importation. The Gothic arches on the throne would place it at least as late as the middle of the century, and the iconography may show local influence, as an Ascension was executed about this time over the central portal of San Martino, probably by the sculptor Guido da Como. The Christ and the angels are much finer than the groups of Apostles and the style has analogies with the angelic hierarchy in the upper part of the Florentine cupola. The Apostles are more hastily done and show the effects of the restoration of 1829, but they still bear striking resemblances to the groups of seated Apostles of the Last Judgment at Florence. A figure of the Virgin must have occupied the space

between the two groups, destroyed when the Gothic window was cut through.

[148]G. Trenta, *I musaici del duomo di Pisa e i loro autori*, Florence, 1896; Venturi, *op.cit.*, V. p.217 ff.; Van Marle, *op.cit.*, I, p.454; Toesca, *op.cit.*, II, p.1003 ff.; Soulier, *op.cit.*, p.151; Nicholson, *op.cit.*, p.45 ff.; Mather, *op.cit.*, p.65 ff.; R. Papini, *Pisa*, Rome, 1912.

Cimabue was in Pisa in 1301 working together with the Luccan, Giovanni di Apparecchiato on a *maestá* of the Madonna for the church of Santa Chiara. From 1302 to 1303 he executed the figure of St. John in the cathedral apse. A certain Francesco da San Simone di Porta a Mare, perhaps a Florentine, who with the aid of others had already worked on the apse in 1300, completed the Christ of the center in a rather dry Byzantine manner (see L. Tanfani Centofanti, *Notizie di artisti da documenti pisani*, Pisa, 1902, p.186). Salmi (*art.cit.*, note 23) would identify this artist with the Francesco who on May 14th, 1298 was "maestro dell'opera del mosaico" at the Florentine Baptistery and received an order from the Consuls of the Arte di Calimala not to work for the duration of their consulship (Frey in *Vasari, op.cit.*, p.330).

Although the St. John has been very generally accepted as by Cimabue, Richter (*Lectures in the National Gallery*, London, 1898) says "but for the evidence of the above mentioned document, no one would now dream of ascribing the work in its present condition (especially the St. John, a most interesting figure) to any great master." Nicholson, however, who has recently studied the mosaic agrees with the consensus of opinion that it is not greatly restored and that it "is in every way characteristic of Cimabue."

The Assumption of the right transept is in fairly good condition although it has been shortened at the base. The Madonna is holding her girdle and there must have been a St. Thomas to receive it. The Annunciation shows restoration but not enough to change the style of the work Papini (*op.cit.*, p.52) ascribes both mosaics to the school of Siena. Venturi (*Storia*, V, p.241 ff.) sees the influence of Giovanni Pisano. Mather (*op.cit.*, p.65) finds a strong Sienese influence which could not be before 1325 and suggests that they may be by a certain Vicino who signed the Madonna in the great apse in 1321. Finally, Berenson (*op.cit.*, p.580) attributes them to Traini.

[149]For the Roman mosaics in this chapter see the works of De Rossi, Venturi, Wilpert, and Van Marle already cited. The latest criticism may be found in Toesca, *op.cit.*, II, p.925 ff.

[150]E. Müntz in *Revue archéol.*, Sept. 1882; G. M. Zimmermann, *Giotto und die Kunst Italiens im Mittelalter*, Leipsiz, 1899, p.126. Zimmermann

would date it at the beginning of the thirteenth century but the style is much more that of the early twelfth century, and it also appears to be earlier than the apse of Santa Maria in Trastevere.

[151] Wilpert, *op.cit.*, II, p.516 ff., thinks that it was in large part copied from the original mosaic of the sixth century. The iconography has much in common with early lost mosaics in Campania (see note 82) and goes back in origin to Syria or Palestine.

[152] Ciampini, *op.cit.*, II, p.164; C. R. Morey, *op.cit.*, p.16 ff.

[153] *Musaici cristiani*, p.48; Van Marle, *op.cit.*, I, pp. 179 and 417; Toesca, *op.cit.*, III, p.927; E. Mâle, *L'art religieux en France au XIIIe siècle*, Paris, 1923, p.185, who considers that the motif of the Coronation of the Virgin was derived from France where it had such a vogue in the later Romanesque and Gothic periods. But it may possibly have been in use in Italy at a much earlier time. Torriti's Coronation in the apse of Santa Maria Maggiore may repeat an earlier theme, and there are the remains of a similar motif in the early frescoes of Santa Maria Antigua.

[154] A. Muñoz, *Frammento di mosaico a S. Bartolommeo all' Isola in Roma*, in *L'Arte*, 1904.

[155] E. Müntz in *Revue de l'art chrétien*, IX, 1898; Wilpert, *op.cit.*, II, p.549 ff. For the apse of St. Peter's see references under note 49 and Toesca, *op.cit.*, III, p.970 and note 36, p.1032. It is probable that Venetians worked on this apse as well as that of St. Paul's. Honorius III's letter to the Doge asks for two masters in addition to those already sent, and the fragments preserved at Poli are in the Byzantine-Venetian style and quite different from the earlier Roman work at Santa Maria in Trastevere. Toesca thinks that a head in the Museo Barracco at Rome, labelled "Byzantine Empress: sixth century." may be the head of the personification of the Church, who together with the Pope, was depicted as worshipping the enthroned Lamb. The style is very close to the head of the Pope preserved at Poli. The façade of St. Peter's was restored by Gregory IX, 1227-1241, and a colossal head of a saint, now in the Museo Petriano, resembling but not identical with the heads of Apostles from the apse of St. Paul's, may be a fragment of this work.

For the apse of St. Paul's see E. Müntz in *Revue de l'art chrétien*, IX, 1898; Wilpert, *op.cit.*, II, p.549 ff. The lower part shows much less restoration than the rest, particularly in the *Hetimasia* and adjacent angels where the style is similar to that of the early work at St. Mark's.

In the chapel to the left of the choir there is a small, finely executed mosaic of the Madonna and Child, very Byzantine in style and perhaps contemporary with the apse (Wilpert, *op.cit.*, p.558 and Van Marle, *op.cit.*, I, p.421).

[156] Van Marle, *Il musaico del Duomo di Spoleto*, in *Rassegna d'arte*, 1921; In the Museum of Cortona there is a mosaic of the Madonna which probably once adorned the market-place. This is a much restored and inferior work of the latter part of the twelfth century (Toesca, *op.cit.*, III, p.1014). It is possible that Solsternus was one of those Venetians who at about this time were working on the apses of Old St. Peter's and St. Paul's at Rome. This would account for the strong and rather un-Roman Byzantine style.

[157] The best general account of the work of the Cosmati may be found in A. Muñoz, *Roma di Dante*, Milan-Rome, 1921. See, also, Toesca, *op.cit.*, III, p.826 ff. and note 57 and 58, p.903, for recent bibliography and a list of monuments.

[158] P. Stanislao, *La Cappella Papale di Sancta Sanctorum*, Grottaferrata, 1919.

[159] See Van Marle, *Italian Schools*, I, p.499 for other references.

[160] *Op.cit.*, II, p.981.

[161] The work of Torriti, both as mosaicist and painter, is admirably summarized by Toesca (*op.cit.*, II, p.979 ff.) and includes the most recent bibliography concerning the artist and his school.

[162] In addition to the general references see Gerspach in *Gazette des Beaux-Arts*, Feb., 1890, and E. Müntz in *Revue archéol.*, 1879, p.109 ff.; Ph. Lauer, *Le palais du Latran*, Paris, 1911, p.212 ff.; G. Rohault de Fleury, *Le Latran au Moyen Age*, Paris, 1877, Pl.2 (for a mosaic of Our Saviour, formerly on the façade of the church, and probably by a follower of Torriti).

[163] Toesca, *op.cit.*, II, p.987 ff.; Van Marle, *Italian Schools*, I, p.490.
This is the only authentic work by Rusuti, although frescoes in the Upper Church at Assisi have been ascribed to him. If we are able to identify Rusuti with the Filippo Bizuti mentioned in documents which have now disappeared (B. Proust, *Quelques documents sur l'histoire des arts en France*, in *Gazette des Beaux-Arts*, XXV, 1887, p.358; H. Moranville, *Peintres romains pensionnairs de Phillippe le bel*, in *Bibliot. de l'École des Chartres*, XLIII, 1887, p.631) we find that in 1308 he was working in France, at Poitiers, for Philippe le Bel, together with his son Giovanni and a certain Nicolas Desmaz (De Marzi). The three artists are mentioned again in 1317, and Giovanni alone, until 1322. De Rossi's investigations (*op.cit.*) place the decoration of the façade between 1288 and 1318. The lower series of mosaics were ascribed by Vasari to Gaddo Gaddi (cf. Milanesi in *Vasari, Le Vite*, I, pp.336 and 346) but Vasari's confused account, the bad condition of the work itself, and the absence of any authentic works by Gaddi (see note 145) make it impossible to substantiate this attribution. There is not enough difference between the upper and the lower series to deny the possibility of Rusuti having supervised the whole of the work.

However, Cavalcaselle (*C. and C.* Douglas ed., II, p.24 ff.), Van Marle (*Peinture romaine,* p.221) and Mather (*op.cit.,* p.28 ff.) follow Vasari and attribute the lower series to Gaddo. Mather sees many stylistic analogies between these and the mosaics in the Florentine Baptistery, but the figures in the Baptistery mosaics are more lively and less static, more linear and less modelled and are much closer to the Byzantine-Venetian style.

[164] Mather, *op.cit.,* p.7 and Fig.13.

[165] For Pietro Cavallini see Venturi, *Storia,* V, p.141 and p.217, note 1, and *Musaici cristiani,* p.47 ff.; S. Lothrop, *Pietro Cavallini,* in *Memoirs of the American Academy in Rome,* II, 1918; Van Marle, *Italian Schools,* I, p.483 ff.; and, especially, Toesca, *op.cit.,* II, p.981 ff. and note 39 for the latest criticism of his style and additional bibliography relating to his work and influence primarily as a painter. See, also, A. Busuioceanu, *Pietro Cavallini e la pittura romana del duecento e del trecento,* in *Ephemeris Dacoromana, annuario della Scuola Romena di Roma,* III, 1925; C. R. Morey, *op.cit.,* p.48 ff. Wilpert (*op.cit.,* I, pp.628 and 756) sees no Byzantine iconography in these mosaics in spite of the fact that they follow it closely, even to details, except in a few instances, as in the Nativity, where the "taberna meritoria," interpolated below the Virgin, refers to the local legend of a fountain of oil gushing forth at the spot where the present basilica was erected.

There are two series of seventeenth-century wash drawings of these mosaics in the Vatican Library; one by Ecclissi (*Cod. Vat. Barb.,* 2010, fol. 16) and the other by A. Ciacconio (*Cod. Vat. Lat.,* 5408). There is a second set by Ecclissi in the Library at Windsor which has been published by Morey (*op.cit.*).

As the mosaics of the façade of San Paolo were ordered by Pope John XXII, 1316-1334, they would be among Cavallini's last works. There is a seventeenth-century drawing of them in the Vatican (*Cod. Vat. Lat., 5407, fol. 63*).

[166] A. Muñoz, *Reliquie artistice della vecchia basilica Vaticana a Boville Ernica,* in *Bollettino d'arte,* 1911; L. Venturi, *La Navicella di Giotto,* in *L'Arte,* 1922.

[167] There is a brief general account of the fourteenth century as a whole in Gerspach, *op.cit.,* pp.151-160.

[168] Dalton, *op.cit.,* p.416; Diehl, *Manuel,* II, p.793 ff. and in *Gazette des Beaux Arts,* 1904-5 and in *Études byzantines,* p.392 ff.; A. Leval, *Les principales mosaïques, peintures et sculptures, existant à Kahriè-Djami, à Constantinople,* Constantinople, 1886; Kondakof, *The Mosaics of the Kahriè Djami,* Odessa, 1881 (Russian); F. J. Schmitt, *Mosaics and Frescoes of the Kahriè Djami,* in *Bulletin of the Russian Archæological Institute of Constantinople,* VIII, 1902, and XI, 1906 excellent plates); *ibid, Kahriè Djami,* Sophiä,

1906; Russian); *ibid*, *La renaissance de la peinture byzantine au XVIe siècle*, in *Revue archéol.*, 1912, II; A. Muñoz, *I musaici di Kahrie-djami in Constantinopoli*, in *Rassegna italiana*, 1906; Rüdell, *Die Kahrie-Dschamisi in Konstantinopel*, Berlin, 1908; Ainaloff, *Byzantine Painting in the Fourteenth Century*, Leningrad, 1917 (Russian); *Mosaics and Frescoes in Kahriè-Djami, Constantinople, copied by Dmitri Ismailovitch*, publ. by Victoria and Albert Museum, 1928; J. Ebersolt, *Trois nouveaux fragments de mosaïques à Kahriè-Djami*, in *Rev. de l'Art Ancien et Moderne*, 1929; R. Byron, *New Mosaic in the Karieh: Dormition of the Virgin*, in *Burlington Magazine*, 1933; H. E. del Medico, *La Komésis de Kahriè Djami*, in *Rev. archéol.*, 1933; Muratoff, *op.cit.*, p.152 seq.

[169] Diehl, *Manuel*, II, p.804.

[170] Ebersolt, *Étude sur la topographie et les monuments de Constantinople*, in *Revue archéol.*, II, 1909, p.37 ff.

[171] Diehl, *Manuel*, II, p.804 ff.; Toesca, *op.cit.*, II, p.927 ff.; Saccardo, *op.cit.*, p.139 ff.; Muratoff, *op.cit.*, p.157; R. Tozzi, *I mosaici del Battistero di San Marco a Venezia e l'arte bizantina*, in *Bollettino d'arte*, 1933.

These mosaics were restored from 1867 to 1880, the Birth of St. John was entirely remade about 1628, and there are many other minor restorations from the seventeenth century onward. Fragments of the old mosaics which were replaced are now preserved in the Museo Marciano.

[172] L. Fumi, *L'Orcagna e il suo preteso mosaico nel museo di Kensington*, in *Revista d'arte*, III, 1905.

[173] Gerspach, *op.cit.*, p.160.

[174] For a general account see Gerspach, *op.cit.*, pp. 161-210.

[175] Paoletti di Oswaldo, *Raccolte di documenti inediti*, Padua, 1895; Venturi, *Storia*, VII 3, p.100; H. Thode, *Andrea Castagno in Venedig*, in *Festschrift für Otto Bendorf*, Vienna, 1898; L. Testi, *op.cit.*, II, p.13 seq.; G. Fiocco, *Michele Giambono, Venezia*, I, Milan-Rome, 1920; Van Marle, *op.cit.*, VII, p.358; Berenson (*op.cit.*, p.229) ascribes these mosaics to Giambono but considers that in the Dormition, the Christ, the Madonna, the two Apostles each side of the bier, and the medallions in the frieze, are Mantegnesque.

[176] Wilpert, *op.cit.*, I, p.340; Venturi, *Musaici cristiani*, p.57; G. Frizzoni, *Melozzo da Forli, ispiratore di una insigne opera di decorazione*, in *Bollettino d'Arte*, 1916.

[177] Gerspach, *op.cit.*, p.181 ff.; Venturi, *op.cit.*, p.58.

[178] The only complete account of these later Venetian mosaics is that of Saccardo, *op.cit.*, p.49 ff. More or less contemporary information about the seventeenth and eighteenth century mosaicists may be found in Bartolomeo Baronchello, *La Chiesa Ducale di S. Marco colle notizie del suo innalza-*

mento, spiegazione de' Mosaici ed Iscrizione etc., Venice, 1753 and A. M. Zanetti, *Della Pittura Veneziana e delle Opere pubbliche de Veneziani Maestri,* Venice, 1771.

[179]Saccardo, *op.cit.,* p.87.

[180]*Op.cit.,* p.89.

[181]*Op.cit.,* p.105 ff.

[182]See Gerspach, *op.cit.,* pp.186-210; Venturi, *op.cit.,* p.58.

[183]The best general account is still that of Gerspach, *op.cit.,* p.211 ff.; see, also, A. Blanchet, *op.cit.,* p.218 ff., and Sir Wm. B. Richmond's article, *Mosaic,* in *Encyclopedia Britannica,* XI edition.

[184]Saccardo, *op.cit.,* p.110 ff.

[185]Gerspach, *op.cit.,* p.218 ff.

[186]Gerspach, *op.cit.,* p.223 ff.

[187]E. P. Betz, *Religious Mosaics,* in *The Western Architect,* 1927.

[188]W. F. Paris, *The Mosaics in the Frontal Colonnade of the Detroit Public Library,* in *The Architectural Record,* 1921.

[189]See L. Dordoré, *Notes sur la mosaïque,* in *L'Amour de l'art,* 1928; Ch. Mauméjean, *La Mosaïque,* in *Renaissance de l'art,* 1929; R. Cogniat, *Carrelages et mosaïques,* in *Art et Décoration,* 1932.

[190]A brief account of some of the modern German and Swedish mosaics may be found in A. Hoff, *Christliche Mosaikbildkunst,* Berlin, 1927; R. Lindeman, *Zu den Mosaikbildern von Max Schwarzen und Hans Gött für den dampfer Europa,* in *Die Kunst,* 1930; W. Michel, *Kirchliche Mosaiken von Josef Eberz,* in *Deutsche Kunst. u. Dek.,* 1930; W. Witthaus, *Das Shellhaus in Hamburg; Mosaikbilder von W. Peiner in der Halle,* in *ibid,* 1931; C. G. Heise, *Mosaiken von Frans Masereel,* in *Die Kunst,* 1932. These last are Belgian.

[191]R. Fry, *Modern Mosaic and Mr. Boris Anrep,* in *Burlington Magazine,* 1923; H. Furst, *Anrep's Pavement in the National Gallery,* in *Apollo,* 1929; *ibid, Boris Anrep and His Mosaics,* in *Artwork,* 1929; E. Hutton, *Mosaics in Westminster Cathedral,* in *Burlington Magazine,* 1934; *Mosaic Pavement in the East Vestibule of the National Gallery, London, by Boris Anrep,* in *the Architectural Review,* 1930; R. Maccoll, *Modern Life in Mosaic: Boris Anrep at the National Gallery,* in *Creative Art,* May, 1930

[192]See G. A. Wagner, *Mosaic, Its Material and Technique,* in *The Western Architect,* 1927 and A. E. Floegel and K. Reid, *The Design and Application of Mosaic,* in *Pencil Points,* 1927.

BIBLIOGRAPHY

The bibliography includes all works and articles in periodicals consulted with the exception of some general books of reference and guide books in current use.

BIBLIOGRAPHY

Abel, F. M., *Notes d'archéologie chrétienne sur le Sinaï*, in *Revue biblique*, 1907.

Agazzi, A., *Il mosaico in Italia*, Milan, 1926.

Agnellus, *Liber Pontificalis sive Vitae Ravenatum* (IX century), in Muratori, *Rerum italicarum scriptores*, II, Milan, 1723.

Ainaloff, D. B., *Mosaics of the Fourth and the Fifth Centuries* (Russian), Leningrad, 1895.

    and Riedin, *The Cathedral of Santa Sophia at Kiev* (Russian), Leningrad, 1899.

    Hellenistic Origins of Byzantine Art (Russian), Leningrad, 1900.

    The Mosaics of the Baptistery of Albenga, in *Vizantieski Vremenik*, VIII, 1901.

    Byzantine Painting in the Fourteenth Century, Leningrad, 1917. (Russian)

    Die Mosaiken des Michaelsklosters in Kiew, in *Belvedere*, 1926.

Alemanni, *De Lateranensibus Parietinis restitutis*, Rome, 1625; with an appendix, Rome, 1756.

Amadesi, G. L., *Metropolitana di Ravenna*, Bologna, 1748.

Amorosa, A., *Le basiliche cristiane di Parenzo*, Parenzo, 1895.

Antonelli, G., *Sul modo di tagliare ed applicare il musaico*, Venice, 1858.

Antoniadi, M., *Description of St. Sophia* (in Greek), Athens, 1907.

Appell, J. W., *Christian Mosaic Pictures; A Catalogue of Reproductions in the South Kensington Museum*, London, 1876.

Artaud, F., *Histoire abrégé de la peinture en mosaïque, suivie de la description des mosaïques de Lyon et du Midi de la France*, Lyons, 1835.

Aubert, E., *Les mosaïques de la cathedrale d'Aoste*, in *Annales archéologiques*, XVII, 1857.

Aurigemma, S., *I mosaici di Zliten*, Rome-Milan, 1926.

    "In a Roman Villa at Zliten," in *Art and Archæology*, 23, 1927.

Auroux, E., *Les mosaïques de la grande mosquée de Damas et les fouilles du moyen Euphrate*, in *L'amour de l'art*, Nov., 1929.

Baldoria, *La cappella del Zenone a Santa Prassede in Roma*, in *Archivio Storico dell'arte*, IV, 1891.

Ballu, A., *Les ruines de Timgad*, Paris, 1911.

Barbet de Jouy, H., *Les mosaïques chrétiennes des basiliques et églises de Rome*, Paris, 1857.
Barbier de Montault, X., *La mosaïques du Dôme à Aix-la-Chapelle*, in *Annales archéologique de Didron*, XXVI, Paris, 1869.
    Les mosaïques des églises de Ravenne, Paris, 1897.
Baronchello, B., *La Chiesa Ducale di S. Marco* etc., Venice, 1753.
Bartolo, A., *Un frammento inedito dei musaici vaticani di Giovanni VII.*, in *Bollettino d'arte*, 1907.
Baumstark, A., *Il musaico degli Apostoli nella chiesa di Grottaferrata*, in *Oriens Christianus*, IV, 1904.
    Palestinensia, in *Römische Quartalschrift*, XXa, 1906.
    I musaici di S. Apollinare Nuovo, in *Rassegna Gregoriana*, 1910.
Bayet, Ch. *L'art byzantin*, Paris, 1904.
Beissel, S., *article on St. Mark's*, in *Zeitschrift für christliche Kunst*, 1893.
Beljajef, D., *Saint Irene*, in *Vizantieski Vremenik*, (published by the Imperial Academy of Sciences), Leningrad, II, 1895, (Russian)
Bell, G. L., *Churches and Monasteries of the Tûr Abdîn*, in *Zeitschrift für Geschichte der Architektur*, IX.
Benesevic, *Sur la date de la mosaïque de la Transfiguration au Mont Sinaï*, in *Byzantion*, I, 1924.
    Mount Sinaï, in *Monumenta Sinaitica*, I, Leningrad, 1925. (Russian)
Benson, E. M., *Mosaics Discovered Near Beirat, Syria*, in *Am. Magazine of Art*, 1934.
Berenson, B., *Italian Pictures of the Renaissance*, Oxford, 1932.
Berenson, Mary, *A Modern Pilgrimage*, London and New York, 1933.
Bertaux, E., *L'art dans l'Italie méridionale*, Paris, 1901.
    Les mosaïques de Daphni, in *Gazette des Beaux-arts*, 1901.
    La part de Byzance dans l'art byzantin, in *Journal des savants*, 1911.
Berthier, Fr. J. J., *L'église de Sainte-Sabine à Rome*, Rome, 1910.
Betz, E. P., *Religious Mosaics*, in *The Western Architect*, April, 1927.
Biagetti, B., *Splendori di arte antica nella Basilica Liberiana rinnovellati dal Sommo Pontefice Pio XI*, in *L'Illustrazione Vaticana*, 1931.
Bieber and Rodenwaldt, *Die Mosaiken des Dioskurides von Samos*, in *Jahrbuch der deutschen archäologischen Instituts*, XXVI, 1911.
Bijvank, A. W., *Het mozaiek in de doopkerk bij de kathedraal te Napels* (with French summary), in *Nederlandsch Hist. Inst. Rome., Med.*, 1931.
Blanchet, A., *La Mosaïque*, Paris, 1928.
    Inventaire des mosaïques de la Gaule (Lugdunaise, Belgique et Germanie), Paris, 1909.
    Étude sur la décoration des edifices de la Gaule romaine, Paris, 1913.

Mosaïque gallo-romaine de Saint-Cyr-sur-Mer, in *Gazette des beaux-arts*, 1924.

Blanchino, F., *De Sacris imaginibus musivi operis a S.Syxto Papa III in Basilica Liberiana constructis* etc. *Dissertationes duae*, Rome, 1727.

Blouet, G.-A., *Thermes de Caracalla*, Paris, 1828.

Boni, G., *Il Duomo di Parenzo e suoi musaici*, in *Archivio storico dell'arte*, 1894.

Boucher, H., and A. Blanchet, *Une nouvelle mosaïque decouverte à Tauroentum*, in *Gaz. des Beaux Arts*, 1930.

Bouet, G., *L'église de Germigny-les-Prés*, in *Bulletin Monumentale*, 1868.

Brehier, L., *L'Art byzantin*, Paris, 1924.

Les mosaïques mérovingiennes de Thiers, Clermont-Ferrand, 1910.

Orient ou Byzance?, in *Rev. archéologique*, 1907.

Bricarelli, C., *San Marco*, in *Civiltá Cattolica*, 1915.

Briggs, M. S., *Newly Discovered Syrian Mosaics*, in *Burlington Magazine*, 1931.

Bulard, M., *Peintures et mosaïques de Delos*, in *Monuments Piot*, XIV, 1908.

Busuioceanu, A., *Pierto Cavallini e la pittura romana del duecento e del trecento*, in *Ephemeris Dacoromana, annuario della Scuola Romena di Roma*, III, 1925.

Byron, R., *Hidden Splendour; Mosaics in St. Sophia in Constantinople*, in *Art Digest*, 1932.

New Mosaic in the Karieh: Dormition of the Virgin, in *Burlington Magazine*, 1933.

Cabrol, F., *Dictionnaire d'archéologie chrétienne et de liturgie*, Paris, 1909.

Cagnat, R., *Diane et Actéon sur une mosaïque africaine*, in *Centenaire de la Société nationale des Antiquairies de France*, Paris, 1904.

Une nouvelle mosaïque decouverte en Tripolitaine, in *Journal des Savants*, 1924.

and Chapot, V., *Manuel d'archéologie romaine*, Paris, 1920, vol. II.

Campbell, W. A., *Excavations at Antioch-on-the-Orontes*, in *Am. Journal of Archæol.*, 1934.

Carducci, *Sul grande musaico recentemente scoperto in Pesaro*, Pesaro, 1866.

Cecchelli, C., *Origine del mosaico parietale Cristiano*, in *Architettura e Arti decorative*, 1922.

Roman Mosaics (translated by E. Savinio), in *Formes*, 1930.

Chamot, M., *Damascus Mosaics*, in *Apollo*, 1931.

Chehab, M., *Decouverte d'une mosaïque byzantine*, in *Gaz. des Beaux Arts*, 1933.

Chirico, Mme. S. de and H. E. del Medico, *Les Mosaïques du narthex de Sainte Sophie*, in *Gaz. des Beaux Arts*, 1934.

Ciampini, J., *Vetera Monimenta*, etc., Rome, 1690, 1697.

2nd edition, Rome, 1747.

De sacris aedificiis a Constantino Magno constructis, Rome, 1693.

Clausse, G., *Basiliques et mosaïques chrétiennes*, Paris, 1893.
Clermont-Ganneau, Ch., *La mosaïque juive de Aïn-Doûq*, in *Comptes-rendus de l'Académie des Inscriptions et Belles-Lettres*, Paris, 1919.
Clute, E., *Craftsmanship in Cosmati Mosaic*, in *Architecture*, 1934.
Cocchi, A., *Le chiese di Firenze*, Florence, 1903.
Cogniat, R., *Carrelages et mosaïques*, in *Art et Decoration*, 1932.
Conton, L., *Torcello*, Venice, 1927.
Crostarosa, P., *Osservazione sul mosaico di Santa Pudenziana*, in *Nuovo Bollet. d'archeol. crist.*, 1895.
Crowe, J. A., and Cavalcaselle, G.B., *A New History of Painting in Italy*, London, 1864 (edited by Langton Douglas, London, 1903.)
Crowfoot, J. W., *Churches at Jerash*, Jerusalem, 1931.
Dalton, O. M., *Byzantine Art and Archæology*, Oxford, 1911.
    East Christian Art. Oxford, 1925.
Dami, L., *La basilica di San Miniato al Monte*, in *Bollettino d'Arte*, 1915.
Davidsohn, R., *Forschungen zu Geschichte von Florenz*, Berlin, 1896.
    Das älteste Werk der Franciscaner-Kunst, in *Rep. für Kunstwissenschaft*, XXII, 1899.
Demus, O., *Uber einige venezianische Mosaiken des 13 jahr-hunderts*, in *Belvedere*, 1931.
    Die Mosaiken von San Marco in Venedig, 1100-1300, Vienna-Leipzig, 1935.
Deperis, P., *Il Duomo di Parenzo e i suoi mosaici*, in *Atti e memorie della Soc. Istriana di Arch. e Stor. Patr.*, X, 1894.
Didron M., *Manuel d'iconographie chrétienne*, Paris, 1845.
Diehl, Ch., *Mosaïques byzantines de Saint-Luc*, in *Mon.Piot*, III, 1897.
    Sainte-Sophie de Salonique, in *ibid.*, XVI, 1909.
    Les mosaïques de Saint-Demetrius de Salonique, in *ibid.*, XVIII, 1911.
    L'Église et les mosaïques du couvent de Saint-Luc en Phocide, Paris. 1889.
    Venise, Paris, 1915.
    Le Tourneau, and H. Saladin, *Les monuments chrétiens de Salonique*, Paris, 1918.
    Études byzantines, Paris, 1905.
    Les origines orientales de l'art byzantin, in *L'Amour de l'Art*, 1924.
    Manuel d'art byzantin, 2d ed., Paris, 1925-6.
    Ravenne, Paris, 1927.
    L'Art chrétien primitif et l'art byzantin, Paris and Brussels, 1929.
    La peinture byzantine, Paris, 1933.
Diez, E., and O. Demus, *Byzantine Mosaics in Greece, Hosios Lucas and Daphni*, Cambridge, Mass., 1931.

Dobbert, E., *Analysis of Riedin's criticisms on St. Mark's*, in *Repertorium für Kuntswissenschaft*, XXI, 1898.

Dordoré, L., *Notes sur la mosaïque*, in *L'Amour de l'art*, 1928.

Duchesne, ed., *Liber Pontificalis*, Paris, 1886.

Dunand, M., *Rapport sur une mission archéologique au Djebel Druze*, in *Syria*, VII, 1926.

Duthuit, G., *Byzance et l'art du XII siècle*, Paris, 1926.

Dütschke, H., *Ravennatische Studien*, Leipzig, 1909.

Ebersolt, J. *Étude sur la topographie et les monuments de Constantinople*, in *Revue Archéol.*, II, 1909.

    Le grand palais de Constantinople et le livre des cérémonies, Paris, 1910.

    and Thiers, *Le églises de Constantinople*, Paris, 1913.

    Les arts somptuaires de Byzance, Paris, 1923.

    Trois nouveaux fragments de mosaïques a Kahrie-Djami (with English summary), in *Revue de l'art ancien et moderne*, 1929.

Enlart, C., *Manuel d'archéologie française*, Paris, 1919.

Fabia, P., *Mosaïques romaines des Musées de Lyon*, Lyons, 1923.

    Recherches sur les mosaïques romaines de Lyon, Lyons, 1924.

Fabri, F., *Le Sagre memorie di Ravenna*, Venice, 1664.

Fasioli, O., *I mosaici di Aquileia*, Rome, 1915.

Filangieri di Candida, A., *I restauri dei musaici del Battistero di S. Giovanni in Fonte*, in *L'Arte*, 1898.

Fiocco, G., *Michele Giambono, Venezie*, Milan-Rome, 1920.

Floegel, A. E., and Reid, K., *The Design and Application of Mosaic*, in *Pencil Points*, March, 1927.

Fontana, G., *Mosaici della primitiva epoca delle chiese di Roma*, Rome, 1870.

Fossati, *Aya Sofia*, London, 1852.

Frey, K., *Vasari*, Part I, vol. I, Munich, 1911.

Friend, A. M., Jr., *The Portraits of the Evangelists in Greek and Latin Manuscripts, Part II*, in *Art Studies*, 1929.

Frizzoni, G., *Melozza da Forli, ispiratore di una insigne opera di decorazione*, in *Bollettino d'arte*, 1916.

Frothingham, A. L., *The Monuments of Christian Rome*, New York, new ed., 1925.

    Les mosaïques de Grottaferrata, in *Gazette archéol.*, 1883.

Fry, R., *Modern Mosaic and Mr. Boris Anrep*, in *Burlington* Magazine, 1923.

Furietti, G. A., *De Musivis vel pictoriae artis origine*, Rome, 1752.

Furst, H., *Anrep's Pavement in the National Gallery*, in *Apollo*, IX, 1929.

    Boris Anrep and His Mosaics, in *Artwork*, 1929.

Galante, G.-A., *I musaici del battistero di Napoli*, in *Nuovo Bollettino di arch. crist.*, 1900.
Galassi, G., *La cosidetta decadenza nell'arte musiva ravennate*, in *Felix Ravenna*, 1914.
    Roma o Bisanzio, Rome, 1930.
Garrucci, R., *Storia del'arte cristiana nei primi otto secoli della Chiesa*, Prato, 1872-1880.
Gauckler, P., *Domaine des Laberii à Uthina*, in *Monuments Piot*, III, 1897.
    Les mosaïques virgiliennes de Sousse, in *ibid*, IV, 1898.
    Mosaïques tombales d'une chapelle de martyrs à Thabraca, in *ibid*, XIII, 1907.
    Opus musivum in Daremberg et Saglio, *Dictionnaire des antiquities*, vol. III, Paris, 1877 seq.
Gayet, A., *L'art arabe*, Paris, 1893.
George, W. S., *The Church of Saint Eirene at Constantinople*, London, 1912.
Germer-Durand, *Décoration de la basilique de Bethléem*, in *Échos de Nôtre-Dame de France*, 1891.
Gerola, G., *Il mosaico absidale della Ursiana*, in *Felix Ravenna*, V, 1912.
Gerspach, M., (article on technique), in *Gazette des beaux-arts*, 1880.
    La mosaïque, Paris, 1882, (2d edition, 1886).
    La mosaïque absidéale de St. Jean de Latran, in *Gazette des beaux-arts*, 1890.
Ghigi, Sac. Sante, *Il Mausoleo di Galla Placidia*, Bergamo, 1910.
Glück, H., *Die christliche Kunst des Ostens*, Berlin, 1923.
Gombosi, G., *Il più antico ciclo di mosaici di San Marco*, in *Dedalo*, 1923.
Graber, André, *La Décoration byzantine*, Paris and Brussels, 1928.
Gravina, D., *Il Duomo di Monreale*, Palermo, 1859, et seq.
Grisar, H., *Il mosaico di Santa Pudenziana a Roma coll'edifici dei luoghi santi*, in *Civiltá Cattolica*, III, 1895 and XII, 1897.
    Il tempio nel mosaici di Santa Maria Maggiore, in *ibid.*, XII, 1897.
    Il Sancta Sanctorum, Rome, 1907.
    Roma alla fine del mondo antico, Rome, 1908.
    Il musaico dell'Oratorio di San Venanzio, in *Civiltá Cattolica*, 1898.
de Gruneisen, W., *Le Portrait. Traditions hellenistiques et influences orientales*, Rome, 1911.
Gsell, S., *Monuments antiques de l'Algérie*, Paris, 1901.
Guthe, Dr. *Die Mosaikkarte von Madaba*, Leipzig, 1906.
Haas, K. v., *Die Mosaiken im Dom von Triest*, Vienna, 1859.
Hamlin, T. F., article *Mosaic*, in *Encycl. Brit.*, XIV ed., 1929.
Harbeson, J. F., *Design in Modern Architecture; Stained Glass and Mosaic*, in *Pencil Points*, 1930.

Haseloff, A., *I musaici di Casaranello*, in *Bollettino d'Arte*, 1907.

Heise, C. G., *Mosaiken von Frans Masereel*, in *Die Kunst*, 1932.

Heisenberg, A., *Die alten Mosaiken der Apostelkirche und der Hagia Sophia*, in Ξένια of the National University of Greece, 1912.
    Grabeskirche und Apostelkirche; zwei Basiliken Konstantins, Leipzig, 1908.

Hermanin, F., article *Cavallini* in Thieme-Becker, *Künstler-Lexicon*, vol. VI, 1912; superseding his article on Cavallini in *Le gallerie italiane*, Rome, 1902.

Herzfeld, *Genesis der islamischen Kunst*, in *Der Islam*, I, 1910.

Hettner, F., *Mosaic of Monnus at Trier*, in *Westdeutsche Zeitschrift für Geschichte und Kunst*, X, 1891.

Hinks, R., *Roman Carpets*, in *Architectural Review*, 1931.

Hoff, A., *Christliche Mosaikbildkunst*, Berlin, 1927.

Hutton, E., *Mosaics in Westminster Cathedral*, in *Burlington Magazine*, 1934.

Ippel, A., *Mosaikstudien*, in *Deutsch Archaol. Inst. Mitt. Rom*, 1930.

Jackson, F. H., *The Shores of the Adriatic, the Austrian Side*, London, 1908.

Jackson, T. G., *Byzantine and Romanesque Architecture*, Cambridge, 1920.

Jacoby, A., *Das geographische Mosaik von Madaba*, Leipzig, 1905.

Jatta, M., *Le rappresentanze figurate delle provincie romane*, Rome, 1908.

Jessen, P., *Die Darstellung des Weltgerichts bis auf Michelangelo*, Berlin, 1883.

Jubaru, F., *La decorazione bacchica del Mausoleo di Santa Costanza*, in *L'Arte*, 1904.

Kaufman, K. M., *Handbuch der christlichen Archäologie*, 3d ed. Paderborn, 1922.

Kisa, A., *Das Glas im Altertume*, Leipzig, 1908.

Kondakof, N., *Voyage to Sinai* (Russian), Odessa, 1882.
    The Mosaics of the Kahrié Djami, (Russian) Odessa, 1881.

Kraus, F.-X., *Geschichte der christlichen Kunst*, Freiburg, 1896.

Kreutz, G. and L., *La Basilica di San Marco in Venezia esposta*, etc. Venice, 1843.

Kühnel, E., *Die Mosaiken der Omayadenmoschee in Damaskus*, in *Der Cicerone*, May, 1930.

Kunstle, C. B., *Das Mausoleum von Santa Costanza und sein Mosaiken nach De Rossi*, in *Römische Quartalschrift*, 1890.

Kurth, J., *Die Wandmosaiken von Ravenna*, Leipzig, 1901.

Larbarte, J., *Le palais imperiale de Constantinople*, Paris, 1861.

Laborde, A. de., *Description d'un pavé en mosaïque . . . d'Italica*, Paris, an X (1802).

Lafaye, G., *Inventaire des mosaïques de la Gaule; Narbonnaise et Aquitaine*, Paris, 1909.
    Mosaique de Saint-Romain-en-Gal, in *Revue archéologique*, 1892.

Lasareff, V., *Early Italo-Byzantine Painting in Sicily*, in *Burlington Magazine*, 1933.

Lauer, Ph., *Le palais du Latran*, Paris, 1911.

Laurière, J. de, *L'abside de St. Jean de Latran*, in *Bulletin Monumental*, V série, VII, 1879.

Lazzarini, V., *Una incrizione Torcellana del secolo VII*, in *Atti del R. Istituto Veneto di Scienze, Lettere ed Arti*, 1914.

Leclerq, H., article *Art byzantin* in Cabrol, *Dictionnaire d'archéologie chrétienne*, Paris, 1909.

Le Coeur, Ch., *Mosaïques de Jurançon et de Bielle (Basse-Pyrénées)*, Pau, 1856.

Lefort, L., *La mosaïque de Ste. Prudentienne à Rome*, in *Revue archéol.*, II, 1874.
 Nouvelles observations sur la mosaïque de Ste. Pudentienne, in *Nuovo Bullett. d'archéol. crist.*, 1896.

Legrand, E., ed., *Revue des études grecques*, IX, 1896. Description by Constantine the Rhodian of the lost mosaics of the Church of the Apostles).

Leib, B., *Rome, Kiev et Byzance à la fin du XIe siècle*, Paris, 1924.

Lersch, L., *Das Kölner Mosaik*, Bonn, 1846.

Lethaby and Swainson, *The Church of Sancta Sophia, Constantinople*, London and New York, 1894.

Leval, A., *Les principales mosaïques, peintures et sculptures, existant à Kahrié-Djami, à Constantinople*, Constantinople, 1886.

Liber Pontificalis Ecclesiae Ravennatis in *Monumenta Germaniae Historica*, Hanover, 1878.

Lindemann, R., *Zu den Mosaikbilden von Max Schwarzer und Hans Gott für den dampfer Europa*, in *Die Kunst*, 1930.
 Max Unolds Mosaikbilder für den Dampfer Europa, in *Die Kunst*, 1930.

Lorey, E. de, *Les mosaïques du VIIIe siècle de la mosquée des Omeiyades à Damas*, in *Cashiers d'art*, vol. 4, no. 7, 1929.
 A Novel Aspect of Byzantine Art of the Eighth Century; Mosaics in Mosque of the Omayyads at Damascus, in *Parnassus*, May 1930.
 The Mosaics of the Mosque of the Omayyads at Damascus, in *Syria*, 1931.
 L'hellènisme et l'Orient dans les mosaïques de la mosquée des Omaiyades, in *Ars Islam*, 1934.

Loriquet, Ch., *La Mosaïque des Promenades et autres trouvées à Reims*, Rheims, 1862.

Los Rios, J.-A. de, *Mosaics gentiliscos; mosaico de Galatea en Elche*, Madrid, 1877.

Lothrop, S., *Pierto Cavallini*, in *Memoirs of the American Academy in Rome*, II, 1918.

Lowrie, W., *Monuments of the Early Church*, new ed., New York, 1923.

Maccoll, R., *Modern Life in Mosaic: Boris Anrep at the National Gallery*, in *Creative Art*, May, 1930.

Maillart, M., *L'Art byzantin*, Paris, Garnier fr., no date.

Mâle, E., *L'Art religieux du XIIe siècle en France*, Paris, 1922.
    L'Art religieux du XIIIe siecle en France, Paris, 1923.

Marçais, G., *Manuel d'art musulman*, Paris, 1926.

Marconi, P., *Il mosaico pesarese di Leda*, in *Bollettino d'arte*, 1933.

Marrucchi, O., *Le recente scoperte nel Duomo di Parenzo*, in *Nuovo Bulletino di archeologia cristiana*, 1896.
    Sta. Agata dei Goti, in *Giornale Arcadico*, 1891.

Di Marzo, *Delle belle arti in Sicilia dai Normani sino alla fine del secolo XIV*, Palermo, no date.

Mason, J. A., *Turquoise Mosaic from Northern Mexico*, bibliog. for the Pennsylvania Museum, Jan., 1929.

Mather, F. J. Jr., *The Isaac Master. A Reconstruction of the work of Gaddo Gaddi*, Princeton, 1932.

Mauméjean, Ch., *La Mosaïque*, in *Rennaissance de l'art*, 1929.

Mayes, W. E., *Removing a Roman Pavement*, in *Museums Journal*, 1933.

McKinney, R. J., *Museum Enters Archæological Field: Mosaic from a Roman Villa at Antioch, Syria*, in *Baltimore Mus. N. Rec.*, 1934.

Medico, H. E., del, *La Koimesis de Kahrié Djami*, in *Revue Archéol.*, 1933.

Mella, E., *Il Battistero di Agrate conturbia e di Albenga*, in *Atti della Soc. di Arch. e Belli di Torino*, 1883.

Merlin, A., *Inventaire des mosaïques de la Gaule et de l'Afrique*, Paris, 1915.
    La mosaïque du seigneur Julius à Carthage, Paris, 1923. (Extr. *Bulletin archéologique*, 1921).
    and L., Poinssot, *Deux mosaïques de Tunisie à sujets prophylactiques, Museé du Bardo*, bibliog. *f il plan Acad. Inscr. Paris mon. et Mem.*, vol. 34, 1934.

Michel, R., *Die Mosaiken von Joseph Ebertz*, in *Deutsche Kunst und Dekoration*, 1930.

Migeon, G., *Les mosaïques de la grande mosquée de Damas*, in *Revue Archéologique*, 1929.

Milanesi, Gaetano, *Del arte del vetro pel musaico* (XVI century), *reprinted*, Bologna, 1864.

Milanesi, G., ed., *Le vite di Vasari*, Florence, 1878-85.

Millet, *Byzance et non l'Orient*, in *Rev. archéologique*, 1908.

Millet, G., *L'Art byzantin* in Michel, *Histoire de l'art*, Paris, 1905 and 1908. vols. I and II.
 Mosaïques de Daphni, in *Mon. Piot*, III, 1897.
 Les mosaïques de Daphni, Paris, 1899.
 Recherches sur l'conographie de l'Évangile, Paris, 1916.
Millin, A. L., *Description d'une mosaïque antique du Musée Pio-Clementin*, Paris, 1829.
Moranville, H., *Peintures romains pensionnairs de Phillippe le Bel*, in *Bibliot. de l'École des Chartes*, XLIII, 1887.
Morassi, A., *La chiesetta di Santa Mario Formosa o del Canneto a Pola*, in *Bollettino d'Arte*, Rome, 1924.
Morey, C. R., *Lost Mosaics and Frescoes of Rome of the Mediæval Period*, Princeton-Oxford, 1915.
 The Sources of Mediæval Style, in *The Art Bulletin*, 1924.
Morgan, Th., *Romano-British Pavements*, London, 1886.
Morris, E. H., *The Temple of the Warriors at Chichen Itzá*, Carnegie Institute, Washington, D. C., 1931.
Muñoz, A., *Frammento di musaico a S. Bartolommeo all'Isola in Roma*, in *L'Arte*, 1904.
 I musaici di Kahrie-djami in Constantinopoli, in *Rassegna Italiana*, 1906.
 San Giovanni in Fonte, in *L'Arte*, 1908.
 Reliquie artistiche della vecchie basilica Vaticana a Boville Ernica, in *Bolletino d'arte*, 1911.
 Sant'Agatha dei Goti, Rome, 1923.
Müntz, E., *La Mosaïque chrétienne pendant les premiers siècles*. Paris, 1893.
 Notes sur les mosaïques chrétiennes de l'Italie, in *Revue archéol.*, 1874-1893, viz: *Santa Prassede*, 1875; *Oratory of John VII*, 1877; *Des éléments antique dans les mosaïques romaines du moyen âge*, 1879; *Triclinium of the Lateran*, 1884; *San Paolo fuori-le-mure*, 1898.
 Les mosaïques byzantines portatives, in *Bulletin monumental*, Caen, 1886.
 The Lost Mosaics of Rome, and *The Lost Mosaics of Ravenna*, in *American Journal of Archæology*, 1885 and 1886.
Muratoff, P., *La pittura bizantina*, Rome (no date).
Navone, G., *Di un mosaico di Pietro Cavallini in S. Maria Transtiberiana* etc., in *Arch. dell Soc. Rom. di Stor. Patr.*, 1877.
Neumann, G., *Die Markuskirche in Venedig*, in *Preussische Jahrbuch*, 1892.
Neuss, Wm., *Die Kunst der alten Christen*, Augsburg, 1926.
Newcomb, R., *The Art of the Mosaicist*, in *The Western Architect*, April, 1927.

Nicholson, A., *Cimabue*, Princeton, 1931.
Nogara, B., *I mosaici antichi conservati nel palazzi del Vaticano e del Laterano*, Milan, 1910.
Oligier, L., *Due mosaici con S. Francesco delle chiesa di Aracœli in Roma*, in *Archivio Francisc. Hist.*, IV, 1911.
Ongania (edit.), *La basilica di San Marco a Venezia*, Venice, 1878-1893.
Orlandos, A. C., *Monuments byzantins de Chios*, Athens, 1930.
Oswaldo, P. di, *Raccolte di documenti inediti*, Padua, 1895.
Ouspenski, F. L., *Recently Discovered Mosaics at St. Demetrius*, Salonika; *Izvjestija (Bulletin of the Russian Archæological Institute of Constantinople)*, XIV, 1908.
Pachtere, F. G. de, *Inventaire des mosaïques de la Gaule et de l'Afrique*, vol. III, (*Afrique proconsulaire, Numidie, Maurétanie*), Paris, 1911.
Papageorgiou, P. N., *St. Demetrius*, in *Byzantinische Zeitschrift*, XVII, 1908.
Papini, R., *Pisa*, Rome, 1912.
Paris, W. F., *The Mosaics in the Frontal Colonnade of the Detroit Public Library*, in *Architectural Record*, 1921.
Parker, H., *Mosaic Pictures in Rome and Ravenna*, Oxford, 1866.
Pavlovsky, A. A., *Iconographie de la chappelle palatine*, Paris, 1895.
    Ibid, in *Revue archéol.*, XXV, 1894.
Perdrizet and Chesnay, *La métropole de Serres*, in *Mon. Piot*, X, 1904.
Phillips, L. M., *Form and Colour*, London, 1915.
Pierce, H. and R. Tyler, *L'Art byzantin*, Paris, 1932.
Poinssot, L. and Lantier, R., *Les mosaïques de la maison d'Adriane à Carthage*, in *Monuments Piot*, XXVII, 1924.
Pozzi, J., *Les mosaïques de Sainte-Sophie*, in *Beaux Arts*, 1933.
    La réapparition des mosaiques de Sainte-Sophie, in *Revue Archéologique*, 1934.
Prévost, *La basilique de Théodulfe et la paroisse de Germigny-des Prés*, Orleans, 1889.
Prost, B., *Quelques documents sur l'histoire des arts en France*, in *Gazette des Beaux-Arts*, XXXV, 1887.
Puig y Cadafalch, J., *L'arquitectura romanica a Catalunya*, Barcelona, 1909-1918.
Quaresimus, *Elucidatio Terrae sanctae*, Rome, 1639.
Quitt, J., *Der Mosaikencyclus von San Vitale*, in *Byzantinische Denkmaler*, Vienna, III, 1903.
Ratti, A., *Il piu antico ritratto di S. Ambrogio*, Milan, 1897.
Reau, L., *L'Art russe*, Paris.
Renan, A., *Torcello*, in *Gazette des beaux-arts*, 1888.
Renan, E., *Mission de Phenicie*, Paris, 1864-1874.

Ricci, C., *Ravenna*, Bergamo, 1902.
 La chiesa di San Michele "ad Frigiselo" in Ravenna, in *Rassegna d'arte*, V, 1905.
 Il Mausoleo di Galla Placidia in Ravenna, Rome, 1914. (Also in *Bollettino d'Arte*, 1913-14)
 Appunti per la storia del mosaico, in *Bollettino d'Arte*, 1914.
 Il battistero della Cattedrale (Ravenna), Rome, 1932.

Rice, D. Talbot, *New Light on Byzantine Portative Mosaics*, in *Apollo*, 1933.

Richa, G., *Notizie istoriche delle chiese fiorentine*, Florence, 1754.

Richmond, Sir Wm. B., article *Mosaic* in *Encycl. Brit.*, XI ed., 1910.

Richter, J. P., *Die Mosaiken von Ravenna*, Vienna, 1878.
 Quellen der byzantinischen Kunstgeschichte, Vienna, 1897.
 Lectures in the National Gallery, London, 1898.
 and A. C. Taylor, *The Golden Age of Classical Christian Art*, London, 1904.

Riedin, E. K., *The Mosaics of the Churches of Ravenna*, (Russian) Leningrad, 1896.

Riegel, A., *Die spätrömische Kunstindustrie*, Vienna, 1901 (new ed. 1927)
 Stilfragen, Berlin, 1893.

Riolo, G., *Dell-artifici o pratico dei mosaici antichi e moderni*, Palermo, 1870.

Rivoira, G., *Le origini dell'archittetura lombarda*, Rome, 1901, translated under title *Lombardic Architecture: its origin and development*, by G. McN. Rushforth, London, 1910.

Robertson, A., *The Bible of St. Mark's*, London, 1898.

Rohault de Fleury, G., *Le Latran au Moyen Age*, Paris, 1877.

Rolffs, W., *Geschichte der Malerei Neapels*, Leipzig, 1910.

Romanelli, P., *Leptis Magna*, Rome, 1925.

Rossi, G. B. de, *Musaici cristiani e saggi dei pavimenti delle chiese di Roma anteriori al Secolo XV*, Rome, 1870-1893.
 Musaico d'un battistero presso la cattedrale di Die, in *Bolletino di archeologia cristiana*, V, 1867.
 La basilica di S. Stefano Rotondo etc., Rome, 1886.
 Della decorazione interna del Mausoleo Constantiniano della via Nomentana appellato Santa Costanza, in *Bollett. dell'Istit. di Corresp. Archeol.*, 1889.

Rothschild, E. F., and Wilkins, E. H., *Hell in the Florentine Baptistery Mosaic and in Giotto's Paduan Fresco*, in *Art Studies*, 1928.

Rouard, E., *Rapport sur les fouilles faites à Aix*, Aix, 1843.

Rubeus, *Historiarum Ravennatum*, Venice, 1589.

Rüdell, *Die Kahrié-Dschamisi in Konstantinopel*, Berlin, 1908.

Rutter, F., *Mosaics in the Dome of St. Sophia, Constantinople*, in *International Studio*, 1930.
Saccardo, P., *Les Mosaïques de Saint-Marc à Venise*, Venice, 1897, and in Ongania, *La Basilica di San Marco*, vol. III, Venice, 1878-93.
Saladin-Migeon, *Manuel d'art musulman*, Paris, 2d ed., 1926.
Salazaro, D., *Monumenti dell'arte meridionale d'Italia*, Naples, 1882.
Salmi, M., *I mosaici del "Bel San Giovanni" e la pittura del secolo XIII a Firenze*, in *Dedalo*, February, 1931.
Salzenberg, W., *Altchristliche Baudenkmäler von Konstantinopel*, Berlin, 1854.
Sangiorgi, G., *Il Battistero della basilica Ursiana di Ravenna*, Rome, 1900.
Saville, M. H., *Turquois Mosaic Art in Ancient Mexico*, New York, 1922.
Scaglia, S., *I musaici antiche della basilica di Santa Maria Maggiore*, Rome, 1910.
Schlumberger, G., *L'Épopée byzantine*, Paris, 1896-1905.
Schmarzow, A., *Der Kuppelraum von Santa Costanza in Rom* etc., Leipzig, 1904.
Schmit, Th., *The Panagia Angelokistos*, in *Izvjestija*, XV, 1911.
  Die Koimesis-Kirche von Nikaia, Berlin and Leipzig, 1927.
  Mosaics and Frescoes of the Kahrié djami, in *Izvjestija*, (published by the Imperial Academy of Sciences, Leningrad) VIII, 1902 and *ibid.*, XI, 1906 (Russian).
Schmitt, F. J., *Kahrié djami* (Russian), Sophia, 1906.
  The Mosaics of the Monastery of St. Luke, (Russian) Kharkof, 1914.
Schulten, A., *Die Mosaik-Carte von Madaba*, Berlin, 1900.
Schultz, B., *Die Kirchenbauten auf der Insel Torcello*, Berlin, 1927.
Schultz, Weir, and Barnsley, S. H., *The Monastery of St. Luke in Stiris in Phocis*, London, 1901.
  The Church of the Nativity at Bethlehem, London, 1910.
Serradifalco, duca di, *Il Duomo di Monreale*, Palermo, 1838.
Sexton, R. W., *Mosaic Art; an Old Decorative Medium*, in *California Arts and Architecture*, 1931.
Sherrill, C. H., *Mosaics*, London, 1932.
Smirnof, J. I., *The Mosaics of Cyprus*, in *Vizantieski Vremenik*, IV, 1897. (Russian)
  The Mosaics of Santa Sophia, Salonika, in *ibid.* V, 1898.
Soulier, C., *Les influences orientales dans la peinture toscane*, Paris, 1924.
Sorrentino, A., *La basilica di Santa Restituta in Napoli*, in *Bollettino d'Arte*, 1909.
Spreti, *De amplitudine, eversione et restauratione urbis Ravennae*, Ravenna, 1793-1796.
  Compendio istorico dell'arte di compone i musaici con la descrizione de' musaici . . . nelle basiliche di Ravenna etc., Ravenna, 1804.

Stanislao, P., *La Cappella Papale di Sancta Sanctorum*, Grottaferrata, 1919.
Stein, Sir Aurel, *Ancient Khotan,* London, 1907.
Strong, E., *Art in Ancient Rome.* 2 vols., London, 1929.
Strzygowski, J., *Nea Moni auf Chios*, in *Byzantinische Zeitschrift*, V, 1896, and in *Vizantieski Vremenik*, VI, 1899.
    Das neu-gefundene Orpheus-Mosaik in Jerusalem, in *Zeitschrift des deutschen Palestina-Vereins*, XXIV, 1901.
    Orient oder Rom, Leipzig, 1901.
    Antiochenische Kunst, in *Oriens Christianus*, 1902.
    Felsendom und Aksamoschee, in *Der Islam*, II, 1910.
    Ravenna als Vorort aramaischen Kunst, in *Oriens Christianus*, 1915.
    Ursprung der christlichen Kirchenkunst, Leipzig, 1920. (Translated with notes by Dalton under title *East Christian Art*.)
Sukenik, J. L., *Discovery of an Ancient Synagogue, Beth Alpha, Palestine*, in *Art and Archæology*, 1932.
Swift, E. H., *Byzantine Gold Mosaic*, in *Am. Journal of Archæol.*, 1934.
Trafrali, O., *St. Demetrius, Salonika*, in *Revue archéol.*, 1909, II and 1910, I.
    Thessalonique, des origines au XIV siècle, Paris, 1919.
Tanfani Centofanti, L., *Notizie di artisti da documenti pisani*, Pisa, 1898.
Tarlazzi, A., *Memorie sacre di Ravenna*, Ravenna, 1852.
Terzi, Amari, and Cavallari, *La Cappella di S. Pietro nella reggia di Palermo*, Palermo, 1889.
Testi, L., *Storia della pittura veneziana*, Bergamo, 1909.
Testi Rasponi, A., ed., *Agnellus, Liber Pontificalis*, in *Raccolta degli Storici italiani*, Milan, 1924 *et seq.*
Thieme und Becker, *Allgemeines Lexikon der bildenden Künstler*, Leipzig, 1910 seq.
Thode, H., *Andrea Castagno in Venedig*, in *Festschrift für Otto Bendorf*, Vienna, 1898.
Tikkanen, J. J., *Die Genesismosaiken von San Marco in Venedig*, Helsingfors, 1889; *ibid.*, in *Acta Societatis Scientiarum Fennicæ*, Helsingfors, 1889; and in *Archivio Storico dell'arte*, 1888.
Toesca, P., *Storia dell'arte italiana*, Turin, 1915 seq.
    La pittura e la miniatura nella Lombardia, Milan, 1912.
Tomai, T., *Historia di Ravenna*, Venice, 1580.
Tozzi, O., *Storia della basilica di Santa Maria Maggiore*, Rome, 1904.
Tozzi, R., *I mosaici del Battistero di San Marco a Venezia e l'arte bizantina*, in *Bollettino d'arte*, 1933.
Trenta, G., *I musaici del duomo di Pisa e i loro autori*, Florence, 1896.
Vailhé, S., *La mosaïque de la Transfiguration au Sinaï est-telle de Justinien?*, in *Revue de l'Orient chrétien*, II, 1907.

Van Berchem, Marg., and E. Clouzot, *Mosaïques chrétiennes*, Geneva, 1924.
 The Mosaics of the Dome of the Rock and of the Great Mosque at Damascus. (transl. by K. A. C. Creswell, reprint from *ibid., Early Muslim Architecture*, Oxford, 1932.)
 art., *Damascus*, in *Monuments Piot*, 1930.
Van Marle, R., *La Peinture romaine au moyen-age*, Strassburg, 1921.
 The Development of the Italian Schools of Painting, The Hague, vol. I, 1923.
 Il musaico del Duomo di Spoleto, in *Rassegna d'arte Umbra*, 1921.
Van Millingen, A., *Byzantine Churches in Constantinople*, London-New York, 1912.
Venturi, A., *Storia dell'arte italiana*, Milan, 1904 seq.
 Musaici cristiani in Roma, Rome, 1925.
Venturi, L., *La Navicella di Giotto*, in *L'Arte*, 1922.
Villefosse, A. H. de, *Lycurge et Ambrosie; mosaïque découverte à Sainte-Colombe-lez-Vienne (Rhone)*, in *Annuaire de l'École pratique des hautes-études*, Paris, 1907.
 Mosaïque de Phoebus à Sens, in *Comptes-Rendus de l'Academie des Inscriptions et Belles-Lettres*, 1910.
Vincent and Abel, *Bethlehem*, Paris, 1914.
Vitet, L., *Dissertation sur les mosaïques chrétiennes*, in *Journal des Savants*, 1862 and 1863.
 Les Mosaïques chrétiennes de Rome.
De Vogüé, Marquis de, *Les Églises de Terre-Sainte*, Paris, 1860.
 Le temple de Jérusalem, Paris, 1864.
Voss, G., *Das jungste Gericht in der bildenden Kunst des frühen Mittelalters*, in *Beiträge zur Kunstgeschichte*, VIII, Leipzig, 1884.
Wagner, G. A., *Mosaic, Its Material and Technique*, in *The Western Architect*, April, 1927.
Weerth, M. D., *Specimens of the Geometrical Mosaic of the Middle Ages with a Brief Historical Notice of the Art*, London, 1848.
Der Wettbewerb für Mosaiken für dem Kongresssaal des Deutschen Museums, in *Der Kunst*, Feb., 1935.
Whittemore, Thomas, *The Mosaics of St. Sophia at Istanbul*, Oxford, 1933.
Wickhoff, F., *Der Apsismosaik in der Basilica des Heilige Felix zu Nola*, in *Römische Quartalschrift*, 1889.
 Die Wiener Genesis, Vienna, 1895.
Wiegand, *Die Geburtskirche in Bethlehem*, Leipzig, 1911.
 Sinai, Berlin, 1920.
Wilkins, E. H., *Dante and the Mosaics of his "bel San Giovanni,"* in *Speculum*, II, 1927.

Wilmowsky, J. N. von, *Römische Mosaiken aus Trier und dessen Umgegend*, Treves, 1888.
    Die römische Villa zu Nennig und ihr Mosaik, Bonn, 1865.
Wilpert, J., *Die römischen Mosaiken und Malereien der Christlichen Bauten vom IV bis XIII Jahrhundert*, Freiburg, 1917.
    La decorazione della Basilica Lateranense, in *Riv. di Archeol. Christiana*, 1921.
Witthaus, W., *Das Shellhaus in Hamburg; Mosaikbilder von W. Peiner in der Halle*, in *Deutsche Kunst und Dekoration*, 1931.
Wheeler, R. E. M., *Experiment in Removing a Fragment of a Roman Pavement*, in *Museums Journal*, 1933.
Wlha and Niemann, *Der Dom von Parenzo, Vienna*, (no date).
Wolanska, J., *Ein römisches mosaik aus Balacza*, in *Oesterische Archaol. Inst. Jahresh.*, 1929.
Woodruff, H., *Iconography and Date of the Mosaics of La Daurade*, in *Art Bulletin*, 1931.
Woolley, C. Leonard, *The Development of Sumerian Art*, London, 1935.
Wulff, O., *Die Koimesiskirche in Nicäa und ihre Mosaiken*, Strassbourg, 1903.
    Altchristliche und byzantinische Kunst, Berlin, 1914-18.
    Die Mosaiken der Nea Moni von Chios, in *Byzantinische Zeitschrift*, XXV, 1925.
    Das Ravennatische Mosaic von San Michele in Affricisco im Kaiser Friedrich-Museum, in *Jahrbuch der Königlich preuszischen Kunstsammlungen*, XXV, 1904.
Zanetti, A. M., *Della Pittura Veneziana e delle Opere publiche de Veneziani Maestri*, Venice, 1771.
Zimmermann, G. M., *Giotto und die Kunst Italiens im Mittelalter*, Leipzig, 1899.

GLOSSARY AND INDEX

GLOSSARY

Anastasis. Term used in East Christian or Byzantine art for the scene which in the West is called the Harrowing of Hell, or, Descent into Hell. Usually connected with the apocryphal Gospel of Nicodemus (ch. xviii) where John the Baptist is said to have foretold the descent of Our Lord into Hell.

Bema. The rudimentary transept of the Early Christian basilica.

Deesis. In Byzantine art, term used for a symbolic group of Christ, the Virgin, and St. John the Baptist.

Dormition. Term used in Byzantine art for the Death of the Virgin whose body lies on a bier round which the Apostles are grouped. Christ stands in the center holding in His arms the soul of His mother, represented as a diminutive human figure.

Ecclesia ex Circumcisione. Terms used to denote the Jewish Church.

Ecclesia ex Gentibus. Term used to denote the Church of the Gentiles.

Etimasis or *Hetimasia*. Means "Preparation of the Throne" and alludes to the coming of Our Lord as Judge. In early examples the throne has upon it a sacred monogram or scroll; then, an open book replaces the scroll, and finally, in fully developed Byzantine iconography, a diadem and the instruments of the Passion are added and it usually appears in Last Judgement scenes.

Labarum. The Constantinian standard upon which was represented the sacred monogram of Christ.

Narthex. A vestibule of one or more stories, usually open and colonnaded at the front, and placed before a building.

Orant. Term used in Early Christian and Byzantine art to denote a standing figure, front view, with the arms raised in the act of prayer.

Pantocrator. In fully developed Byzantine iconography, the type of Our Lord as Judge of humanity.

Pendentive. An inverted, triangular, concave piece of masonry used to support a section of a dome.

Squinch. A slab or small arch thrown across the angle of a square or polygon to render its shape more nearly round in order to receive the base of a dome.

Traditio Legis. Scene in which Our Lord gives the Law to St. Peter and St. Paul who stand to right and left, the book or scroll being actually handed to St. Peter.

Triclinium. The Roman dining-room, so-called because it was furnished with three couches.

Triumphal arch. The arch immediately in front of the apse of a church.

INDEX

	Page
A-anni-padda, temple of	28
Abd al Melek, Caliph	127
"Academy of Plato"	49
Aegeans	30
Agra	31
Aïnaloff	229
Ainay, church at, pavement	233
Aix-la-Chapelle, palace	154
Albenga, baptistery	118–119
All-Saints Church, Richmond, Va.	257
Altar-pieces, St. Peter's	247
American Church of St. Paul, Rome	257
Anrep, Boris, pavements by	261
Anthée, mosaic from	43
Antioch, pavements	52–53
as a radiating center	103, 104, 123
Antoniazzo Romano	240
Aphrodosius, legend of	74
Apocrypha	159
Apollonius, mosaicist	203
Aquileia, pavement	53
Aquino, mosaic, note 128	
Ara Pacis	52
Archbishop's Palace, Ravenna	97–98
Arena Chapel, Padua	203
Arian Baptistery, Ravenna	101
Ark of the Covenant, see Germigny-des-Prés	
Arta, church of the Paregoritissa	230
Autun, pavements from	43
Avignon, papal court removed to	222
Aztecs	32
Azulejos	30
Babylonian Captivity	232
Bacchus, Triumph of	64
Bagdad	132
Baldovinetti, Alesso	239
Baptistery of the Orthodox, Ravenna	89–91
Barberini, Cardinal	144
Bartoli, Cosimo, painter	223
Basilica Ursiana, Ravenna, apse	102, 200
Baths of Caracalla	72
Baybars, mosque of, Damascus	132
Belloni	254
Bembo, chronicle of	191
Benedict XIII, pope	245
Benedict XIV, pope	144
Berlin, Excelsior Hotel, Roman bath	260

	PAGE
Bernini	245
Bernward, bishop, see Hildesheim	
Bertaux	122
Bethlehem, church of the Nativity	174–175
Bianchini, the	242, 243
Bithynia, see Nicaea	
Blashfield, Edwin	257
Blue Mosque, see Dome of the Rock	
Bohemia	233
Boni, G., quoted 40, note 9	
Borghese Gallery, see Paul V	
Boscoreale, villa from	108, 130
Boulogne-sur-Mer, mosaics from	43
Bouquet, Louis	259
Boville, Ernica, San Pietro Ispano, Giotto's angel	223
Brading, pavement	51
Brooklyn Museum, mosaic	217
Brosses, Charles de, quoted	248
Burne-Jones, Sir Edward	257
Caesar	176
Calendra, G.	245
Caligula	53
Campo Santo, Pisa, frescoes	206
Cappella Palatina, Palermo	181–183
Cappuccini, church of the, Rome	223
Capua, cathedral	187
Capua, see San Prisco	
Casaranello, basilica	119
Caspar, Karl	260
Castagno, Andrea del	238
Catacomb mosaics	56
Cavaliere d'Arpino	245, 246
Cavallini	188, 209, 212, 213, 217, 218, 221–222, 237
Cefalù, cathedral, apse	179, 180
Central American mosaics	31
Cézanne	258
Charlemagne	102, 143, 144, 152, 154
Charles VIII	240
Chester, cathedral	256
Chicago, Oriental Theater	261
Avalon Theater	261
Chichen Itzá, plaque from	32
Chinili Kiosk, Constantinople	30
Chios, Nea Moni	169, 170
Chora, church of the, see Kahrie Djami	
Choricus of Gaza	54, 112
Chosroes	62
Ciampini	63, 76, 83, 102, 137, 144, 145, 150, 154, 211
Cimabue	201, 205, 209

INDEX

	PAGE
Cingria, Alexandre	259
Cirencester, pavement	51
Ciriacus, catacomb of	56
Civil War, American culture after the	256
Civita Castellana, cathedral	216
Clayton and Bell	256
Colonna, palace, moasic	217
Colors, range of	41
Constanti, Tarragona, mosaics	122
Constantia	64
Constantine	59
Constantine the Rhodian	112, 160

Constantinople
- Holy Apostles, church of 111–112, 159
- Fetiye Djami 230
- Kahrie Djami 227–229
- St. Irene 112–113
- St. Sophia 42, 110–111, 162–163

Contarini, doge	191
Copenhagen, mosaics	260
Cordova, mosque	132
Cortes	31
Cortona, Museum, Madonna, note 156	
Cosmas, Giovanni, mosaicist	216
Cosmati, the	188, 215
Cotanello, stone from	43
Crispus	64
Cristofari, Fabius	245
Cristofari, P. P.	245
Crusades, the	227
Curzon, M. de	254
Currier Gallery of Art, Manchester, N. H.	262
Cyprus, see Panagia Angelokistos and Panagia Kanakaria	
Dalton	27, 161
Dante	203
Daphne, pavements, note 13	
Daphni	172–174
dome	172
Feasts of the Church	173
narthex	173, 174
David, painter	253
Decôte	259
Decree of 1648, Venice	39
Delhi, tombs and mosques at	30, 31
Delos	47
Denis, Maurice	259
Des Moines, Iowa, State Capitol	258

Detroit
- Public Library 258
- Fisher Building 261
- MacCabees Building 261

	PAGE
Diehl	89, 123, 159, 165, 228
Dielman, Frederick	257
Diodato, mosaicist	188
Dioskourides, mosaic by	49
Dome of the Rock, Jerusalem	42, 127–129
octagonal arcade	128
circular arcade	128
drum	128
style	129
Dordoré, quoted, 259 and note 1	
"Doves" of the Capitoline	49
Ducas, Maria	227
Duccio	149, 201, 209
Duellberg, Ewald	260
Durande de Mende, tomb of, Rome	216, 217
Early-Christian style defined	60–62
Ecclesia ex Circumcisione	61
Ecclesia ex Gentibus	61
Egyptian mosaics	29
El-Aksa, mosque, Jerusalem	175
El-Hakim, Caliph	132
emblema	49
English XIX century mosaics	255–256
Ephesus, Council of	74
Erfurt, cathedral	255
Eski-Djouma, Salonika	110
Essen, Altkatholischen Kirche	260
Evans, Sir Arthur	29
Faulkner, Barry	262
Faun, house of the	50
Feather mosaics	32
Felix IV, pope	134
Ferrara, mosaic, note 137	
Fetiye Djami, Constantinople	230
Filadelfi, mosaic of the	52
Flavius Vopiscus	40, 50
Flemish miniatures	231
Florence	
Baptistery	201–205
Cathedral	205
Ghirlandaio, mosaics by	239
Opera del Duomo, mosaics in	176, 240
San Miniato	205
Florentine Baptistery	201–205
"scarsella"	201, 202
dome	202–205
Florentine intarsia	31
Foro Claudio, apse	237
Forseth, Einar	260
Fossati	110
Fountain niches, Pompeii	54

INDEX

	PAGE
Fournier	255
Fourth Style, Pompeii	108, 130
Fra Jacopo Francescano, mosaicist	201, 203
France, XIX century mosaics	253–255
Francesco, mosaicist	232
Frankfurt am Main, Frauen-Friedenskirche	260
Friedenskirche, Berlin, see San Cypriano, Murano	
Frosinone, see Boville Ernica	
Fry, Roger, quoted	36
Gaddo Gaddi	204, 205, 220, 221
Gaeta, mosaic, note 128	
Galla Placidia	87
Mausoleum of	87–89
Garnier, Charles	254
Garrucci	117
Gaudin	259
Gaugin	258
Geneva, St Paul's	259
Genoa, San Matteo	206
Gentile da Fabriano	238
George, Walter	40
German XIX century mosaics	255
Germigny-des-Près, apse	152
Gerspach	241, 254
Gessi, de	245
Ghiberti	137, 222
Ghirlandaio, David, mosaics	240
Ghirlandaio, mosaics	239
quoted	38
Giambono, Michele	238, 239, 244
Giggleswick, chapel	256
Giotto	203, 222, 223
Giovanni, Cosmas, mosaicist	216
Glass	41
Glass factories, Murano	231
Gonsalvo Rodriguez, tomb of, Rome	216, 217
Gospels, source of iconography	61
Goths	81
Grand Palais, Paris	255
Great Mosque, Damascus	129–132
Great Panel	130
Style	131
Gregory of Tours	153
Grijalva, Juan de	31
Grimaldi, drawings	137, 145
Grottaferrata, Rome	171, 172
Guard's Chapel, St. James' Park	256
Guilbert-Martin	259
Hadrian's Villa, vault	54

	PAGE
Hagia Paraskeoi, see Eski-Djouma, Salonika	
Hagia Paraskevi, see St. Demetrius, Salonika	
Hague, the, mosaic by Thorn Prikker	260
Hamlin, definition of mosaic, by, note 1	
Haseloff	119
Heisenburg	159
Hieron II	53
Hilarius, Pope	78
Hildesheim, mosaics of Bernward	233
Hohenlohe, Prince Max von	260
Holy Apostles, church of, Constantinople	111–112, 159
Holy Land, mosaics of	62
Holy Redeemer, church of the, Detroit	257
Holy Sepulchre, church of	62, 67
Homburg, Erlöserkirche	255
Honorius I, pope	133
Honorius III, pope	200
Hosios Lucas, Phocis	163–165
mosaics	164
style	165
Houses of Parliament, St. George	256
Huesca, tombal mosaic	122
Hylas and the Nymphs	48
Hypogeum, Via Po	66
Iconography	
Early Christian	59–62
Byzantine	157–160
Impressionism	258
India	30
Indriomeni, Marco Greco, artist	192
Innocent I, pope	133
International School	231
International Telephone and Telegraph Building, New York	261
Isfahan, portal of the Misjid-i-Shah	30
Issus, battle of, from Pompeii	49
Istanbul, see Constantinople	
Irving Trust Building, New York	262
Jackson, T. G.	256
Jacobello del Fiore	238
Jacopo, mosaicist	215, 216
Jaroslav	165
Jean de Ganai, Président	240
Jerash, pavements, note 13	
John IV, pope	134
John VII, oratory of	137–139
Virgin, Florence	137
Fragments	138
Adoration of Magi	138
John of Malta	215
John Zimesces, emperor	163

INDEX

	PAGE
Junius Bassus, basilica of	48
Jurançon, pavement	51
Justinian	87
portrait of	95
Kabr Hiram, pavement	64
Kahrie Djami, Constantinople	227–229
Kaiser Wilhelm Memorial Church, Berlin	255
Khotan, frescoes, note 55	
Kibel, restoration by	89, 90
Klein, César	260
Knossos, Lesser Palace at	29
Kondakoff	228
Koran	128
Krakow, Czartoryski Museum, mosaic, note 133	
Kutchuk Aya Sofia, see SS. Sergius and Bacchus	
Laberii, Villa of the	52
Labouret	259
La Dourade, Tours, church	153
La Farge, Bancel	257
La Farge, John	256, 257
Lascari, Salvatore	262
Lateran, the,	
nave	84
apse	218–219
Lateran Baptistery, apse	68
Latins, the	227
Leland Stanford University, California	258
Lello, mosaicist	187, 206
Leo XII, pope	245
Leopoldo dal Pozzo	244
Liber Pontificalis	63, 83, 136
Library of Congress, Washington, D. C.	257
Lillebonne, pavement	51
Livia, house of, Primaporta	130
Lorenzetti, the	206
Lorey, Eustache de	129
Lost mosaics	
Rome	83, 84
Ravenna	102
Louvre, main stair-case	254
Lourdes, Basilica	254
Lucca, see San Frediano	
Lucifer	203
Luigi di Pace	241, 244
Lyons, Nôtre-Dame de Fourvières	254
Madeleine, the, Paris, apse	254
Magne, Henri-Marcel	254
Maitani, Lorenzo	232
Mantegna	238

	PAGE
Marienburg, Marien-Kirche, mosaic	234
Marien-Kirche, see Marienburg	
Marienwerder	233
Marseilles, New Cathedral	254
Martorana, church of the, Palermo	180–181
Mather	221
Mauméjean, the brothers	259
Mausoleum of Galla Placidia	87–89
building	87
vaults	87, 88
St. Lawrence	88
Good Shepherd	88
style	89
Maxentius, temple of	79
May, Maria	260
Mehmet Fatih, mosque	112
Meiere, Hildreth	258
Melozzo da Forli	240
Menology of Basil II	165
Merson, Luc-Olivier	254
Mesarites	112, 160
Messina, cathedral, apse	185–186
Messina Museum, see San Gregorio, Messina	
Metochites, Theodore	227, 228
Metropolitan Life Insurance Building, Ottawa	262
Metropolitan Museum	108
Mexican mosaics	31, 32
Middle Ages, enthusiasm for	251
Milan	
Sant' Ambrogio	117–118, 200–201
San Lorenzo	116–117
Millet	159, 172, quoted, 228, 229
Miniature mosaics	176
Minoans	29
Mistra, frescoes	227, 229
Modern architecture	262
Moguls	31
Mohammed II	111
Mohammedan mosaics	30
Molkenboer	260
Monnos, pavement by	51
Monophysites	111
Monreale, cathedral	183–184
Monte di Giovanni di Miniato, mosaicist	240
Monza ampullae	62
Morgan, Charles L.	261
Moro, Giovanni	251
Morosini, tomb of, in SS. Giovanni e Paolo, Venice	232
Mosaic, definition of	35
color, possibilities for	35
technique of	37–44

	PAGE
materials of	40–44
range of colors	41, 42
Mosque of Omar, see Dome of the Rock	
Mount Athos, mosaics	170
Mount Sinai, see Monastery of St. Catherine	
Munich, Maximilianeum	255
National Theatre	255
Munio da Zamora, tomb of, in Santa Sabina	217
Muñoz	119, 120
Muqaddasi, quoted	130, 131
Murano, see SS. Maria e Donato and San Cypriano	
Musée Cluny	240
Muziano da Brescia	38, 245
National Catholic Cathedral, Washington, D. C.	257
National Gallery, London, pavement	261
Nativity, church of the, see Bethlehem	
"Navicella" by Giotto, St. Peter's	222–223
Nazarene school	255
Nea Moni, see Chios	
Nebbia, Cesare	246
Nemi, lake of	53
Nennig, pavement	51
Neo-Classicism	251
Neon, Archbishop	89
New Church, Constantinople	159
Nicaea, church of the Dormition	167–168
Nicephoras Gregoras	228
Nicephoras Phocas	132, 163
Nolde, Emile	260
North Italian painting	231
North Prussia	233
Northern Africa, pavements	51
Northern Europe, mosaics	233
Norwegian mosaics	260
Nymphaeum, Via Tiburtina	55
Ocean liners, mosaics on	260
Ohio State Building, Columbus	262
Old St. Peter's, apse	214
Olynthus	30
pebble mosaics	47
Opéra, Paris	254
Opus musivum	48
Opus sectile	31, 48
Opus tessellatum	48
Opus vermiculatum	48
Orcagna, Andrea	232
Orpheus	51
Orvieto, cathedral, façade	55–56
Ostia, "Sylvanus" from	232

	PAGE
Paduan school	238
Palaeologus, Andronicus, emperor	227
Palaeologi, the	227
Palermo	
Camera di Ruggero	184–185
Cappella Palatina	181–183
Cathedral	185
Martorana	180–181
La Zisa	184
Palestrina, pavement from	49
Panagia Angelokistos, Kiti, Cyprus	160–161
Panagia Kanakaria, Cyprus	161
Panthéon, Paris, apse	254
Paregoritissa, church of the, see Arta	
Parenzo, basilica	114–116
ciborium, note 133	
Pascal I, pope	145
Pasteur, tomb of	254
Paul V, portrait of	247–248
Paulus Diaconus	136
Pebble mosaics	30
Pechstein, Max	260
Persian mosaic tiles	30
Peru, early burials in	32
Peruzzi, Baldassare	240
Pescennius Niger, mosaic of	53
Petrus, mosaicist	239
Phillips, L. March, quoted, note 2	
Piave, pebbles	43
Pietro da Cortona	245
Pinturicchio	240
Pisa, Cathedral, apse	205–206
Pisanello	238
Pisano, Andrea	232
Pliny	50
Pola, see Santa Maria del Canneto	
Poli, Cappella dei Conti	214
Pordenone	242
Portative mosaics, see miniature mosaics	
Post Impressionism	258
Poynter, L. J.	256
Posen, Schlosskapelle	255
Pozzulana	38
Prague, cathedral, mosaic	233
Pseudo-Matthew, account of	72
Presbyterian churches, Rochester, N. Y.	257
Prikker, Johan Thorn	259
Protevangelium of St. James	227
Procopius quoted	112
Provenzale da Cento	245, 246

INDEX

	PAGE
Ptolomey Philopator	53
Pueblos	32
Quimper, cathedral	259
Rameses II, temple of	29
Raphael, mosaic in Santa Maria del Popolo	240–241
Ravenna	
Archbishop's Palace	97–98
Arian Baptistery	101
Basilica Ursiana	200
Galla Placidia, mausoleum	87–89
Lost mosaics	102
Orthodox Baptistery	89–91
Sant'Apollinare in Classe	98–101
Sant'Apollinare Nuovo	91–95
San Michele	101–102
San Vitale	95–97
Renaissance, the	237
Reparatus, Archbishop	100
Restorations, recent	251–252
Revoil	254
Rheims, "Mosaic of the Promenade"	51
Ricci, Sebastiano	244
Rochester, N. Y., Savings Bank	261
Rockefeller Center, New York	262
Roger, chamber of King, see Royal Palace, Palermo	
Roman art defined	62
Romanos II, emperor	164
Romanticism	251
Rome	
Colonna Palace, mosaic	217
John VII, oratory of	137–139
Lateran apse	218–219; nave, 84
Lateran Baptistery	68
Old St. Peter's, apse	214
Sant'Agata dei Goti	84
Sant' Agnese	133–134
Sant' Andrea Catabarbara	84
San Bartolommeo all' Isola	213
San Bastianello	237
St. Calixtus	56
Santa Cecilia	150–151
San Cesareo	246
San Clemente	209–211
San Crisògono	217–218
SS. Cosma e Damiano	79–81
Santa Costanza	63–65
Santa Croce in Gerusalemme	240–241
Santa Francesca Romana	211–212
St. John the Evangelist, oratory	78
San Lorenzo-f-l-m	82–83
San Marco	151–152
Santa Maria in Aracœli	217, 218
Santa Maria in Cosmedin	216
Santa Maria in Domnica	149–150
Santa Maria di Loreto	246
Santa Maria del Popolo, Raphael	240–241

	PAGE
Santa Maria Scala Cœli	246
Santa Maria in Travestere	212–213, 221–222
SS. Nereo de Achille	145
San Paolo-f-l-m.	77–78, 214–215
St. Peter's	213, 214, 245–247
San Pietro in Vinculi	136–137
Santa Prassede	145–149, 216
Santa Pudenziana	66–67
Santa Sabina	76
Santo Stefano Rotondo	135–136
Santa Suzanna	144
San Teodoro	134
San Tommaso in Formis	215
St. Venantius, oratory	134–135
Triclinium of Leo III	144
Vatican Library, Apostles' Heads	144
Vatican Studio	245, 252–253
Rossi, G.-B. de, quoted	152
Rossi, Girolamo, historian	96
Royal Palace, Palermo, chamber of King Roger	184, 185
Russia, XIX century mosaics	253
Rusuti	220
Sacré-Coeur, Paris	254
Sant' Agata, Ravenna	102
Sant' Agata dei Goti, Rome	84
Sant' Agnese, Rome	133–134
Sant' Ambrogio, Milan, chapel of St. Victor	117–118
apse	200–201
Sant' Andrea Catabarbara, Rome	84
Sant' Apollinare in Classe, Ravenna	98–101
apse	99
Reparatus	100
Abraham and Melchisedec	100
Sant' Apollinare Nuovo, Ravenna	91–95
Life of Christ	91–93
Prophets	93
Processions of saints	93, 94
Portrait of Justinian	95
St. Bartholomew's, New York	257
San Bartolommeo all' Isola, Rome	213
San Bastianello, Rome, apse	237
St. Calixtus, lost mosaics	56
St. Catherine, monastery of	113
Santa Cecilia, Rome, apse	150–151
San Cesareo, Rome	246
San Clemente, Rome	209–211
SS. Cosma e Damiano, Rome	79–81
apse	79, 80
arch	81
Santa Costanza, Rome	63–65
dome	63
ring-vault	64
apses	65
San Crisògono, Rome, mosaic	217–218
Santa Croce in Gerusalemme, Rome	240–241

INDEX

	PAGE
San Cypriano, Murano	199
St. David, Salonika	110
St. Demetrius, Salonika	109, 110
St. Denis, lateral portal	233
St. Eusebius, crypt of	156
St. Felix, Nola, basilica	121
Santa Francesca Romana, Rome	211–212
San Frediano, Lucca	205
St. John the Evangelist, oratory of, Rome	78
St. George, Salonika	107–108
San Giovanni in Fonte, see Baptistery of Soter	
San Gregorio, Messina	186
St. Irene, Constantinople	112, 113
St. Isaac, cathedral of, Leningrad	253
San Lorenzo, Milan, chapel of St. Aquilinus	116–117
San Lorenzo-fuori-le-mura, Rome	82–83
St. Louis, cathedral	257
San Marco, Rome, apse	151–152
Santa Maria dell' Ammiraglio, see Martorana	
Santa Maria in Aracœli, Rome, tomb in	217
lateral portal	218
Santa Maria del Canneto, Pola	116
Santa Maria in Cosmedin, Rome, baldachino	216
Santa Maria in Domnica, Rome, apse	149–150
SS. Maria e Donato, Murano	199
Santa Maria di Loreto, Rome	246
Santa Maria Maggiore, Rome	69–76
nave mosaics	70–72
triumphal arch	72–73
date	75
technique	76
apse	219–220
façade	200–221
restoration	38
Santa Maria Maggiore, Ravenna	102
Santa Maria Nuovo, see Santa Francesca Romana	
St. Mary Pammakaristos, see Fetiye Djami	
Santa Maria del Popolo, Chigi Chapel	240–241
Santa Maria Scala Cœli, Rome	246
Santa Maria in Trastevere, Rome, apse	212–213
façade	213
Cavallini	221–222
St. Mark's, Venice	191–196
general scheme	192
early work	192
central cupola	193
west dome	193
east dome	193
life of Christ	194
narthex	194, 195
Cappella Zeno	195, 196
façade	196
Baptistery	230–231

	PAGE
Cappella di Sant' Isidoro	231
Chapel of the Mascoli	238
Apocalypse vault	243
Leopoldo dal Pozzo	244
Giovanni Moro	251
Salandri	252
Società Salviati	252
St. Martin, Tours, church	153
St. Matthew's, Washington, D. C.	257
San Matteo, Genoa	206
St. Michael, Kiev	167
San Michele in Affricisco, Ravenna	101–102
San Miniato, Florence	205
SS. Nereo ed Achille, Rome, arch	145
San Paolo-fuori-le-mura	77–78
triumphal arch	77–78
apse	214–215
St. Paulinus, description by	121
St. Paul, Minn., State Capitol	258
St. Paul's, London	248, 256
St. Peter's, Rome, mosaics	245–247
crypt, mosaic in	213–214
San Pietro Chrysologo, see Archbishop's Palace, Ravenna	
San Pietro Ispano, see Boville Ernica	
San Pietro in Vinculi, Rome	136
Santa Prassede, Rome	146–149
triumphal arch	146
apsidal arch	146, 147
apse	147
chapel of San Zeno	147–149
Madonna and Child	216
San Prisco, Capua, chapel of Santa Matrona	121–122
Santa Pudenziana, Rome	66–67
Santa Restituta, Naples	187, 188
Santa Sabina, Rome	76
St. Sergius, Gaza	112
SS. Sergius and Bacchus, Constantinople	112
San Silvestro, Tivoli, apse	237
St. Sophia, Constantinople	42, 110–111
narthex	110–111
lunette of Leo VI	162
lunette over South Portal	162, 163
St. Sophia, Kiev	166
St. Sophia, Salonika	139–140
Ascension in dome	169
Santo Stefano Rotondo, Rome	135–136
St. Stephen, Gaza	112
Santa Susanna, Rome, apse	144
San Teodoro, Rome	134
San Tommaso in Formis, Rome	215
St. Venantius, oratory, Rome	134–135
San Vitale, Ravenna	95–97
apse	95

INDEX

	PAGE
arch	95
vault	95–96
walls	96
panels of Justinian and Theodora	97
Saladin	175
Salandri, Liborio	252
Salerno, cathedral	186–187
façade	186
apses	186–187
Salonika	107
Eski-Djouma	110
St. David	110
St. Demetrius	109–110
St. George	107–108
St. Sophia	139–140, 169
Salzenburg	110
Samarkand, mosque of Chah-Sindeh at	30
Sancta Sanctorum, Rome, chapel	216
Sanctuaire de Sainte-Thérèse de l'Enfant Jesus, Paris	
Sandhurst, Military College	259
Sansovino, Jacopo	261
Sassanian winged motif	242
S. S. "Bremen", mosaic	128
S. S. "Kungsholm", mosaic	260
Scheffler, Rudolph	257, 261
Schevenigen, Holland, St. Antonius	260
Selvo, Domenico, doge	191
Seneca	40, 50
Serbia, Cathedral of Topola	260–261
Seres, Metropolitan	170
Sicily, general	179
Siena, cathedral, façade	232
Sisinius, legend of	210
Skovgaard, Joakim	260
Smirnoff	161
Società Salviati	252
Solsternus, mosaicist	215
Sosus of Pergamon, pavement by	50
Soter, Baptistery of, Naples	119–120
South Kensington Museum, studio	256
mosaic by Orcagna	233
Spartian, *Historia Augusta*	53
Spoleto, cathedral, façade	215
Stefaneschi, cardinal	222
Stevens, Alfred	256
Stockholm, Town Hall	260
Strzygowski	27
Suger, the abbot	233
Sumerian mosaics	27–29
reliefs	29
"Sylvanus" of Ostia	55–56
Sylvester I, pope	133

	PAGE
Symonds, J. A., quoted	36
Syracuse, Museum, mosaic, note 125	
Syro-Palestinian school, note 85	
Tabarka, Morocco	51, 122
Tafi, Andrea, mosaicist	203
Tankiz, mausoleum of, Damascus	132
Tarragona, tombal mosaics	122
Tate Gallery, pavement	261
Teano, tombal mosaic, note 83	
Tel-el-Yehudia, capitals, at	29
Temple Emmanuel, New York	258
Teutonic Order	234
Theodoric	87
Théodulfe, abbot	152
Tigress and Bull, from the Capitoline	48
Tikkanen	195
Timgad, "*Mosaïque de la Piscine*"	52
Tintoretto	242
Titian	242, 243
Toesca	117, 118, 194, 204
Tombal mosaics	122
Topola, see Serbia	
Torcello, cathedral	196–199
vault	196–197
apses	197
Last Judgment	197–199
Torriti	209, 218, 219, 220, 221, 237
Traini, Francesco	206
Trecento	149
Trecento, painting	229
Trial of 1573	243
Triclinium of Leo III, Rome	144
Trieste, Cathedral	199–200
Cappella del Sacramento	199
Cappella di San Giusto	199–200
Trier, pavement	51
Trinity College Chapel, Washington, D. C.	257
Tuscan painters, early	204
Ugonio	65
Union Terminal Station, Cincinnati	262
Ur, Standard of	29
Urban VIII, pope	247
Ursiana, Basilica, see Basilica Usiana, Ravenna	
Uthina, pavement	51
Valencia, tombal mosaic	122
Van Berchem, Marg.	40, 42, 131
Van Gogh	258
Vanni, Cecco, mosaicist	232
Vasari	203, 204, 205, 220, 239, quoted 240, 241

INDEX

	PAGE
Vassalletti, the	188
Vatican Library, Apostles' heads	144
Vatican Studio	245, 252–253
Vatopedi, Catholicon	171
Crucifixion	176
Vedder, Elihu	257
Venturi	133, 136, 145, 185, 213
Veramin, mosque at	30
Veronese, Paolo	242
Venice, general	191
Santa Maria della Salute, mosaic, note 133	
Vienna, Church of the Minorites, Leonardo's Last Supper	253
Vigeland, Emanuel	260
Vladimir, Prince of Kiev	165
Vogüé, de	175
Walid I, Caliph	129
Warka, Ziggurat tower at	27
courtyard	28
Warriors, temple of the	32
Wartburg, the	255
Watts	256
Westminster Cathedral, London	261
Whittemore, Thomas	40, 42, 111, 162
Wiley, F. J.	258
Wilpert	117, 119, 134
Woodchester, pavement	51
Woolley	28, 29
Wren, Sir Christopher	248, 256
Xenophon, Catholicon	171
Zancarron, capilla del, see Cordova, mosque	
Zisa, the, Palermo	184
Zliten, pavements	52
Zuccati, the	242, 243
Zuccato, Francesco	242

ROMAN PAVEMENT PLATE 1

1. NAPLES MUSEUM. ACADEMY OF PLATO FROM TORRE ANNUZIATA

ROMAN PAVEMENTS PLATE II

2. MUSEO DELLE TERME. HEAD OF MEDUSA
3. POMPEII. RECLINING DOG
4. PAVEMENT FROM THE BATHS OF CARACALLA
5. CAPITOL MUSEUM. "PLINY'S DOVES"
6. TIMGAD. MOSAÏQUE DE LA PISCINE
7. ZLITEN (TRIPOLI). DETAIL OF PAVEMENT

POMPEII—OSTIA PLATE III

8. POMPEII. FOUNTAIN NICHE
9. NAPLES MUSEUM. FOUNTAIN NICHE
10. NAPLES MUSEUM. MOSAIC COLUMN
11. LATERAN MUSEUM. "SILVANUS" FROM OSTIA

SANTA COSTANZA   PLATE IV

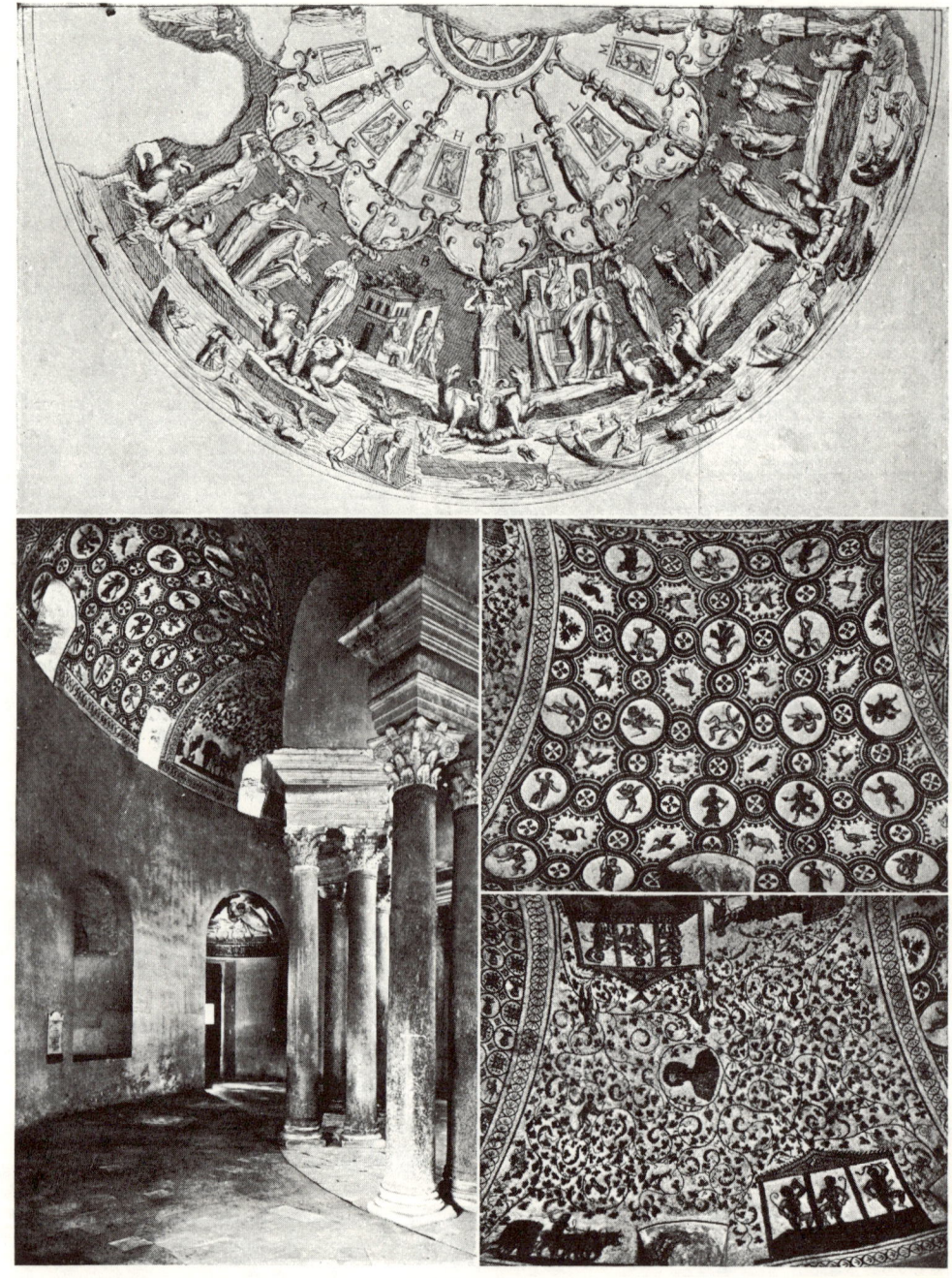

12. CIAMPINI'S ENGRAVING OF THE DOME
13. GENERAL VIEW OF THE VAULT
14. DETAIL OF THE VAULT. DECORATIVE PATTERN
15. DETAIL OF THE VAULT. VINTAGE SCENE

ROME—FIFTH CENTURY PLATE V

16. SANTA COSTANZA. LEFT APSE 17. SANTA COSTANZA. RIGHT APSE
18. SANTA PUDENZIANA. APSE 19. LATERAN BAPTISTERY. APSE
20. SANTA MARIA MAGGIORE. GENERAL VIEW OF THE NAVE

SANTA MARIA MAGGIORE PLATE VI

21. ABRAHAM AND THE THREE ANGELS
22. SANTA MARIA MAGGIORE. SEPARATION OF ABRAHAM AND LOT   23. MARRIAGE OF MOSES AND SEPHORA

SANTA MARIA MAGGIORE   PLATE VII

24. GENERAL VIEW OF THE TRIUMPHAL ARCH
25. DETAIL OF THE ARCH   26. DETAIL OF THE ARCH
27. DETAIL OF THE PRESENTATION

SANTA SABINA—SAN PAOLO   PLATE VIII

28. SANTA SABINA. GENERAL VIEW OF MOSAIC
30. SANTA SABINA. DESTROYED MOSAIC OF THE ARCH FROM CIAMPINI
29. SANTA SABINA. ECCLESIA EX CIRCUMCISIONE   31. SAN PAOLO FUORI-LE-MURA. APSE AND TRIUMPHAL ARCH

SS. COSMA E DAMIANO   PLATE IX

33. APSE AND TRIUMPHAL ARCH   34. CHRIST, DETAIL
35. RIGHT HALF OF THE APSE
32. LATERAN BAPTISTERY. VAULT   36. LEFT HALF OF THE APSE
37. SAN LORENZO FUORI-LE-MURA. ARCH

GALLA PLACIDIA   PLATE X

39. GENERAL VIEW OF THE MOSAICS OF THE VAULTS
38. EXTERIOR OF MAUSOLEUM
40. STAGS DRINKING
41. MARTYRDOM OF ST. LAWRENCE
42. THE GOOD SHEPHERD

BAPTISTERY OF THE ORTHODOX   PLATE XI

43. DOME, BAPTISM OF CHRIST. THE APOSTLES, THRONES AND ALTARS
44. BAPTISM OF CHRIST   45. THE INTERIOR

SANT'APOLLINARE NUOVO PLATE XII

46. LEFT WALL OF NAVE
47. RIGHT WALL OF NAVE
48. DETAIL OF LEFT WALL
49. DETAIL OF RIGHT WALL

SANT'APOLLINARE NUOVO PLATE XIII

50. THE MULTIPLICATION OF BREAD
51. THE SEPARATION OF THE SHEEP FROM THE GOATS

SANT'APOLLINARE NUOVO PLATE XIV

52. THE LAST SUPPER 53. THE KISS OF JUDAS

SANT'APOLLINARE NUOVO   PLATE XV

54. VIRGIN ENTHRONED   55. CHRIST ENTHRONED

SAN VITALE   PLATE XVI

56. SANT'APOLLINARE NUOVO. PORTRAIT OF JUSTINIAN
57. SAN VITALE. CHRIST ENTHRONED
58. SAN VITALE. VAULT
59. SAN VITALE. ST. MATTHEW AND ST. MARK WITH THEIR SYMBOLS

60. ABEL AND MELCHISEDEK, MOSES AND ISAIAH
61. ABRAHAM AND THE THREE ANGELS
62. SOFFIT OF THE ARCH. DETAIL, SAINTS AND MEDALLIONS
63. JUSTINIAN AND HIS COURT

SAN VITALE PLATE XVIII

64. THEODORA AND HER COURT 65. THE EMPRESS THEODORA AND ATTENDANTS

ARCHIEPISCOPAL PALACE PLATE XIX

66. VAULT
67. INTERIOR
68. VAULT AND APSE
69. BUSTS OF FEMALE SAINTS
70. MILITANT CHRIST

SANT'APOLLINARE IN CLASSE PLATE XX

71. APSE AND TRIUMPHAL ARCH. THE TRANSFIGURATION

SANT'APOLLINARE IN CLASSE PLATE XXI

73. CONSTANTINE IV AND REPARATUS
72. ST. URSUS
74. SACRIFICE OF MELCHISEDEK
75. THE ARIAN BAPTISTERY. CUPOLA
76. SAN MICHELE IN AFFRICISCO. APSE

SALONIKA PLATE XXII

78. ST. GEORGE. LEO AND THE FLUTE-PLAYER PHILIMON
77. ST. GEORGE. DECORATION OF THE DOME   80. ST. DEMETRIUS AND THE FOUNDERS
79. ST. DEMETRIUS. ST. DEMETRIUS AND TWO CHILDREN

SALONIKA—CONSTANTINOPLE   PLATE XXIII

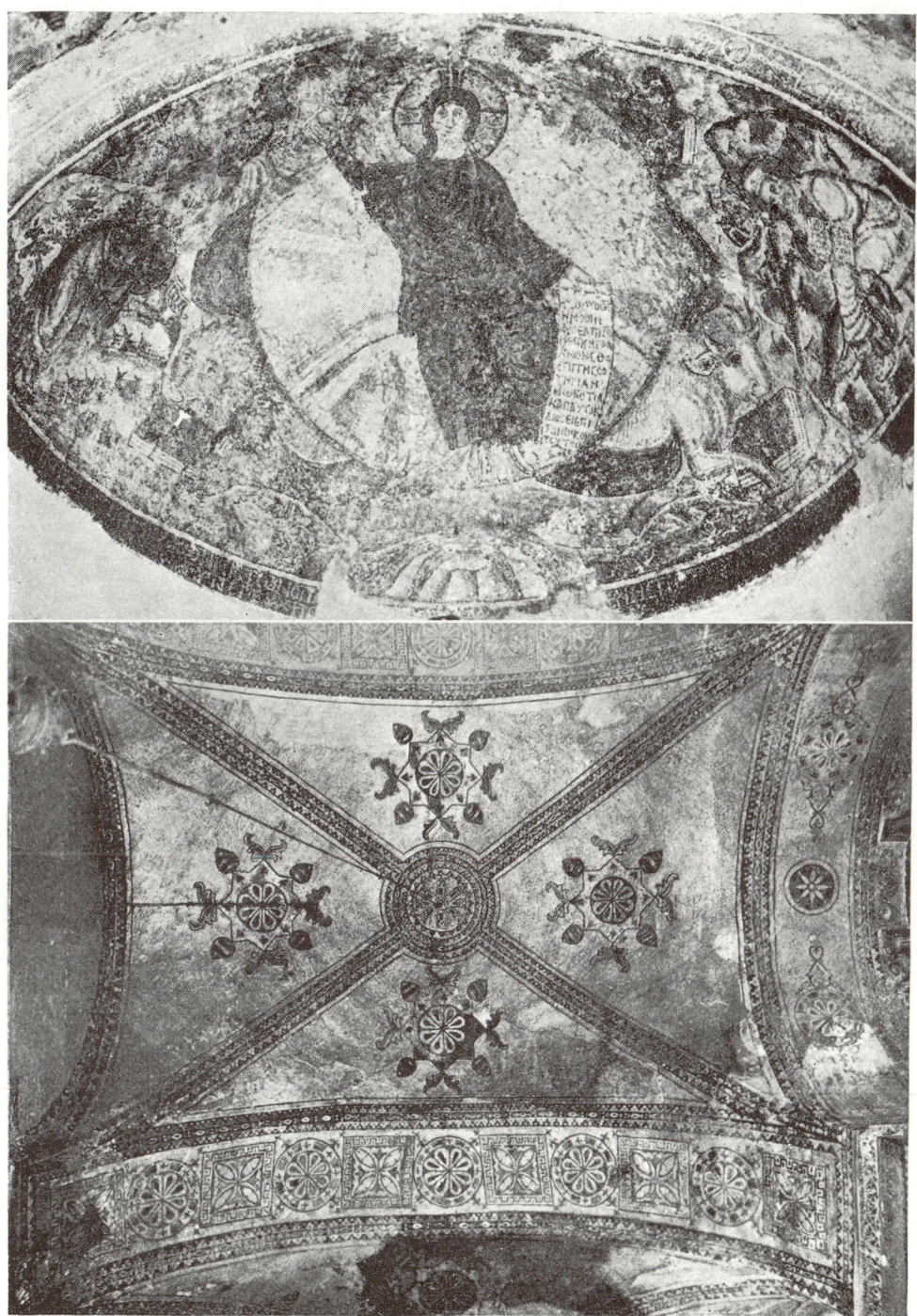

81. ST. DAVID. VISION OF EZECHIEL   82. ST. SOPHIA. NARTHEX. VAULT

CONSTANTINOPLE—SINAI—PARENZO   PLATE XXIV

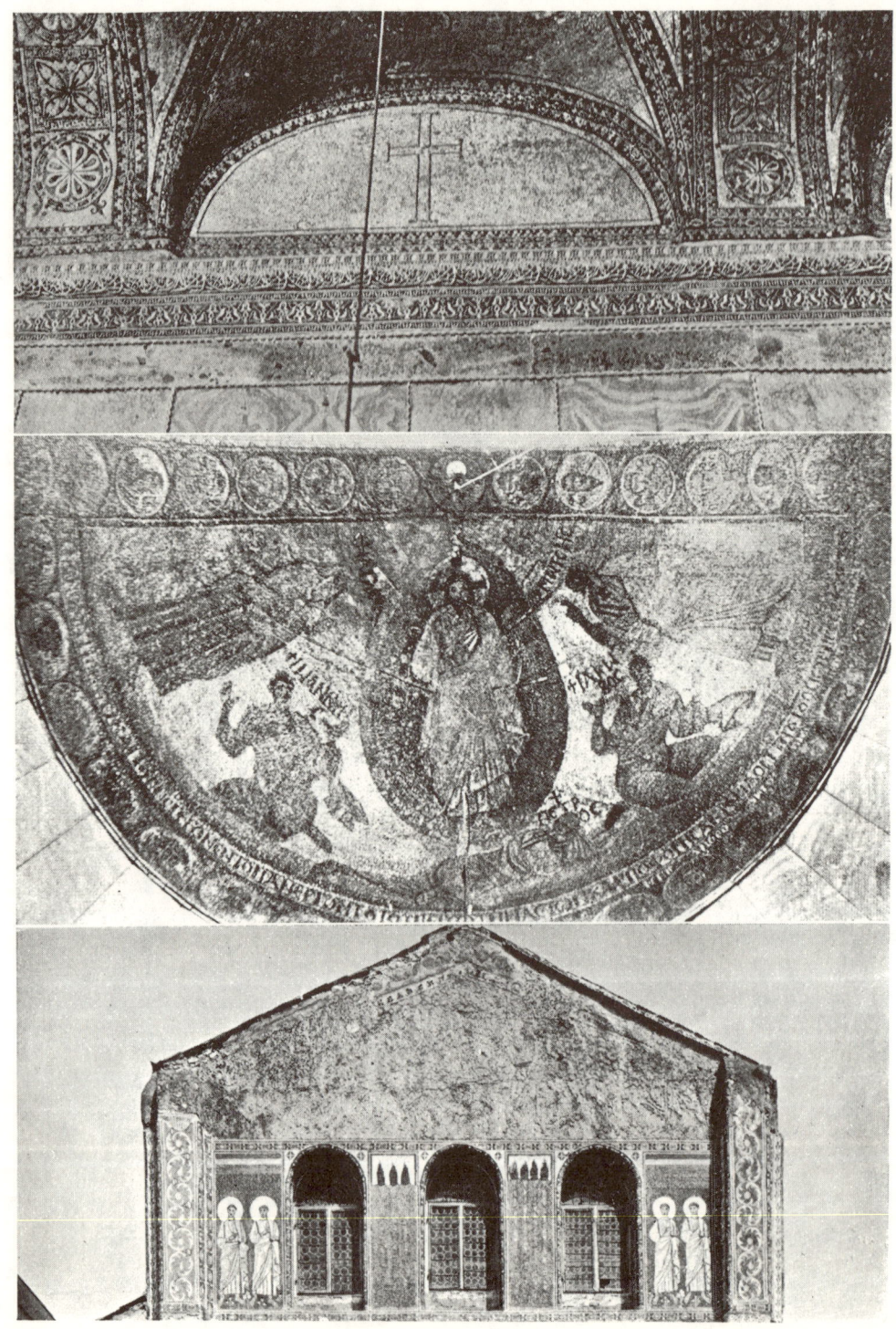

83. ST. SOPHIA. NARTHEX. CROSS
84. MONASTERY OF ST. CATHERINE. DETAIL OF THE APSE
85. PARENZO. FAÇADE

PARENZO　　　　　　　　　PLATE XXV

86. APSE AND TRIUMPHAL ARCH. MADONNA AND CHILD ENTHRONED WITH ANGELS, SAINTS AND DONORS

PARENZO PLATE XXVI

87. DETAIL OF THE APSE

88. ANNUNCIATION 89. VISITATION

MILAN—ALBENGA—CASARANELLO PLATE XXVII

90. SAN LORENZO. CHRIST AND THE APOSTLES
91. SAN LORENZO. APSE
92. SANT'AMBROGIO. CHAPEL OF ST. VICTOR. CUPOLA.
93. SANT'AMBROGIO. CHAPEL OF ST. VICTOR. ST. AMBROSE
94. ALBENGA. BAPTISTERY. DETAIL
95. CASARANELLO. CUPOLA

NAPLES—TARRAGONA PLATE XXVIII

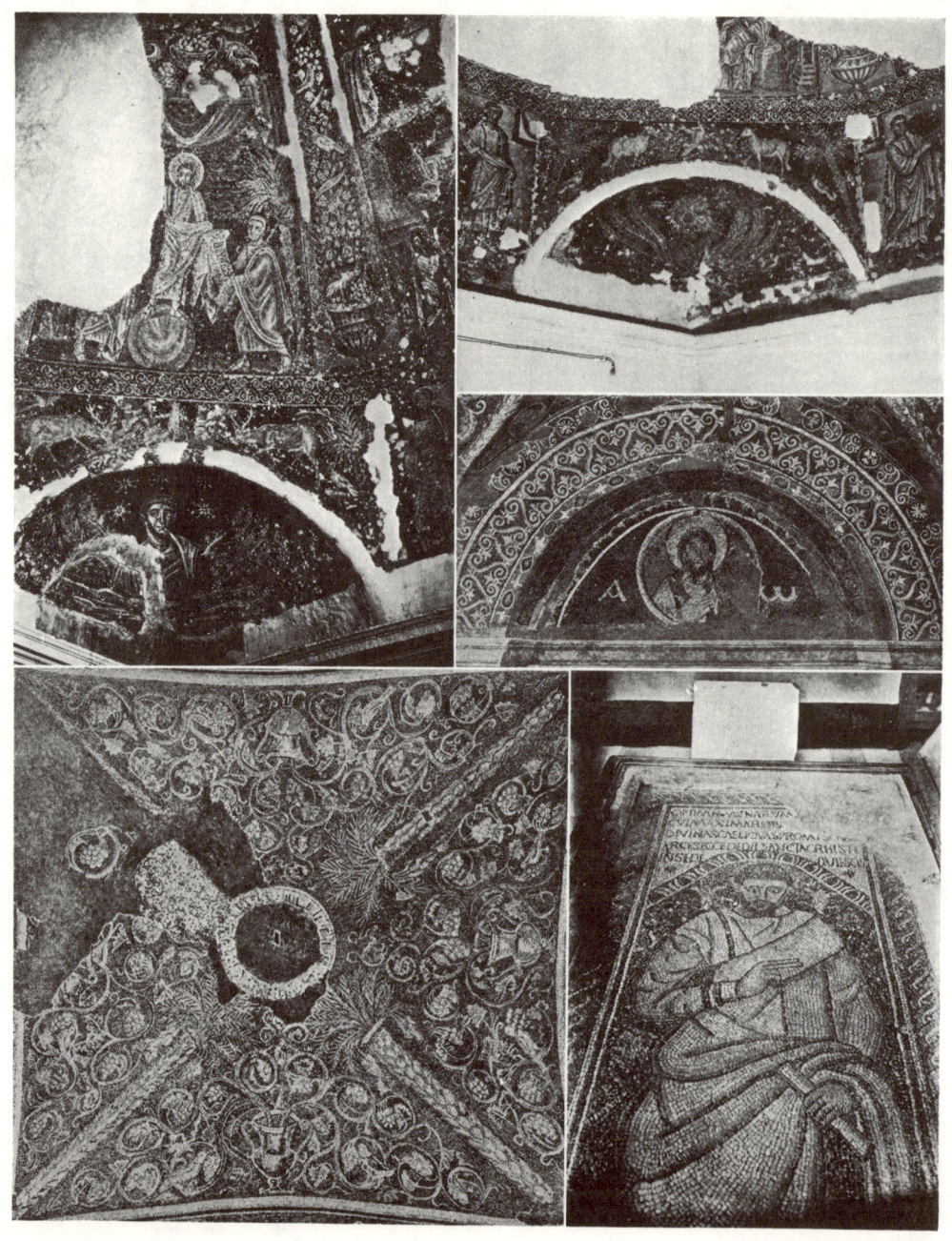

96. SAN GIOVANNI IN FONTE. CHRIST AND ANGEL
99. CAPUA. SAN PRISCO. VAULT
97. SAN GIOVANNI IN FONTE. THE LION
98. CAPUA. SAN PRISCO. CHRIST
100. TARRAGONA. TOMBAL MOSAIC

"DOME OF THE ROCK" PLATE XXIX

101. OCTAGONAL ARCADE. DETAIL
103. THE DRUM. DETAIL
102. CIRCULAR ARCADE. DETAIL

DAMASCUS—CORDOVA PLATE XXX

104. THE GREAT MOSQUE. THE GREAT PANEL
105. THE GREAT MOSQUE. THE FOUR TREES 106. CORDOVA. MOSQUE. FAÇADE OF THE MIHRAB

107. SANT'AGNESE. APSE   108. SAN TEODORO. APSE
109. ORATORY OF ST. VENANTIUS. APSE AND TRIUMPHAL ARCH
110 ORATORY OF ST. VENANTIUS. GROUP OF SAINTS   111. ORATORY OF ST. VENANTIUS. GROUP OF SAINTS

ROME—SEVENTH CENTURY   PLATE XXXII

112. SANTO STEFANO ROTONDO. APSE
113. SAN PIETRO IN VINCOLI. ST. SEBASTIAN
114. ORATORY OF JOHN VII. FAÇADE FROM CIAMPINI
115. FLORENCE. SAN MARCO. VIRGIN AS ORANT

ROME—SEVENTH CENTURY PLATE XXXIII

116. MUSEO PETRIANO. PORTRAIT OF JOHN VII
117. MUSEO PETRIANO. ST. PETER PREACHING
118. LATERAN MUSEUM. THE WASHING OF THE INFANT CHRIST
119. SANTA MARIA IN COSMEDIN. ADORATION OF THE MAGI

ROME—SALONIKA PLATE XXXIV

121. ROME. TRICLINIUM OF THE LATERAN. APSE
120. SALONIKA. ST. SOPHIA. VIRGIN IN THE APSE   122. ROME. VATICAN CRYPT. CHRIST BLESSING

ROME—NINTH CENTURY   PLATE XXXV

123. SS. NEREO ED ACHILLE. TRIUMPHAL ARCH
125. SANTA PRASSEDE. THE HEAVENLY JERUSALEM   126. SANTA PRASSEDE. THE TWENTY-FOUR ELDERS
124. SANTA PRASSEDE. THE APSE AND THE TRIUMPHAL ARCH

ROME—NINTH CENTURY PLATE XXXVI

127. SANTA PRASSEDE. FAÇADE OF THE CAPPELLA SAN ZENO
128. SANTA PRASSEDE. VAULT   129. SANTA PRASSEDE. FEMALE SAINTS

NINTH CENTURY PLATE XXXVII

130. SANTA MARIA IN DOMINICA. APSE
131. SANTA CECILIA. APSE
132. SAN MARCO. APSE
133. GERMIGNY-DES-PRÉS. APSE
134. AIX-LA-CHAPELLE. DECORATION OF THE DOME

135. NARTHEX. LUNETTE OVER THE ROYAL DOOR
136. NARTHEX. LUNETTE OVER THE SOUTH PORTAL

HOSIOS LUCAS PLATE XXXIX

137. THE PANTOCRATOR 138. THE MADONNA AND CHILD IN THE APSE
139. DESCENT OF THE HOLY GHOST WITH TRIBES IN THE PENDENTIVES

140. KIEV. THE PANTOCRATOR
142. NICÆA. VIRGIN OF THE APSE.
141. KIEV. COMMUNION OF THE APOSTLES
143. NICÆA. ARCHANGELS

SALONIKA—CHIOS—SERES PLATE XLI

144. NICÆA. VIRGIN AS ORANT
145. SALONIKA. ST. SOPHIA. CUPOLA
146. CHIOS. NEA MONI. BAPTISM
147. CHIOS. NEA MONI. ANASTASIS
148. SERES. COMMUNION OF THE APOSTLES

GROTTAFERRATA PLATE XLII

149. PENTECOST 150. DEESIS

DAPHNI   PLATE XLIII

151. PANTOCRATOR   152. TRANSFIGURATION
153. ENTRY INTO JERUSALEM

DAPHNI PLATE XLIV

154. CRUCIFIXION 155. ANASTASIS
156. PRAYER OF ST. ANNA

MINIATURE MOSAICS   PLATE XLV

158. FLORENCE. BARGELLO. CHRIST
159. LOUVRE. TRANSFIGURATION

157. FLORENCE. OPERA DEL DUOMO. PANELS OF THE TWELVE FEASTS

CEFALÙ PLATE XLVI

160. CATHEDRAL. APSE   THE PANTOCRATOR WITH THE VIRGIN, ARCHANGELS AND APOSTLES BELOW

CEFALU — THE MARTORANA PLATE XLVII

161. CEFALÚ. CATHEDRAL. VAULT
163. THE MARTORANA. CUPOLA
162. THE MARTORANA. INTERIOR
164. THE MARTORANA. NATIVITY

THE MARTORANA—CAPPELLA PALATINA PLATE XLVIII

165. THE MARTORANA. DORMITION
167. THE MARTORANA. SS. JAMES AND PAUL
166. KING ROGER CROWNED
168. CAPPELLA PALATINA. INTERIOR

CAPPELLA PALATINA PLATE XLIX

169. CUPOLA, CHRIST AND ARCHANGELS
170. APSE, THE PANTOCRATOR
171. NAVE, CREATION OF ADAM AND EVE
172. NAVE, ENTRY INTO JERUSALEM

CAPPELLA PALATINA—MONREALE PLATE L

173. NAVE, SCENE FROM THE LIFE OF ST. PAUL
175. MONREALE. APSE
174. NAVE, HEAD OF ST. GREGORY
176. MONREALE. NAVE, OLD TESTAMENT SCENES

177. NAVE, DETAIL OF THE CREATION
178. WILLIAM II OFFERS THE CHURCH TO THE VIRGIN   179. CHRIST CROWNING WILLIAM II

OTHER SICILIAN MOSAICS PLATE LII

180. PALERMO. LA ZISA
181. LA ZISA. DETAIL OF FRIEZE
182. PALERMO. PALACE. CAMERA DI RUGGERO
183. CAMERA DI RUGGERO, DETAIL
184. MESSINA. CATHEDRAL. MAIN APSE

SALERNO—NAPLES PLATE LIII

186. SALERNO. CATHEDRAL. ST. MATTHEW
185. MESSINA. VIRGIN AND CHILD FROM SAN GREGORIO 187. NAPLES. S. RESTITUTA. VIRGIN AND CHILD

ST. MARK'S PLATE LIV

189. THE ASCENSION CUPOLA
188. INTERIOR
192. THE CHRIST EMMANUEL CUPOLA
190. THE ASCENSION CUPOLA. THE VIRGIN
191. THE PENTECOST CUPOLA
193. DETAIL OF PROPHETS

ST. MARK'S PLATE LV

194. DEESIS
195. ENTRY INTO JERUSALEM
197. THE BODY OF ST. MARK CARRIED TO THE SHIP
196. ANASTASIS AND INCREDULITY OF THOMAS
198. ANGELS ABOVE THE TREASURY DOOR

ST. MARK'S PLATE LVI

201. LIFE OF ABRAHAM
199. NARTHEX. THE CREATION CUPOLA 203. SCENE FROM THE LIFE OF ST. MARK
200. THE ANIMALS GOING INTO THE ARK 202. LIFE OF MOSES
204. TRANSLATION OF THE BODY OF ST. MARK

TORCELLO   PLATE LVII

205. CATHEDRAL. VAULT. ANGELS SUPPORTING MEDALLION OF THE LAMB
206. CENTRAL APSE   207. LATERAL APSE

TORCELLO   PLATE LVIII

208. LAST JUDGMENT

MURANO—TRIESTE—RAVENNA PLATE LIX

209. MURANO. SS. MARIA E DONATO. APSE
212. TRIESTE. CAPPELLA DI SAN GIUSTO. APSE
210. TRIESTE. CAPPELLA DEL SACRAMENTO. APSE
211. TRIESTE. CAPPELLA DEL SACRAMENTO. DETAIL
213. RAVENNA. PALACE. VIRGIN AS ORANT

RAVENNA—MILAN—FLORENCE　　　PLATE LX

214. RAVENNA. PALACE. HEAD OF ST. JOHN　　215. MILAN. SANT'AMBROGIO. APSE
216. FLORENCE. BAPTISTERY. VAULT OF THE "SCARSELLA"
217. BAPTISTERY. MADONNA AND CHILD, DETAIL　　218. BAPTISTERY. ST. JOHN THE BAPTIST

THE FLORENTINE BAPTISTERY   PLATE LXI

219. GENERAL VIEW OF THE DOME

THE FLORENTINE BAPTISTERY　　PLATE LXII

221. CHRIST ENTHRONED
220. DECORATION BELOW THE LANTERN
222. DETAIL OF THE "HELL"
223. BIRTH OF ST. JOHN

FLORENCE PLATE LXIII

224. BAPTISTERY. DETAIL OF HEAD
228. SAN MINIATO. FAÇADE
225. BAPTISTERY. THE PROPHET JOEL
226. CATHEDRAL, LUNETTE. CORONATION OF THE VIRGIN
227. SAN MINIATO. APSE

229. LUCCA. SAN FREDIANO. ASCENSION
230. PISA. CATHEDRAL. APSE

MEDIÆVAL ROMAN MOSAICS   PLATE LXV

232. SAN CLEMENTE. APSE, DETAIL
234. SANTA MARIA IN TRASTEVERE. APSE
236. SANTA MARIA IN TRASTEVERE. DETAIL OF
       THE FAÇADE
231. SAN CLEMENTE. APSE AND TRIUMPHAL ARCH
233. SANTA FRANCESCA ROMANA. APSE
235. SANTA MARIA IN TRASTEVERE. JEREMIAH
       AND ISAIAH

MEDIÆVAL ROMAN MOSAICS   PLATE LXVI

237. ST. PETER'S. FRESCO OF THE OLD APSE   239. SAN PAOLO FUORE-LE-MURA. APSE
240. SAN PAOLO FUORE-LE-MURA. HEAD OF APOSTLE
238. POLI. CAPPELLA CONTI. INNOCENT III.   241. SAN TOMMASO IN FORMIS. CHRIST AND TWO SLAVES
242. CIVITA CASTELLANA. LUNETTE

MEDIÆVAL ROMAN MOSAICS PLATE LXVII

243. SANCTA SANCTORUM. VAULT
245. STA. MARIA SOPRA MINERVA. TOMB OF DURANDE   244. SANTA PRASSEDE. VIRGIN AND CHILD
246. STA. MARIA MAGGIORE. TOMB OF RODRIGUEZ

MEDIÆVAL ROMAN MOSAICS   PLATE LXVIII

247. BROOKLYN MUSEUM. MADONNA
249. SAN CRISÒGONO. MADONNA AND CHILD
248. STA. SABINA. TOMBSTONE OF ZAMORA
250. STA. MARIA IN ARACŒLI. LUNETTE
251. THE LATERAN. APSE

252. STA. MARIA MAGGIORE. APSE
254. STA. MARIA MAGGIORE. DORMITION   253. STA. MARIA MAGGIORE. APSE. DETAIL
255. STA. MARIA MAGGIORE. FAÇADE, CHRIST ENTHRONED

MEDIÆVAL ROMAN MOSAICS　　　PLATE LXX

256. STA. MARIA MAGGIORE. DREAM OF POPE LIBERIUS
257. STA. MARIA IN TRASTEVERE. BIRTH OF THE VIRGIN
258. STA. MARIA IN TRASTEVERE. NATIVITY

259. STA. MARIA IN TRASTEVERE. DORMITION   261. BOVILLE ERNICA. ANGEL
260. ST. PETER'S. THE "NAVICELLA"

THE KAHRIE DJAMI   PLATE LXXII

262. CUPOLA. CHRIST AND PROPHETS
265. THE MAGI BEFORE HEROD

263. THEODORE METOCHITES AT THE FEET OF CHRIST
264. DORMITION

KAHRIE DJAMI—FETIYE DJAMI   PLATE LXXIII

266. KAHRIE DJAMI. ANNUNCIATION   268. CUPOLA OF THE FETIYE DJAMI
267. KAHRIE DJAMI. THE HIGH-PRIEST GIVES THE WOOL TO THE VIRGIN

FETIYE DJAMI—ST. MARK'S—MARIENBURG PLATE LXXIV

269. FETIYE DJAMI, DETAIL OF CHRIST
270. ST. MARK'S, BAPTISTERY. CHRIST, ANGELS AND SERAPHIM
271. ST. MARK'S, BAPTISTERY. HEROD'S FEAST   272. MARIENBURG. VIRGIN AND CHILD

THE ITALIAN RENAISSANCE   PLATE LXXV

273. ST. MARK'S, CHAPEL OF THE MASCOLI. BIRTH OF THE VIRGIN AND PRESENTATION
275. FLORENCE. CATHEDRAL. ANNUNCIATION
276. FLORENCE. MUSEO DEL OPERA. ST. ZENOBIUS
274. ST. MARK'S, CHAPEL OF THE MASCOLI. DORMITION
277. ROME. STA. CROCE IN GERUSALEMME. VAULT

THE ITALIAN RENAISSANCE   PLATE LXXVI

278. ROME. STA. MARIA DEL POPOLO. CUPOLA
279. ST. MARK'S. DETAIL OF THE PARADISE   281. ST. PETER'S. DETAIL OF THE DOME
280. ST. MARK'S. MOSAIC BY LEOPOLDO DAL POZZO

ROME—AMERICA PLATE LXXVII

284. DETROIT. CHURCH OF THE HOLY REDEEMER
282. FAÇADE OF SAN PAOLO FUORI-LE-MURA
283. ROME. APSE OF THE AMERICAN CHURCH BY BURNE-JONES
285. ST. LOUIS. CATHEDRAL. DETAIL
286. NEW YORK. ST. BARTHOLOMEW'S. DETAIL

FRANCE—GERMANY PLATE LXXVIII

287. PARIS. DETAIL OF MOSAIC BY THE BROTHERS MAUMÉJEAN
288. THE HAGUE. MOSAIC BY THORN-PRIKKER
289. GERMANY. THE THREE WISE MEN, BY EWALD DUELLBERG
290. FRANKFORT-AM-MAIN. TOWER OF THE FRAUEN-FRIEDENSKIRCHE
291. SS. "BREMEN", MOSAIC IN BALL-ROOM
292. STOCKHOLM. THE "GOLDEN HALL" BY EINAR FORSETH

ENGLAND—AMERICA PLATE LXXIX

293. LONDON. 35 UPPER BROOK STREET. PAVEMENT BY BORIS ANREP
295. ROCHESTER SAVINGS BANK 294. PAVEMENT BY BORIS ANREP. NATIONAL GALLERY

RECENT AMERICAN MOSAICS   PLATE LXXX

296. NEW YORK. INTERNATIONAL TELEPHONE AND TELEGRAPH BUILDING
297. OTTAWA. METROPOLITAN LIFE INSURANCE BUILDING
298. CINCINNATI. UNION TERMINAL STATION
299. NEW YORK. AN INTERIOR OF IRVING TRUST BUILDING
300. NEW YORK. ROCKEFELLER CENTER. MURAL